Advances
in **COMPUTERS**
VOLUME 7

Contributors to This Volume

WILLIAM R. BOZMAN
WAYNE A. DANIELSON
RUTH M. DAVIS
JOHN C. MURTHA
ARNOLD C. SATTERTHWAIT
ANDRIES VAN DAM

Advances in
COMPUTERS

EDITED BY
FRANZ L. ALT
National Bureau of Standards
Washington D.C.

AND
MORRIS RUBINOFF
University of Pennsylvania
and
Pennsylvania Research Associates
Philadelphia, Pennsylvania

VOLUME 7

ACADEMIC PRESS · New York · London – 1966

Copyright © 1966 by Academic Press Inc.
ALL RIGHTS RESERVED.
NO PART OF THIS BOOK MAY BE REPRODUCED IN ANY FORM,
BY PHOTOSTAT, MICROFILM, OR ANY OTHER MEANS, WITHOUT
WRITTEN PERMISSION FROM THE PUBLISHERS.

ACADEMIC PRESS INC.
111 Fifth Avenue, New York, New York 10003

United Kingdom Edition published by
ACADEMIC PRESS INC. (LONDON) LTD.
Berkley Square House, London W.1

LIBRARY OF CONGRESS CATALOG CARD NUMBER: 59-15761

Second Printing, 1968

PRINTED IN THE UNITED STATES OF AMERICA

Contributors to Volume 7

WILLIAM R. BOZMAN, *National Bureau of Standards, Washington, D.C.*

WAYNE A. DANIELSON, *The University of North Carolina at Chapel Hill, Chapel Hill, North Carolina*

RUTH M. DAVIS, *Office of Director of Defense Research and Engineering, Department of Defense, Washington, D.C.*

JOHN C. MURTHA, *Westinghouse Electric Corporation, Baltimore, Maryland*

ARNOLD C. SATTERTHWAIT, *Program in Information Science, Washington State University, Pullman, Washington*

ANDRIES VAN DAM, *Moore School of Electrical Engineering, University of Pennsylvania, Philadelphia, Pennsylvania*

Preface

As the third generation of computers begins to make its impact felt on the business and technological world, the time has come for a broad review of the recent developments in computer hardware and software that have contributed to the new generation. The current volume of *Advances in Computers* accordingly presents a comprehensive critical review of programming language processors, a detailed review and evaluation of hardware systems with multiple cooperating digital and/or analog processing units, and an up-to-the-minute description of computer-driven displays and their use in real-time on-line man-machine problem solving. The review will continue in Volume 8 with a survey and detailed discussion of time-sharing systems and the various means by which these systems are designed to accommodate large numbers of remote users in a seemingly simultaneous mode.

In this volume, the article by Ruth Davis on programming language processors carefully delineates their common theoretical and conceptual foundations and bridges the gap between mathematical linguistics and programming language processor design. The author points to the attention paid to syntax and pragmatics through the use of unambiguous vocabularies and structures, and the formal specification of actions to be executed by the computer. She notes, however, that semantics is either nonexistent or artificially introduced in programming language processors to date. A discussion of the historical development and current features of these processors is followed by enumeration of measurement criteria for their analytic evaluation. A companion article by Arnold Satterthwait discusses several specific programming systems in the U.S.A. which have been directed toward machine translation studies. These systems include COMIT, MIMIC, the Wayne system, SNOBOL, and LRS; the article provides detailed descriptions and illustrative applications of each of them.

In John Murtha's article on highly parallel computer complexes, he distinguishes among memory-organized, network, and multiple-computer systems. He discusses parallel network complexes with many identical processors and a single central control, such as the Unger and Solomon systems, and contrasts them with distributed control networks of interconnected identical modules with independent control, such as proposed by Holland. Special-purpose systems receive lengthy consideration, including pattern recognizers, list processors, differential equation solvers, optical correlators, maximum likelihood processors, and both

PREFACE

serial and parallel signal processors. The article takes into account and interrelates the use of digital and analog hardware and the corresponding software considerations.

Andries van Dam's article is primarily concerned with erasable visual displays and man-machine cooperation. Careful attention is paid to the subtle conceptual distinctions underlying the various properties of light and the factors entering into visual communication. Detailed consideration is given to the computer system, the display buffer, command decoding, and display generation and presentation. Considerations entering into time-sharing from multiple remote displays are also presented. Uses of visual displays are discussed from the viewpoints of on-line programming, computer-aided instruction, and computer-aided design.

Recent advances in computer applications are represented in this volume by two articles on copy editing and typesetting. These provide a brief description of the current state of computer-based automation in the publishing industry, with emphasis on principles, techniques, and methods for preparing computer output for publication. Six real-life examples serve to illustrate the process.

FRANZ L. ALT
MORRIS RUBINOFF

July, 1966

Contents

CONTRIBUTORS	v
PREFACE	vii

Highly Parallel Information Processing Systems
JOHN C. MURTHA

1. Introduction	2
2. Parallel Network Computers	10
3. Distributed Control Networks	22
4. Limited Application Parallel Processors	34
5. Multiple Instruction Stream/Multiple Function Machines	68
6. Programming Languages for Highly Parallel Machines	84
7. Translation Techniques	91
8. Parallel Processing Techniques and Algorithms	100
References	113

Programming Language Processors
RUTH M. DAVIS

1. Introduction	117
2. Features of Programming Languages	119
3. Rules, Syntactical Techniques, and Grammatical Models for Decoding Programming Languages	128
4. Historical Development of Programming Language Processors	141
5. Features of Programming Language Processors	147
6. The Conventional Programming Language Processor	159
7. The Syntax-Directed Programming Language Processor	163
8. List Processors	167
9. Evaluation of Programming Language Processors	173
10. Concluding Remarks	175
References	177

CONTENTS

The Man-Machine Combination for Computer-Assisted Copy Editing
WAYNE A. DANIELSON

1. Introduction	181
2. Computerized Line Justification	182
3. Computerized Hyphenation Programs	183
4. Advantages Claimed for Computerized Typesetting	187
5. Editing and Proofreading in Existing Systems	187
6. Editing in Experimental Systems	188
7. An Experimental Edition Planner	190
8. Conclusions	192
References	192

Computer-Aided Typesetting
WILLIAM R. BOZMAN

1. Publication of Computer Output	195
2. Preparation of Computer Tapes for Typesetting	198
3. Examples of Computer-Prepared Typesetting	199
4. Hyphenless Justification	205
5. Conclusion	206
References	206

Programming Languages for Computational Linguistics
ARNOLD C. SATTERTHWAIT

1. Introduction	209
2. Languages for Machine Translation	212
3. A Sentence-Parsing Program in COMIT	227
References	238

Computer Driven Displays and Their Use in Man/Machine Interaction
ANDRIES VAN DAM

1. Introduction and History	239
2. Display Technology	242
3. Man/Machine Interaction	278
References	287
Bibliography	289
Author Index	291
Subject Index	295

Contents of Volume 1

General-Purpose Programming for Business Applications
  CALVIN C. GOTLIEB

Numerical Weather Prediction
  NORMAN A. PHILLIPS

The Present Status of Automatic Translation of Languages
  YEHOSHUA BAR-HILLEL

Programming Computers to Play Games
  ARTHUR L. SAMUEL

Machine Recognition of Spoken Words
  RICHARD FATEHCHAND

Binary Arithmetic
  GEORGE W. REITWIESNER

Contents of Volume 2

A Survey of Numerical Methods for Parabolic Differential Equations
  JIM DOUGLAS, JR.

Advances in Orthonormalizing Computation
  PHILIP J. DAVIS AND PHILIP RABINOWITZ

Microelectronics Using Electron-Beam-Activated Machining Techniques
  KENNETH R. SHOULDERS

Recent Developments in Linear Programming
  SAUL I. GASS

The Theory of Automata, a Survey
  ROBERT MCNAUGHTON

Contents of Volume 3

The Computation of Satellite Orbit Trajectories
  SAMUEL D. CONTE

Multiprogramming
  E. F. CODD

Recent Developments in Nonlinear Programming
  PHILIP WOLFE

Alternating Direction Implicit Methods
  GARRETT BIRKHOFF, RICHARD S. VARGA, AND DAVID YOUNG

Combined Analog-Digital Techniques in Simulation
  HAROLD K. SKRAMSTAD

Information Technology and the Law
  REED C. LAWLOR

Contents of Volume 4

The Formulation of Data Processing Problems for Computers
  WILLIAM C. MCGEE

All-Magnetic Circuit Techniques
  DAVID R. BENNION AND HEWITT D. CRANE

Computer Education
  HOWARD E. TOMPKINS

Digital Fluid Logic Elements
  H. H. GLAETTLI

Multiple Computer Systems
  WILLIAM A. CURTIN

Contents of Volume 5

The Role of Computers in Election Night Broadcasting
  Jack Moshman

Some Results of Research on Automatic Programming in Eastern Europe
  Władysław Turski

A Discussion of Artificial Intelligence and Self-Organization
  Gordon Pask

Automatic Optical Design
  Orestes N. Stavroudis

Computing Problems and Methods in X-Ray Crystallography
  Charles L. Coulter

Digital Computers in Nuclear Reactor Design
  Elizabeth Cuthill

An Introduction to Procedure-Oriented Languages
  Harry D. Huskey

Contents of Volume 6

Information Retrieval
  Claude E. Walston

Speculations Concerning the First Ultraintelligent Machine
  Irving John Good

Digital Training Devices
  Charles R. Wickman

Number Systems and Arithmetic
  Harvey L. Garner

Considerations on Man versus Machine for Space Probing
  P. L. Bargellini

Data Collection and Reduction for Nuclear Particle Trace Detectors
  Herbert Gelernter

Advances
in **COMPUTERS**
VOLUME 7

Highly Parallel Information Processing Systems*

JOHN C. MURTHA

Westinghouse Electric Corporation
Baltimore, Maryland

1. Introduction 2
   1.1 General Design Objectives 2
   1.2 Design Concepts 7
2. Parallel Network Computers 10
   2.1 SOLOMON I 11
   2.2 SOLOMON II 13
   2.3 Potential Parallel Network Developments 20
3. Distributed Control Networks 22
   3.1 The Holland Machine 23
   3.2 A Modified Holland Machine 27
   3.3 Multilayer Distributed Machine 29
   3.4 A Multidimensional Machine 31
   3.5 Von Neumann's Cellular Logic 33
4. Limited Application Parallel Processors 34
   4.1 Pattern Processors 34
   4.2 Associative Processors 39
   4.3 Differential Equation Processors 49
   4.4 Optical Processors 58
   4.5 Maximum Likelihood Processors 60
   4.6 Signal Processors 65
5. Multiple Instruction Stream/Multiple Function Machines . . 68
   5.1 The Ideal Multifunction Machine, IT 70
   5.2 Associative Logic Parallel System (ALPS) 71
   5.3 Schwartz's Machine 73
   5.4 Conway's System 76
   5.5 Variable Structure Parallel Computers 79
6. Programming Languages for Highly Parallel Machines. . . 84
   6.1 A Parallel Network Language 85
   6.2 A Language for Processing Two-Dimensional Patterns . . 89
   6.3 Concurrent ALGOL 90
7. Translation Techniques 91
   7.1 Translation for Distributed Control Machines . . . 91
   7.2 Algorithmic Decomposition 96
   7.3 Translation for Parallel Networks 99
8. Parallel Processing Techniques and Algorithms 100
   8.1 Parallel Network Processing 100
   8.2 Algorithms for Highly Parallel Machines 109
   References 113

* This work was partially supported by the Office of Naval Research under contract NOnr 4575 (00)

JOHN C. MURTHA

1. Introduction

The purpose of this article is to review the main body of work in the organization of highly parallel information processing systems. This work is very broad in scope, ranging from memory organized systems to various network systems and multiple computer systems. The memory organized systems work is closely tied to the manufacturing technology of batch fabrication [*34*].

Section 1 is a discussion of the general objectives of the research, the types of systems that are being developed, and the general problems faced. Sections 2, 3, 4, and 5 cover parallel networks, distributed control networks, limited application parallel processors, and multiple instruction stream/multiple function systems. Sections 6, 7, and 8 discuss parallel languages, translation techniques, and algorithms.

1.1 General Design Objectives

There are three primary design objectives being pursued in research in highly parallel processors. Probably the most significant of these is to obtain a radical increase in computing power, perhaps several orders of magnitude, within the existing component technology. This increase is expected to be obtained from (a) using more components and (b) obtaining better utilization of these components. Costs are expected to be held down because cheaper parts and manufacturing techniques can be used.

Unusual computing power can be obtained in only two ways: either by using unusually fast components or using many (perhaps) slower components in parallel. The latter approach can be both cheaper and more effective. Figure 1 shows the general trend in the cost versus speed capabilities of memories in late 1964. This curve will shift with time but is expected to retain its essential shape. Similarly, unusual component speeds require expensive and developmental techniques.

A second aspect of the component cost factor as it relates to organization is illustrated in Fig. 2. It shows the relation between number of devices used and number of logic stages for a 23-bit addition. The number of logic stages and the propagation delay of the logic element determine the add time. As an example, 3 adders with 10 stages each can be built with roughly the same component count as a single adder with 5 stages (only twice as fast). This is of course not the whole story. For example, because of memory constraints, it is more difficult to supply a single stream of operands to the extremely fast adder than multiple parallel streams to slower adders.

Figure 3 shows how the component cost factors can relate to the system

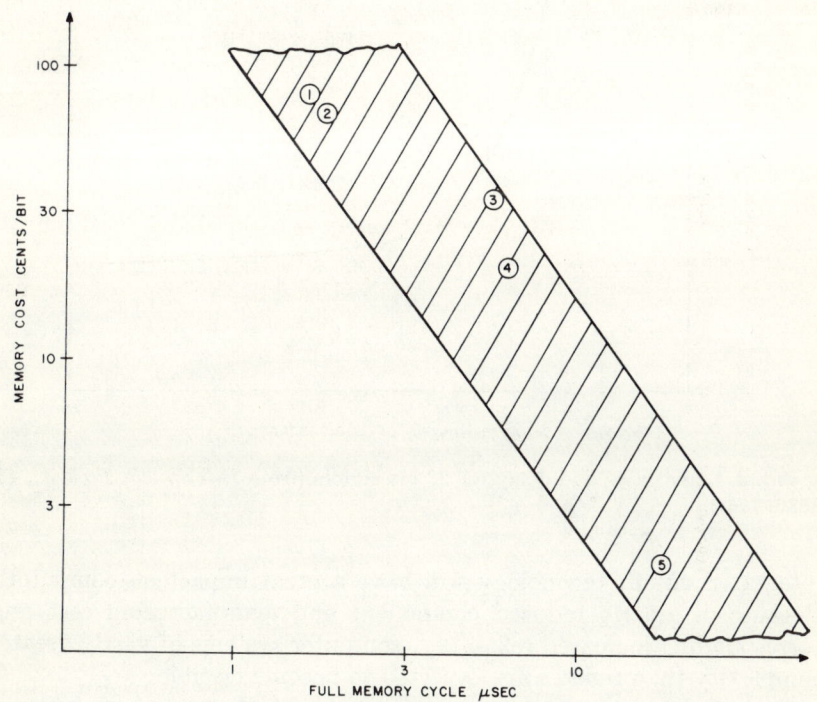

Fig. 1. Random access memory cost, 1964: 1, Philco 212, 1.6×10^6 bits, 1.5 μsec cycle; 2, IBM 7094, 10^6 bits, 2 μsec cycle; 3, GE 235, 3.3×10^5 bits, 6 μsec cycle; 4, CDC 1064A, 1.6×10^6 bits, 6.4 μsec cycle; 5, Ferroxcube mass memory, 5×10^6 bits, 15 μsec cycle (available 1965).

cost effectiveness. A representative highly parallel machine (SOLOMON II) is compared with a group of conventional machines in bit handling capability (additions per second times word length) versus cost. The data are taken from the *Computer Characteristics Quarterly* [2]. It should be noted that this chart ignores the very important factor of how efficiently the computer can be used in practice including software, data flow efficiency, input/output flexibility, and relative bookkeeping requirements.

The second major objective being pursued is to take advantage of the rapid development of batch fabrication technology. It has been widely recognized that the full development of batch fabrication and

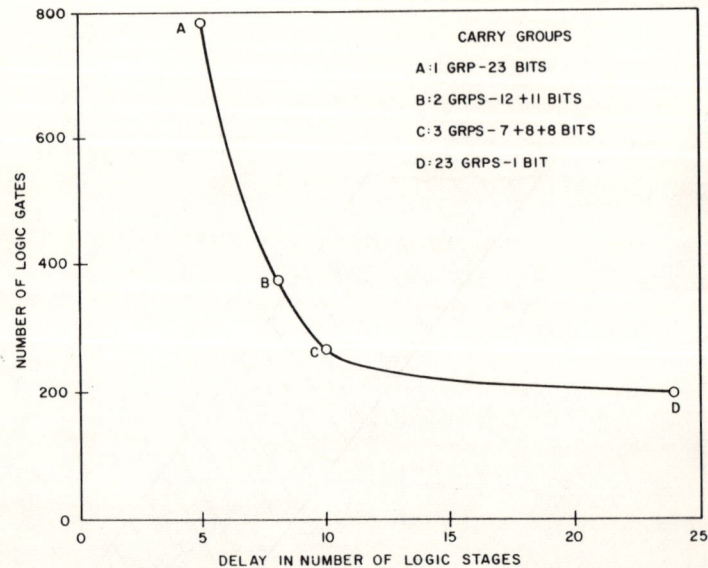

FIG. 2. Logic gates and delay for 23 bit adders (from *Bell System Tech. J.*, **43**, 2080, 1964).

integrated circuit technology will have a great impact on computers. Because of greatly reduced component and manufacturing cost and corresponding increased reliability, computer systems of vastly greater complexity than today's are expected to become feasible.

Part of this potential has been realized with the passage from transistor to integrated circuits of the single gate per package variety. In fact, it is this development which makes reasonable a computer of the SOLOMON type. The future developments in integrated circuit technology will determine the feasibility of more advanced computer concepts. Within the next few years, it will probably be possible to manufacture basic circuit devices with perhaps two orders of magnitude greater complexity than the integrated circuits of today and with a reliability comparable to today's single circuit. Because of the ease with which these circuits can be fabricated, the component technology can be expected to force a repetitive structure onto the computer. At present, such a repetitive structure occurs at the gate level, all logical devices being constructed from a few variations of the same basic integrated circuit.

The changes in technology can be best summarized in terms of the following factors. First, integrated circuit logic speed: With certain exceptions, the power of a given machine organization is determined by

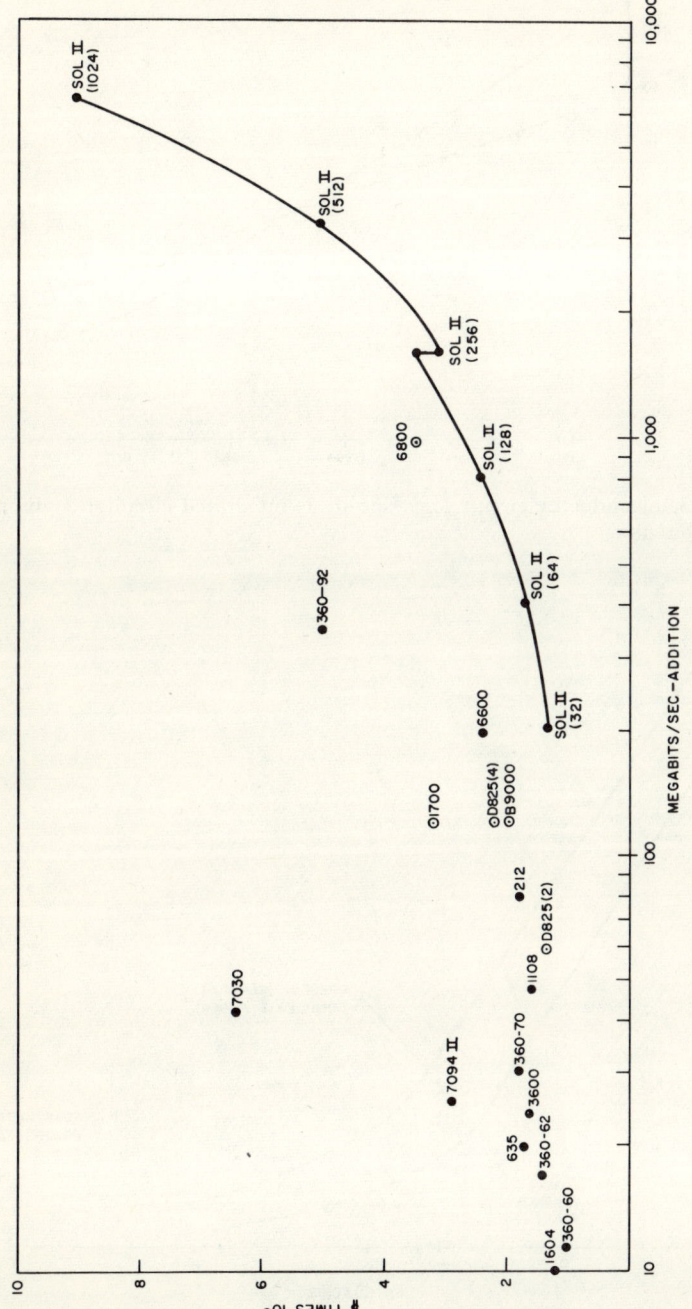

FIG. 3. Cost versus potential processing capability.

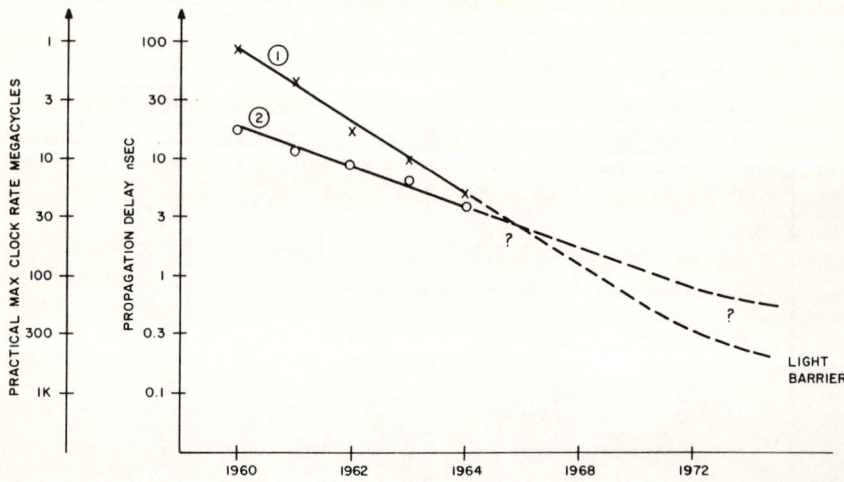

FIG. 4. Semiconductor circuit logic speed: 1, integrated circuits; 2, discrete transistor circuits.

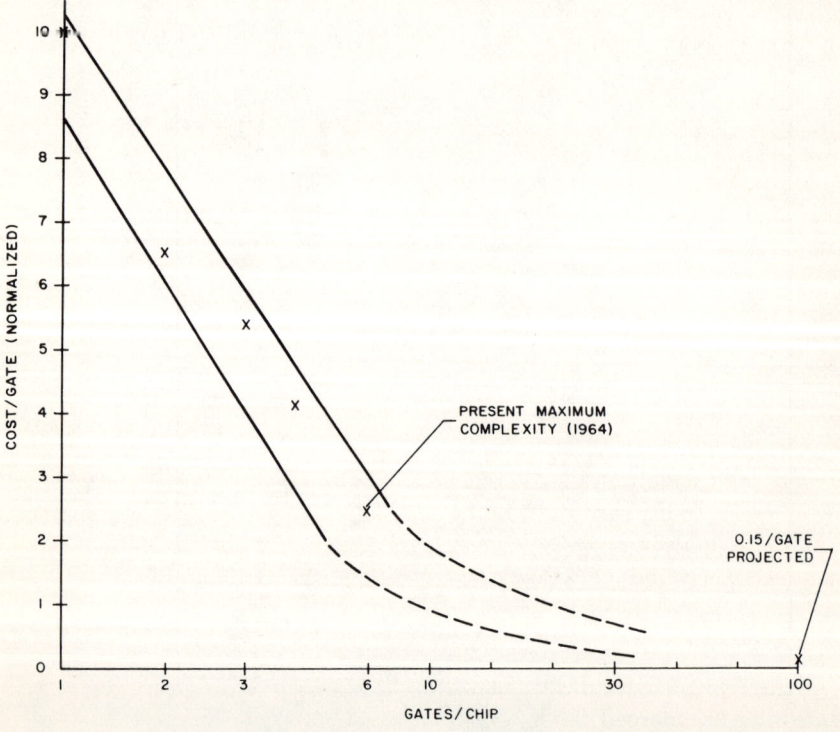

FIG. 5. More gates per chip reduces gate cost.

the propagation delay through the switching device. As this delay falls, the speed of the computer can be increased proportionally. This applies to both conventional and highly parallel machines. A projection of circuit propagation delay is shown in Fig. 4. Second, cost of the device: This factor, together with reliability, limits the number of components that can be used in a computer. The likely evolution of the integrated circuit and its effect on the cost factors are shown in Fig. 5. This curve is based on the assumption that a highly repetitive structure is used. Third, memory speed: Generally, the faster the machine the faster the memory must be. Evolution of memory speed is shown in Fig. 6.

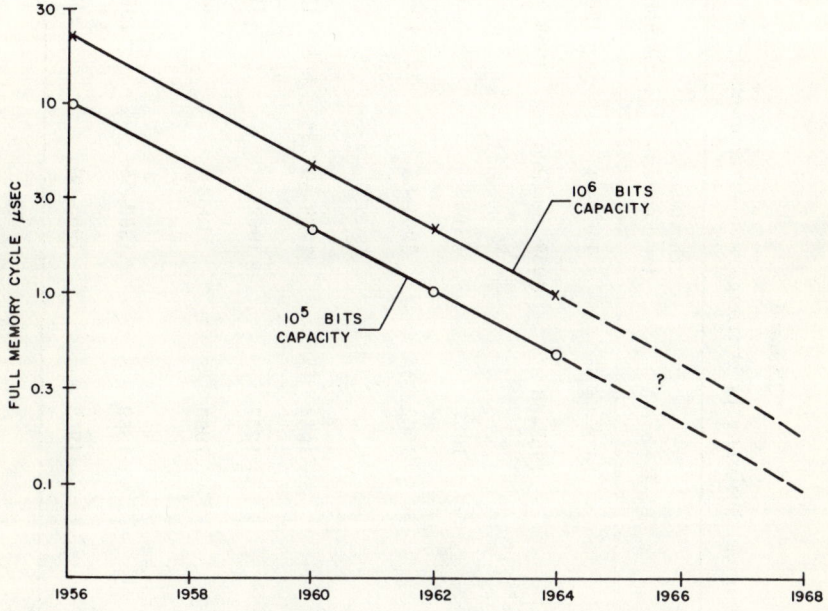

FIG 6. Random-access memory speed versus time.

A third motivating force is the desire to reflect more closely the structure of widely used algorithms. Some of the most important areas of interest today are the numerical solution of partial differential equations, matrix processes, and the processing of data structures such as precedence and phrase structure languages, trees, and lists.

1.2 Design Concepts

A number of basic design concepts in highly parallel machine organization have emerged. These concepts are to a large degree independent, in that each can be used in a system whether or not the others are. They

TABLE I

GENERAL SUMMARY OF ANTICIPATED DEVELOPMENT

	Research	Hardware development	Demonstration	Operationally used
Parallel networks	1958–64	1961–64	1962–64	1966–68
Distributed control networks	1958–66	1968 (possible)	1969 (possible)	—
Limited application machines:				
Pattern processors	1957	1962	1965	1966
Associative processors	1962	1964–65	1965–66	—
Differential equation processors	—	—	—	—
Optical processors	1954	1958–59	1960	1960
Maximum likelihood processors	1957	1962–	1962	—
Signal processors (parallel, digital)	1963	1963	1967–68	—
Multiple instruction/function machines:				
Variable structure	1959	1962–65	1965–66	—
Multiple instruction systems	1962	1965–66	1966	1966–67

HIGHLY PARALLEL INFORMATION PROCESSING SYSTEMS

TABLE II
STATUS SUMMARY

	Present status	General problems
Parallel networks	General development completed, some hardware exists, hardware being built	Requires operational experience and future software development
Distributed control networks	Further research necessary, no hardware built	Depends on continued evolution of integrated circuit technology
Limited application machine:		
Pattern processors	Further research necessary, hardware has been built	Probably too special purpose
Associative processors	Demonstration hardware being built	Utility needs to be demonstrated; software and experience lacking
Differential equation processors	Operationally used	Limited range of applicability and flexibility
Optical processors	Operationally used	Flexibility needed
Maximum likelihood processors	Research hardware built	Probably too limited in concept
Signal processors (parallel digital)	Operationally used	Lower cost needed to compete with other less flexible alternatives
Multiple instruction/multiple function machines:		
Variable structure	Hardware being built	Operating experience necessary, further software development
Multiple instruction systems	Some hardware exists, more being built	Software and experience lacking in more highly parallel areas

9

are multiple bit processing, multiple parameter processing, multiple instruction stream processing, and multiple function processing.

By multiple bit processing is meant the conventional parallel by bit processing. Multiple parameter processing involves a single instruction stream which is executed simultaneously by many arithmetic units, each operating on different parametric values of the same data type. This approach is used in parallel network machines, associative processors, and most limited application highly parallel processors.

Multiple instruction stream processing involves using parallel instruction sources with related control and execution logic provided for each instruction stream. Many different approaches have been proposed, differing primarily in the manner in which the different instruction streams are integrated and the degree to which data are available to all processors. Machines in this case include distributed control networks and multiple computer systems.

Multiple function processing refers to the use of special purpose subsystems which can operate simultaneously under programmer control. This includes systems such as the GAMMA 60, systems with special I/O subsystems and probably should include variable structure machines.

There are, of course, additional parallelism techniques which have been used to speed up various systems. They include separating instruction and data memory, look ahead and overlapping of instruction, and overlapping of memory modules.

A brief summary of the development status of highly parallel hardware and the general development problems is given in Tables I and II.

2. Parallel Network Computers

The parallel network was conceived with the recognition first, that the really large-scale computing jobs are generated from the repetitive execution of the same algorithm over and over on different pieces of data, and second, that much of the cost of conventional computing is tied up in the control logic. The parallel network takes advantage of both factors. Many simple, identical processors are each programmed by a common central control in such a way as to directly simulate the fundamental physical processes. The concept is illustrated in Fig. 7.

The basic process which is to be executed upon different data drives the network through a single program in the common control. Each of the processors which comprise the network then executes the process with its own data.

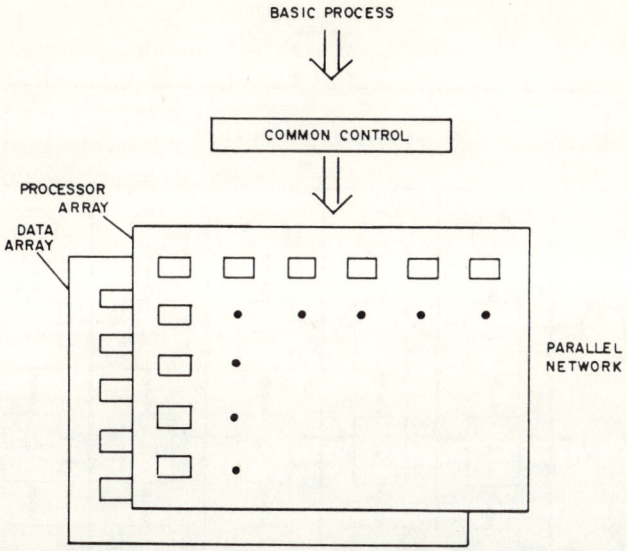

FIG. 7. Multiple parallel execution of a basic process on different pieces of data.

2.1 SOLOMON I

The heart of the SOLOMON I system [4, 60, 61] is the network of processing elements illustrated in Fig. 8. The system consists nominally of 1024 of these processing elements in a 32×32 array. Each Processing Element (PE) is a complete minimized serial-by-bit arithmetic and logical unit that is capable of performing a full complement of arithmetic and logical instructions on a pair of binary digits at a time. Each PE may contain up to 16,382 bits of data storage in modules of 4096 bits. Word length is completely variable from 1 to 128 bits as determined by the contents of a Variable Word Length Register accessible to the programmer.

Each PE has the option of playing either an active or passive role during an instruction cycle on the basis of its own state in the mode control method described later. These processing elements are identical and the system is composed of modules of an arbitrary number of PE's. Each PE is connected by serial data busses (the heavy lines in Fig. 9) to its four nearest neighbors permitting the interchange of data stored in the PE memories.

The geometry of the basic 32×32 array of PE's is illustrated by first considering the array as a plane where $N(i, j)$ represents the ith row and jth column. Several array interconnection variations can be selected by the programmer. These are listed as follows:

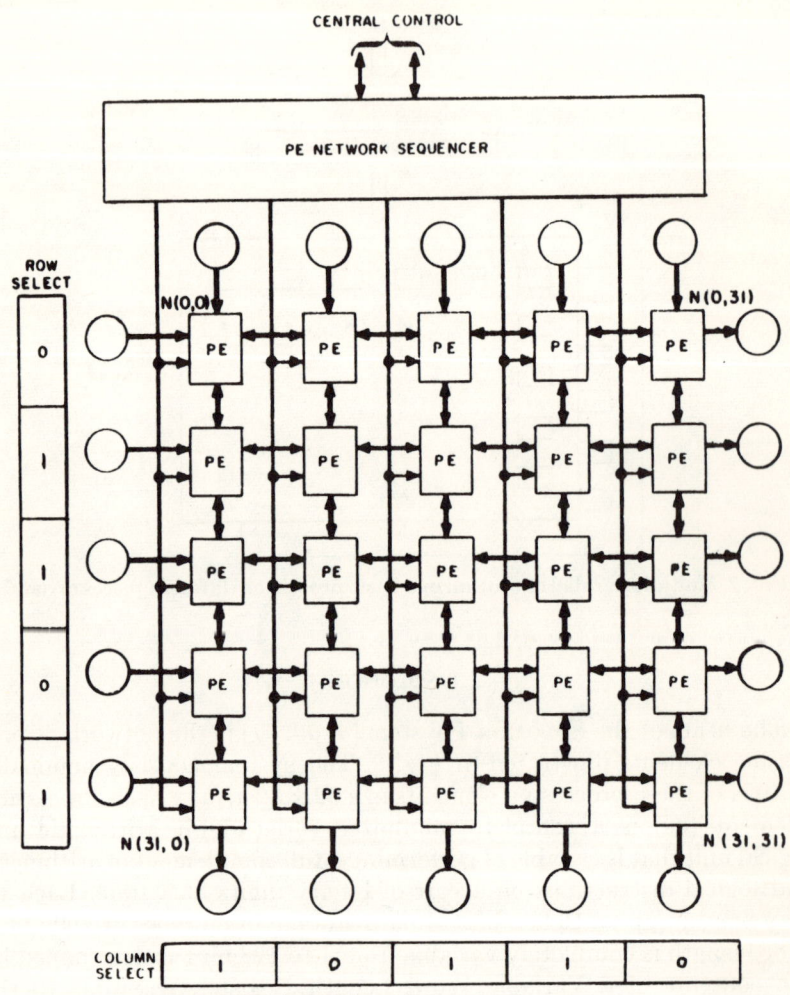

Fig. 8. SOLOMON I parallel network.

(1) Processing elements in column $N(i, 31)$ can be connected logically to the corresponding PE's in column $N(i, 0)$ resulting in the formation of a cylindrical array.

(2) Likewise the row $N(0, j)$ can be connected logically to the row $N(31, j)$ and a second cylinder formed.

(3) The first two options can be combined with the net result being that the PE array is formed into a torus.

(4) An additional option is available to the programmer which forms the PE array into a single straight line of 1024 PE's. That is, the specific

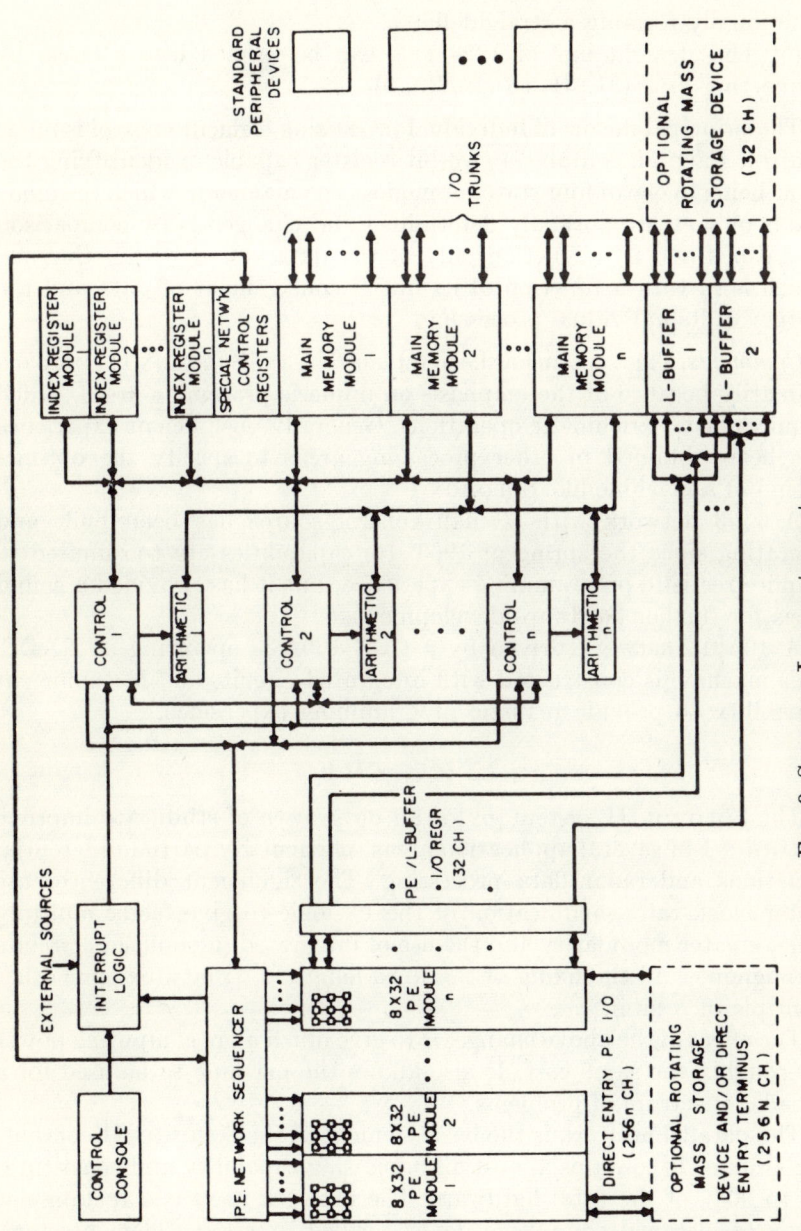

Fig. 9. Solomon I computer system.

PE designated by $N(i, 31)$ is logically connected to PE $N(i + 1, 0)$ functionally forming a straight line.

(5) The straight line of 1024 PE's can be formed into a circle by connecting PE $N(31, 31)$ to PE $N(0, 0)$.

The principal means of individual processing element control is mode control. Each PE contains a two-bit register capable of identifying the PE as being in one of four states or modes. The manner in which the mode states of a PE are normally determined and changed is by comparison operations and is a function only of the data stored within that PE, which is in turn a function of its initial consignment of data and the history of its individual processing.

Comments. This system has been replaced by the SOLOMON II approach primarily because of the emphasis on numeric processing areas, which requires faster arithmetic operations. Generally, insufficient experience has been obtained in other processing areas to specify the optimal design of a machine like SOLOMON I.

A 3×3 network with a small control source has been built and operating since the spring of 1963. Its capabilities are too limited to acquire realistic programming experience, but it has provided a sound basis for further hardware development.

A 10×10 network driven by a CDC 160A is operating at RADC. This machine is constructed with integrated circuits and has sufficient capability to provide realistic programming experience.

2.2 SOLOMON II

The SOLOMON II system [62] is an outgrowth of studies to improve SOLOMON I in several application areas, particularly partial differential equations and radar data processing. The significant differences are faster clock rate, modification of the PE logic to give faster multiply time, greater modularity and the use of integrated (monolithic) circuits throughout, and the fixing of the word length at 24 bits (or some other multiple of 8 bits).

The effect of the above changes is to give much more computing power for roughly the same cost. It also allows the machine to be used for a broader spectrum of problems.

The parallel network is the basic element of the SOLOMON II computing system. It contains almost all processing capability and constitutes up to 90% of the total hardware. The network itself is a rectangular array of identical computing devices called processing elements (PE). Each of these can perform all the arithmetic and logical processes normally associated with a general-purpose computer. Furthermore, each PE has its own data memory which serves as its working storage.

HIGHLY PARALLEL INFORMATION PROCESSING SYSTEMS

2.2.1 Flow of Instructions

The principal units in the SOLOMON II system are shown in Fig. 10. The Network Control Unit (NCU) performs the system control function. Programs for the network are stored in the Program Memory which is separate from the PE memory. The NCU obtains network instructions one at a time from the program memory and either sends them to the Network Sequencer or executes the instruction itself. The network

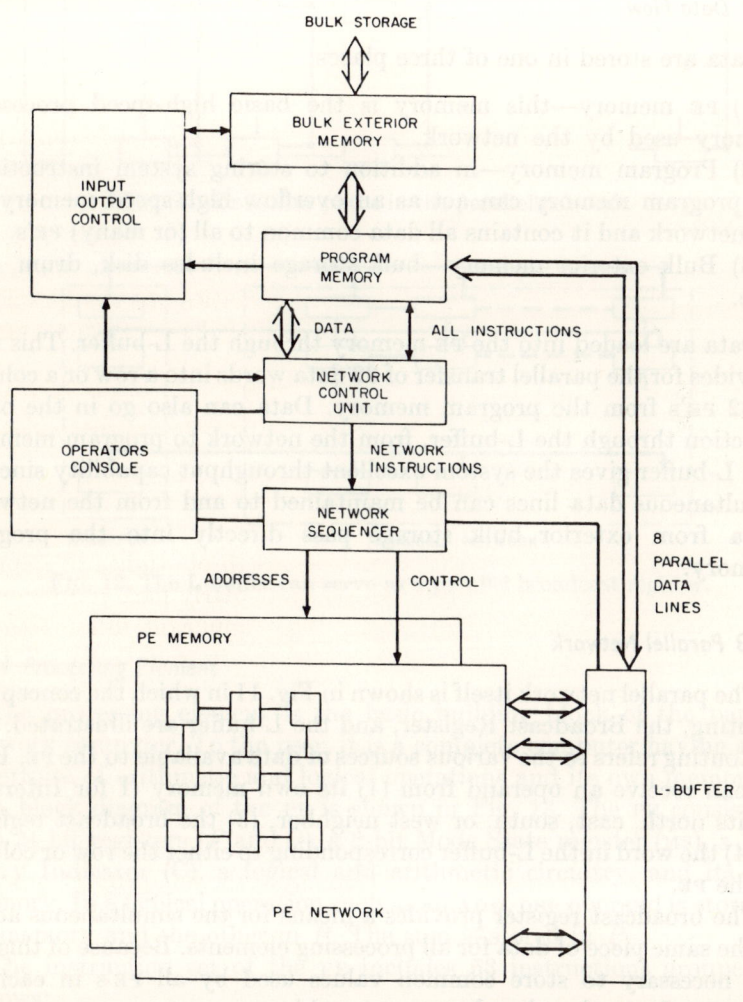

FIG. 10. SOLOMON II system.

15

(2) Fixed point arithmetic—addition, subtraction, multiplication, division, sign operations, and shifts within P and Q.

(3) Boolean operations—AND, OR, exclusive OR, NOT.

(4) Mode control—mode status can be set unconditionally or by comparison of data stored in the PE.

Operation times for these operations are:

Multiply	19.1 μsec
Any compare	3.8 μsec
Any command that writes into memory	3.8 μsec
Divide	84.6 μsec
Shifts	3.3 to 16.4 μsec
Other	3.4 μsec

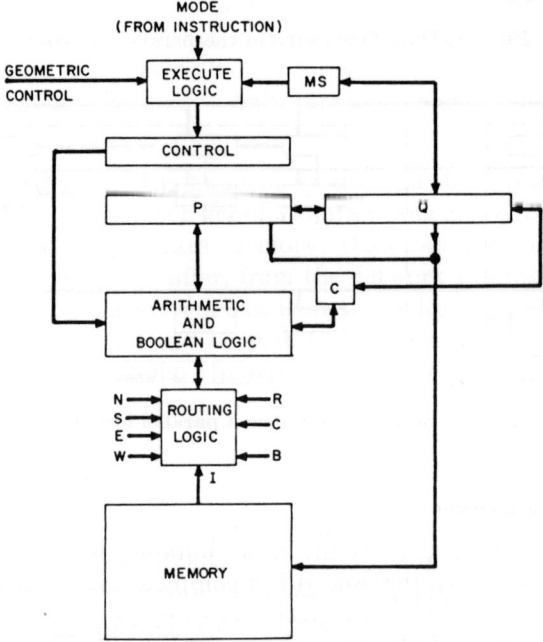

FIG. 13. The processing element.

2.2.5 Mode Control

The mode state register (MS) is a register which sets the operating status of the PE to one of four states or modes, 0, 1, 2, or 3. Each network instruction then indicates which PE modes are to be effective. Thus, when the network executes an operation, each PE in an effective mode performs the operation, while all others do nothing.

The mode of a PE can be set by conditional or unconditional mode changing instructions. For example, a PE can be set to a particular mode if its P register contains zero. The mode state register is addressable so that mode data can be transferred to and from PE memory. By this means an arbitrary number of different mode states can be effectively programmed.

2.2.6 The Input/Output System

The input/output system is designed to provide throughput consistent with the computing power of the parallel network. The path of data, shown in Fig. 14, is from bulk exterior storage to the program memory, to the L-buffer (LB), to the network. The path between the LB and the

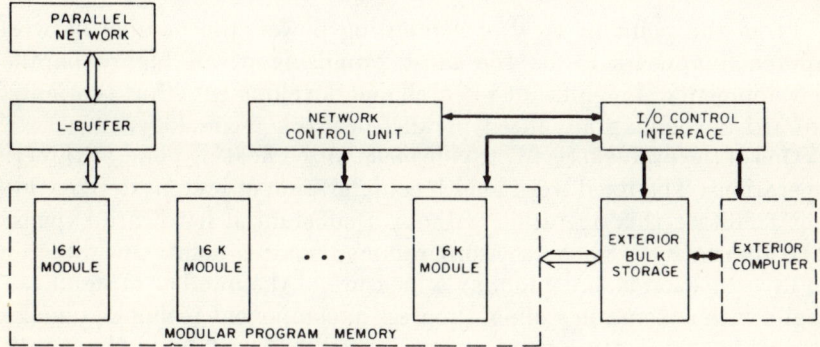

Fig. 14. Input/output data flow.

Program Memory (PM) is 96 bits. The number of bits accessed per program memory cycle is 192. The 96-bit path between the LB and the PM allows data to be transferred to the network. In approximately 3.8 μsec, thirty-two 24-bit data words can be transferred between the LB and network. Between the LB and program memory, eight 24-bit words (192 bits) are transferred per memory cycle. Four 1-μsec memory cycles will transfer 32 data words to the L-buffer.

Program memory is modular in blocks of $16K$, each of which can be independently accessed. To maintain peak data flow to and from the network, one module is connected to exterior storage while another is communicating with the network. Roles are periodically exchanged.

A generalized I/O controller interface provides for communication to a general-purpose computer or an independent input/output system. Instructions to the I/O controller are passed through the program memory. The SOLOMON II system thus has the capability of being used as a peripheral parallel computation device for a wide variety of conventional general-purpose computers or of standing alone as a powerful parallel processor depending upon the problem mix or system requirements of the user. This approach is necessary to allow the system to reflect the operating requirements over the wide range of application of the network.

Comments. The SOLOMON II system is the most powerful highly parallel system. Extensive programming and hardware experience has been acquired; design has been almost completed. It can be expected that a full scale SOLOMON II (or decendent) will be operating in a production role within several years.

2.3 Potential Parallel Network Developments

From the point of view of computing power, the parallel network approach appears to be the most promising of all highly parallel developments. A significant research and development effort is oriented toward developing advanced parallel network technology.

One of the problems is to provide mechanized floating point arithmetic operations. The fixed word length configuration of present designs does not facilitate this operation without a substantial hardware expense. The alternative is of course a programmed floating point. One direction of investigation is in combining a measure of the number of significant digits with automatic scaling. Progress in component technology makes it certain that floating point operations will be practical in the parallel network in a short time.

A second problem is to obtain more flexible data distribution in the network. Present configurations have either four or six nearest neighbors. Channels also exist from each PE to exterior registers. In several applications, however, more flexible data flow between PE's is desired. For example, in the iterative solution of certain partial differential equations (alternating directions) it is desirable that each PE be able to obtain operands from all other PE's. Several methods have been proposed to achieve this capability and it appears that the cost may be quite realistic. The capability will also broaden the spectrum of system applications.

A third area of interest is higher operating speed in the PE. Several directions are being investigated. One of these is to include more parallelism in the PE. For example, the PE multiply speed of SOLOMON II is in part achieved through parallel rather than serial arithmetic. Another direction is to increase the clock speed. The general difficulty here is that memory speed must be increased. One way that this can be done is by overlapping several slower memories. Progress in memory technology can be expected to improve this parallel network capability.

HIGHLY PARALLEL INFORMATION PROCESSING SYSTEMS

A fourth problem is to allow independent memory access within the PE's. Memory costs are a large fraction of the total hardware costs of the parallel network and in fact the whole approach depends, from a cost point of view, on common PE memory addressing. Furthermore, practical programming requirements also restrict the memory addressing scheme. For example, it is impractical at this time to consider writing programs in which each PE must have a separate stream of data addresses flowing into it.

The programming element of the problem can be solved if the independent memory access is provided within the framework of indexing. In this design the common memory address transmitted to all PE's is modified by an index value stored within the PE. The effective address used in each PE therefore can be different. It appears that this approach is as general as is needed.

The hardware problems are not so easily solved. No idea has been presented which gives promise of solving all of them within reasonable cost bounds. However, further developments (particularly cost reductions) in associative or distributed logic memories can provide the solution.

A direction of development interest is toward facilitating multiple instruction streams directing the network, that is, a limited form of distributed control. Specifically, in some applications, mode control is used to effect a branch in the control process. The separate branches of the process must be followed sequentially with mode control used to associate each PE with the appropriate branch. The effect is to reduce the hardware utilization factor, since only a fraction of the PE's operate in each branch. The ultimate objective is to provide the means for the separate branches of the control process to be followed in parallel, thereby raising the hardware utilization factor.

The brute force method is to have multiple sequencers with mode control used to associate each PE with the proper sequencer. Among other things this gives rise to problems with memory organization. Several other suggestions have been made that may eventually turn into realistic hardware.

It should be emphasized that the requirement for both the independent control and the independent memory access has not been clearly demonstrated. It has been found that in practical programming it is generally possible to get around these problems by using different processing techniques.

A final development which would have great significance for parallel networks is a practical large memory which has two separate accessing structures as does the present L-buffer. Such a memory would serve as both the PE memory and program memory. Presently data must be loaded first into program memory and then passed to PE memory through the L-buffer.

In addition to answering the fundamental problem of inadequate computing power, the parallel network makes several other important contributions. The most significant of these is an important reduction in cost per operation. There are several reasons for this. First, beyond a certain speed, component costs rise very rapidly with increases in operating speed. With the parallel network, computing capacity is obtained through parallelism rather than through developmental extremely high speed component technology. This allows the component requirements, and hence costs, to be brought into balance with the total system capabilities. For example, integrated circuitry is used throughout in SOLOMON II. Also, the high degree of hardware modularity simplifies manufacture, assembly, and checkout of the computer.

The second major contribution is that for the first time a truly modular computing system is available. Growth in computing capacity can be achieved by increasing the network size without a major effect on software. Thus, the size of the parallel network can be changed to reflect an increase (or a decrease) in computing load without affecting in any way the basic process which drives the network.

J. H. Pomerene at IBM is reported to be constructing a Parallel Network Digital Computer (PNDC) with 32 processing elements. It differs from SOLOMON II in that the processors are fully parallel by bit, word length being 32 bits. It is alike in that it has such elements as the broadcast register and mode control. As with SOLOMON II the limit of processing power is the memory. A $\frac{1}{2}$-μsec cycle time core memory is being used with access to thirty-two 32-bit words per cycle. The add time of the PE is about 400 nsec and the multiply time about 1.3 μsec. By reducing the number of PE's, it becomes more feasible to buffer between the arithmetic unit and memory. A high-speed 32 word flip-flop storage is being used for this. By using the higher speed memory and the buffer, a speed advantage of 3 times is gained over the 256 PE SOLOMON II which probably will cost about the same.

Several other advantages are gained in going to the small number of processors and the parallel by bit arithmetic. First, more flexible routing is practical. Second, a smaller number of processors is more flexible in its application, and third, a distributed control mode is more practical.

3. Distributed Control Networks

Distributed control machines consist of an array of many identical modules or processing elements each of which can independently execute an instruction. This machine organization was first proposed as a conceptual rather than a practical device to provide a formal basis for theoretical investigations in automata theory and computability. Such a machine is designed to execute an arbitrary number of programs or subprograms simultaneously. Since Holland first proposed the distributed control approach in 1958, several investigators have attempted to recast the idea to make it more practical.

The most important problems in the original organization are the large amount of hardware and the low utilization factor. Several proposals have been made to reduce the hardware, generally by compromising the distribution of control. A second, perhaps equally important problem, is programming the machine.

3.1 The Holland Machine

The machine [32, 33] is a two-dimensional array of identical simple modules. Each module contains a simple storage register and several auxiliary registers and can communicate in several ways with its north, east, south, and west neighbors. Each module can be thought of as having two relatively independent sections. The upper section is memory and control, while the lower section governs the general communications functions giving a dual network effect as shown in Fig. 15.

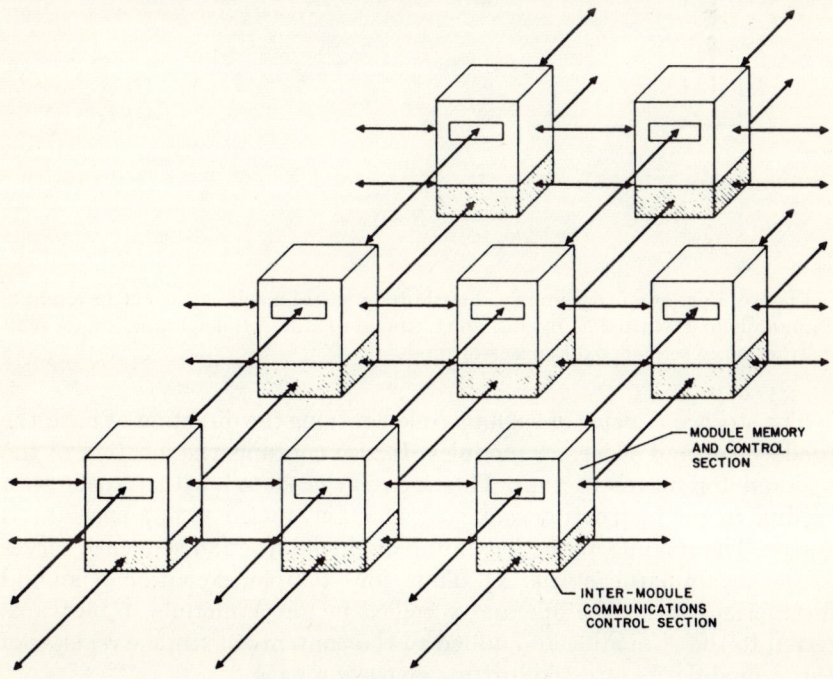

FIG. 15. Holland machine network.

A sequence of instructions is stored in an arbitrary line of modules, with one instruction stored in each storage register. These instructions are executed one at a time along one direction of the line of successors. The active instruction is contained in the storage register of a module in the active (X) status. This module is placed into X status (turned on) by its predecessor, namely a north, south, east, or west neighbor. It interprets the data in its storage register as an instruction and executes it. It then passes its activity to its successor in the program sequence, one of its nearest neighbors. An arbitrary number of modules may be active.

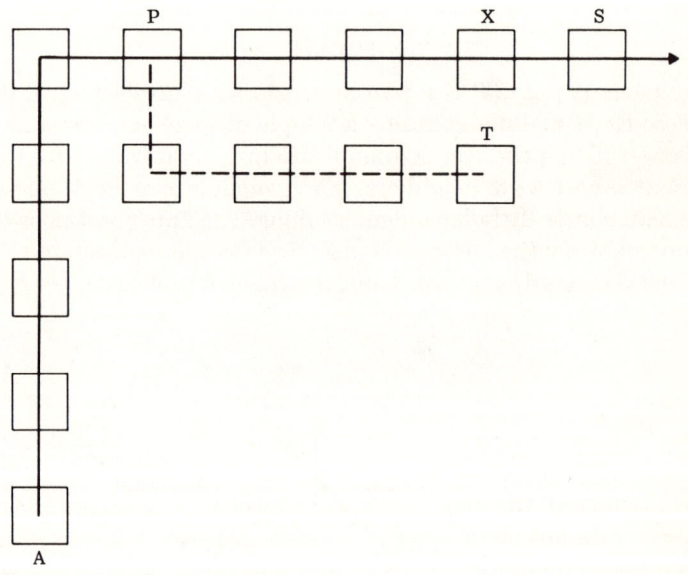

Fig. 16. Part of a program in a distributed control machine: X, active module; P, module in P status; T, operand or terminal module; A, accumulation; S, next instruction in sequence for successor module.

The storage register of each module contains the direction of both the predecessor and successor modules. It also contains the location of the operand for its instruction. This location is stated with respect to a module in the instruction sequence which is labeled as in a special (P) status. The module at the beginning of the instruction sequence serves as the accumulator (status A). Thus, for example, execution of an add instruction causes the operand specified in the X module to be transferred to the A module and added to the contents of storage register of the A module. Figure 16 illustrates part of a path.

The operation at each time step is divided into three phases. In phase one, the module storage register can be set to a value supplied by an external source. During phase two, an active module determines the location of the operand. A path is gated open from the A module to the operand. During phase three, the active module executes the instruction in its storage register.

Several rules must be incorporated into the hardware to insure that there is no interference between programs. For example, independent paths to separate operands may cross through a module but independent paths may not start at the same module.

A total of eight instructions is included: arithmetic add, store the value in A into a given operand, transfer on minus, iterate segment (used for path building), set registers, record registers, no order, and stop.

Comments. As noted previously this machine has several severe problems which prevent it from being a practical device. The most important is that a very large amount of hardware is required to achieve reasonable computing capability. Because of programming difficulties much of the hardware at any given time will not be used. No way has been found to achieve a high hardware utilization factor. Furthermore, because of the complexity of the module, it does not appear that in the near future it will be possible to make a module as a single monolithic circuit.

As another example of a practical difficulty, path lengths to operands may be both very short and very long. The clock rate of the system must be slow enough to account for the longest path. This has the effect of further reducing the hardware utilization factor. An asynchronous operation does not seem feasible because of programming problems.

The programming problem is also very severe. While progress in developing algorithms for converting present-day computer languages into a Holland machine language is being made, the gap between what is needed and what is available is too large for practical consideration in the near future.

A rough gate count [9] for the modules of this machine has been made at the University of Michigan giving about 1200 gates per module. This is based on the assumption of serial data transfer and a 40-bit word. There is a possibility that this module eventually can be constructed as a single monolithic integrated circuit. At this time (late 1964) it is possible to make 1200 gates on a single one square inch monolithic substrate. However, this ignores the yield problem in that only perhaps 90% of these circuits would be good. Several possibilities exist for getting around this. First, a factor of 2 reduction in the linear dimensions of each gate can be achieved in the near future, allowing perhaps 5000 gates per square inch. It may be possible to test these gates individually, then connect only good ones to produce the full module. This will be at best a rather expensive process.

A second possibility is to use redundant circuit logic, perhaps majority logic, with four gates used for each functional gate (a total of 5000 gates). Assuming a total of 50 faults in the substrate gives a yield of good modules of about 1 in 4. Thus, the cost per module would be roughly four times the cost of one complete process. A cost of perhaps $100 each in large quantities might therefore be anticipated. With a 10,000-module machine, the hardware cost would be $1 million, not totally unreasonable.

It is also constructive to estimate the operation times. The multiply operation is not mechanized and must be programmed. It is also not a representative operation for this machine. The add time is a more suitable operation time. This time depends on the path length from operand to accumulator. An average value of 200 modules per path is reasonable. Each module will have about 10 gating levels giving about 2000 gates through which the signal must propagate. Assuming 10 nsec per gate gives 20 μsec.

The 10,000-module machine is at best a minimum practical system since it includes both data and instruction storage, a small total for a very high speed computer.

A comparison of the Holland machine with a conventional computer has been made at Michigan for the problem of inverting an $M \times M$ matrix. The results are summarized in Table III. A measure of effective-

TABLE III

COMPARISON OF A CONVENTIONAL COMPUTER WITH A HOLLAND MACHINE

	Conventional computer	2-Dimensional Holland
Number of instruction words and temporary storage	150	$5-9M^2$
Instructions plus data	$M^2 + 150$	$6-10M^2$
Minimum possible length of program	$5M^3$	$3M^2$
Maximum number of instructions executed in parallel	1	$5M$
Total words times length of program	$5M^3$	$18-30M^4$

ness is given as the number of words of storage times the program length (proportional to running time). The 10,000-module machine will handle a 30 × 30 matrix. The result that conventional organization is superior for this type of processing is clear.

3.2 A Modified Holland Machine

Comfort [11] has proposed a modification of the Holland machine which has a better hardware utilization factor and which is easier to program. His approach is to use two types of modules, called A modules or A boxes, and storage modules. The A modules provide arithmetic and logic capability, while the storage modules provide instruction and data storage. The A modules are placed along one side of an array of storage modules as shown in Fig. 17. A single A box serves several columns of storage modules, and a switch is included to switch between columns. The A boxes correspond to the accumulator modules of the Holland machine. Storage modules consist of a single word storage register together with data and instruction communication logic.

The basic instruction and data storage concepts of the Holland machine are retained. An instruction sequence must start with an A box. The line of successors is determined by a 2-bit "next instruction address" which indicates which of the four nearest neighbors contains the next instruction address. During instruction execution, the instruction (stored in the storage register) is sent back along the line of predecessors to the A box at the beginning of the sequence.

Operands are retrieved in a manner similar to the Holland path building approach. A path starts at a P module in the instruction sequence and stops at a termination point T. These modules are connected by a sequence of horizontal and vertical path segments. Paths are formed through communication logic in the storage module. The operand in the T module is gated down the path to the P module and from there to the A box. A somewhat different and more flexible path building procedure than in Holland's machine is used.

Also, a richer instruction repertoire is made available since the instruction execution need only be mechanized in A boxes. The instruction word is 36 bits including the instruction code and path building data which are equivalent to the operand address. A total of 31 different instructions are defined including arithmetic, logical, and instruction sequence codes plus various control operations.

Comments. This approach gives a reduction in hardware of roughly four times by removing arithmetic and decoding logic from the array modules. It also simplifies the programming problem primarily through the richer instruction repertoire. Very little, if any, flexibility is given

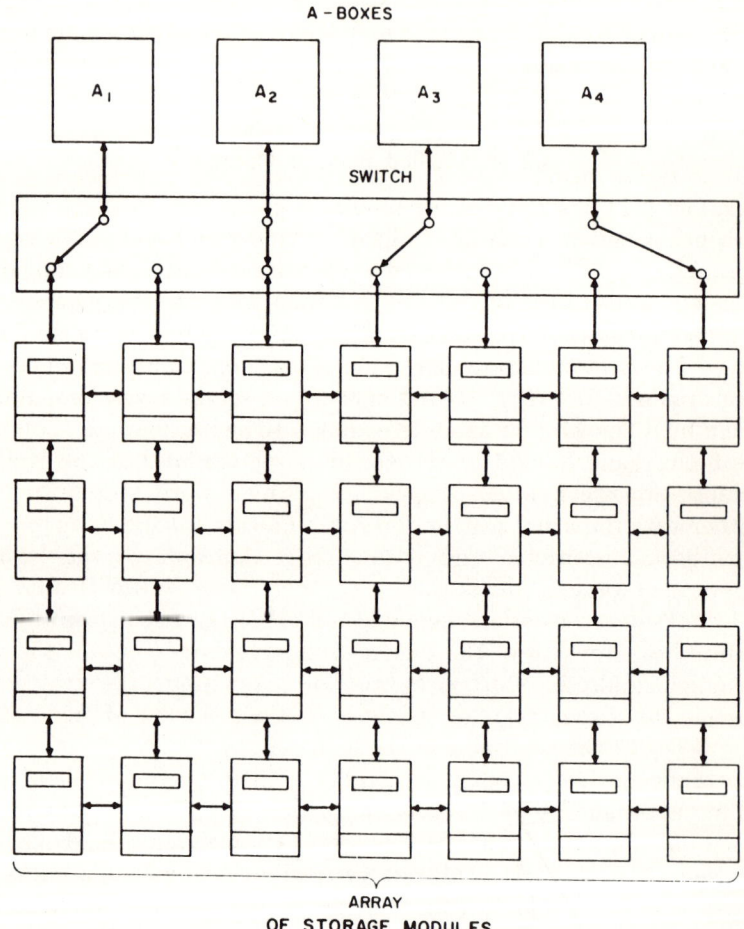

Fig. 17. Network computing system.

up and thus this approach (as a practical machine) is definitely superior to a pure Holland machine.

Many variations in hardware can be seen for this machine, such as having more than a single word of storage in a storage module. It appears that it will become possible in perhaps three years to build this machine with enough modules (10^4) to be perhaps practical. It therefore would be desirable to continue system and optimization studies. One aspect of the organization that should receive attention is the poor hardware utilization. It does not seem possible to have as much as perhaps one-twentieth of the hardware active on the average. Another element to be considered is mechanization methods. For example, magnetic core is now a cheaper way of storing data than the active logic assumed in the proposed configuration.

3.3 Multilayer Distributed Machine

An iterative array machine has also been proposed by Gonzales [28] at the University of Michigan. It is a modified Holland machine with improvements in path building. A look-ahead capability is also suggested.

The look-ahead capability is provided by the multilevel aspect of the machine. It consists of three layers of modules (each similar to Holland's) arrayed in a rectangular network. The layers are: a program layer in which data and instruction are stored—one word per module; a control layer which decodes instructions; and a computing layer in which arithmetic, logical, and geometrical operations are performed. The layers are identical, with one word of storage in each layer. A direct communication path exists between each of the three modules in corresponding positions in the three layers as shown in Fig. 18. In a

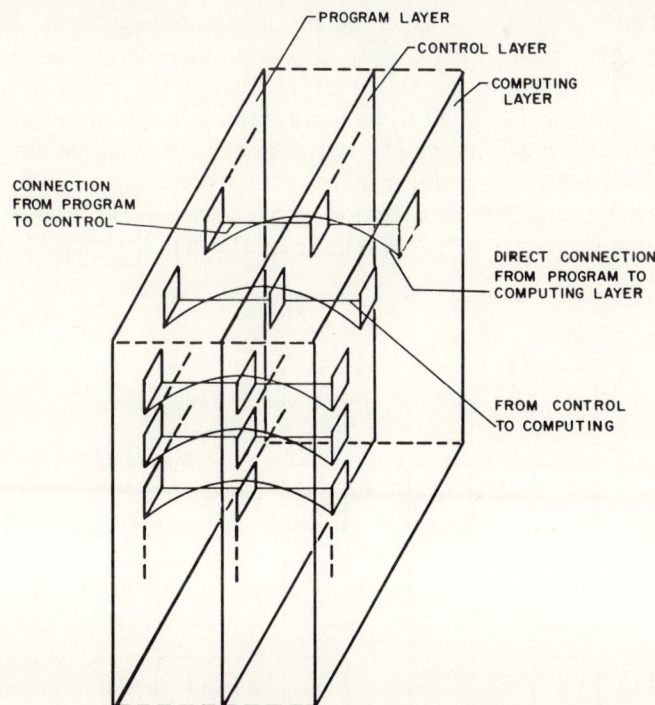

FIG. 18. Connections between layers.

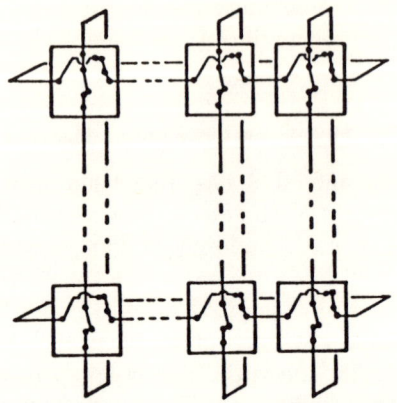

Fig. 19. Column and row information lines.

typical instruction execution cycle, an instruction is passed from a module in the program layer to all modules in the control layer which are to be active. The instruction is decoded in the control layer. Data are passed from modules in the program layer to modules in the computing layer. The instruction is executed in the computing layer. While the computing layer is executing an instruction, the control layer is working on the next instruction and the program layer on the one after next.

The machine is intended to be programmed in the same general way as the Holland machine. In the initial state, a continuous information path exists between modules in rows and columns of each plane as shown in Fig. 19. The instruction defines the operator and operand modules and causes a connection to be established between the operator

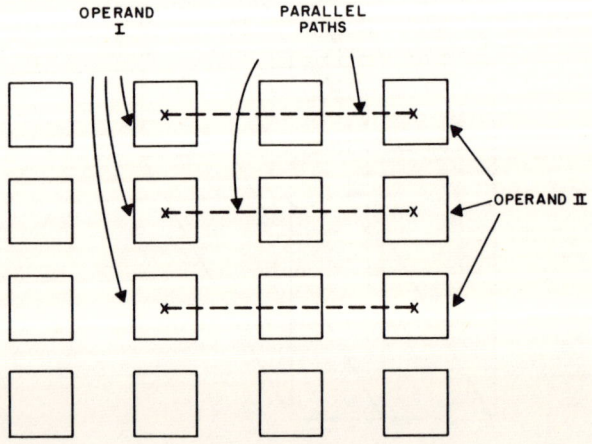

Fig. 20. Typical operating state.

module and operand module. A typical operating state, with three parallel paths, is shown in Fig. 20. Operand II modules execute the instruction operating on data in their own registers and the data in operand I modules, with the result stored in operand II modules. The instruction set proposed is limited to load, add, complement, and store. The module interconnection capability allows a one-to-one, one-to-many, and many-to-many connections. Thus the store operation can directly effect the geometical operations of copy, extend, reproduce, and displace. Each instruction specifies the module containing the next instruction.

Comments. The same general problems which exist for the Holland machine also exist for this machine, namely, excessive hardware requirements and difficulty of programming. It is also not clear that the hardware required for the look-ahead (multilayer) is justifiable. Otherwise, the same general considerations applicable to the Holland machine apply here.

The additional path building capability over the Holland concept appears to be most suitable to geometric operations. However, for this type of processing the parallel network is believed to give better hardware utilization.

3.4 A Multidimensional Machine

This machine proposed by Squire at the University of Michigan [65] can be characterized as a Holland machine with more intermodule connections. The connections give the network the topology of an n-dimensional cube with a module placed at each vertex and with direct connections between the adjacent vertices. A total of 2^n modules is used. The modules are also made more capable than the Holland module without a commensurate increase in hardware. As with the Holland machine, each module contains one word of storage used either for data or instructions. This word is $5(n+1)$ bits long. The module also contains arithmetic and logical circuitry, timing and control, and path connection logic as shown in Fig. 21.

The instruction word consists of five fields, two of which contain an operation code and three contain addresses. Two of these addresses designate two operands; the third specifies the next field. Each address is n bits (where 2^n is the number of modules) plus an additional bit to indicate whether the address is indirect. If the address is indirect, each of the five fields in the word named in the address field serve as addresses unless the field is all zero. Each indirect address can also be indirect thus giving a pyramid with a potential splitting factor of 5 at each level.

Any of the three initial addresses can be indirect including the next instruction.

The instruction set includes the four basic arithmetic operations with floating point mechanized. A total of 19 instruction codes is defined, including logic, sequencing, input, and output. Byte operations on the $(n + 1)$ bit fields are allowed for the addition, subtraction, logical, and sequencing operations. Through the indirect addressing and byte capability, the fields can be used as index registers.

Information flow in the machine is illustrated in Fig. 22. An add operation is to be executed in module R with the contents of Y to be added to the contents of the register specified in the indirect address X, namely, X_1 and X_2. The next instruction is contained in module S. Paths are connected from R to X and from there to X_1 and X_2, from R to Y, and from R to S.

A great deal of special hardware must be provided to prevent interference of paths. First of all, each of the three address fields in the instruction must be provided with separate path structures to avoid interference. Second, several different instructions may either refer to the same operand simultaneously or use a module as part of a path. Flip-flop storage must be provided to allow incoming data words to be saved together with priority logic. A total of $n^2 + 5n$ bits must be used per module for this purpose. For example, with 4096 modules, $n = 12$

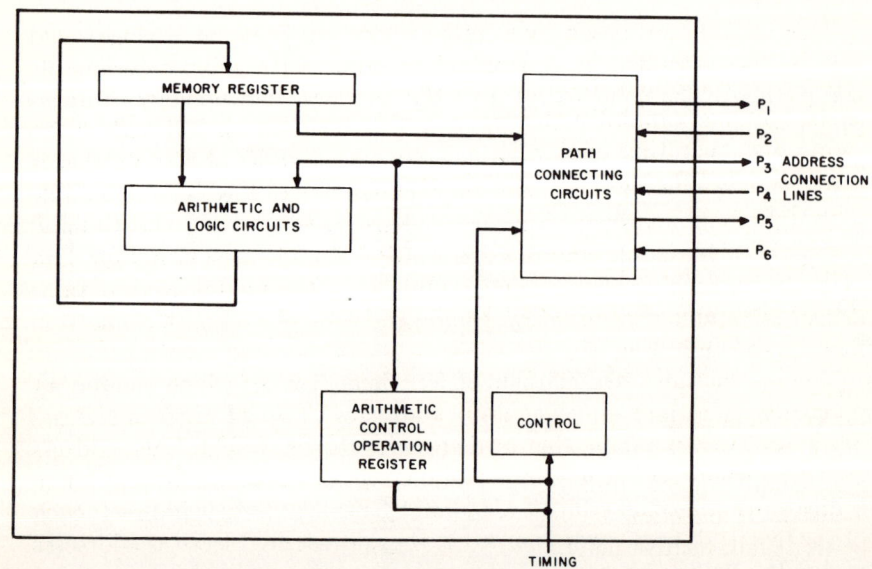

Fig. 21. Function and flow.

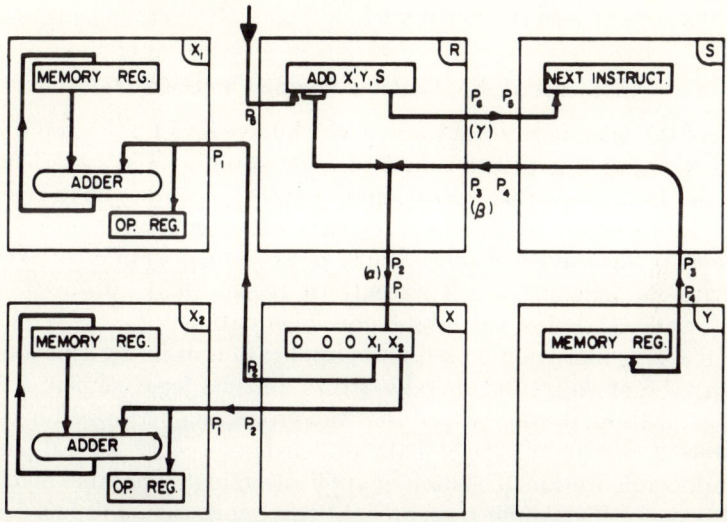

Fig. 22. Information flow during execution.

and each module contains 226 bits of storage for switching and a 69-bit instruction/data word. About 400 logic elements are also used.

Comments. This approach seems well beyond practical hardware limits until appropriate bit storage can be provided at a realistic cost. However, the Michigan studies have demonstrated that the improved path building capabilities give a definite advantage both in programming and operating efficiency. For example, for the matrix inversion process noted for the Holland machine, the minimum possible program length to invert an $M \times M$ matrix is $3M + 1$, as compared to the $3M^2$ for the planar array. The measure of effectiveness is $24M^3$ as compared with 18 to $30M^4$. This factor still compares unfavorably with conventional computers and other parallel machines.

3.5 Von Neumann's Cellular Logic

Von Neumann [7, 8] in about 1952 first suggested a two-dimensional iterative circuit machine. This work has been the inspiration for much of the subsequent thinking in highly parallel machines. This machine consists of a rectangular array of cells each one of which is connected with its four nearest neighbors. Time is considered to be discrete and the state of a cell at time $t + 1$ is a function of its own state and the states of its neighbors at time t. Von Neumann calls this function the "transition rule." Each cell has a total of 29 states. Von Neumann made extensive investigations of various problems in the theory of automata based on the properties of this cellular model.

4. Limited Application Parallel Processors

One of the most important factors which have held up the application of highly parallel machines is lack of understanding and experience in their use. Because of this, many highly parallel machines have been designed in response to the requirements of specific problems. These problems include most of those which press the capabilities of existing conventional machines such as pattern recognition, information retrieval, and solution of partial differential equations.

By focusing attention on a limited application, it is often possible to simplify the machine and thereby utilize unusual logic elements. As to the organization, it may be said that the processing performed by these machines generally has the global parallelism of a more general parallel network configuration. The limited application highly parallel machines can be classified by application area, by mechanization, and to a certain extent by organizational properties. For convenience both application area and means of mechanization are used in this review.

4.1 Pattern Processors

Some of the earliest work in highly parallel processing was done for problems in pattern recognition. The first published work was by Unger [70] in 1958 in which a rudimentary parallel network approach was proposed.

These machines are designed broadly for the extraction of basic characteristics of the pattern such as local and global topological properties. Particularly in the case of the ILLIAC III, machine design efforts have been supplemented by work in the software area. The machines are characterized by having (1) little internal memory (only a few bits per cell), (2) little mechanized arithmetic capability, and (3) a rectangular two-dimensional structure with direct neighbor connections.

4.1.1 Unger Machine I

The machine was proposed by Unger in 1958 [see 70–72]. It is a rectangular network of identical modules each controlled by a common central control unit (global control). The module consists of a 1-bit accumulator, a small random access memory of perhaps 6 bits and some elementary logical capability. Inputs can be broadcast from the central control or entered directly into each of the module accumulators.

As originally envisioned, the module instructions included one-bit logical operations, the capability to store and load the accumulator from memory, and data shift operations to north, east, south, and west modules. Link and expand instructions are provided which are essentially local topological processes used, for example, to fill out a line which is not complete because of noise in the input pattern. For these instructions connections between modules exist in a diagonal direction in addition to the horizontal and vertical.

Comments. The machine was conceived as a pattern recognition device in which each resolution cell of the two-dimensional input pattern is processed by a corresponding cell in the two-dimensional computer array. Initial investigation has been oriented toward the methods of using the machine to discover local and global pattern features. The concepts proposed have been realized in later more ambitious hardware programs, most notably SOLOMON II and ILLIAC III.

4.1.2 Illiac III

The ILLIAC III [47] is a pattern recognition computer being studied and constructed at the University of Illinois Digital Computer Laboratory. A main processing unit of this computer is the Pattern Articulation Unit (PAU) which is a two-dimensional, programmable, iterative array (32×32). It is a special purpose device designed for preprocessing of two-dimensional patterns. It is augmented by an unconventional core memory which gives the array an associative memory capability.

4.1.2.1 Data flow. The processing capability of the PAU can best be seen by reference to the repertoire of network instructions and the resulting operations performed in the individual module. The network is microprogrammed with the instruction divided into four fields of 10 bits each.

The first 10-bit field controls the logical processing performed by the module. Bits 1 and 3 control complementing of the output and input, respectively (labeled C and $\bar{C}$ in Fig. 23). Bit 4 controls the "flash through" which bypasses the module (labeled F). The remaining bits in the first field control the logical processes called "bubbling" by which the number of 1's in the module storage are counted. The remaining three 10-bit fields determine (1) which of the eight nearest neighbors will be inputs to the module, (2) which of the 1-bit registers in the module will be loaded, and (3) which of the 10-bit registers will be unloaded to the output bus.

The Transfer Memory (TM) is 54 words of 1 bit each which is loaded from, or unloaded into, bit m of the module. An external register, called the "list register," can be directed to compile a list of the modules which have a 0 in the m bit. Data are entered into the network from an edge.

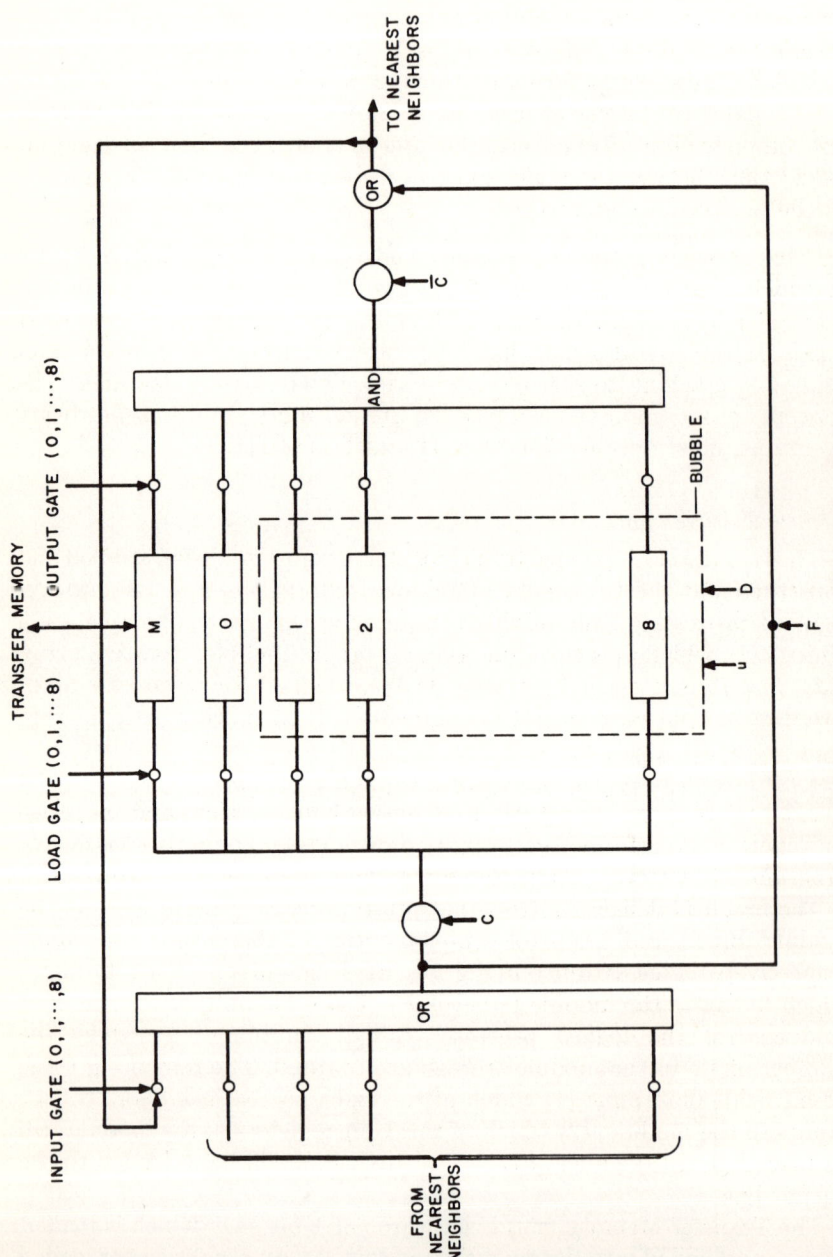

Fig. 23. Diagram of Illiac II PAU module.

The principal logical process performed within the module (excluding data transfer) is called "bubbling." The name is chosen to indicate that the process results in a separation of ones and zeros in the 8-bit bubble system. Zeros bubble to the top. The number of ones can then be counted.

4.1.2.2 Processing capability. The PAU is designed for local processing such as thinning of lines, filling in of lines, and identification of topological features such as an isolated point, an interior point of a line, an end point of a line, and a junction point of a line. This functional capability is ultimately achieved by counting the nearest neighbors satisfying appropriate logical conditions.

An associative capability is also available through the m bit and the list operation. A match of a key is identified by a zero in the m bit. The modules in which a match is made are identified through the list operation. The 54-bit word in the matching module can be directly unloaded to the exterior. The search key is sent a bit at a time to each module in the network.

The ILLIAC III program has been carried to an advanced stage both in the hardware and analysis areas.

4.1.3 Unger Machine II

The single most important feature of this machine is that the modules do not have the memory elements. It is designed as a special purpose network for character recognition.

The basic device is a two-dimensional iterative array switching network. Each module in the array is simple and all modules are identical. No central control is required. It is used as in Fig. 24. Each of the arrays

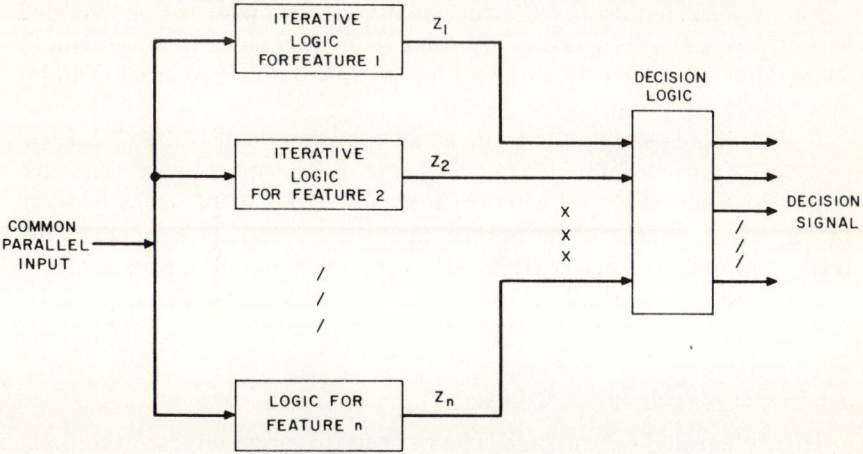

FIG. 24. Multiple iterative arrays for pattern recognition.

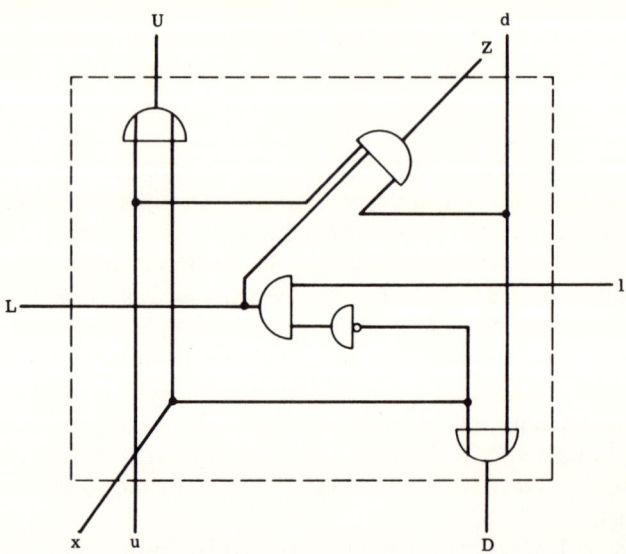

FIG. 25. Module for detecting cavities open to right.

is used to process the input pattern in a different way producing a characteristic output. All of these outputs are then fed into a decision logic. Many two-dimensional topological characteristics can be detected with simple modules. These include, for example, holes and cavities in the pattern such as those in the letters O and E.

As an example, Fig. 25 shows the module used for detecting cavities open to the right. The input signal to the module is x which is a 0 if the pattern is white at the corresponding point in the two-dimensional input, 1 otherwise. The output from the module is Z which is to be summed logically over the entire array. The signals L and l move left from and to the module, respectively, U and u move up from and to, and D and d move down from and to the module.

If the l line is set equal to one at all right-hand cells, the signal will propagate left through $x = 0$ cells and be stopped by $x = 1$ cells. Similarly, a signal $U = 1$ will propagate upward and a signal $u = 1$ will propagate downward. The output signal, $Z = \bar{x}lud$, will appear only if the module is within a cavity open to the right. Similar mechanizations are required for extraction of each of the characteristics needed for recognition.

4.1.4 Iterative Array Switching Circuits

Highly parallel networks [31] have been investigated from the point of view of switching theory. Much of this work has been directed toward development of techniques for the analysis and synthesis of networks that realize a particular mapping of primary two-dimensional input patterns to primary output patterns.

Only limited results have been obtained in developing synthesis methods. Similarly, only limited results have been obtained in the analysis of stability of networks. One of the more important of the results is a demonstration that general analysis and synthesis procedures do not exist. However, the absence of such procedures does not greatly affect the general development of highly parallel systems.

Work on iterative switching arrays is being carried out at CRL by Brookings and Glucksman. They have built several models, 3×3, 4×4, and 5×5, each node consisting of an elementary logical function including NOR, OR, and AND. From these they have constructed basic digital devices such as an adder and an oscillator. Theoretical work emphasis is on developing means for synthesizing a given function using iterative switching arrays. Glucksman has developed techniques for pattern recognition based on Unger's approach.

4.2 Associative Processors

A rather large number of highly parallel associative machines have been proposed. These include associative memories, associative computers, and list processors. Associative memories can be described as storage devices in which sufficient logic is associated with each word of memory to allow a parallel comparison of all words in memory with a single search key.

Associative computers are a natural generalization of associative memories in which enough additional logic is added to each word of storage so that arithmetic operations on the data words can be performed conveniently under global control. There is no clear conceptual difference between either the associative memory, the associative processor, or the parallel network. List processors are designed to search through a list-structured file. The list search may or may not involve parallel comparison.

The application or problem that associative machines are designed to handle is that of retrieval of data which satisfies a set of logical conditions. The logical conditions are generally expressed in terms of a search key together with a relation that is to be satisfied between the search key and the data record to be retrieved. For example, a typical relation is equality between the key and a specific field of the data record to be retrieved, a typical search key is a name, and a typical data record to be retrieved is the employment record of the employee named.

The search problem is inherently a totally parallel process in that all comparisons between the search key and data records in the file can in principle be performed simultaneously. Associative memories and associative computers are designed to perform all comparisons in parallel.

Associative memories can be simulated very effectively using conventional memories and tree- or list-structured files. Several machines have been suggested to facilitate this type of processing. Among them are the multilist central processor [51] and the IBM ADAM. These organizations are not conceived as being highly parallel and therefore are not described.

Landauer [39] has shown that for optimal utilization in processing tree-structured files, the number of branches that emerge from a node should be between 3 and 5. It should be noted that hardware utilization is in some cases less important than speed of retrieval. In the latter case, the list processor could be made highly parallel. The search key would then be compared with each of many branches at a node in parallel, the number of branches at each node being determined more by the available hardware than by considerations of hardware efficiency.

RADC is presently (1965) supporting organization studies of associative processors by Hughes, IBM, General Precision-Librascope, and GE. The general objective is to determine the machine organizations which reflect the requirements of basic search and association processes. Probably the most ambitious hardware development is a cryogenic processor being built by Texas Instruments. It will have 5000 words of 65 bits each with a parallel read cycle time of about 10 μsec. It is expected to be operating in the fall of 1966. RADC is supporting an associative memory development by Goodyear of 2048 words of 48 bits due for completion in January 1966.

4.2.1 Associative Memories

A sizable associative memory must use a nondestructive read so that it is not necessary to rewrite simultaneously all memory locations. The ferrite toroid memory when accessed in the usual way does not meet this requirement, so other memory techniques must be employed. The techniques most frequently suggested are multiaperture ferrite cores and superconductive cryotrons. Semiconductor storage cells also have been suggested. The application of these techniques to the realization of an associate memory has been the subject of considerable research; some of this effort is discussed below.

Perhaps the most promising phenomenon for large-scale associative memories (10^6 bits) is superconductivity. Superconductive or cryogenic techniques are eminently suited to associative memories. Because of the near-ideal properties of superconductive storage elements, little

HIGHLY PARALLEL INFORMATION PROCESSING SYSTEMS

power is required to interrogate all elements simultaneously. Also, superconductive elements are most naturally fabricated through batch fabrication techniques in which many memory elements, interconnections, and even memory addressing logic are formed simultaneously.

One suggested cryogenic associative memory cell is shown in Fig. 26 [*50*]. The associative memory system constructed with these cells would have several modes of operation:

(1) *Comparison*—the contents of all words in the memory can be compared simultaneously. This comparison can be made on any subset of the bits of each word; any bits not pertinent to a particular comparison are masked out.

(2) *Read*—the Read operation must always be preceded by a Comparison operation. If the comparison finds a matching word, the Read operation places this word in an input-output register.

(3) *Write*—this operation also must be preceded by a Comparison operation. Any subset of any word can be written by appropriate masking.

(4) *Comparison bypass*—this operation is used (in the case of multiple matching words) to exclude the first matching word after it has been dealt with.

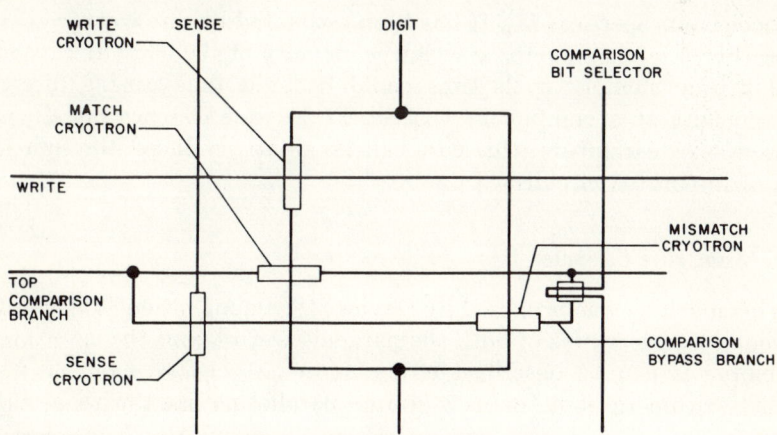

FIG. 26. Associative memory cell.

Small laboratory memories of this type have been built and tested. Based on results obtained, the developers of these memories estimate that it is now feasible to build a 300,000-bit associative memory of this type with a 50-μsec Comparison cycle time. As indicated by the modes of operation discussed above, such a memory would possess a very flexible and powerful associative capability.

Several approaches to obtaining associative memories through magnetic techniques have been suggested. These approaches differ primarily in the nondestructive elements on which they are based. [As previously noted, Nondestructive Read-out (NDRO) is essential.] One approach obtains NDRO from ferrite toroids by driving them with intense pulses for such a short time as to not affect their state [*36*]. A second approach uses "bicore" elements consisting of two superimposed thin film spots [*35*]. One spot is of high coercivity material for storing the bit, the second of low coercivity for sensing. In a third magnetic approach, ferrite multiaperture devices are used [*48*]. At every bit location a zero signal is obtained when stored and interrogation bits are identical and a nonzero signal when they differ. There is word match if there is no signal in a winding linking all elements comprising a word and mismatch otherwise.

The above techniques allow the realization of magnetic associative memories up to about 100,000 bits capacity. Larger sizes become impractical largely because of the amount of power required to drive all elements during interrogation.

An additional technique which has been suggested for associative memories is semiconductor storage cells. Such cells are semiconductor flip-flops with modifications appropriate to achieving the desired associative properties [*42*]. It has been estimated by one worker in this area that a semiconductor associative memory of 400,000 bits capacity and 2 μsec memory cycle time could be built today using discrete components at a component cost of $1.00 to $4.00 per bit. In the reasonably near future, this cost can be greatly reduced through the use of integrated circuitry.

4.2.2 Associative Computer

This machine was proposed by Davies [*18*] among others [*22, 26, 35*]; it combines properties of both the parallel network and the associative memory. It can be described either as an associative memory with added arithmetic logic or as a simple parallel network with a small memory.

As can be seen in Fig. 27, the system configuration is essentially that of the associative memory. The principal deviation is in the control unit and the control module. The control unit performs a role similar to that of the network sequencer in the parallel network. It broadcasts micro-program commands to all control modules. The control module contains the logic for the cell and can be compared to the logic in the PE (although as proposed it is somewhat simpler). The memory module contains the key and operand and thus corresponds to PE memory. The

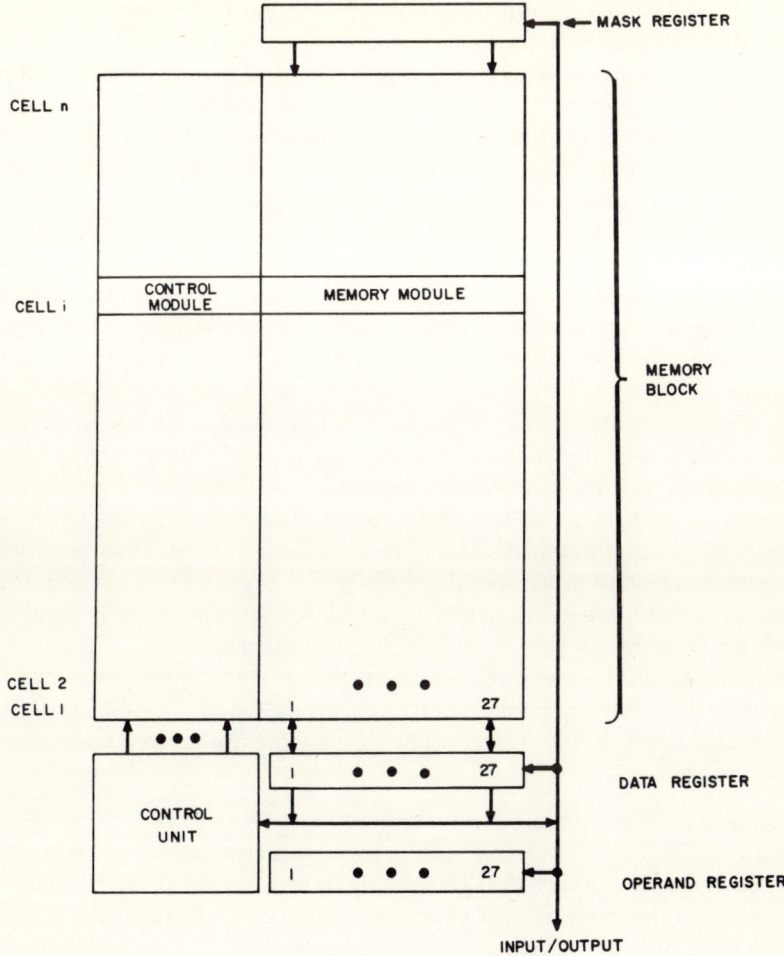

Fig. 27. Associative computer.

word register defines the portion of the word in which the association or computation is performed. The operand register contains data which are to be transmitted (broadcast) to all control modules; for example, keys used in associating are such data.

It is natural to propose that instructions be stored in the associative memory block rather than in a separate program memory. To allow this, the data register is designed to receive the instruction retrieved from the associative memory block and from there route it to the control unit. The data register also receives data retrieved from the memory block. A routing capability is also provided. Each cell can receive data from the adjacent cell, effecting an organization which corresponds to a parallel network with a linear communication topology.

The machine has an instruction repertoire of 31 instructions including associative comparison, logical operations, arithmetic operations—add, subtract, and shift—and sequencing operations. The word length proposed is 27 bits. The first 3 bits are used to label the word as: empty, a data word, an instruction, a mask, or a key. The remaining 24 bits are used for storage. Data words and instructions contain two 12-bit fields. One field is a label. The other 12-bit field contains the data word or instruction. The label is used to allow parallel computation. All pieces of data with the same label can be processed in parallel by a single instruction stream. In a sense, the label corresponds to the PE data memory address.

A program consists of a sequence of instructions, masks, keys, and data words stored in the memory. After each word is retrieved, a tag is activated in the next word in sequence (the adjacent word in the memory), and the tag of the active instruction is turned off.

Several possible extensions have been proposed. First, the machine is presently considered to operate serially by bit. It is suggested that parallel by bit processing can be used. A second variation is to allow modules to communicate with other than adjacent cells.

The proposed mechanization uses cryotron logic. Approximately 100 cryotrons are necessary for each control module and about 7 cryotrons are needed per data bit. Thin film or active logic (integrated circuit) can also be used.

Comments. With some qualifications, it is at least 10 times cheaper to obtain large data storage by ferrite core storage than by an alternate approach and it is likely that this will be true for several years. For this reason, it is desirable that a clear justification be obtained for storing either data or instructions by nonmagnetic core techniques.

It is not clear that improvements cannot be made in the system by either (1) using a separate conventional memory for program store, (2) using a network configuration to improve data accessibility, or (3) using a cheaper storage medium for data. Experimental hardware seems necessary for the evaluation of the associative processor concept.

4.2.3 Intercommunicating cells

This machine proposed by Lee [*41*] is designed as a modular retrieval device with distributed logic. It perhaps qualifies more as a memory than as a full machine.

The organization is shown in Fig. 28. It is constructed from cells, each of which can store one character, connected together into a linear

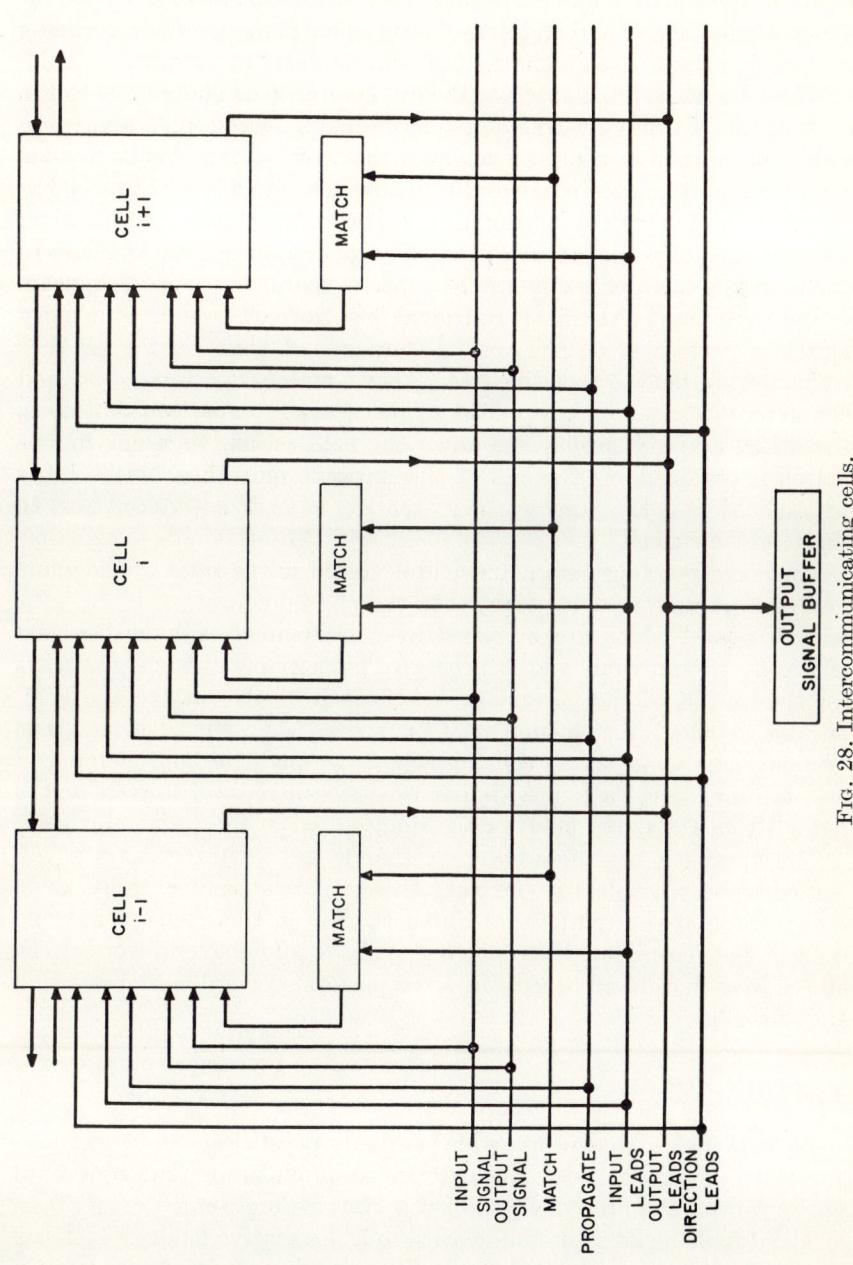

FIG. 28. Intercommunicating cells.

strip. Each cell is under a common control with four types of control leads: input, output, match, and propagate. The cell is either active or inactive. When a cell is active and an input control signal is received, the contents of the input line are stored in the cell, and similarly for output.

When a match signal appears, the cell compares its contents with the contents of the input line. If a match is obtained, the cell sends a signal to a neighboring cell causing the neighbor to become active. When a cell is active and a propagate command is received, a signal is sent to a neighboring cell which then becomes active, the original cell becoming inactive. The direction of propagation is controlled by two control leads: R and L.

Name fields are defined by use of a special character A, which appears at the beginning of the field. Retrieval is performed as follows: First a match is performed on the special character A thus setting all cells which begin a field to an active state. Then a match is performed on each character of the search key, one at a time. As the comparison continues, the initial activity propagates down the field as long as a continuous match is obtained. At the end of this process, only those name fields whose content is the same as the search key have an active cell next to their right-most cell.

The corresponding parameter field is stored to the right of the name field. All parameter fields start with the special character B. All cells with a B and which are preceded by a matching key have been set active by the previous search process. This active cell forms the basis for the output of the parameter field. Each of the characters is retrieved (fetched) in sequence until the special character A is met. The original activity in the B cell propagates through the parameter field as a tag for the retrieved. A similar process can be used to retrieve the name (from the name field) of the item stored in the parameter field.

The approach has the advantage that in two or three years it will probably be possible to construct the cells relatively cheaply using active integrated circuit logic. Further work on this concept is being done at Bell Telephone Laboratories (BTL) to allow several words to be stored in each cell and processing to be performed parallel by bit within the cell [13].

4.2.4 SM1

Barnett at MIT has proposed [3] a highly parallel machine organization for syntax analysis. The machine is modular in that it is built entirely from a simple device called a "double register."

The double register (module) is a simple associative device which can detect elementary logical relations. The module operates on a string of characters presented to it by the input channel as shown in Fig. 29.

HIGHLY PARALLEL INFORMATION PROCESSING SYSTEMS

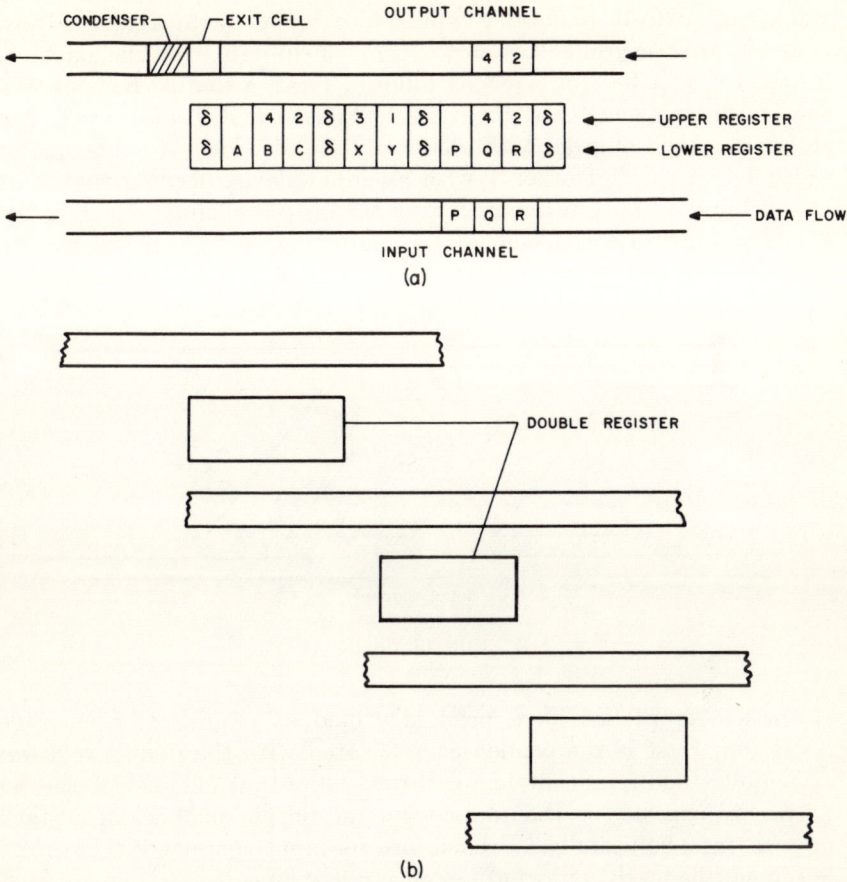

FIG. 29. (a) Double register and (b) stack of double registers.

The module compares the contents of its lower register with the input string and, if a match is found, writes the contents of its upper register on the output channel. The module is divided into fields defined by the character δ in Fig. 29(a). Comparison is by fields. Thus a match must be made for the entire field.

The function of the module is to write the name of the syntactical entity that appears in the input channel on the output channel. Thus the module shown in Fig. 29(a) corresponds in part to a syntactical rule in Backus normal form.

The modules are grouped first into stacks and then into shelves. A stack is an arrangement in which the output channel of each module feeds the input channel of the next module as shown in Fig. 29(b). The stack can perform a more complex hierarchial syntactical analysis.

Stacks are also grouped as shown in Fig. 30 into shelves. The machine, in general, can be conceived as follows: First, a double register is a shelf of order 0 and the shelf shown in Fig. 30, a shelf of order 1. The stacks in a shelf of order 1 also have an order of 1. An SM1 machine of order 1 is a shelf of order 1 with an input device feeding the input channel and an output device fed by the output channel. Machines of a higher order are constructed by combining shelves of order m to obtain a stack of order $m + 1$.

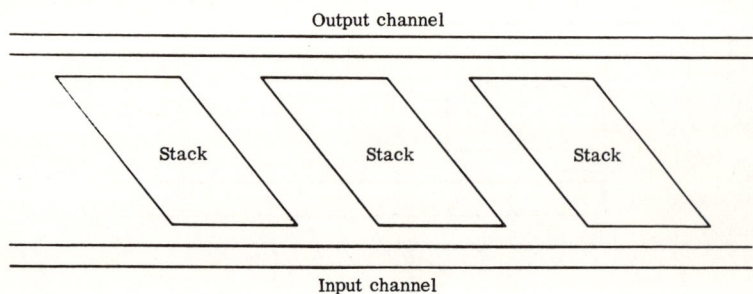

FIG. 30. Shelf.

Further properties have been identified as required for effective operation. First is the condenser associated with the double register. It removes nonsignificant blanks from the output channel. A second property suggested is that data from the output channel of a stack or shelf may be usefully fed back into its input channel. This recirculation can be used to unwind nested input strings.

Both analog and digital mechanizations have been suggested. Possible digital methods for constructing modules are by associative memory techniques and using delay lines. For an analog approach, the module must measure the "distance" between the input and stored signals. A suggested measure is

$$\int_a^b [f(x) - s(x)]^2 \, dx.$$

When this function falls below a threshold, a stored signal is sent out on the output channel.

The machine has a difficulty in the shift register design of the channels. However, the double register itself can now be built as three monolithic circuits and in a short time as a single monolithic device. This would make the organization quite attractive for several applications.

4.3 Differential Equation Processors

The numerical solution of differential equations, particularly partial differential equations, represents a computational load which would appear to justify machine organization optimized for this function. However, the variability of the processing procedures makes general-purpose machines comparatively efficient, and for this reason few special-purpose organizations have been proposed. The most significant work including both hardware and theoretical organization study has been in networks of analog modules. These machines are rather limited in scope of application, and recent thinking has been toward combined systems of analog and digital networks. Extremely powerful processors may evolve from this work.

Several digital computers have been proposed for processing data arrays with particular emphasis on arrays arising from partial differential equations. However, it appears that general-purpose systems are at least equally powerful and more efficient.

4.3.1 Lockheed Machine

A group at Lockheed Missiles and Space Company [Tanaka, 67] has investigated a machine designed for the use of parallel iterative procedures. Generally for such procedures (partial differential equations) data can be laid out in a fixed array in which data dependencies are local. Thus, computation on different areas of the array are relatively independent. Because of this feature, a modular structure with a common central control is suggested.

Other modular machine designs (conceived through the same train of logic) are felt at Lockheed to have serious drawbacks. They are: (1) the relatively fixed interconnection structure among computing modules limits the hardware efficiency and causes serious input/output problems; (2) with specific blocks of memory reserved for specific modules, the total memory capacity cannot be used; and (3) several designs (Holland) have included active memory elements which are more expensive than passive magnetic storage.

4.3.1.1 Organization. The proposed Lockheed machine has two computing subsystems, namely, a general-purpose stored program conventionally organized machine and a multimodule unit as shown in Fig. 31. The configuration of each module is as shown in Fig. 32. The multimodule unit has a common central control which is not a stored program device but is instead a plugboard. The general-purpose unit is used to set up the data in the modules, to supply initial conditions, and to receive output data. The multimodule unit operates autonomously and repetitively after it is started.

Each module has a cyclic memory unit which is continuously scanned by the module. Suggested mechanizations of this memory include magnetic drum, cycled core memory, and microwave delay line. The plugboard control generates a fixed operation sequence which operates on the continuous stream of data presented to the module logic from the memory. This approach has the advantage of using relatively cheap memory. The plugboard control provides a cheap and simple sequencer but at the expense of stored programmed control and a certain loss of flexibility.

The module is also simple (Fig. 32). It is serial with five words of internal storage. Input and output lines are connected to appropriate memory units through the plugboard. The module includes a serial adder, a comparison unit, and a word select. The comparison unit provides feedback to the control unit, and the word select allows for branching. In a typical application, some memory channels are used to store the array of constants while others are used for working storage.

The suggested configuration is for 20 modules each assigned a channel of a 20-channel magnetic drum. The drum rotates at 6000 rpm and contains 20,000 bits per channel. Each channel has one read head and one write head which follows the read head by several words. Postulated is a 20-bit word length, a 1-Mc clock rate, and a resulting 20-μsec add time.

As postulated the machine has no multiply, and a programmed multiply routine would be very slow. This seriously limits the range of

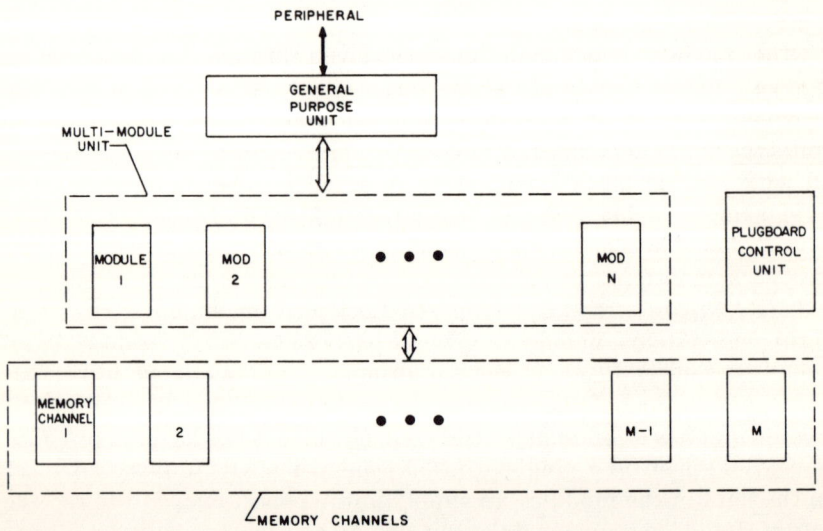

Fig. 31. Array processor.

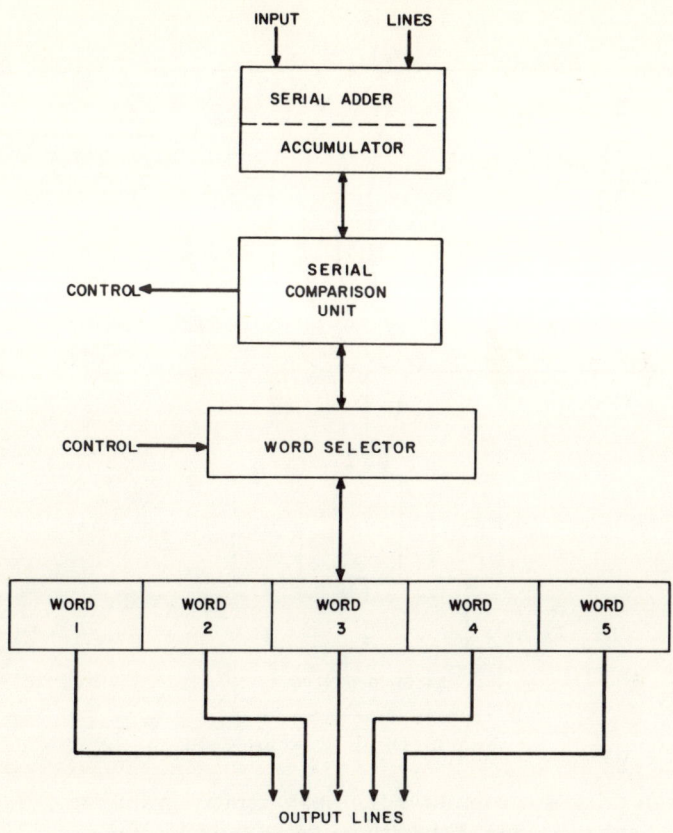

FIG. 32. Processing unit for channel M.

problems. However, with existing components a multiply could be designed without modifying the data rate through the module. The serial memory and plugboard sequencer are the principal elements of the concept which make it a special-purpose unit. This concept was proposed in similar form by Leondes and Rubinoff in 1952 [*43*].

4.3.2 Drum Array Processor

A similar drum machine has been studied by Rosin at the University of Michigan. As with the Lockheed machine, memory is cyclic, and a linear array of processing modules makes iterative passes through the data mapped on the drum storage.

For elliptical equations, each track on the drum represents a column of the points in the grid overlay. One processor is assigned to each track as shown in Fig. 33, and has access to the adjacent tracks. At each grid

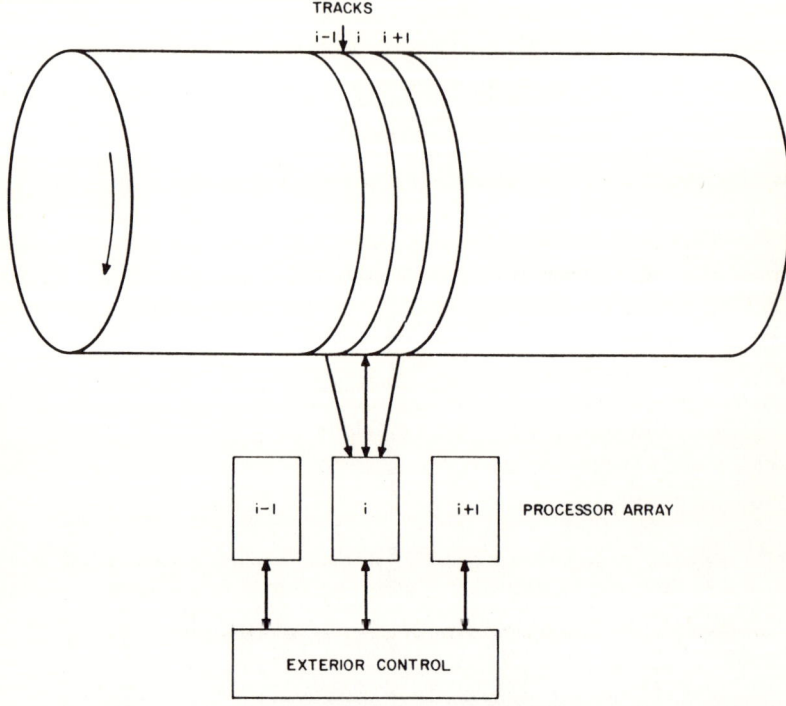

Fig. 33. Drum array processor.

point, the processor computes the next iterative value, $n + 1$, by the conventional averaging of the nth values of the four adjacent grid points. Delay lines are used as temporary storage registers for grid points within the processor. In one revolution of the drum, an entire iteration is performed, giving one new value of each grid point. A slight modification is suggested for over-relaxation methods.

The drum speed proposed is 1500 rpm with 1000 tracks each with 375 words of 40 bits each. The cost figure for the Array Processor alone is $1000 per processor and $330 per drum track. The processor is serial by bit.

The investigation has also been directed toward a Drum Array Processor for random walk solutions of elliptic and parabolic equations. The processor at each point is shown in Fig. 34. It consists of a counter and some logic to move the particles from grid point to grid point. The drum contains the state of the grid point stored in the corresponding storage word. A 200-word 200-track drum is considered. The processor is serial by bit, each processor having about 30 gates and 16 delay lines. A central control device is assumed to provide random numbers and count absorptions.

Comments. The major disadvantage of this concept is the inflexibility of the hardware; the major advantages are speed of operation and low cost. The module is conceived as being a one process device so that the device can be made cheaply enough. However, for the cost considered ($1000 per processor), a processor can be built which can do rather a lot of processing (global control) in the time available, $60/(1500 \times 375) = 100$ μsec per point.

The machine does not seem well suited for the more powerful iterative procedures such as the alternating direction methods. This is a serious practical defect for a differential equation machine as these procedures may converge where the simple iterative methods do not and may converge as much as two orders of magnitude faster than over-relaxation.

A machine similar to this in concept has been independently studied by Raytheon for track initiation in a large weapons system. In that device each rotation of the drum corresponds to a radar scan. Drum storage is mapped onto the coverage volume in several possible ways.

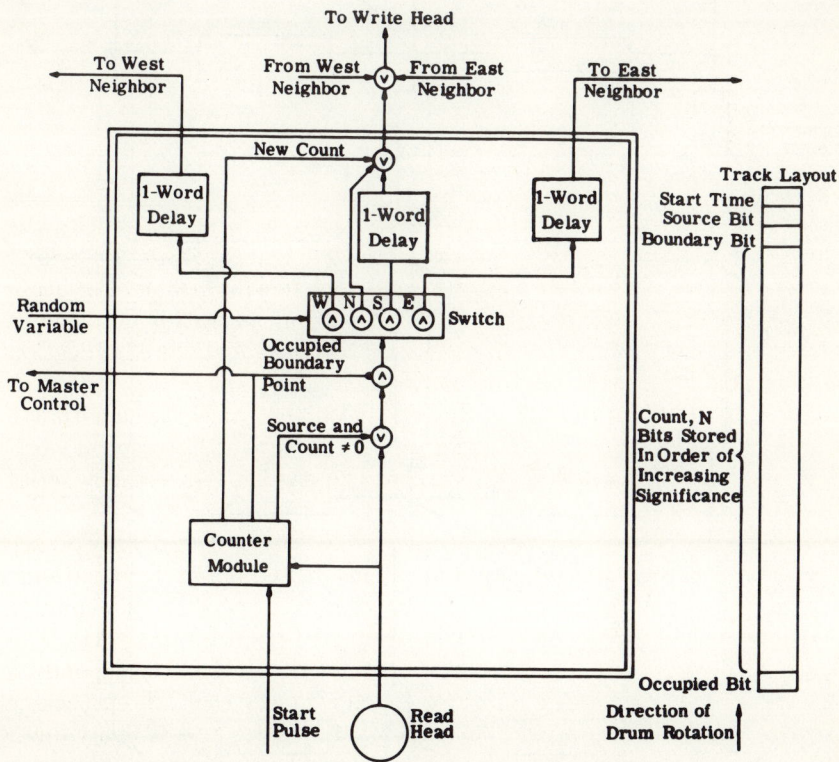

FIG. 34. Concurrent random walk processor.

4.3.3. Resistance Networks

Resistance networks [30] have been used for many years to solve equations of the form.

$$\text{div}\,(p\,\text{grad}\,U) = f(x, y, z, U, k).$$

The network is set up as in Fig. 35, and with nodes of the resistive network corresponding to a point in the standard grid overlay of the region. In the general case, the equation is solved iteratively for the unknown eigenvalue k. The function f is represented by the current source I flowing into the node according to the relation.

$$I = -fh^2/R$$

where h is the distance between the mesh junctions in the grid and R is the local value of the network resistance. The local value of R is proportional to the special function p.

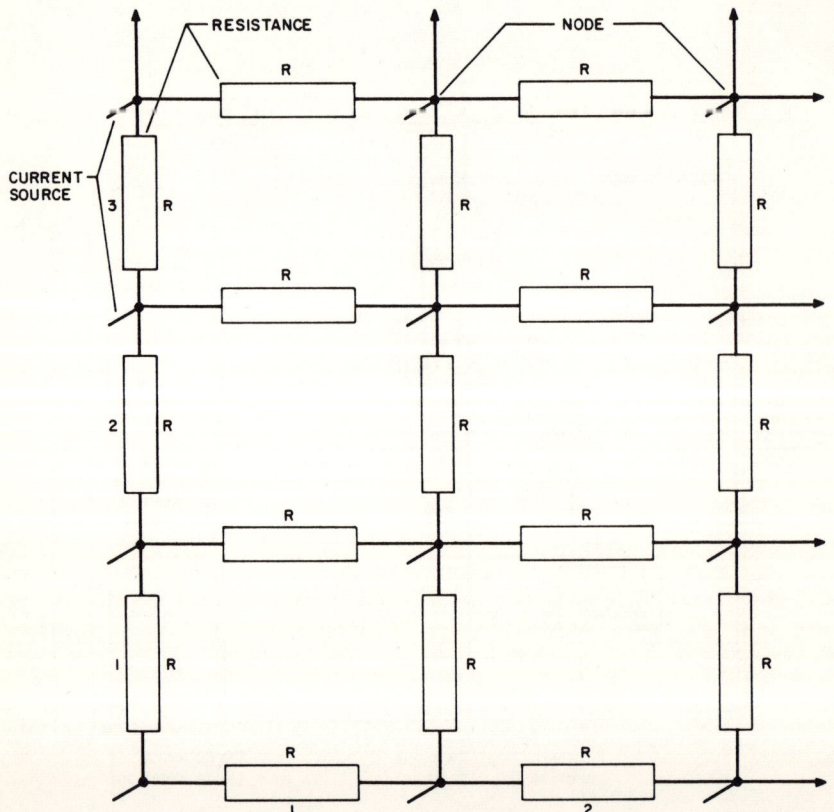

FIG. 35. Two-dimensional resistance network.

Initially an arbitrary guess, f_0, is made for f to give a first approximation U_0. This is used to correct f_0 to f_1 which is then used to compute U_1.

While flexibility is limited, good accuracy can be obtained on the order of one part in 10^4. The low cost is likewise a very favorable factor. However, it is difficult to deal with complex geometries.

4.3.4 Impedance Networks

Impedance Networks [37, 45, 63] can be used to solve a wide range of partial differential equations. Currents and voltages are in general used to represent line, surface, and volume integrals over an infinitesimal cube. Generally, the analogy is established by using Kirchhoff's two laws $\sum i = 0$ and $\sum e = 0$ to represent the divergence and curl operators. Thus, for example, for the resistive network discussed in the previous paragraph, Kirchhoff's laws represent the equations, respectively,

$$\text{div } \rho v = f$$
$$\text{curl } \rho V = 0,$$

where $V = \text{grad } U$ and ρ is a density.

As shown by Kron [37], more general analogies can be constructed for more complex equations. For example, the field equations of Maxwell in two dimensions can be represented as follows:

The curl equations

$$\text{curl } E + \frac{\partial B}{\partial t} = 0$$
$$\text{curl } H - \frac{\partial D}{\partial t} - I = 0$$

are represented by Kirchhoff's laws for electrical meshes and junction pairs, respectively.

The divergence equations

$$\text{div } B = 0$$
$$\text{div } D = \rho$$

are represented by Kirchhoff's laws for magnetic meshes and dielectric junctions pairs, respectively.

The networks for the transverse magnetic and electric modes are shown in Fig. 36.

The equations

$$B = \mu H \qquad D = \epsilon E \qquad I = \sigma E$$

are represented by Ohm's law in these circuits.

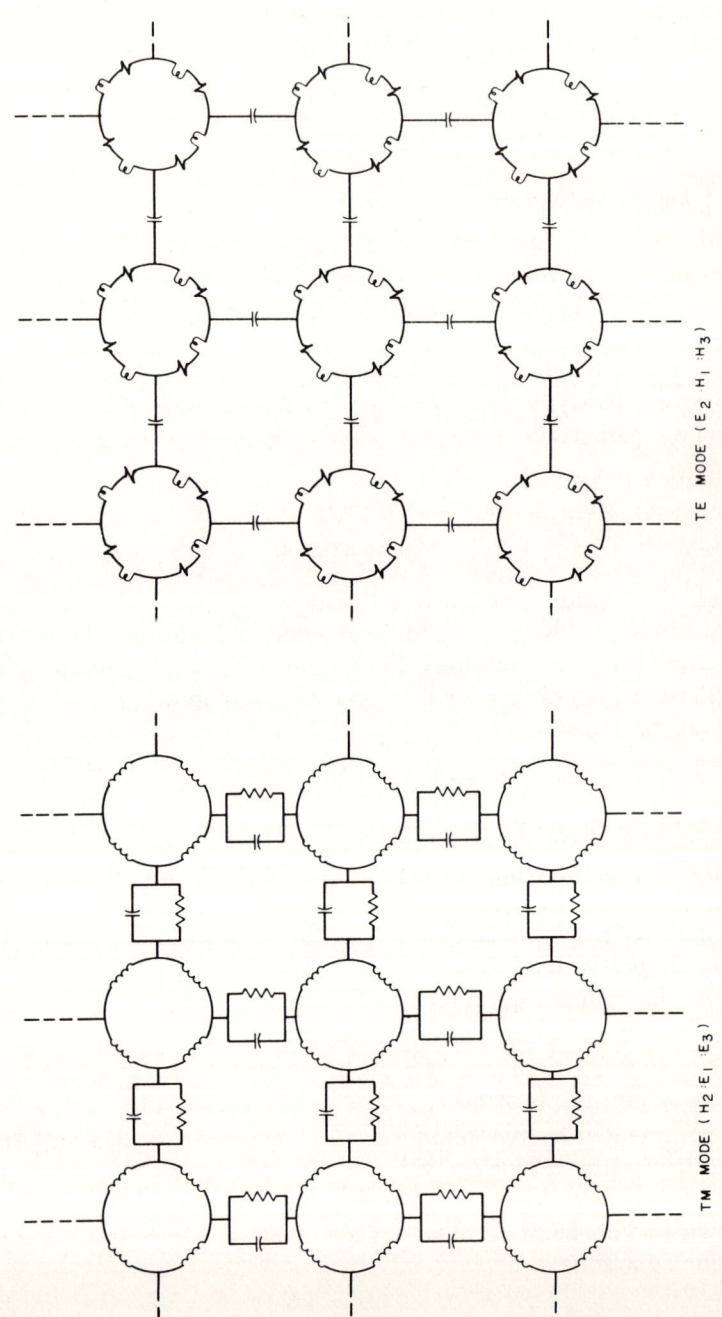

FIG. 36. Simulation of Maxwell's field equations in two dimensions.

Using passive circuit elements, the technique can be applied to partial differential equations that satisfy two conditions. First, they must be linear; that is, their coefficients are not functions of the dependent variable. The second is that they must be a tensor-density equation.

Models have been designed for a wide variety of equations such as the general scalar-potential and vector-potential equations, compressible fluid flow, Maxwell's field equations, Schrödinger's wave equations, and elasticity. Initial value, boundary value, and characteristic value problems can be solved.

Comments. The main limitations are of flexibility and accuracy. Errors arise from statistical deviations of the individual components from their nominal values and from systematic deviations of the network model from the partial differential equations. The statistical errors tend to average out. The systematic deviations depend on the solution region, but for similar cases accuracies can be higher than with other analog techniques such as the electrolytic tank. Typical accuracies are roughly 1%.

While impedance networks are perhaps trivial parallel networks, they have been used for many years on practical problems. In particular, Paschkis at Columbia University has built and used a rather large computer for solving heat flow problems. Also, a computer called CAL-TECH at California Institute of Technology is a general-purpose plugboard-type computer—a kind of variable structure device. It has been used for investigation of transient phenomena in complex systems.

4.3.5 Analog–Digital Techniques

Particularly for time-dependent equations such as the wave equation and more complex two- and three-dimensional equations, a combination of both digital and analog techniques has significant advantage. A very powerful and flexible approach utilizes [*38*] both a parallel network digital computer and a parallel analog network.

In the time-dependent case, the analog network performs the tasks of integrating from time t_n to time $t_n + \Delta t$, that is, one time step. The initial conditions (at time t_n) are supplied to the network by the digital parallel network through a direct module-to-module interface. The values of the independent variable at time $t_n + \Delta t$ are transferred to the digital computer for a further processing. This processing may include generation of time-dependent and nonlinear field variables. From these values, the initial conditions at that time are computed and fed to the analog network for integration to $t_n + 2\Delta t$. Thus, in effect, analog techniques are used for the space variables and the digital techniques for the time variable.

The benefits of this approach are: (1) implicit techniques are used in the analog integration thereby avoiding the usual problems of stability and round off, (2) time-dependent and nonlinear parameters are easily generated by the digital device, (3) solution times are small compared to the all-digital approach, and (4) more flexibility is obtained than with an all-analog system. The disadvantage is that of lack of flexibility and programmability of the analog network.

4.4 Optical Processors

A variety of optical processors has been proposed, both analog and digital devices. Such devices are very highly parallel two-dimensional arrays in which the number of parallel channels is limited only by the number of positions which can be resolved over the system aperture. Extremely high data handling capabilities can be achieved (well beyond any conventional approach) because of the high degree of parallelism and also because wide-band data can flow continuously through each channel.

4.4.1 Digital Optical Processors

Figure 37 shows a typical digital operation in which the Boolean function

$$x \cdot a = x_1 a_1 + x_2 a_2 + \cdots + x_n a_n$$

is evaluated. The variables x and a take the values of either 0 or 1.

The x and a planes are transparencies which do or do not transmit light to represent the values 1 and 0. Complements are obtained as negatives. The detector is a small region of a film or a photocell. By appropriate selection of functions or complements, the logical operations of AND, OR, NAND, and NOR can be obtained. These functions are sufficient to form any more complex logical function such as ordinary arithmetic functions.

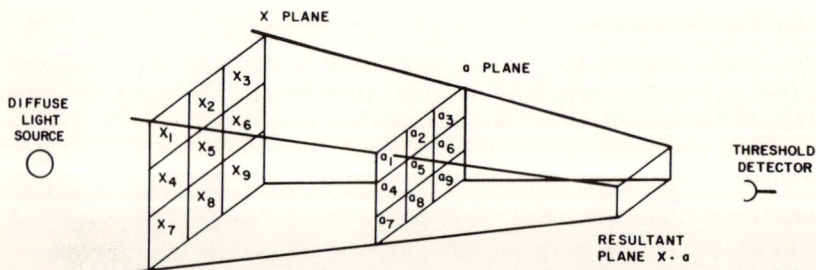

FIG. 37. Cross-correlation by optical means.

The most significant disadvantage of the optical processor is the time delay associated with developing photographic film to produce transparencies and their complements. This is significant for multilevel logic processes such as an add operation but has been mitigated by the use of devices such as closed circuit television to provide feedback of carries.

To compare [Barnum and Knapp, *4*, Chapter 3] the digital optical processor with a conventional computer, a single logical operation takes a frame time of about 1/24 (40 msec) in continuous operation. About 10^3 cells can be obtained per linear dimension with 35-mm film giving about 24×10^6 operations per second. Since development time is roughly 1 min with present technology, a continuous "rippled" data stream of at least 24×60 frames must be maintained for continuous operation. There is also a delay of 1 min for each logical level in the process.

4.4.2 Analog Optical Processors

Analog optical processors [*16*, *17*] are generally designed to evaluate an integral such as

$$I(X_0, Y_0) = \int_c^d \int_{a(y)}^{b(y)} f(x, y) g(x - x_0, y - y_0) \, dx \, dy$$

where x_0, y_0, a, b, c, and d are functions of time. This integral includes processes such as cross-correlations, autocorrelation, convolution, and spectral analysis.

Multiplication of two 2-dimensional functions

$$T_1(x, y) \quad \text{and} \quad T_2(x, y)$$

is achieved as shown in Fig. 38(a). Transparency 1 has a transmittance of $T_1(x, y)$ which, when illuminated by a light of intensity I, gives an emergent distribution of $I(x, y) = I_0 T_1(x, y)$. The lens system between T_1 and T_2 with unity magnification thus gives the emergent intensity of $I_0 T_1(x, y) T_2(x, y)$. Integration over a plane is accomplished by imaging the region of integration onto a detector [Fig. 38(b)].

Coherent optical techniques give a great deal more flexibility. Such devices utilize a point source of light (or a laser) rather than a diffuse source so that relative phases in various parts of the system are time invariant.

The significance of the coherent approach arises from the fact that a Fourier transform relation exists between the light amplitude distribution at the front and back focal planes of a lens used in such systems. This allows integral transform operations to be performed very conveniently. Transparencies are used to modify the spectral content of the complete signal. Complex transmittances are obtained by varying

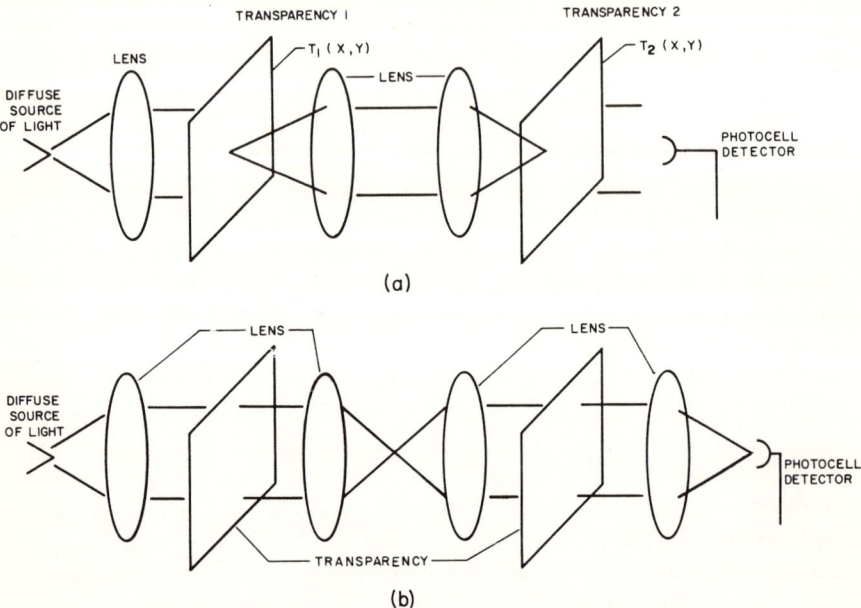

FIG. 38. Optical multiplication and integration techniques: (a) multiplication of T_1 by T_2 and (b) two-dimensional integration.

the optical density (amplitude modulation) and the optical thickness (phase modulation).

Applications include real time data processing of very wide-band signals (100 Mc) and computation of functions which involve Fourier or Laplace transforms, cross-correlations, autocorrelations, and similar functions. The technology has a long history of development and use going back as far as 1953. The most significant limitation is that such a system is not programmable and is dependent on photographic data handling. There is however a wide range of lens configurations and techniques which can give a rather wide range of processing.

4.5 Maximum Likelihood Processors

Numerous highly parallel machines [29] have been proposed for purposes of adaption and recognition. By and large these devices are highly parallel in the sense that they are composed of many computing modules. They are also usually networks in that either nearest neighbor or more complex direct-wired connections are utilized; and finally, they often have (or could have) a global (common) control. (A discussion of how the classification process can be performed on a machine with global control is given in Section 8.1.5.) Generally, also, little attention has been given to these devices from a computer organization point of view. This is perhaps because the orientation of the designers is more toward the theoretical or laboratory model rather than the practical machine.

Furthermore, because the theoretical models have been relatively incomplete, no attempt has been made to pull the various theoretical objectives and suggested mechanizations into a generalized system.

In order to understand the configuration of these machines, it is necessary to state briefly the theoretical model [59] upon which much of this specialized machine work is based. Essentially the objective is to determine which of several classes a given measurement belongs to; that is, given certain observed characteristics, what is the matching object? The problem arises out of the fact that the measurement is distorted by noise and may in fact not be complete enough to determine the class uniquely. For example, in character recognition the goal is to decide which character in an alphabet is being observed.

The input to the machine is an n-dimensional measurement vector; the output is an m-dimensional decision vector in which generally all components are zero except one. The nonzero component is the "decided" one of the m alternate decisions.

The machine is designed on the basis of (1) *a priori* probability p_l of occurrence of objects in each of C classes, (2) the conditional probability distribution $F(a_i \mid c_l)$ of the measurements a_i associated with each class c_l (as distorted by noise), and (3) a measure of performance or a criterion of optimality. The theory of multiple hypothesis testing of statistical inference provides a formula which optimizes the system according to the criterion of optimality.

The machine determined by this theory is shown in Fig. 39. In the first level, the conditional probabilities $F(a_i \mid c_l)$ are calculated for each of the C characters. The risk assigned to each decision is then calculated in the second level as the weighted sum

$$X_i = \sum_{l=1}^{C} (w_{il} p_l F(a_i \mid c_l))$$

In the final layer, the minimum risk signal is selected—one decision signal is 1, all others 0. A generalized approach is to apply a transformation to the signal space which must be applied also to the measurement vector. This transformation is designed to separate the means of the class probability distributions and also to peak these distributions (lower their standard deviations).

Such a system (Fig. 39) computes the relative probability, given the measurement, that the observed object is in a specific class. This is done for each of the C possible classes. The computation of the

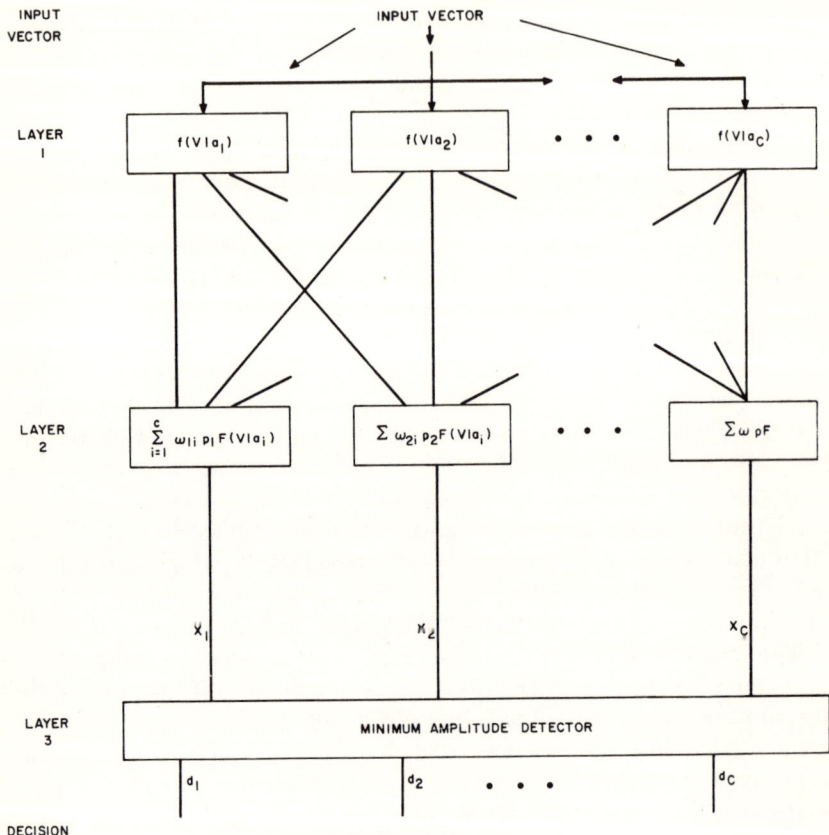

Fig. 39. Maximum likelihood processor.

probability for each class is independent of the others thus providing a large degree of parallelism.

There are several problems associated with the realization of the ideal system shown in Fig. 39. First, the storage requirements for an arbitrary system can easily exceed practical limits. Second, the probability distribution may not be known. When this is the case, the machine must perform the additional task of measuring these distributions. (It may also have the task of selecting the classes.)

It can be said that the devices that have been proposed in this general area by and large perform single functions such as making probability distribution measurements or decisions according to limited procedures. It may also be said that a more general purpose machine such as a parallel network with appropriate characteristics could perform the same functions efficiently and with a great deal more experimental flexibility.

4.5.1 CHILD

A representative machine of this class [56] is being constructed at RADC. It consists of a rectangular array of modules as shown in Fig. 40. The input is an n-dimensional measurement vector S_i applied at one side. The output is an m-dimensional binary decision vector.

Each row of modules corresponds to a decision class. Each module M_{ij} of row j compares its corresponding component of S (S_i) with two thresholds which it maintains, θ upper and θ lower. If the component of

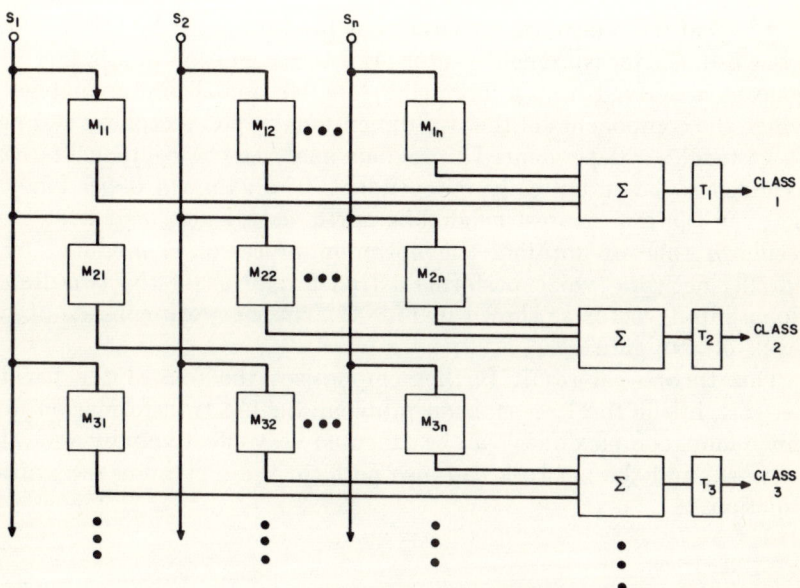

FIG. 40. CHILD functional diagram.

S is between these limits, the module transmits a signal W_{ij} to the row summer. The row summer adds all signals received from modules in its row. If a threshold is passed, a positive decision signal is given which indicates that the object falls in the class defined by the row (class j). That is, recognition is obtained if

$$\sum S_{ij}\omega_{ij} \geq T_j \quad \text{where } S_{ij} = 1 \quad \text{if } \theta_{ij\,\text{lower}} \leq S_i \leq \theta_{ij\,\text{upper}}$$
$$= 0 \quad \text{otherwise}$$

Each module thus partitions the n-dimensional input signal space by two parallel hyperplanes perpendicular to axis i. All modules in the row act together to partition the signal space into multiple regions which, together with the weights and threshold, define the acceptance region. The thresholds $\theta_{ij\text{ upper}}$, $\theta_{ij\text{ lower}}$, and T_k are determined by a learning process.

The module is an analog device. The extraction of characteristics which serve as the analog input measurement vector is not performed by the machine. The actual measurements are also not made by the machine. The analog configuration gives a continuous signal space which may have some bearing on system effectiveness.

4.5.2 Generalization Proposed by Chow

A logical transformation network has been proposed by Chow [10] to transform the measurement vector prior to recognition processing. This concept is derived from a more complete decision theoretic analysis in which the components of the two-dimensional input vector are assumed to be neighbor-dependent. In previous analyses the components were assumed to be statistically independent. The assumed dependency is between the four nearest neighbors, north, east, south, and west. As a result of this assumption, the optimum processor is modified by a parallel network which performs a transformation of the two-dimensional input vector as shown in Fig. 41. This network consists of two levels of AND gates.

This theoretical result further emphasizes the role of the parallel network in the total recognition problem. Such a transformation (and much more complex ones) can be executed very effectively by a parallel network, and the network can also perform the remaining recognition function.

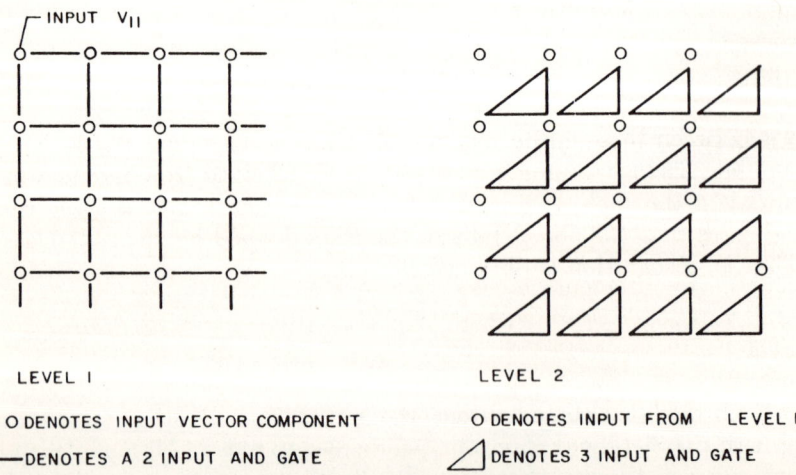

Fig. 41. Transformation network.

4.6 Signal Processors

Radar and sonar systems provide a requirement for highly parallel machines designed for real time or near real time signal processing. Generally the problem is to compare various stored ideal signal forms with the received signal. Specifically, the integral

$$\int |f(x) - g_i(x)| \, dx$$

is to be evaluated for a large range of indices i. Since each value of i corresponds to a complete integral, this is an ideal application for a parallel network.

The process is a matched filter. Each of the values of i represents a different value of a physical quantity such as range rate. The minimum of the integral occurs at the value of i for which $g_i(x)$ most closely matches $f(x)$. The functions $f(x)$ and $g(x)$ are ordinarily complex.

Both analog and digital processors have been proposed, but to date only analog systems have proved practical because of the magnitude of the computation problem. The most advanced of the analog systems are optical processors which have a great deal of flexibility and computational power. More conventional analog systems are arrays of filters, each filter corresponding to a different parameter value.

For radar application, digital signal processors can only be used for nonreal time applications, where accuracy and flexibility requirements are beyond the analog capabilities. Examples are target measurement systems in which the signal processing must be very accurate. Distortion and nonlinearities in the total sensor system are removed by the digital processor. In this application the general purpose parallel network is required.

4.6.1 Westinghouse Parallel Network Signal Processor

Sonar systems are another matter. Not only are signal velocity and bandwidths consistent with present digital technologies, but the variability of the medium and other conditions generate flexibility and accuracy requirements beyond analog technology. A special purpose parallel network is under study at Westinghouse [75].

The parallel network is designed to perform all data processing in the sonar receiver. The block diagram is shown in Fig. 42. The antenna is a conformal phased array. The incoming waveform is sampled directly through the A/D converter and fed into a buffer. The parallel network performs the beam forming, narrow band filtering, pulse compression, log FTC, and thresholding. The processing varies with type of signal and operating environment. Post-detection maximum target likelihood threat analysis is also performed on a nonreal time basis.

The computer is a parallel network derived from the Westinghouse SOLOMON II. The major variation results from the requirement to minimize equipment cost, thus some general-purpose capability is removed.

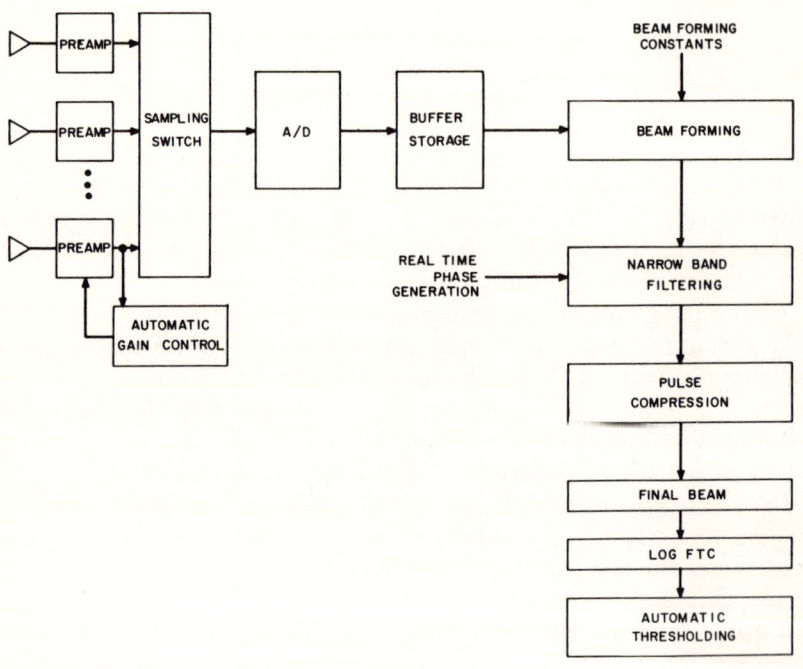

FIG. 42. General digital receiver concept.

Design trade-off studies are under way. It appears that memory of roughly 256 words of 12 bits per network processor is required. The L-buffer and broadcast register are unchanged. The multiply instruction is used at a very high rate and its operation time determines the number of PE's necessary to meet all time constraints. For this reason, attention is being given to using nonstandard multiply techniques such as modular arithmetic and hybrid analog.

4.6.2 Solenoid Array

A special-purpose [6] hybrid digital-analog machine has been built at Sylvania which has 2000 parallel correlation channels of 1428 bits each. The parallel correlation time is 2.7 μsec. The machine evaluates

$$T_j = \sum_{k=1}^{M} W_{jk} U_k, \qquad j = 1, \ldots, 2000,$$

where W_j are the stored signals and U_k are the components of the input signal. Accuracy is about 2%.

The machine consists of a linear array of long thin solenoids. Each solenoid is associated with a component of the input vectors as shown in Fig. 43. The analog input voltage drives the solenoid which thus determines the magnetic solenoid field. The number of turns of the jth component around the kth solenoid determines W_{jk}. The voltage induced in the secondary winding is thus $W_{jk} U_k$. The terms are summed by wiring the secondaries in series.

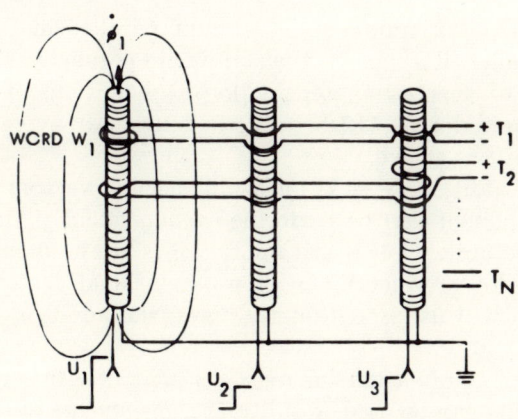

Fig. 43. Solenoid array.

The main problem associated with this device is inflexibility since the values of W_{jk} are determined by the number of turns on the solenoid. In an attempt to eliminate this problem several solenoids are appropriately connected and driven by the same input component. Each solenoid is wound with a different number of windings, and appropriate combinations are used to achieve a range of turns. For example, the values 1, 2, 4, and -7 give all integer values between 7 and -7. Unfortunately, this approach is still rather inflexible.

The solenoid is a very effective device for generating $W_{jk} U_k$ rapidly and cheaply. For certain special purposes where flexibility and accuracy are less important and particularly where great processing speed is important, this approach has considerable merit.

5. Multiple Instruction Stream/Multiple Function Machines

A number of attempts have been made to design a large-scale machine composed of many smaller computers which can operate together on a single problem or separately on smaller problems. A good deal of hardware has been built including the Burroughs D825 and its antecedents, the Bull Gamma 60, Pilot, the RW400, the Nike X Larc [14, 44], and others. A description of these machines is given by Curtin [15].

The principal system design problem is to achieve a consistently high effective hardware utilization factor. This seems to require that it be possible to operate in parallel at the algorithm level which demands great flexibility in the flow of instruction and data. Several examples must be given at this point to show the orientation of the machine designer.

(1) Addition of n numbers, Maximum parallelism is achieved by adding in parallel all $n/2$ pairs, then adding in parallel pairs of pairs, etc. The number of successive steps is $[\log_2 n] + 1$. Thus, if $n = 1024$, 10 steps are required and 512 arithmetic units. An average of $n/\log_2 n$ arithmetic units is active.

(2) Vector addition, $\mathbf{V} + \mathbf{U}$ for n-dimensional vectors. The addition for each component can be performed independently, one component per arithmetic unit. Thus n arithmetic units are used.

(3) Vector dot product $\mathbf{V} \cdot \mathbf{U}$ for n-dimensional vectors. The multiplication step will use n arithmetic units, the addition step as in (1) above.

(4) Gaussian elimination for an $n \times n$ matrix. An average of $\frac{1}{3} n^2$ arithmetic units can be used to subtract the elements of the first row of the coefficient matrix from each of the elements of the following row, thereby reducing the matrix to triangular form in the usual way. As the form becomes more and more close to the triangular in the course of the reduction, the number of active arithmetic units decreases. Search for the maximal element for pivotal elimination can also be performed in parallel using at first n^2 arithmetic units and subsequently a decreasing number.

(5) Matrix multiplication $C_{ij} = \sum_{k=1}^{n} A_{ik} B_{kj}$ $(i, j = 1, n)$. This operation requires a total of n^3 multiplications and $n^3 - n^2$ additions. At most n^2 processors are required to achieve full parallelism. Time required is n multiplication times and $n - 1$ addition times.

A summary of the degree of concurrency in a group of commonly occurring arithmetic algorithms is presented in Table IV. The columns headed local and global control indicate the need or lack of need for individual control capability in each processing unit. More specifically,

TABLE IV

SUMMARY OF OPERATIONS

Description	Local control	Global control	Sequential time	Concurrent time	Maximum concurrency
(1) Sum or product of N numbers		X	$N - 1$	$[\log_2 N]$	$N/2$
(2) Evaluate Nth degree polynomials			$2N$	$2[\log_2 N]$	N
(3) Multiply vector by matrix		X	$2N^2$	$[\log_2 N] + 1$	N^2
(4) Multiply two matrices		X	$2N^3$	$[\log_2 N] + 1$	N^3
(5) Matrix inversion	X		$5N^3$	$3N$	$2N^2$
(6) Solving systems of linear equations	X		$5N^2(N + K)$	$3N$	$2N(N + K)$
(7) Solving ordinary differential equations		X	$12N^2K$	$4(4 + \log_2 N)K$	$N^2/2$
(8) Least squares fit		X	$2NK^2 + 5K^3$	$2N + 3K$	$2K^2$
(9) Compute the Nth prime		X	$N[\ln N]^2$	N	$N/[\ln N]$
(10) Unordered search		X	$2[\log_2 N]$	4	$2N$
(11) Sort N elements		X	$N[\log_2 N]$	$2N$	$4N$
(12) Evaluating Fourier series		X	$CS:N$	$[\log_2 N] + CS + 2$	$2N$
(13) Neutron diffusion equation					
2-dimensional			$21N^3$	$6N$	$4N_2$
3-dimensional			$30N^2$	$9N$	$4N$
(14) Neutron transport equation	X		$2N^2 + KN$	$2[\log_2 N] + [\log_2 K]$	$2N^2$
(15) Eigenvalues of a matrix			$30N^3$	$18N$	$2N^2$

69

if during concurrent operations, each processor is executing the same instruction, an X appears in the global column.

The principal system design problem is to achieve a consistently high effective hardware utilization ratio. For example, in the Gaussian elimination algorithm a decreasing number of arithmetic units is needed, giving a poor utilization factor unless the unused units can be used for another task.

Several ideas have been investigated for solving this problem.

(1) The separate arithmetic units are tied together so that they can function either together or separately. As many units are used as are necessary for the problem which has the highest priority or largest size. The remaining machines are left on their own, processing their own smaller "background" problems. These problems are interrupted when the machine is needed for group processing.

(2) A hardware device is provided for automatic traffic management. For example, push-down stacks can be used to queue data and instructions and associative memories used to call data and instructions as needed.

(3) A variable machine structure is used in which the inventory of hardware building blocks is allocated to processing tasks according to an assignment algorithm.

5.1 The Ideal Multifunction Machine, IT

Much of the mathematical work performed to develop new algorithms for highly parallel machines has been based on the assumed use of highly integrated multiple processor machines. The ideal multifunction machine IT provides a consistent basis for comparing these algorithms. It also defines the ultimate hardware objectives.

The machine IT consists of an ensemble of n processors and a supervisory control unit. Each processor in the ensemble can perform any sequence of the operations of which it is capable without regard to the sequence being performed by any other processor. However, any processor can be made cognizant of the operations or results of the operations of any other processor or group of processors. In short, the processors function in the best possible manner in a given situation. A measure of the parallelism inherent in an algorithm is given by the number of processors which is needed to minimize the time required to complete the algorithm multiplied by the time required to complete the algorithm.

It is difficult to evaluate or compare algorithms for any real computer. One of the major difficulties is in estimating the running time. Optimum coding with respect to storage assignment and precomputation of

HIGHLY PARALLEL INFORMATION PROCESSING SYSTEMS

repeatedly used quantities greatly affects running time. Coding considerations are removed from the evaluation of algorithms by comparing algorithms on the ideal machine.

Properties of a processor in IT:

(1) No time is required for fetching, storing, or moving operands between registers.

(2) The time required for addition, subtraction, multiplication, etc., is independent of the sign or magnitude of the operands. Each operation may have a specific length of time associated with it.

(3) No time is required for loading index registers or the indexing phase. For example $A_{ij} \pm B_{mn}$ requires one addition time as does $C \pm D$.

(4) No time is required for incrementing, testing, or jumps in iterations. For example, matrix multiplication

$$C_{ij} = \sum_{k=1}^{N} A_{ik} B_{kj} \quad i = 1, \ldots, N; \quad j = 1, \ldots, N$$

takes N^3 multiplication times and $N^3 - N^2$ addition times. Of course, this computation could be performed by an IT system with N^2 processors in N multiplication times and $N - 1$ addition times.

(5) Storage is assumed large enough to hold the program, data and results, and temporary storage locations for the complete algorithm. The algorithm is thus compute-limited and no input-output timing need be considered.

(6) A class of associative operations is available within the common pool of storage for the IT system. These operations include: find the maximum (minimum) element and supply the element and/or its subscripts to some IT processor. Another is supply all elements between two thresholds to processors as fast as they accept the elements, etc.

(7) The IT computing system automatically divides up computation among its processors so that as many processors are used as are needed to perform the job in the minimum time.

5.2 Associative Logic Parallel System (ALPS)

5.2.1 Objectives and Organizations

The stated design objectives [46] are for a machine which is highly reliable, modular, and more easily programmed than conventional multimachine complexes. It also is intended to take advantage of cryogenic mass fabrication technology and is designed around associative memory elements.

The system (Fig. 44) is organized to utilize the inherent local parallelism in decomposed algorithms. The computer module includes both control and arithmetic types. An arbitrary number of computer modules

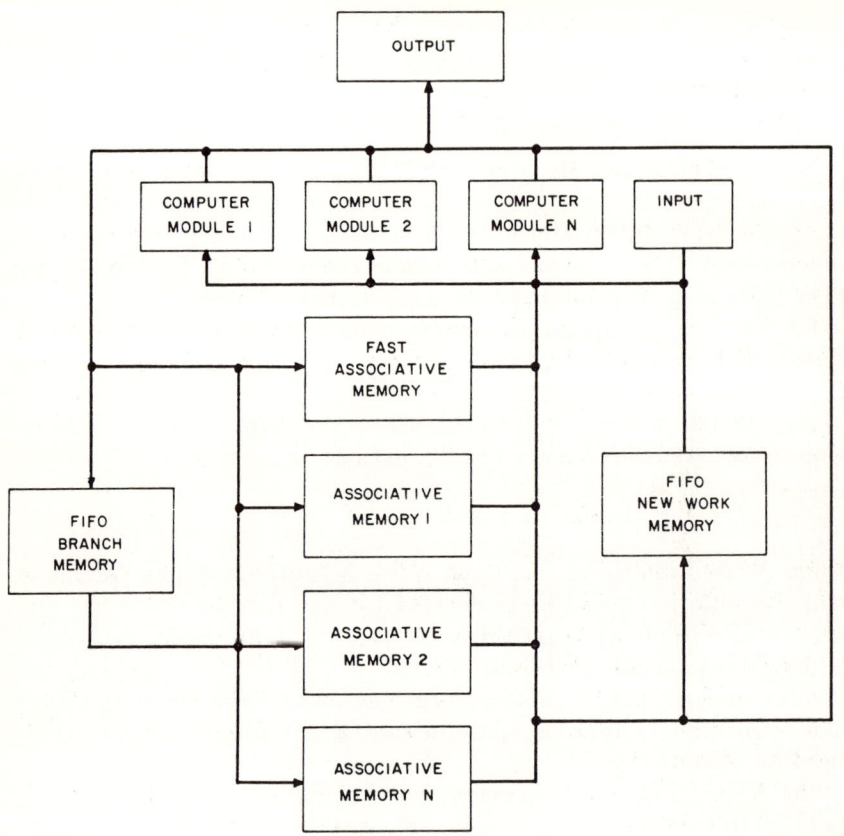

Fig. 44. Associative logic parallel system (ALPS).

is used. Memory is associative with an arbitrary number of memories. First In–First Out (FIFO) memory is also utilized to queue both data and instructions.

Computer modules are intended to operate independently on different segments of the same algorithm. Supervision is provided by the programmer through a binary tree program structure which reflects the tree structure of the algorithm. There is therefore no central control. Interconnections allow simultaneous transfer of data among independent functional parts.

5.2.2. Instruction and Data Flow

Instructions (and data) are stored in the associative memories. They are retrieved as required through a tag field in the instruction which defines the location of the instruction in the tree. Instructions are retrieved when the data to which they refer are available to be operated on. The location of the data in the tree indicates the instruction which refers to the data through a label in the tag field. Initially, all data are marked as ready to be processed. Processing proceeds on one or more trees and their branches as computer modules become available. A control field is used in both data and instruction words to prevent simultaneous call by two units.

Comments. This machine seems to provide an excellent approach to the traffic handling problem which arises in many a computer system. It appears that this idea could be used with profit in other systems in which there are multiple semi-independent processing paths.

In addition to the problem of availability of adequate associative memory, the systems problems have not yet been deeply investigated. In this respect, data flow studies appear to be the next step with an objective of optimizing hardware and demonstrating utility of the concept.

Independent investigations in programming principles correlate well with the ALPS approach. Squire's algorithm for the conversion of ALGOL programs into a tree language would be suitable for this machine.

5.3 Schwartz's Machine

Schwartz [57, 58] at the Courant Institute of New York University has proposed a very large scale multiple machine concept. The essential idea is the data conveyor by which the modules are connected. The system is composed of 64 modules and is relatively inflexible as to numbers of modules. Each module is conceived to be a conventional general computer without program or data memory. Figure 45 is a diagram of the AT-1 computer. The main conveyor provides the path for data and instructions to flow between the set of processors, the set of memory modules, and the set of input-output channels. The processor operates synchronously with each cycle being as long as the longest instruction in the processors' repertoire (can easily be made asynchronous).

To fetch an instruction or data word, each processor places the address of the required word in the section of the conveyor which is "opposite" it. Each conveyor section includes an address part, a message part, and a code part. The address part is set to the requested address, and the code part to "read-memory." The conveyor rotates, placing the read requests successively opposite each memory module for possible action.

In this system each memory module includes buffer storage for up to six read requests per fetch cycle. A memory accepts a read request for

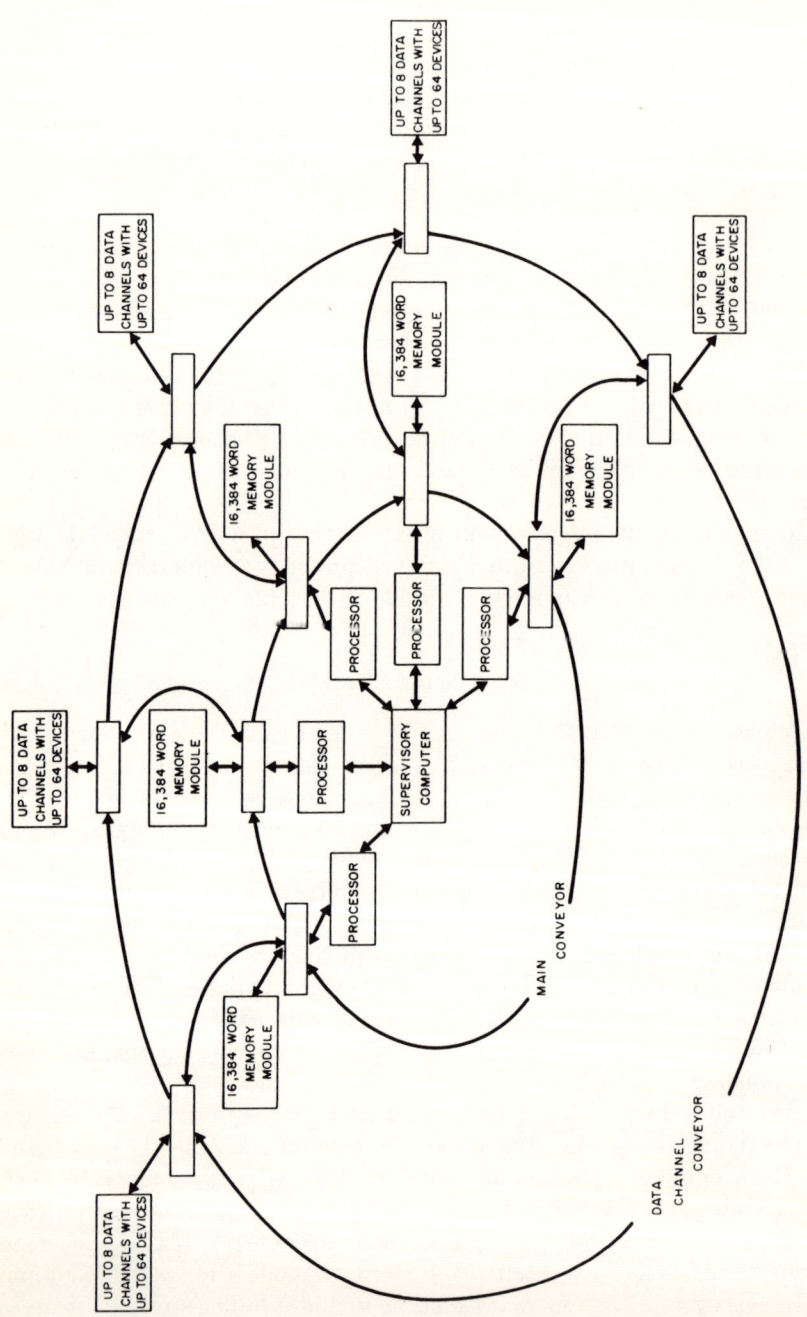

Fig. 45. Schwartz's machine, AT 1.

a word in its memory by storing the address in this buffer and changing the code in the conveyor to indicate that the request has been processed. Subsequent requests for the same word are ignored since one request for a particular word is sufficient to insure its subsequent distribution.

After the conveyor has completed one revolution, it revolves again to pick up and distribute the fetched results to the processors. During this cycle, each processor compares its read-request address with the address part of the successive conveyor positions, and accepts the data when the addresses match—but only if the code part indicates that the request has been processed. Requests can remain unprocessed because some memory module received requests for more than six distinct words. In such an instance, the conveyor must continue to rotate until all requests have been satisfied. Statistically, assuming a random distribution of 64 requests among 64 modules this should be necessary only about 4% of the time.

The data channel conveyor provides the communication path between one I/O device and another. Data words can supposedly be transferred between devices without any other explicit control. No description is given of the buffering means used when two devices of unlike speeds are to be used in this manner. In any case, requests for communication between the I/O subsystem and the memory subsystem are also handled, at least initially, via the data channel conveyor. When these requests occur, they are placed on the data channel conveyor along with the requests for transfer of data values between I/O devices. One rotation suffices to distribute the latter. When the processors are in their execution phase and thus are not using the main conveyor the data channel conveyor transfers these read and/or store requests to the main conveyor which rotates a sufficient number of times to process them in the normal manner. Replies from satisfied requests are transferred back to the data channel conveyor for distribution. These activities will sometimes delay the processors in storing results or obtaining their next instructions.

Comments. The conveyor is an alternative to the conventional crossbar method of connecting modules with each other. Analysis of hardware and processing time for the conveyor indicate that the crossbar is more efficient. The conveyor uses about four times as many gates and takes slightly longer to route data.

The machine generally has the advantages and disadvantages of nonglobal machines in that slightly more general applicability is achieved by having both joint and separate operation. It has the disadvantage of not having a total computing power consistent with hardware used. Thus, the hardware utilization efficiency depends on the problem environment. In general, it is indicated that the machine would have application where many small problems separately justify 64 individual computers. The conveyor then provides the means for using the available combined power on a single large problem. Several additional features are desirable to facilitate programming.

(i) Each processor should have the ability to execute "cut" instructions similar to those for the GAMMA 60. This would facilitate interprogram control when a subset of the processors is operating on a single program.

(ii) The programs should be capable of running synchronously or asynchronously with respect to stepping their instruction counters. Thus compiler-generated programs could merge sequences of instruction and results by counting instructions rather than determining real time for a sequence of instructions (Squire's algorithm, Section 7). Also, separate programs or noncritical parts of the same program could run each processor at maximum capacity in the asynchronous mode.

5.4 Conway's System

A system [12] somewhat similar to ALPS has been proposed by Conway. He has suggested several ideas for improving programmability and data flow of a nonglobal system.

First, a set of instructions is provided to control branching to parallel paths in an algorithm. These are called "fork" and "join" instructions. The fork instruction appearing in a primary instruction sequence commands another processor to begin executing another specified instruction sequence in parallel. The join instruction serves to reestablish the single instruction sequence by delaying further processing past the join point until both of the parallel processes have reached the join point.

Figure 46 shows a typical fork-join pair. A secondary parallel process is established in a second independent processor. The join instruction delays the further processing of the primary instruction stream until the secondary process is complete. The join instruction is placed at the end of each of the parallel instruction sequences and acts as a transfer instruction. The delay is controlled as follows: The fork instruction sets a counter to 2. The join instruction decrements this counter by 1. Further processing is delayed until the counter reaches 0. Any number of forks may be executed, each one upping the number of processors by 1.

The major problem associated with this approach is that if a single conventionally organized memory is used, instructions cannot be obtained from the memory fast enough to support more than a very few

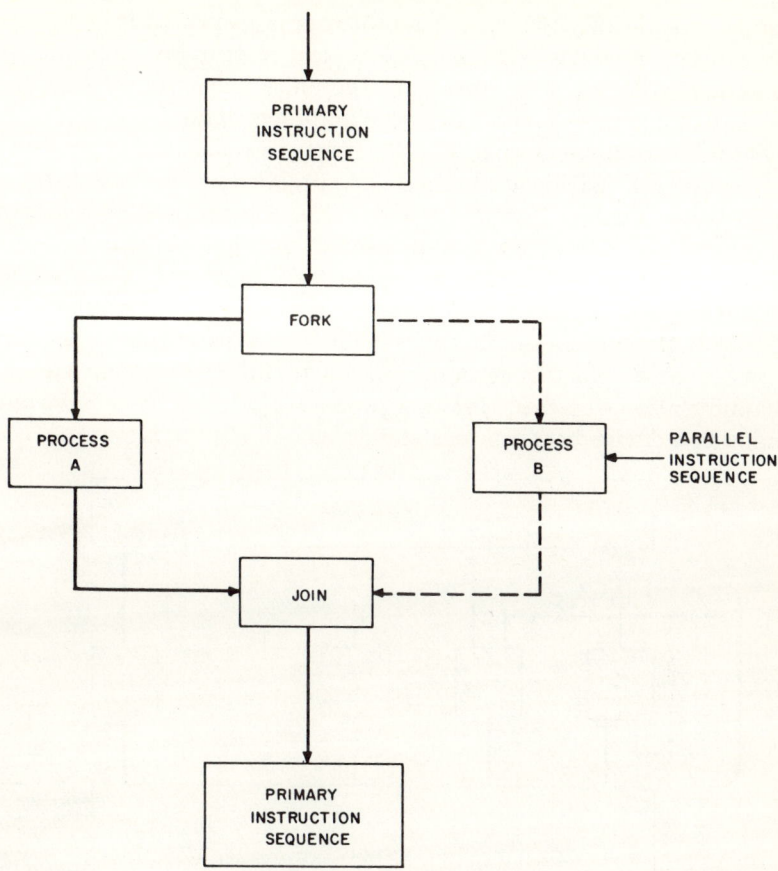

Fig. 46. Fork-join instruction pair.

processors. A similar problem exists for data since each processor must have access to all data.

The suggested solution is to divide the memory into small independently accessed memories. An appropriate subset of these memories is assigned to each parallel instruction sequence. (These may of course be completely independent programs.) A multiple bus (or possibly crossbar) arrangement is used to allow any processor to communicate with any memory module. This thereby ensures that instruction and data can be supplied at a rate sufficient to keep them busy. (Problems can still occur if many processors require data from the same module simultaneously.)

Each processor has a small associative memory which preserves program and data integrity. Each instruction sequence is given a number and the associative memory maps these numbers onto the allowed storage modules. By this means, a processor is prevented from accessing any storage modules not assigned to the instruction sequence it is executing. Allocation of storage is therefore achieved by writing all associative memories with the same mapping data.

The full system is shown in Fig. 47. It consists of special Input/Output Processors (IP), Arithmetic Processors (AP), Memory Modules (MM), and a number of Central Processors (CP). The central processor assists in the allocation of processing sequences to processors. This is done as follows: Each fork establishes a request for a processor. These requests are queued and assigned to processors as they become available on a priority basis. A processor becomes available for reassignment whenever it comes to a join instruction. The CP performs the logic and data communication necessary for this process. The dispatcher is an interconnection device between CP's and AP's.

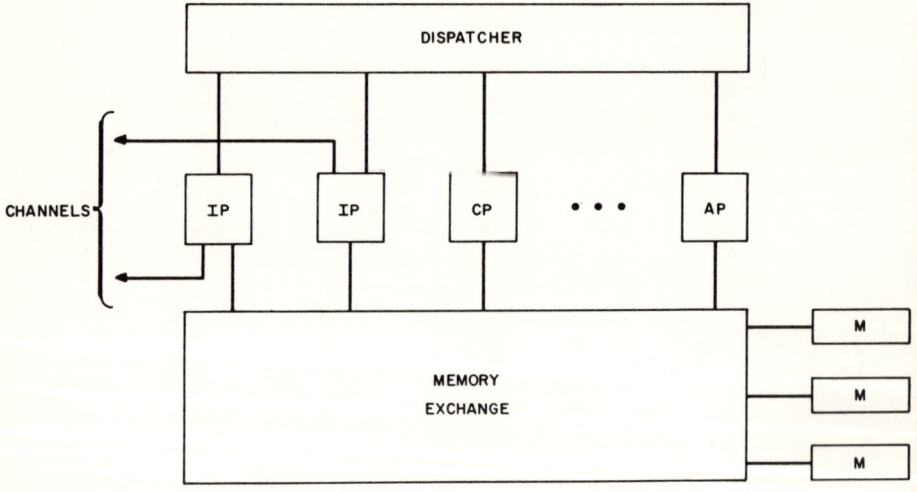

FIG. 47. Conway's multicomputer system.

Comments. As with most of the highly parallel machine proposals, important systems questions have not been studied. Some of the questions that should be investigated are:

(1) Memory organization. Memory is one of the very important cost elements of any large-scale system. Breaking it up into many independently accessible modules will sharply increase the amount of memory hardware (addressing, sense amplifier, drive circuits). A variety of alternate approaches has been suggested based on other memory organizations (e.g., associative) and other data communication devices (e.g., conveyor) to solve this problem.

HIGHLY PARALLEL INFORMATION PROCESSING SYSTEMS

(2) Communication and data routing. A good deal of hardware is tied up in this function as outlined.

Programming requirements fit very well with the algorithmic decomposition processes discussed in 7.2.

5.5 Variable Structure Parallel Computers

From the point of view of efficiency of utilization of hardware, no general-purpose organization is as effective for any job as a special-purpose organization designed specifically for that job. It is, therefore, natural to attempt to develop a variable structure computer which can be adapted (or adapt itself) to the specific problem at hand.

5.5.1 *The UCLA Machine*

Several proposals have been put forward for such a machine, the most significant parallel approach being that by Estrin [*1, 20, 21*] of UCLA in 1960. This proposal is to provide an inventory of high-speed substructures which can be used as required to produce a problem-oriented system with capabilities beyond the capabilities of general-purpose systems. The machine is oriented to take advantage of algorithmic parallelism.

5.5.1.1 Organization and control. A fixed (F) general-purpose computer is included in the system to perform input/output functions, to permit the use of existing programming languages and subroutine libraries, and to perform complex, but not time consuming, parts of the computational task.

The variable structure computer (V) is used to gain speed in generally less complex iterative procedures. It uses various (possibly special-purpose) techniques such as wired programs, unconventional circuits and circuit interconnections, unconventional number representations, and parallelism. Real time structural changes are permitted. The basic system configuration is shown in Fig. 48. The variable structure is highly parallel in that it has (potentially) many arithmetic units.

Communication and control between the F and V are an essential part of the concept. The principal control elements are shown in Fig. 49. Within the variable structure there are three levels. The lowest generates elementary (micro) commands in the arithmetic unit. One such control is used for each arithmetic unit. The next higher control level provides instructions to the lower level for the execution of subroutines such as the generation of elementary functions, complex arithmetic, and matrix operations. Additional higher control levels may be included which can be stored program devices. The highest control level is the system supervisor. It then provides control to both F and V. It also controls data

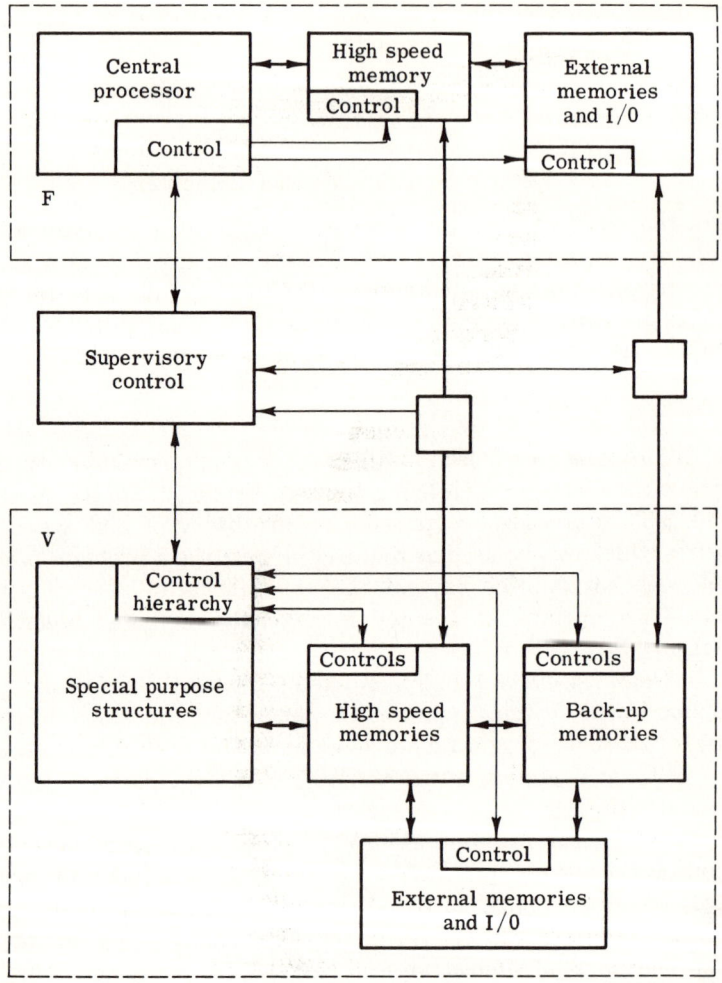

Fig. 48. Block diagram of the F + V system.

exchanges between F, V, peripheral equipment, and between units within V. The supervisory control is a stored program unit.

Comments. Extensive effort has been expanded in various study and design programs. A system is being constructed at UCLA. The fixed system is a 7090; the variable system is modular. This modularity will allow for system growth.

Effort has been applied to developing an understanding of the organization requirements for a spectrum of significant problem areas. Additional study has been directed toward the problem of assignment of subcomputations to the autonomous computing structures of the variable structure system. This study has covered the selection of computing structure, system organization, and assignment and sequence of computation to structural elements. This problem is closely related to the multiprogramming problem. A successive approximation assignment technique has been developed using directed graph theoretic techniques. It takes into consideration the numbers of traversals through various computational loops.

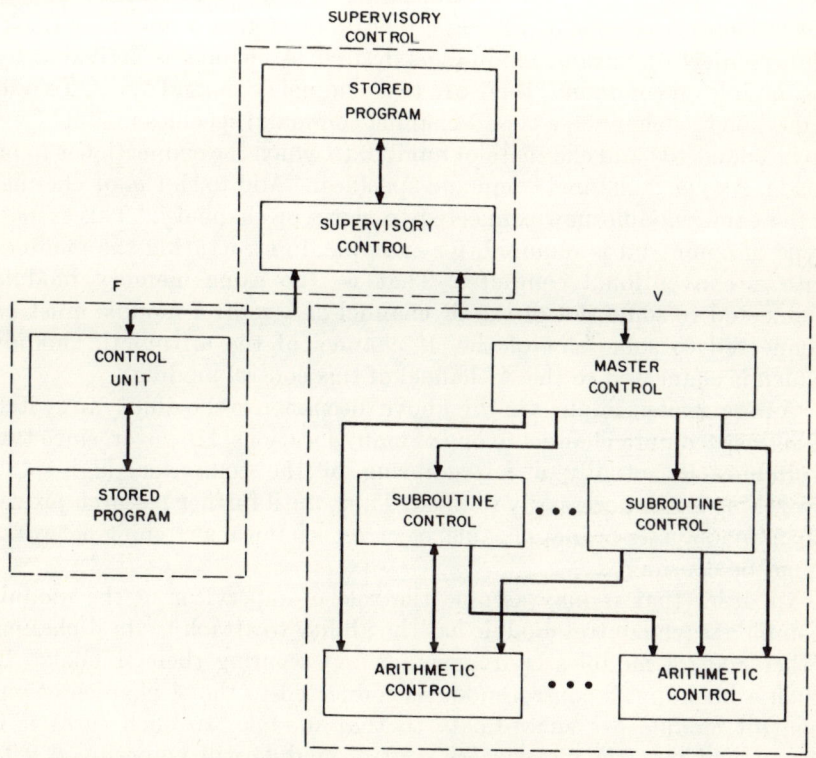

FIG. 49. F + V control hierarchy.

5.5.2 Functional Unit Modular Machine

A second variable structure system has been proposed by R. L. Beadles at Westinghouse to give the same machine both local and global parallelism capability. The computer organization consists of at least four types of functional unit modules connected appropriately for the set of problems under solutions at a given time. These functional unit modules can be connected to form either many semi-independent conventional computers operating simultaneously on different programs as a multiple instruction processor, or as a parallel network computer with one central supervisory module and one program in which many modules perform the same operations simultaneously. All of these structuring capabilities are incorporated as an integral part of the computer system design.

5.5.2.1 Organization. Associated with the various types of functional unit modules to be described are interconnecting devices called hooks and channels. Type A hooks can be connected only to type A channels and provide control paths. Type M hooks can be connected only to type M channels and provide data paths. A channel of either type has several slots, each one of which may be connected to a matching hook, thus connecting various modules as desired. A channel is activated by its module on command; there are two channel command types. To add a module to a channel, a type 1 channel command specifies module type to be connected and channel slot number to which the connection is to be made. A type 2 channel command specifies: "Add to slot m of channel k the same module now connected to slot n of channel j." This second type of command is required, for example, in structuring the modules into a conventional computer. That is, the same memory module connected to some slot of the M channel of a control module must be connected to some slot of the M channel of the arithmetic module which is connected to the A channel of this control module.

A requirement implicit in the above discussion is the ability to switch a high-speed data channel to one of many locations. However, since this switching is actually a restructuring of the computer, high-speed switching is not necessarily implied. Thus, until further research proves them inadequate or inapplicable, electromechanical switching networks must be considered.

In order that it may assume the role of supervisor of the module complex, each control module has the ability to attach to its A channel other control modules by requesting and securing their A hooks. In such a hookup, all control modules connected to the A channel of one control module are subordinate to that module. In such cases it is envisioned that the supervisory control module will be occupied with processing priorities while relegating to the other control modules the function of controlling the arithmetic modules active on those programs being executed under control of that supervisory module.

A conventional computer can be assembled by using one of each of the four module types as follows:

(a) *Control module*: to two slots of the A channel of the control module, attach the A hook of the I/O module and the A hook of the arithmetic module. To a slot on the M channel of the control module, attach the M hook of the memory module. Leave the A hook of the control module floating.

(b) *Arithmetic and I/O modules*: to a slot on the M channel of the arithmetic module and to a slot on the M channel of the I/O module connect the M hook of the memory module which is attached to the M channel of the control module.

The above connections completely specify the conventional computer.

A parallel network type of computer (say, 3 by 3 PE's) can be built from the functional modules as follows:

(a) Choose one Control Module (CM) and nine Arithmetic Modules (AM's), numbering the AM's AM(1, 1) through AM(3, 3) in the usual matrix notation.

(b) Connect to the M channel of the CM an MM, giving the equivalent of central memory.

(c) Connect the A hook of AM's(1, 1) through (3, 3) to the CM through some slot (the same slot for each AM) of the A channel of the CM.

(d) To slot 1 of the M channel of AM(I, J) connect an MM and number it MM(I, J) giving each AM (each PE) its own memory.

(e) To slot 2 of the M channel of AM (I, J) connect MM$(I + 1, J)$, thus giving AM(I, J) a *south* neighbor. To slot 3, connect MM$(I, J - 1)$ for *west* neighbor. To slot 4, connect MM$(I + 1, J)$ for *north* neighbor. To slot 5, connect MM$(I, J + 1)$ for *east* neighbor.

(f) To slot 6 of the M channel of each AM, connect that MM which is connected to the CM, thus giving the equivalent of the parallel network broadcast capability.

Both of the computer structure examples above are, of course, single program types; they are given only to indicate the flexibility of the modules under discussion.

Comments. The four module types are sufficiently powerful and flexible to allow the construction of various digital computer configurations. The practical design and implementation of these modules at an allowable cost is yet to be studied in detail. Certainly, the design of these modules to conform closely to their equivalents in conventional computer is not the ideal design. For example, the program counter is ordinarily considered to be a part of the control unit of an ordinary computer. In contrast, the program counter equivalent for the modular machine is probably best incorporated in the memory module, for it is in this module that program restart addresses will be stored when programs are interrupted by higher priority ones. When such a low priority program can become active again, its restart address is available immediately to the control module now attached to it (which, in general, can be different from the original control module executing this program).

One of the questions that must be answered is what degree of complexity for individual modules maximizes the advantages of the concept for a given class of problems. It appears now that the ancillary equipment required to give a module the desired flexibility will be considerable. If this is indeed the case, then the computational capability of each module must be considerable to achieve a balanced design. Consequently, the organization would, at this time, appear to be better suited to problems requiring large amounts of computation.

Similar design problems are yet to be solved for the channels. A channel of either type as now conceived has the ability to accept and execute commands; it is apparent that such a channel is relatively complex. Just how complex an A channel is and how it differs from an an M channel is not known. Further study is also necessary to define the switching networks which connect hooks to channel slots for obtaining a desired computer configuration. It is not yet known whether these networks should be distributed as integral parts of channels or whether they would be better considered as separate entities, perhaps as a centrally located switching network.

6. Programming Languages for Highly Parallel Machines

The essential feature of problem- or process-oriented languages is that they must be well suited to the specification of the process and independent of the machine characteristics. At this stage of machine development, however, the process, its descriptive language, and the machine organization are not separable.

This problem has several facets. First, and least significant, algorithms are not available at present to translate processes as specified in existing languages (e.g., ALGOL) into programs for highly parallel machines. Second, the parallel processes are generally most naturally defined in a language which reflects the parallel aspects of the process. This is particularly true for processes which involve the local or global geometrical and topological properties associated with data arrays. As an example, for sequential machines, the program for the conventional relaxation process for Laplace's equation over a two-dimensional grid includes a nested pair of DO loops for running through rows and columns of the grid. When this grid is mapped onto a two-dimensional parallel network, these DO loops are eliminated. It is then convenient to describe the relaxation process as averaging the north, south, east, and west grid points. The third difficulty with conventional languages is that they do not provide enough information about the process for a translator to be efficient.

The following approaches to languages for highly parallel machines have been suggested. In one, network hardware oriented terms are permitted. The second avoids hardware references by using a two-dimensional data array to reference implicitly specific hardware elements. Both of these are oriented toward the natural processes performed on multidimensional data arrays. In the third language approach, the object is to provide the additional information needed by the translator to apply conventional languages to unconventional machines.

6.1 A Parallel Network Language

One direct approach to the language problem for parallel networks is to extend an ALGOL-like language so as to provide the terms necessary to specify data processing performed by a parallel network. The programmer is thereby provided the means to define the process in a way natural to the machine organization.

For example, data are often used in a rectangular array such as in the solution of partial differential equations. In an array of this kind, it is necessary to describe relations between grid points such as north, north-east, etc. It is desirable that the programmer be able to express these concepts in ways consistent with natural usage.

A language based on this approach has been studied at Westinghouse for a parallel network processor such as SOLOMON. It is a direct extension of ALGOL in the sense that ALGOL is a subset of the network language. Because of this, conventional translation techniques can be used.

Westinghouse studies have indicated some of the required extensions as follows:

(1) *Data descriptions:* The format of PE data words must be defined both as to range and type. The format may be defined with a statement

FORMAT N1,N2

where N1 and N2 are unsigned integers which indicate the number of bits in the fractional part and exponent. The range may be defined with a statement such as

RANGE N1,N2

where N1 and N2 are unsigned integers and give the upper and lower bounds. To define integer variables in the PE array, a statement such as

PE INTEGER V1

is required and to define a real variable

PE REAL A.

Thus, for example, to define a 5-bit integer in the PE array, we write

PE INTEGER V1 RANGE 1,32.

To provide array storage allocation, write

>   PE ARRAY v1(N1,N2)

where N1 and N2 give the upper and lower bounds of a single dimension array. For example,

>   REAL PE ARRAY A(1,9) FORMAT 28.8

defines an array with nine 36-bit words.

(2) *Configuration statements:* A configuration statement is necessary to define the topology of the array. Thus, write

>   PE TOPOLOGY s1

where s1 is one of the following

>   PLANAR, LINEAR, TOROIDAL, SPHERICAL, HORIZONTAL CYLINDER, VERTICAL CYLINDER.

(3) *Label:* It is often necessary to identify a particular PE or class of PE's by its coordinates. Thus

>   PE(I,J)

means the PE in row I and column J (following SOLOMON PE coordinate conventions); I and J can be expressions. Thus, PE (1,1) is the upper left hand PE and A(PE(1,1)) means the variable A in PE(1,1).

It is also necessary to have relative PE labels, that is, labels of PE's relative to specific PE's. Thus, N, S, E, W, NE, NW, SE, SW, and B are relative labels standing for north, etc., and B for base (the relative reference PE itself). Examples of the use of these labels are

>   A(S) ; I(NE)

where A and I are PE variables.

(4) *Geometry control:* Geometry control in SOLOMON is basically used to control PE's according to externally derived patterns. These patterns can be expressed by a statement such as

>   PE INDEX v1 = v2 STEP v3 UNTIL v4

where v1, v2, v3, and v4 are expressions, and have the same meaning as in sequential ALGOL except that a PE INDEX results (ordinarily) in an activation of a geometry control register rather than performance of a loop. As an example:

>   M = 0
>   PE INDEX I = 1 STEP 2 UNTIL P,
> J = 1 STEP 1 UNTIL Q
>   M(PE(I,J)) = 1

will result in the PE INTEGER, M, being set to 1 in alternate rows.

(5) *Mode control:* The statements already covered include a full capability to use SOLOMON mode control. Mode control capability is achieved via the PE INTEGER. Thus, in the previous illustration, M would be an integer stored in the array or a mode value depending on its use in the program. If its arithmetic value is used, it must appear in PE storage, while when used in tests of PE status, it would be loaded into the mode register. No programming restrictions on the range or number of PE INTEGERS are necessary.

(6) PE *status tests:* It is necessary to provide for tests of PE status, including branching on existence or nonexistence of PE's satisfying a Boolean condition. Thus, IF ANY and IF NO statements are contemplated. For example,

$$\text{IF ANY M} = 1 \text{ OR A} = 0 \text{ THEN K} = \text{M(N)}$$

means if there are any PE's for which the PE INTEGER (mode) M = 1 or the real variable A = 0 then set the PE INTEGER, K, of all PE's equal to the value of M in the north PE.

(7) *Mixed PE and non-PE expressions:* Sequential variables will be understood to be defined in the SOLOMON control processing unit. Examples of mixed expressions and statements follow.

$$\text{IF M} = 3 \text{ AND Y} = 0 \text{ THEN}$$
$$\text{X(B)} = \text{X(N)}$$

means if the mode of a PE is 3 and if Y is 0 where Y is a central or non-PE variable, then set X of the PE to the value of X in the north PE.

$$\text{IF M(N)} = 1 \text{ AND K(B)} = 2 \text{ THEN}$$
$$\text{X(N)} = \text{Y,}$$

where X is a PE variable and Y a central variable, means if the mode (M) of the north PE is 1 and the mode (K) of the PE itself is 2, then broadcast Y to the north PE and store it in location X.

(8) *Further examples:*

(a) A(B,1) = (A(B,2) + A(B,4) + A(N,6) + A(S,8))/4.

This process occurs in the relaxation solution of the Laplace equation with 9 points assigned to each PE in the one-dimensional array A.

(b) AKK = 0
FOR K = 1 STEP 1 UNTIL 9 DO
 AKT = MAX (A(PE(I,J),K))
 IF AKT > AKK THEN AKK = AKT
END

With I and J defined as in (4) above, AKK (central variable) is set to the maximum of all elements of A in the alternate rows of the PE array.

(c)   PE INDEX N5 = 1 STEP 1 UNTIL Q
      PE TOPOLOGY TOROIDAL
      FOR N3 = 1 STEP 1 UNTIL Q DO
      BEGIN
      AIK = A (PE(1,N3),N4)
      CK = AIK/AKK
      IF (1 = ALROW(N3)) THEN
      A(PE(1,N5),N3) = A(PE(1,N5),N3) −
                         A(PE(1,N5),N4)*CK
      END

This program step, a part of Gaussian elimination, eliminates elements below the main diagonal. The pivotal element is in row N4 and ALROW defines rows below the diagonal.

While it is apparent that the above statements allow a wide range of processing capability, not enough experience has been gained to demonstrate that they have singular value or cover the spectrum of processing capability. However, they constitute a natural extension of ALGOL and thereby allow full use to be made of previous language efforts. Further, it is expected that similar extensions to languages like COBOL and JOVIAL can readily be made.

Once the basic language requirements have been defined, the next step is to develop the syntax tables. These tables completely define all grammatical rules both to the programmer and to the machine. Syntax tables are metalinguistic formulas which are typically in Backus normal form. Such tables have been given for ALGOL, FORTRAN, COBOL, and others.

Syntax tables, extending the sequential ALGOL syntax, have been written for the language described above. These tables have proved rather lengthy because they define all allowed mixtures of PE and central expressions. Thus, for example, the expression

$$Y = X(B)$$

is not allowed when Y is a central variable and X a PE variable. Similarly,

$$IF\ X(B) = 0\ THEN\ Y = 0$$

is not allowed if X is a PE variable and Y is central, while it is if Y is a PE variable. These difficulties are avoided by defining types of expressions depending on whether they have a sequential or a parallel value. Thus, MAX operating on a parallel valued expression produces a sequential valued expression and SIN operating on a parallel valued expression is parallel valued. Expressions such as IF M = 1 AND Y = 0 THEN, where M is a PE variable and Y central, must be followed by PE operations.

Comments. This language will, when fully defined and modified to reflect experience, provide a convenient programming language for parallel networks analogous to present-day languages. Further, since it is a natural extension of present concepts, little learning will be necessary and conventional compiling techniques are applicable although syntax tables are large.

However, this is an interim solution in several respects. First, the more significant problem is the translation of conventional languages into programs for highly parallel machines of which parallel networks are an example. Because it has a conventional syntax structure and allows precise specification of the parallel process, this language provides a convenient short-term way of getting around this problem but does not meet the ultimate objectives. Second, the language is highly machine-oriented, not even being suited to all highly parallel concepts. Several data array description languages may perhaps be a better approach to a parallel network language.

6.2 A Language for Processing Two-dimensional Patterns

A significant step is being taken at the Digital Computing Laboratory of the University of Illinois in developing processing algorithms and a problem-oriented language for parallel network processing of two-dimensional pictures. The procedures are based on the formalism of syntactical models developed for programming languages for conventional computers. The structure is designed with the ILLIAC III Pattern Articulation Unit in mind but is applicable to a more general parallel network machine.

6.2.1 Description

This approach [49] is a pattern recognition technique based on topological properties of the pattern rather than on its statistical properties (Section 4.5). Because of this, the processing produces a structured description of the input picture rather than a single "yes," "no," or "don't know" decision. The procedure is applicable to two-dimensional binary patterns made up of thin linelike elements.

The initial step in processing is to discover and identify local topological properties such as line elements, terminals, junctions, crossings, bends, and curves. Higher order topological relations between these elements are then established and identification is made on the basis of all these relations. The topological relations are defined according to the structured rules used in conventional syntax models. The first step, identifying local topological properties, is strongly parallel network oriented. It results in the conversion of the pattern into a graph with labeled vertices and branches.

The programming language has been specified as a direct extension of ALGOL. It conforms to the requirement of being machine-independent. A set of primitive operations is defined which operates on two-dimensional pictures as primitive operands.

Higher order expressions and functions are defined in terms of the preventive operands and operations. These definitions are given in conventional notation (Backus normal form) and conform to the requirements for syntax directed compilers.

In order to avoid references to specific processing modules, operations are defined on both a picture (argument) and a context, giving a new picture as output. The context is also a binary two-dimensional pattern. When used in Boolean operations, the arrangement of 1's and 0's in the context pattern serves to identify operational modules. Thus, the context pattern serves the same purpose as mode control.

The primitive operations include the following: set operations, which are binary Boolean operations between two pictures; neighborhood operation, which establishes direction of line elements; threshold operations, which are the basis for counting and arithmetic; connectivity operations, which determine connectivity; and input/output operations.

6.3 Concurrent ALGOL

The decomposition algorithm developed by Squire [see Garner, *27*] for translating ALGOL for highly parallel machines has several limitations which arise from the source language ALGOL. For example, there is no way in conventional ALGOL to specify whether a CALL modifies its arguments. Because of this, the translator must assume that any expression which appears after the CALL and which contains arguments of the CALL cannot be evaluated until after the CALL has been completed even if a module is available for the evaluation of the expression.

To get around this, he has investigated an extended ALGOL which will allow the programmer to state explicitly which statements can be executed concurrently and which must be executed sequentially. These extensions are expressed in Backus normal form and are a rather minor modification to ALGOL.

Specifically, the ampersand is used to indicate that all connected statements (connected by the ampersand) may begin execution when the first statement begins. That is, the computational order is irrelevant in the algorithm. The successor statement is not executed until all connected statements have been completed.
Example:

C = A + B & FOR Q = 1 STEP S UNTIL N DO X (Q) = B (Q).

Commence and halt statements are defined to begin and end execution of multiple concurrent expressions.
Example:

COMMENCE IF X > Y: 51; 57; 512.

Declarations are provided to state independence of variables or arrays. In terms of arguments of procedure calls, the arguments declared to be independent are not affected by the procedure so that in an algorithmic decomposition, the translator can allow references to the arguments in parallel with the execution of the CALL.

7. Translation Techniques

Generally, the problems of translation for highly parallel machines have received little attention. Crude compilers can now be constructed for several types of machines but several basic problems remain. These problems are different for the three classes of highly parallel machines.

7.1 Translation for Distributed Control Machines

The effectiveness of any computer is determined in part by the cleverness of the programmer in utilizing the available hardware to best advantage. However, this factor appears to be of unusual importance for distributed control machines; it is both harder to write an efficient program and more important that the program be efficient.

The increase in versatility achieved through distributed control gives rise to several programming problems not encountered with other machine organizations. Among these are:

(a) *Data and program allocation:* Data are stored relative to a module rather than in a fixed area. Injudicious location of data can result in substantial increases in path building. Similarly, the location and structure of the program and its paths will also strongly affect program efficiency. The design of the path structure is thus at the heart of the programming problem. The translation program (or the coder) must determine the best path between the operating and data modules. Data are then allocated in modules to minimize both the amount of programming necessary to build paths (operating time of the object program) and the amount of hardware tied up by the path structure.

(b) *Programming interactions:* One of the important potential advantages of distributed control is unlimited interactions among many programs. This implies also an increase in the problems of program protection. For example, one program cannot be allowed to destroy critical paths of another independent program.

(c) *Redundant programming:* Redundancy techniques can be used to improve system reliability. This redundancy is completely programmable and thus can be used to the degree required by the application.

7.1.1 Barriers

Figure 50 shows all the possible states of a connecting module in a path. This set of states can allow a barrier to be formed between two regions such that it is impossible to form a path across the barrier without erasing part of the existing path structure. Several examples of barriers are shown in Fig. 51.

Garner's group at Michigan [27] has developed an algorithm by which it can be discovered when a barrier exists and whether two modules are separated by the barriers. He defines a dual segment as the common side of a pair of contiguous modules. The set of all dual segments of a path constitutes its dual path. A set of paths and their duals are shown in Fig. 52. Since each dual segment arises from a corresponding path segment connecting two contiguous modules, no new path can connect

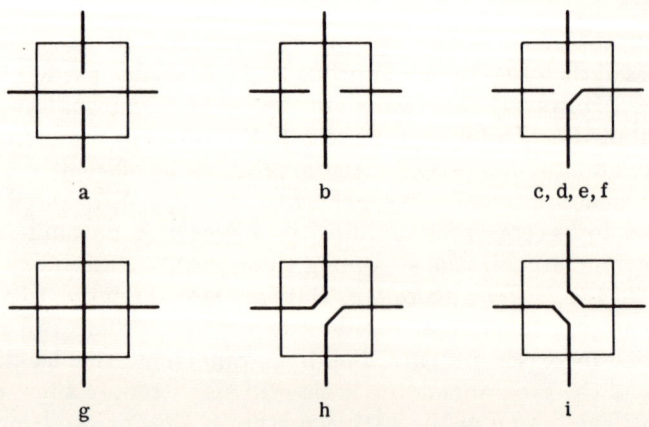

FIG. 50. States of connecting modules.

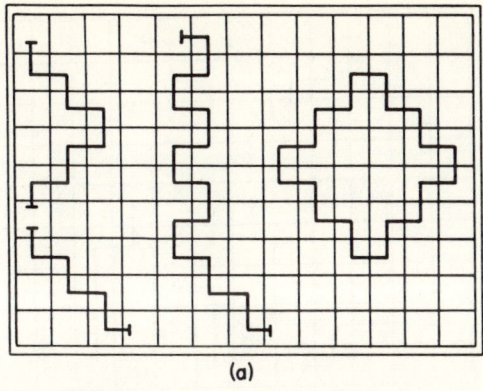

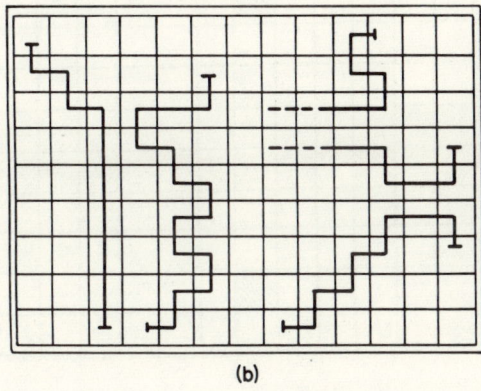

FIG. 51. Examples of barriers: (a) barriers formed by single paths, and (b) multiple path barriers.

them. Thus a barrier exists if a continuous dual path exists which connects two sides or if a continuous dual path is closed.

The algorithmic process is a method for keeping track of dual path segments. Connected dual segments are kept in separate lists and as each new dual segment is created it is added to the appropriate list if it is connected to a dual segment. If not, it starts a new list. If the new segment is connected with several segments, their lists are combined into one.

To discover whether two modules are separated by a barrier, a normal path is constructed between them. A normal path consists of one horizontal segment and one vertical segment connecting the modules regardless of whether it interferes with other existing paths. If this path contains an odd number of segments in common with the barrier, the modules are separated by the barrier.

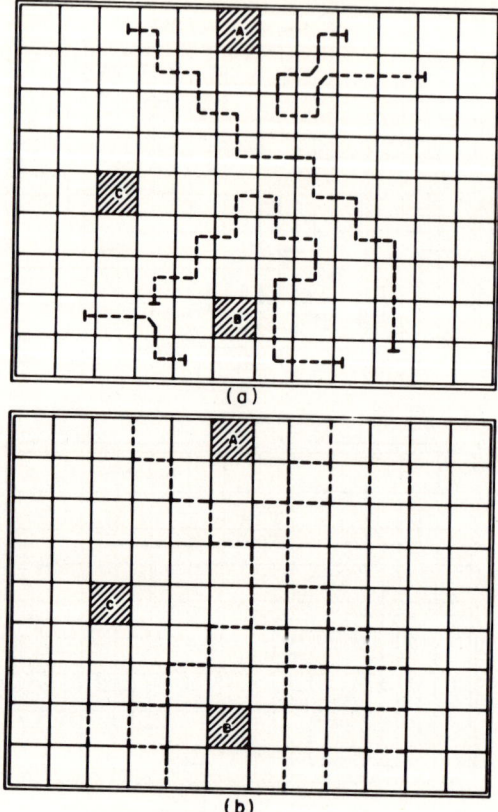

Fig. 52. (a) Paths and (b) their duals.

7.1.2 Optimization of Path Structure

A path connecting the operand with the active module must be defined by the translator for each instruction to be executed. It appears that it is not possible to adopt a simple strategy for developing the path structure. To illustrate the problem, one such strategy is to generate a new path to each operand from each active module leaving all paths formed. The large number of paths that are formed quickly make it impossible to discover new connections through the existing paths. Since many operations can be expected to be repetitive, it is not desirable to break existing paths. An alternate strategy is to gain access to new operands by adding or deleting modules from the termination. However, this also will involve much duplicated path building. No definite optimum strategy for developing the path structure has been stated.

Significant results have, however, been obtained for the more restricted problem of constructing the path of minimum length between two given modules. This problem is simplified by restricting admissible paths to those called "nonregressive." These paths are those which are traced in one direction (or sense) horizontally and in one direction vertically. The path is not allowed to track back in the opposite direction. All such paths have the same length and thus the problem is simplified to that of constructing an allowable nonregressive path. This is done in two steps: first, the elimination of zones of modules which are nonacceptable as path components, and second, the actual path tracing.

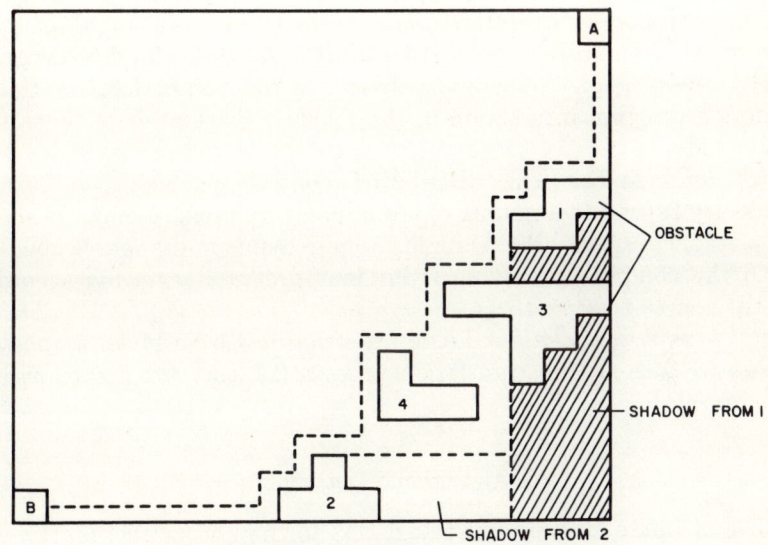

Fig. 53. Shadowing process to determine path.

Elimination of zones which are nonacceptable is done by a shadowing technique as shown in Fig. 53. The objective is to connect module A with module B. A priority is arbitrarily chosen of horizontal segments over vertical (relative to module B). This establishes a trial path along the right vertical and lower horizontal sides of the allowed rectangular region. Then, for every obstacle contiguous to the right side, its leftmost point is determined. Then, a vertical line is drawn to the lower side, and the region below the obstacle and to the right of the line is shadowed. This has been done for region 1 in Fig. 53. The same is then done for obstacles contiguous to the lower side. Repeating this process gives the path shown.

Comments. The algorithms developed by Garner [27] provide the basis for a compiler for a distributed control machine, at least with an appropriate source language that specifies the algorithmic parallelism to be used. However, at the present time, the object program for a large and complex process will be rather inefficient. It also does not seem that the potential subtle program interactions that might be used with many parallel programs can be used. A few of the areas of further research effort to improve the translation process are indicated below.

(a) *Path building:* The complexity of the path building process indicates that further attention might be given to hardware modifications of the path building concept. It appears that the full path building capability of the Holland approach with accessibility between all modules is more a theoretical than necessary or useful capability. For example, a compromise such as Comfort's [*11*] does simplify programming in addition to reducing hardware. At this point, the potential for complex program interaction in the Holland machine is of theoretical value only.

(b) *Redundancy:* The distributed control machine can provide arbitrary types and amounts of redundancy by programming. It should be possible to specify the reliability requirements in the source language with the compiler providing redundant program segments according to the source specifications.

(c) *Aids to compilation:* Little attention has been given to possible hardware aids to the translation process (at least for highly parallel machines).

7.2 Algorithmic Decomposition

The ultimate objective in translators for highly parallel machines is to be able to accept programs written in conventional programming languages such as FORTRAN and produce an efficient operating program on the highly parallel machine. In order to do this, it is necessary for the translator to analyze the program to determine the local and global parallelisms that can be used by the machine.

Some investigation of the algorithms necessary for this process has been performed by Squire [see *27*]. He has described a modification of the conventional precedence scan procedure to give the maximal local (and therefore global) parallelism in the process. This process appears to have application to all highly parallel machines.

The machine is considered initially as operating in fixed time increments or cycles during which any type of instruction can be executed. The increments are numbered in sequence starting at zero. The increment during which computation of a variable is begun is called the starting height of the variable. The increment during which the computation is completed is the end height. The algorithm determines the

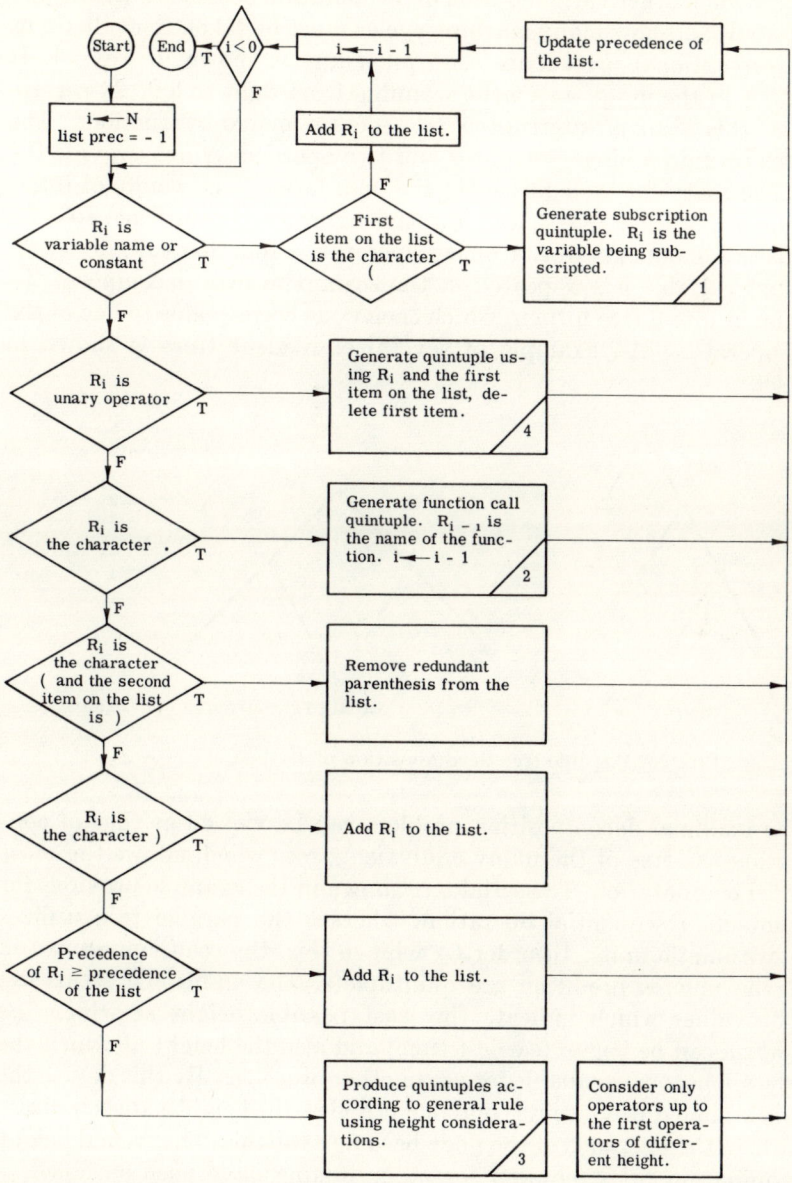

Fig. 54. Conventional precedence scan modified for maximal decomposition.

least possible height at which the variable can be computed by taking into account when other variables used in its definition become available (are computed) and how many machine cycles must be taken to evaluate it.

A conventional precedence scan procedure is shown in Fig. 54. It operates on the input statement scanning from right to left. At certain points, this scan is interrupted to generate macro-instructions. The macros contain a binary operator and two operands which provide the data necessary for later phases in the translation. The points of interruption are labeled 1, 2, 3, and 4 in this figure and occur when either a complete binary operator, a unary operator, a function call, or a subscripted variable has appeared in the scan. The scan decomposes the statement into a tree form in which each node corresponds to one of the four operators. An example of several equivalent trees is shown in Fig. 55.

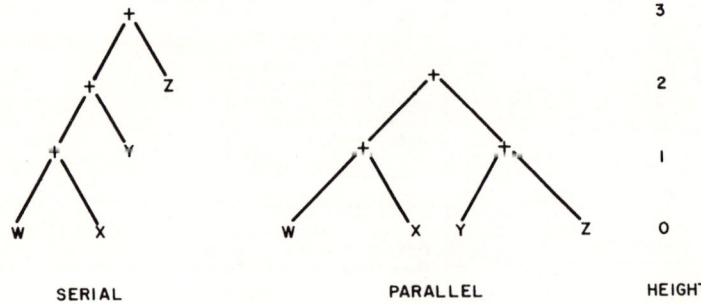

Fig. 55. Possible tree decomposition of $W + X + Y + Z$.

The maximal decomposition problem can be viewed as that of constructing the tree of the many equivalent trees which allows the most parallel computation. The serial tree shown in the example provides for a completely sequential operation, whereas the parallel tree utilizes two arithmetic units. In order to achieve this, the scan is modified in that the macros produced are quintuplets. The additional terms are height values which indicate the least possible height at which the operation can be begun (earliest time) and also the height at which the result will become available for use in other processes. By this device the tree is broken down into its component nodes, the height values indicating where the operands of the node become available. The formal height determination rules required for programming have been specified.

The tree is then assembled according to the limits of the height data and the machine configuration. At present, the scanning and tree assembly process is limited to blocks of statements in the program, where a block contains no possible transfers of a control in or out. That is, all statements in a block are executed or none are. This limitation arises in part because the necessary data for a more complete process are not contained in conventional languages. However, all the necessary data are available at execution time and it is possible to modify the translation so that the tree assembly (and remaining stages of translation) is performed at the time the object program is executed.

Comments. This approach has been partly programmed (on a conventional computer) to demonstrate the operation of the concepts. A lot of additional effort can be expected before an efficient translation process can be achieved. This element of the translation process has very general application but little attention has been given to relating the translation process to the machine configuration.

7.3 Translation for Parallel Networks

At present, the most direct means of obtaining a translator for a parallel network is through a syntax-directed compiler used in conjunction with a language which allows direct specification of the parallel process and its relation to the machine. Several syntax-directed compilers are in development (P. Z. Ingerman at Westinghouse, also Warshall and Shapiro [*73*]) and should be completed for conventional machines in the near future. It will be necessary to make some modifications (for example, in the optimization phases) to reflect the different machine concept.

As indicated earlier, the drawback of the special language approach is that it is highly desirable that conventional languages such as FORTRAN be used. This would allow existing programs to be used on the parallel network with perhaps little reprogramming.

This goal can at least be realized in part. Using Squire's algorithmic decomposition it is possible to identify some of the global parallelism contained in the conventional program; specifically, the global parallelism that arises in the basic algorithm. However, many problems arise.

(1) Experience has shown that much of the parallelism in conventional programs lies rather deeply imbedded and concealed. Typically, a DO loop will provide the multiple elements of a process necessary for a parallel network, each iteration of the loop being assigned to a PE. Generally, however, this loop is a rather complex process with several subloops and data-dependent branches. In order to obtain an efficient program, the logical structures of the subloops and branches generally have to be greatly modified.

(2) Much of the flexibility of the global approach arises because of the possibility of queuing different sets of data to be used with the same

process. The availability of such queues (multiple parameters) brings an important added dimension to the parallelism in the algorithms. The algorithmic parallelism and the parallelism by queuing can be used together. However, generally this possibility cannot be taken advantage of at translation time because it is data-dependent. For example, the best method of matrix multiplication depends on the size of the matrix and the number of matrix products that can be queued up at execution time. The only way that this can be handled is to complete the translation at the time of execution when the data dependency can be established.

(3) To a significant degree, the best algorithm for a specific process depends on the machine. The only thing that can be done about this is reprogramming.

8. Parallel Processing Techniques and Algorithms

To a certain extent, the processing techniques and algorithms that have evolved for conventional machines are not suited to highly parallel machines. The development of both of these depends on actual experience with hardware. Since little operational hardware is available this aspect has been somewhat neglected. Only a partial summary of research results is given.

8.1 Parallel Network Processing

The parallel network computer such as the SOLOMON II system provides great efficiency in data flow and hardware utilization for very large scale data processing problems. This efficiency is obtained through the provision of adequate high-speed memory, parallel channels to bulk storage, multiple access paths to the network, and the network configuration which helps to minimize data flow and bookkeeping. Several principles in the use of parallel networks are illustrated below to show how parallel processing is used in several basic data processing areas.

8.1.1 Matrix Operations

The basic operation of matrix multiplication can be performed by using either the broadcast register, the L-buffer, or only the network. The most efficient approach depends on the size of the matrix in relation to the network.

One way that the broadcast register is used is shown in Fig. 56. In the row-by-column operation used to compute the product matrix

$C = AB$, each PE contains a column of matrix B. One row of matrix A at a time is fed through the broadcast register, one element at a time. Each PE executes the same sequence of instructions, namely,

$$\sum_{j=1}^{N} a_j \cdot b_j,$$

each giving an element of matrix C. Each obtains a_j from the broadcast register and b_j from its own memory. One entire row of matrix C is thus computed simultaneously and left in the network. For full hardware utilization, the number of matrix columns must be either equal to the number of PE's or equal to an integer multiple of the number of PE's. This is essentially the case with very large matrices.

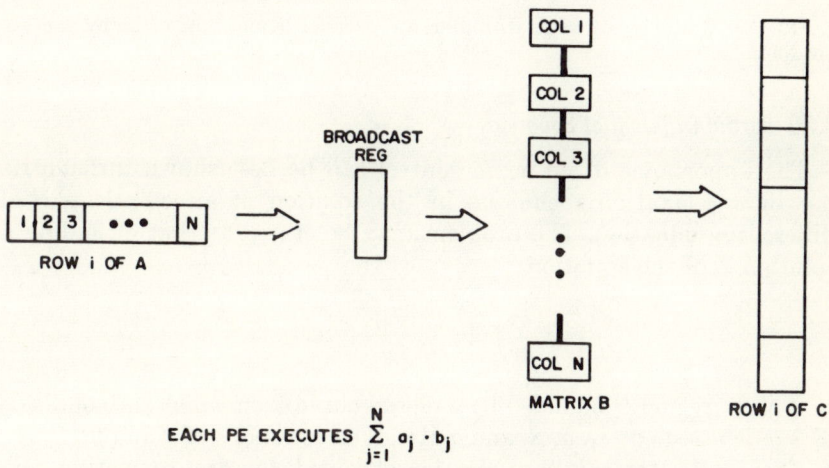

FIG. 56. One method of using broadcast register.

The L-buffer provides a variety of alternative ways of using the network when the matrices do not have as many columns as there are PE's. In this case, there are more but smaller matrices and parallelism is obtained by performing several matrix operations simultaneously. One such method is to use the L-buffer as shown in Fig. 57.

Each row of the network is used for a different matrix, each forming an entire matrix. Specifically, for the matrix product AB, matrix row i of A is loaded element by element into a word of the L-buffer. Matrix B is stored in the corresponding row of the network, one column per PE. For full efficiency, the number of columns in each matrix B must be equal to (or a multiple of) the number of columns of PE's. Thus, high efficiency is achieved with a large number of small matrices.

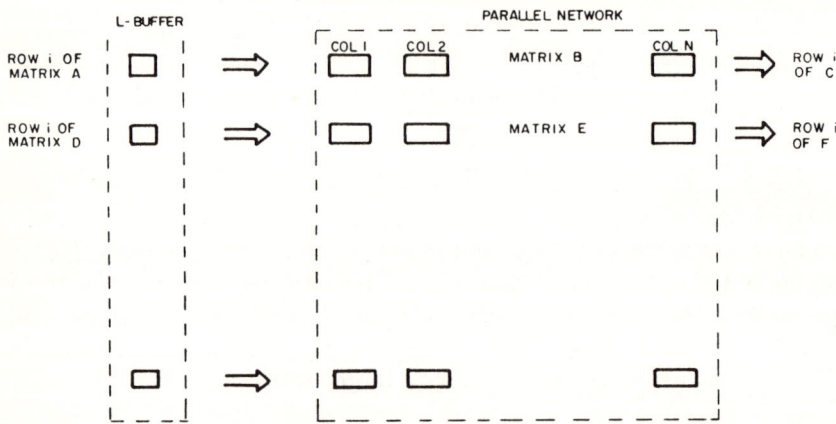

FIG. 57. One way of using L-buffer for parallel evaluation of many matrix products.

8.1.2 Partial Differential Equations

The importance of PE mode control can be best shown through its use in a relaxation technique in the solution of an elliptic partial differential equation. The problem may be stated as that of finding a solution Z of the equation

$$\frac{\partial}{\partial x}\left(D\frac{\partial z}{\partial x}\right) + \frac{\partial}{\partial y}\frac{(\partial z)}{\partial y} + az - S = 0$$

in a plane region G bounded by a closed curve C on which the condition $Z = \sigma$ is satisfied; D, a, S, and σ are given functions of x and y.

The numerical solution can be obtained by approximating this equation by a system of algebraic equations. These equations are obtained by overlaying the region G with a rectangular grid as shown in Fig. 58 and using the finite difference approximation to the partial derivatives. In the resulting system of equations, each point of the grid generally appears as a function of its immediate neighbors. For example, in one simple case,

$$Z_{i,j} = \tfrac{1}{4}(Z_{i-1,j} + Z_{i+1,j} + Z_{i,j-1} + Z_{i,j+1}).$$

The solution in this case can be obtained by an iterative procedure in which the $n+1$ iterative approximation to $Z_{i,j}$ is

$$Z_{i,j}^{(n+1)} = \tfrac{1}{4}(Z_{i-1,j}^{(n)} + Z_{i+1,j}^{(n)} + Z_{i,j-1}^{(n)} + Z_{i,j+1}^{(n)}).$$

Using the parallel network, several neighboring grid points can be stored in each PE, for example, four points per PE as shown in Fig. 59.

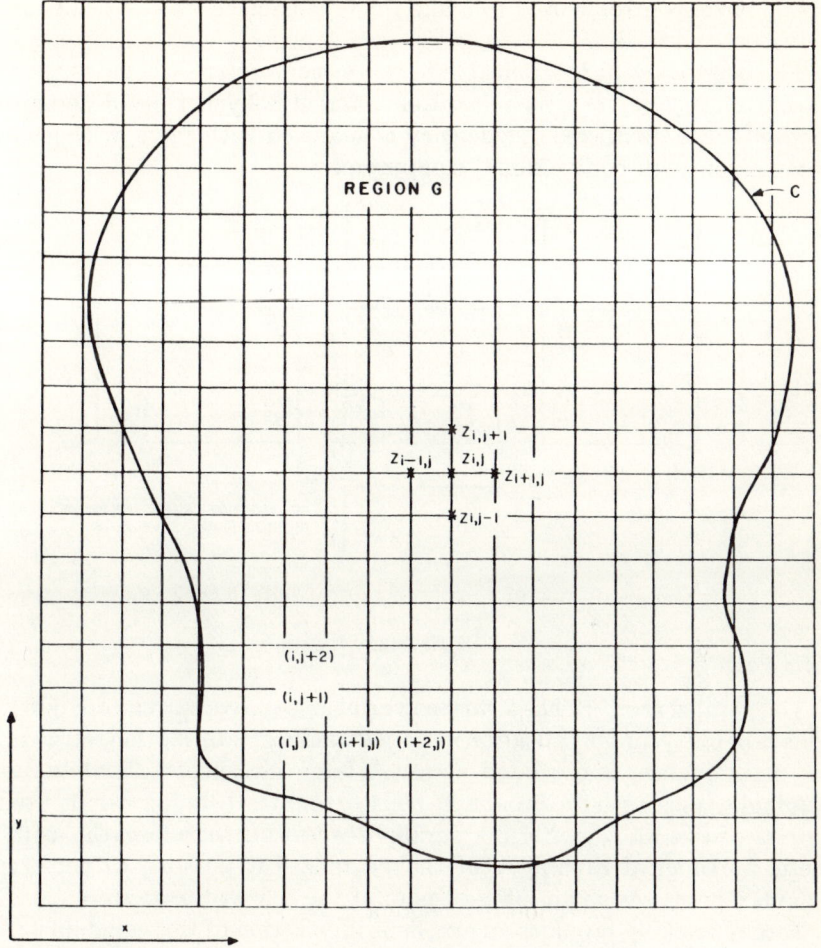

FIG. 58. Grid overlay used for the solution of a partial differential equation.

In this example, four separate steps are executed by the network for $Z^{(n+1)}$ at points 1, 2, 3, and 4 in turn, all 1 points, then 2 points, etc., being done simultaneously. In comparison, with a conventional computer each grid point must be processed separately—one point at a time.

In evaluating $Z^{(n+1)}$, the values of $Z^{(n)}$ are obtained using various routing options. Thus, for 1 points in the iterative procedure described above, $Z^{(n)}_{i,j-1}$ is obtained from the north PE, $Z^{(n)}_{i-1,j}$ is obtained from the east PE, and $Z^{(n)}_{i+1,j}$ and $Z^{(n)}_{i,j+1}$ are stored in the PE itself.

Mode control can be used very effectively to take into account an irregular boundary. For example, if the point labeled B is a boundary

103

point, mode control is used to make that PE inactive when 1 points are being processed.

The basic concept is applicable to the basic iterative schemes such as Jacobi's, successive over-relaxation, and Chebychef semi-iterative methods. A high degree of efficiency is achieved with these methods in comparison with conventional computers.

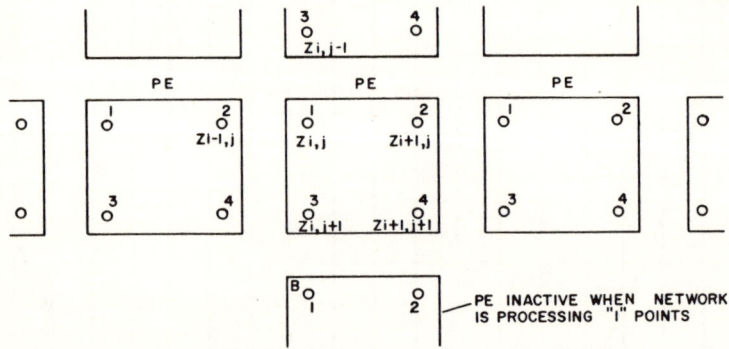

Fig. 59. Storing of neighboring grid points in each PE.

8.1.3 Parallel Search

The parallel network has a very powerful associative search capability. This capability finds application in target tracking, information retrieval, file maintenance, and related areas. A large measure of flexibility is available, since both the broadcast register and the L-buffer can be used with the network to perform a parallel search. Furthermore, the arithmetic and logical capability of the PE makes it possible to perform complex processes as an integral part of the search function.

Target tracking provides an excellent illustration of this capability. A typical problem is to catalog or keep track of targets seen by a radar. One part of this function is to take a target sighting and compare it with each of the targets in the catalog to determine whether or not the target is in the catalog. If not, it is a new target and must be entered into the catalog. This process is called "correlation."

In the parallel network, each target is assigned to a PE, and the coordinates of the sighting are placed in the broadcast register. Each PE then computes the distance between the sighting and each of its target tracks. If for one track this distance is small enough, the sighting is assumed to be of that target. The PE containing this track is then set to a unique mode for further processing. The flow of data is shown in Fig. 60.

The correlation process is performed by the network once for each

HIGHLY PARALLEL INFORMATION PROCESSING SYSTEMS

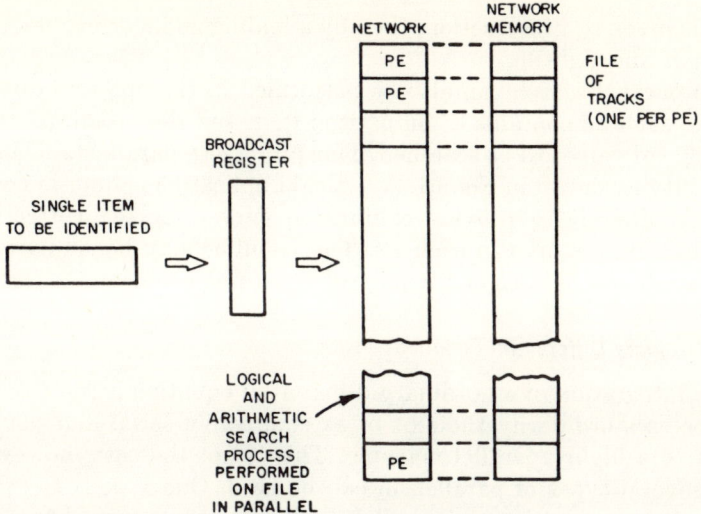

Fig. 60. Parallel network file search.

sighting, taking care of all tracks in parallel. By comparison, a conventional computer must execute the correlation process for each track with each sighting.

The efficiency of the parallel network is shown by its handling of various complexities which arise. For example, track confusion can develop if the sighting is close enough to two targets assigned to two PE's that both PE's are set at the unique mode. However, the fact that more than one track correlates with the sighting can be determined with

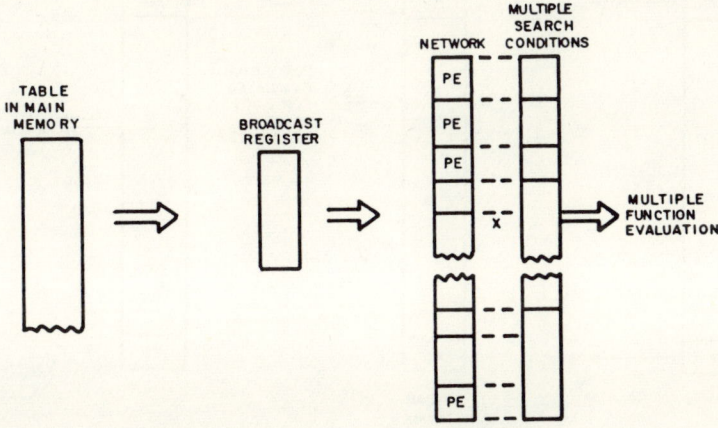

Fig. 61. Parallel table look-up capability.

a single mode test instruction, thereby avoiding an incorrect association of target and sighting.

The parallel search can also be performed in the opposite direction; that is, each PE contains a comparison item and the broadcast register the table of values to be searched. This provides a parallel table look-up capability as shown in Fig. 61. A typical application is function evaluation. Another is to provide calibration curves for the correction of measured data stored in each PE. The L-buffer may be similarly used when each row is assigned a part of the total problem.

8.1.4 Ordinary Differential Equations

The integration of an ordinary differential equation is representative of processes ordinarily thought of as completely serial and not at all suited to a highly parallel machine. This is not the case, however. In fact, several types of parallelism can be used. One type is to evaluate many similar equations in parallel, each equation assigned to a PE. A second is to evaluate a single equation at many points, one point per PE.

A highly parallel system cannot be justified unless a very large computation load exists—typically requiring 10^7 to 10^8 arithmetic operations per second. In this case, it is reasonable to expect that the problem is perhaps a parametric study of a variable defined by the integration of an ordinary differential equation. Examples are the optimization of a

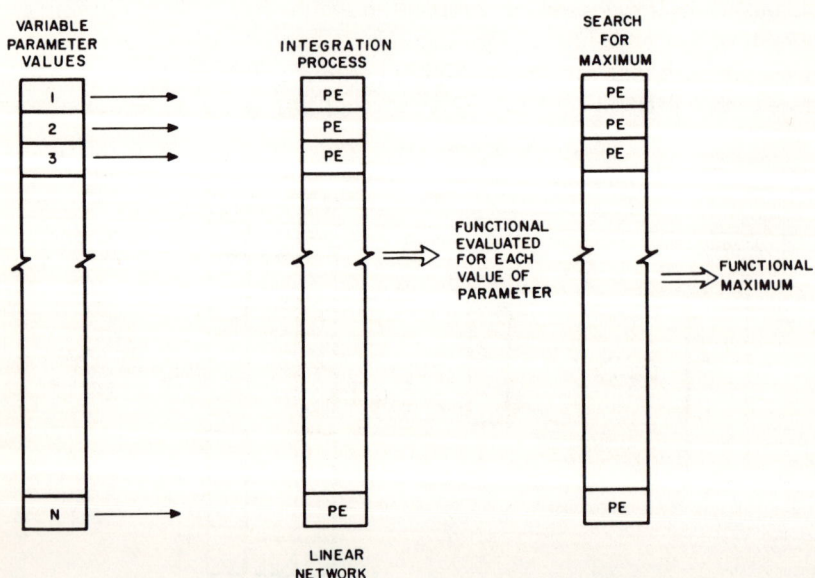

FIG. 62. Parametric search for differential equation functional maximum.

complex missile flight and the stability analysis of an aircraft. The idea is shown in Fig. 62. Selected values of the critical parameter are assigned to the PE's, one value per PE. The integration process is performed using conventional techniques such as the Adams or Range-Kutta methods. At the termination of the integration process, each PE has evaluated the functional of interest and the maximum or minimum is identified.

Picard's methods can be used for the integration of a single equation at many points. Each PE performs the integration at a single point. Studies at Westinghouse [74] have shown that a good utilization of the network is achieved and that the approach compares favorably (is an improvement) with more conventional machines.

8.1.5 Adaptive Networks

A great variety of existing and contemplated adaptive system modules has been studied. Generally, they have been constructed to mirror various characteristics or properties of biological systems and it is the processing concept rather than the hardware mechanization that is significant. From the point of view of computer organization, it is pertinent to evaluate the effectiveness of alternate hardware configuration in executing these adaptive processing algorithms.

A typical network is shown in Fig. 63. The S units represent (binary)

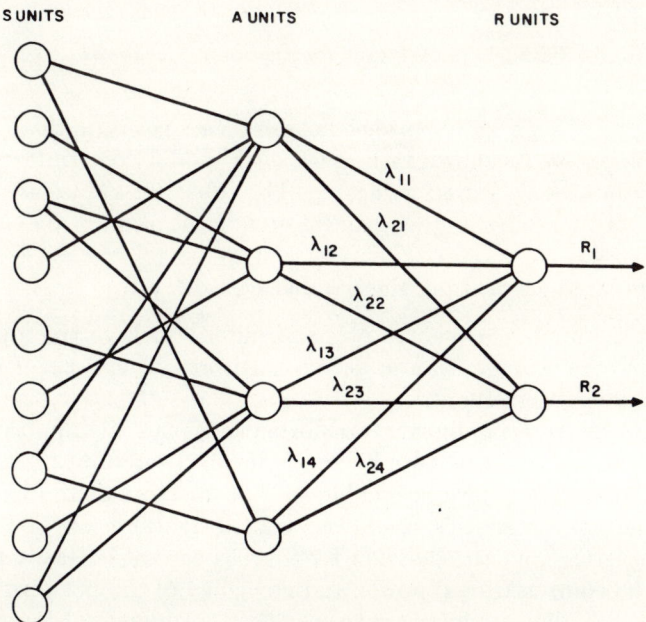

FIG. 63. A simple adaptive network.

sensors, the A units are called associative units each of which produces an output a if a sufficient number of S units that supply it are activated. The R units compute weighted sums of the outputs of the A units. Thus, the output vector is

$$R_m = \sum_{i=1}^{N} a_i \cdot \lambda_{mi}.$$

The vector a is a characteristic of the input pattern which in general is subjected to a coordinate transformation.

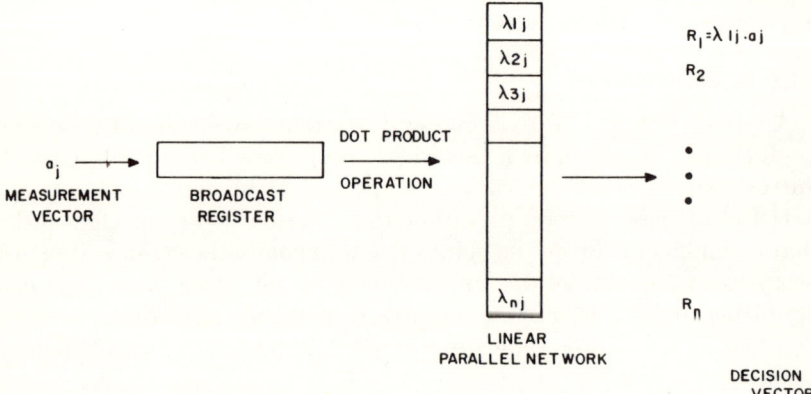

FIG. 64. Parallel network used for maximum likelihood detection.

A machine such as a parallel network can perform this operation quite efficiently. As shown in Fig. 64, each module computes a specific R based on its own stored values λ_{ij}. The subscript values are common inputs to all modules so they can be broadcast, element by element to the network.

The advantages of using the parallel network are:

(1) It is much cheaper to store variables such as the λ-matrix in magnetic core storage than in active hardware. Therefore, many more such values can be stored.

(2) Linear and nonlinear transformations can be applied experimentally to the input pattern by the same hardware unit.

(3) The system is programmable so that far more flexibility is available. The characteristics used, the transformations applied to these characteristics, and the decision techniques can all be easily modified.

(4) The computational power and efficiency of the network makes it possible to realize far larger networks than are practical by other configurations.

(5) Multilevel and variable structure nets can be programmed.

(6) Syntactical structures such as those described by Narasimhan [*49*] can be used for hierarchy of decisions. Similar processes have been developed for associative processors by Fuller [*26*].

8.2 Algorithms for Highly Parallel Machines

Several groups have active research programs in the development and evaluation of algorithms for highly parallel machines. These studies have generally indicated that the processes which have evolved for conventional computers are not necessarily appropriate for highly parallel machines.

8.2.1 Generalized Horner's Rule

The conventional method used for evaluating a polynomial of nth degree

$$p(x) = a_0 + a_1 x + \ldots + a_n x^n,$$

is by a recursive procedure known as Horner's rule. This procedure consists of recursively evaluating for $n, n-1, n-2, \ldots$, to 0, the function

$$b_i = a_i + x b_{i+1}$$

with $b_n = a_n$ and $b_0 = p(x)$. This achieves a nesting which can be written as

$$P(x) = \cdots x(x(a_n(x) + a_{n-1}) + a_{n-2}) + \cdots.$$

It requires n multiplications and n additions. It is, as it stands, totally sequential, since no b_i can be computed until b_{i-1} has been.

It is therefore desirable to modify this rule to take advantage of all the processors in a highly parallel machine, particularly for the locally controlled organization with many semi-independent arithmetic units. This is done as follows [*19*].

If there are k arithmetic units available, each one is used to evaluate the factor

$$b_i = a_i + x^k b_{i+k}$$

where $i = 0, \ldots, k-1$. The terms b_k to b_{n-k} (evaluated previously in parallel) are also $b_i = a_i + x^k b_{i+k}$. The remaining k terms from $n-k$ to n are

$$b_i = a_i.$$

The polynomial can be seen to be

$$p(x) = b_0 + b_1 x + \ldots b_{k-1} x^{k-1}.$$

Using all available parallelism, the effective computing time for large n is n/k multiplications and n/k additions. A similar procedure has also been proposed by Estrin.

8.2.2 Westinghouse Studies

Westinghouse has had several contracts to develop numerical processing techniques and algorithms for advanced computer organizations. Areas investigated include partial differential equations, ordinary differential equations, search techniques, root finding Monte Carlo methods and linear programming [64, 74].

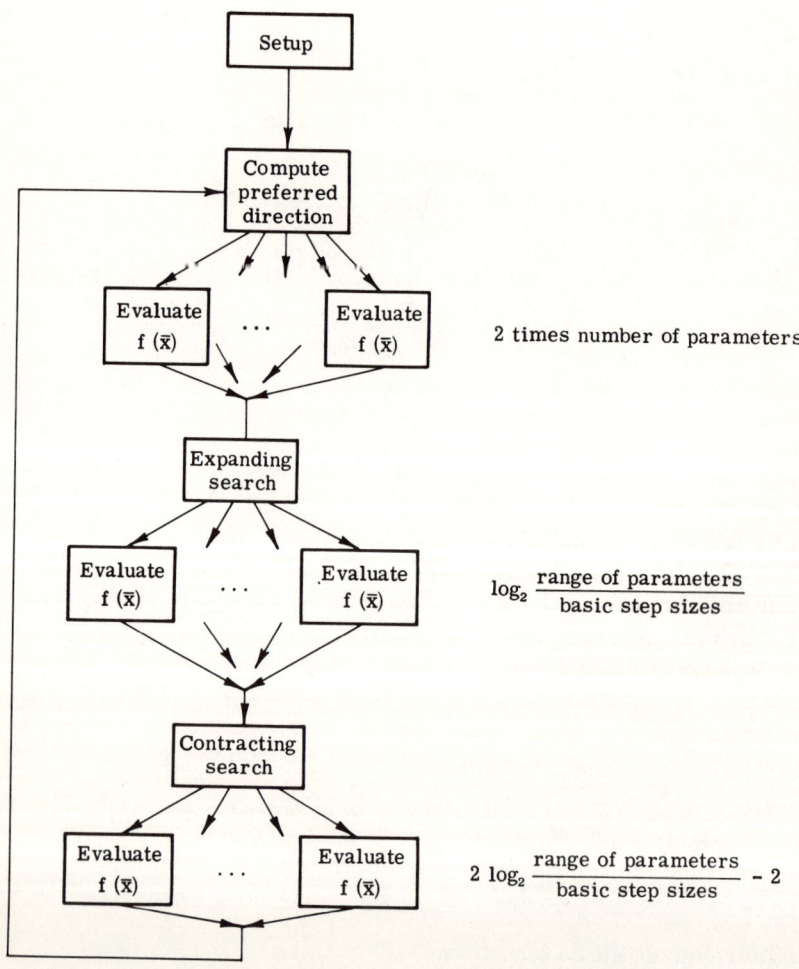

FIG. 65. Parallel algorithm for generalized optimization.

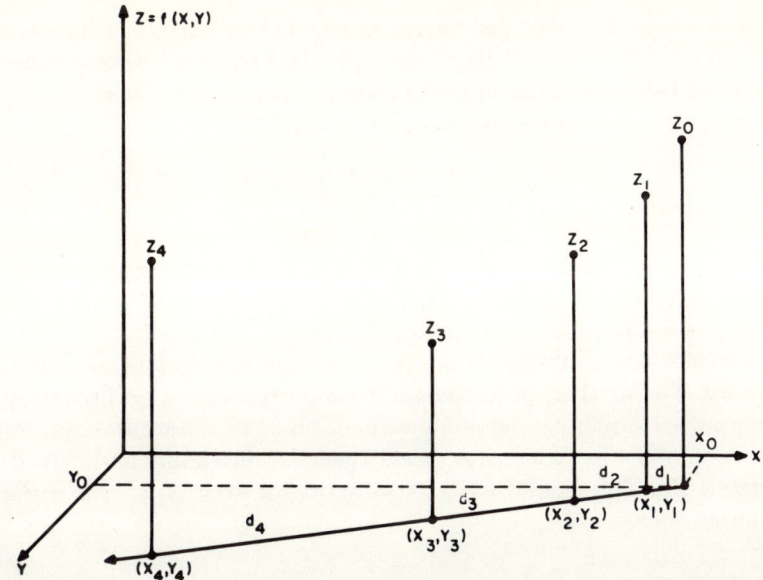

FIG. 66. Expanding search.

One of the results has been to demonstrate the importance of parallel "trial and error" search methods. Squire has developed an algorithm for generalized optimization for parallel machines. The algorithm finds the absolute minima of a very general class of functions including multimodal functions, nonlinear and discontinuous functions, and functions with linear or nonlinear constraints. The general approach is shown in Fig. 65.

In coarse form, the process consists of three steps iterated repeatedly. At each step the function $f(x)$ of the N-dimensional vector x is evaluated in parallel for many values of x. In the first step, a direction of search is determined by evaluating the function at $2N$ points lying on the hypersphere around the current value of x min. The direction is toward the minimum of these $2N$ values of $f(x)$.

The second step is taken along this line. The function is evaluated at k points along this direction where

$$k = \log_2\left(\frac{\text{range of parameters}}{\text{basic step size}}\right)$$

The step sizes are progressively longer by a factor of 2 as shown in Fig. 66. The third step is a contracting search, each step halving the previous step. This step is taken between the 2 values of x around the minimum of $f(x)$ in the second step.

Another search technique based on parallel function evaluation has been investigated for finding roots of algebraic and transcendental equations. Roots are defined as the complex values for z such that $f(z) = 0 + i0$. The method uses the complex integral

$$\frac{1}{2\pi i} \oint_c \frac{f'(z)}{f(z)} dz$$

to determine if a root is present in a region. Each such region containing a root is divided into equal regions which are checked for presence of a root. The number of regions should be equal to the number of modules. The process continues until all roots are determined to the desired accuracy. The method possesses those properties which lend themselves to computers which can evaluate a function at many arguments simultaneously. An algorithm has been specified in detail and coded in FORTRAN IV. The results were very favorable even on a conventional computer.

8.2.3. Monte Carlo Methods

Past experience [68] on conventional computers has shown that for the solution of partial differential equations, Monte Carlo techniques are less efficient in two dimensions than other techniques. However, several reasons exist for reconsidering this conclusion for highly parallel machines. First, because of the parallel nature of the Monte Carlo process, it seems that data flow and computation can be held to a minimum. Second, for higher dimensional problems the amount of computation does not go up as rapidly as it does for more conventional problems. It also provides a method for evaluating the solution at specific points of interest without obtaining the solution at other points.

Several modifications [55] of the conventional random walk techniques have been investigated for highly parallel machines. As an example, one of these suited to boundary value problems for the Laplace equations is the following: Conventionally, particles are introduced at the point where the solution is desired. At each time step, a particle is moved to one of the four adjacent grid points according to a random number. When the particle reaches the boundary of the region, it is absorbed and a new particle is introduced at the solution point. The solution is taken to be the average of the values of the boundary value at the points where the particles are absorbed.

For a parallel machine [74] a new particle is introduced at the solution point at each time step. As time progresses these particles will spread out through the grid. All particles are moved in the same direction at each time step according to a single random number. Multiple particles at a grid point are treated as a single particle of lighter weight. Using a parallel network, each grid point is assigned to a module of the network. For more complex equations, more complexities enter into the process. For example, for the general elliptic equation the transition probabilities are not constant over the entire grid, but are spatial functions of the coefficients of the equation. Thus, each particle must be split into four particles of unequal weight at each time step. Particles which arrive at the same grid point are combined into a single particle with a weight equal to the sum of the weights of the combining particles. For higher order difference schemes, particles must be split in a more complicated way with a fraction of the particle going to each related grid point in the stencil.

REFERENCES

1. Acki, M., Bussell, B., Estrin, G., and Leondes, C. T., Annual summary report of investigation in digital technology research. Dept. of Engineering, UCLA, Rept. No. 62–64 (1964).
2. Adams Associates, *Computer Characteristics Quart*. September (1964).
3. Barnett, M. P., A hypothetical machine for syntax tests. Coop. Computing Lab., MIT, Tech. Note No. 18 (undated).
4. Barnum, A. A. and Knapp, M. A., (eds.), *Computer Organization*. Spartan Books, Washington, D.C. (1963).
5. Bourne, C. P., and Ford, D. F., The historical and predicted state-of-the-art of the general purpose computer. *Proc. WJCC* 17, 1–22 (1960).
6. Brick, D. B., Pick, G. P., and Gray, S. B., A parallel matched filter correlator system for communication and radar. MIL-E-CON, 117–120 (1963).
7. Burks, A. W., Notes on von Neumann's cellular self-reproducing Automaton. Unpublished manuscript, Univ. of Michigan (undated).
8. Burks, A. W., Historical analysis of von Neumann's theories of artificial self-reproduction. Unpublished manuscript (1960).
9. Carroll, A. B., and Comfort, W. T., The logical design of a Holland machine. Internal Rept., Univ. of Michigan (1961).
10. Chow, C. K., A recognition method using neighbor dependence. *IRE Trans. Profess. Group Electron. Computers* 11, 683–390 (1962).
11. Comfort, W. T., A modified Holland machine. IBM Development Lab. Internal Rept. TR 00. 1038 (1963).
12. Conway, M. R., A multiprocessor system design. *Proc. Fall JCC* 24, 139–146 (1963).
13. Crane, B. A., Economics of the DDLM, A batch-fabricated parallel processor. *Proc. IEEE Symp. Batch Fabrication*, pp. 144–149, IEEE, New York (1965).
14. Critchlow, A. J., Generalized multiprocessing and multiprogramming systems. *Proc. Fall JCC* 24, 107–126 (1963).
15. Curtin, W. A., Multiple computer systems. *Advan. Computers* 4, 245–303 (1963).
16. Cutrona, L. J., Optical computing techniques. *IEEE Spectrum* 1, 101–108 (1964).

17. Cutrona, L. J., Leith, E. N., Palermo, C. J., and Porcello, L. J., Optical data processing and filtering systems. *IRE Trans Profess. Group. Inform. Theory* **6**, 386–400 (1960).
18. Davies, P. M., Design for an associative computer. *Proc. Pacific Computer Conf.* **T-147**, 109–116 (1963).
19. Dorn, W. S., A generalization of Horner's rule for polynominal evaluation. IBM Res. Paper No. RC-135 (1961).
20. Estrin, G., Organization of computer systems—The fixed plus variable structure computer. *Proc. WJCC* **17**, 33–40 (1960).
21. Estrin, G., Bussell, B., Turn, R., and Bibb, T., Parallel processing in a restructurable computer system. *IEEE Trans. Electron Computers* **12**, 747–754 (1963).
22. Estrin, G., and Fuller, R. H., Algorithms for content-addressable memories. *Proc. Pacific Computer Conf.*, **T-147**, 118–130 (1963).
23. Estrin, G., and Fuller, R. H., Some applications for content-addressable memories. *Proc. Fall JCC* **24**, 495–508 (1963).
24. Ewing, R., and Davies, P., An associative processor. *Proc. Fall JCC* **26**, 147–158 (1964).
25. Falkoff, A. D., Algorithms for parallel search memories. *J. Assoc. Computing Machinery* **9**, 488 (1962).
26. Fuller, R. H., Associative processor study—interim report. Gen. Precision-Librascope, Glendale, California (1964).
27. Garner, H. L., A study of iterative circuit computers. Univ. of Michigan Inform. Systems Lab. Rept. No. TDR 64 24 (1964).
28. Gonzales, R., A multi-layer iterative circuit computer. *IEEE Trans. Electron Computers* **12**, (1963).
29. Hawkins, J. K., Self-organizing systems—A review and commentary. *Proc. IRE* **49**, Computer Issue, 31–48 (1961).
30. Hechtel, J. R., and Seeger, J. A., Accuracy and limitations of the resistor network used for solution of Laplace's and Poisson's equations. *Proc. IRE* **49**, 933–940 (1961).
31. Hennie, F. C., *Iterative Arrays of Logical Circuits*. Wiley, New York (1961).
32. Holland, J. H., A universal computer capable of executing an arbitrary number of sub-programs simultaneously. *Proc. EJCC* **16**, 108 (1959).
33. Holland, J. H., On iterative circuit computers constructed of microelectronic components and systems. *Proc. Winter JCC* 17, 259–265 (1960).
34. *IEEE, Symp. Batch Fabrication, Proc.* IEEE, New York (1965).
35. Joseph, E. C., and Kaplan, A., Target track correlation with a search memory. *Proc. 6th Nat. Military Electronic Conv. Washington, D.C.*, 255–261, IRE, PGME, New York (1962).
36. Kiseda, J. R., Peterson, H. E., Seelbach, W. C., and Teig, M., *IBM J. Res. Develop.* **5**, 106 (1961).
37. Kron, G., Electrical circuit models of partial differential equations. *Elec. Eng.* **67**, 672–684 (1948).
38. Karplus, W. J., A new active-passive network simulator for transient field problems. *Proc. IRE* **49**, 268–275 (1961); also *IRE Trans. Electron. Computers* **13**, 597–605 (1964).
39. Landauer, W. I. The tree as a stratagem for automatic information handling. Astia Document No. AD 293 888.
40. Lee, C. Y., An algorithm for path connection and its application. *IRE Trans. Electron. Computers* **10**, 346–365 (1961).

41. Lee, C. Y., Intercommunicating cells—Basis for a distributed logic computer. *Proc. Fall JCC* **22**, 130–136 (1962).
42. Lee, E. S., Semiconductor circuits in associative memories. *Proc. Pacific Computer Conf.*, **T-147**, 96 (1963).
43. Leondes, C. T., and Rubinoff, M., Dina, A digital analyzer for Laplace, Poisson, diffusion and wave equations. *Trans. Am. Inst. Elect. Engrs.* **71**, 303 (1952).
44. Lewis, D. R., and Mellen, G. E., Stretching Larc's capability by 100—A new multiprocessor system. *Proc. Symp. Microelectronics and large systems* (ONR and UNIVAC), also *Washington, D.C.*, 1964; *Aviation Week Space Technol.* **81**, No. 22, 49 (1964).
45. Liebmann, G., Electrical analogs. *Brit. J. Appl. Phys.* **4**, 193–200 (1953).
46. Lindquist, A. B., and Seeber, R. R., Mass fabrication, highly parallel systems and associative logic. IBM Development Lab., Internal Rept. (1962); also *Proc. Fall JCC* **24**, 489–493 (1963).
47. McCormick, B. H., The Illinois pattern recognition computer–Illiac III. *IEEE Trans. Electron. Computers* **12**, 791–813 (1963).
48. Minnick, R. C., Magnetic comparators and code converters. *Proc. Symp. Application Switching Theory in Space Technol.*, Sunnyvale, California, (1962).
49. Narasimhan, R., Labeling schemata and syntactic descriptions of pictures. *Inform. Control* **7**, 151–179 (1964).
50. Newhouse, V. L., and Fruin, R. E., A cryogenic data addressed memory. *Proc. Spring JCC* **21**, 89–99 (1962).
51. Prywes, N. S., and Gray, H. J., The multilist system for real time storage and retrieval. *Proc. Munich Congr.*, IFIP 1962 pp. 273–278.
52. Prywes, N. S., Landauer, W. I., Cohen, L. J., and Lefkovitz, D., An automated sea surveillance system. Computer Command and Control Co., Philadelphia, Pennsylvania, Rept. No. 4-101-4 (1964).
53. Rice, T., Computers of the future. *Proc. EJCC*, **16**, 8–14 (1959).
54. Rosin, R. F., An organization of an associative cryogenic computer. *Proc. Spring JCC* **21**, 203–212 (1962).
55. Rosin, R. F., A algorithm for concurrent random walks on highly parallel machines. Cooley Electronics Lab. Univ. of Michigan, Rept. No. TR151 (1964).
56. Sammon, Lt. J. W., and Choisser Lt. J. P., Child—A new adaptive learning machine. *TRD Technol. Briefs* February (1964), USAF, AFSC; also RADC-TDR-63-228 (1963).
57. Schwartz, J., AT-1 parallel computer—Second preliminary version. Unpublished rept. New York Univ. (1964).
58. Schwartz, J., Algorithms in parallel computation. Unpublished rept., New York Univ. (1964).
59. Sebestyen, G. S., *Decision-Making Processes in Pattern Recognition*. Macmillan, New York, 1962.
60. Slotnick, D. L., Borck, W. C., and McReynolds, R. C. The Solomon computer. *Proc. Fall JCC* **22**, 97–107 (1962).
61. Solomon parallel network processor. Westinghouse Electric Corp. Aerospace Division, Baltimore, Maryland, Internal rept. (1962).
62. Solomon II—Parallel network processor. Westinghouse Electric Corp. Rept. No. 1869A, Aerospace Division, Baltimore, Maryland (1964).
63. Spangenberg, K., Electrical network analyzers for the solution of electromagnetic field problems. *Proc. IRE* **37**, 724–729 (1949).

64. Squire, J. S., Tech. Notes 1 through 7, Westinghouse Electric Corp., Aerospace Division, Contract No. AF30(602)3313 (1964).
65. Squire, J. S., and Palais, S. M., Physical and logical design of a highly parallel computer. Univ. of Michigan Information Systems Lab. Tech Note No. 04-794-2-T (1962).
66. Standard EDP Rept. Auerbach Electronics Ins., and BNA, Inc., Washington, D.C. (1964).
67. Tancka, R. I., Research on automatic computer electronics, Vols. I, II, and III Lockheed Missiles and Space Co., Rept. No. RTD-TDR-63-4173, Palo Alto, California (1964).
68. Todd, J., Experiments on the inversion of a 16×16 matrix. *NBS Appl. Math. Ser.* **29**, 113–115 (1953).
69. Turn, R., Assignment of inventory in a variable structure computer. UCLA, Dept. of Engineering Rept. No. 63-5 (1963).
70. Unger, S. H., Pattern detection and recognition. *Proc. IRE* **46**, (1958).
71. Unger, S. H., A computer oriented toward spacial problems. *Proc. WJCC* **15**, 234–239 (1959).
72. Unger, S. H., Pattern recognition using two-dimensional, bilateral, iterative, combinational switching circuits. *Proc. Symp. Mathematical Theory Automata, Polytech. Inst. Brooklyn*, 1962. Wiley, New York, 1963.
73. Warshall, S., and Shapiro, R. M., A general-purpose table-driven compiler *Proc. Spring JCC* **25**, 59–65 (1964).
74. Westinghouse Electric Corp. Contract Repts. Numerical solution of partial differential equations on parallel digital computer. NASA Contract No. NAS5-2730 (1963).
75. Westinghouse Electric Corp., Aerospace Division, Baltimore, Maryland, Internal Document, Application of SOLOMON II in an advanced digital sonar (1963).
76. Yevreinov, E. Z., and Kosarev, Yu. G., High efficiency computing systems. *Eng. Cybernetics* **1**, No. 4 (1963) (translated from the Russian by IEEE).

Programming Language Processors

RUTH M. DAVIS

Office of Director of Defense Research and Engineering
Department of Defense, Washington, D.C.

1. Introduction 117
2. Features of Programming Languages 119
   2.1 Factors Related to the Effectiveness of Languages . . . 119
   2.2 Classifications of Programming Languages 122
   2.3 Dependence of Programming Languages upon Computer Design . 127
3. Rules, Syntactical Techniques, and Grammatical Models for Decoding
   Programming Languages 128
   3.1 General Comments 128
   3.2 Formal Description of a Programming Language . . . 130
   3.3 Grammatical Models and Ambiguity Considerations . . 137
4. Historical Development of Programming Language Processors . . 141
5. Features of Programming Language Processors 147
   5.1 Types of Language Processors 147
   5.2 Programming Language Processor Terminology . . . 153
6. The Conventional Programming Language Processor . . . 159
7. The Syntax-Directed Programming Language Processor . . . 163
8. List Processors 167
   8.1 General Comments 167
   8.2 Fundamental Features of List Processors 168
   8.3 List Processor Organization 172
9. Evaluation of Programming Language Processors 173
10. Concluding Remarks 175
    References 177

1. Introduction

This article is a summary of lecture notes on Programming Languages and Programming Language Processors. The lectures have been presented each year since 1962, and the subject field has evolved so rapidly that a major revision of the notes was required each year.

The emphasis through the article will be on theoretical or conceptual considerations underlying the design of programming language processors. In this regard, little attempt is made to describe individual existing programming language processors. Rather, common foundations underlying all processors of a given type and conceptual differences separating the various types of programming language processors are stressed. Efforts are made to bridge the gap between mathematical linguistics and programming language processor design. The often inseparable aspects of programming languages and their processors are pointed out, and a great deal of attention is paid to the syntactic specifications of programming languages [24, 48, 66].

The phrase "programming language processor" has evolved from a succession of terms such as "interpreter," "assembly routine," "translator," and "compiler" advanced by program analysts over the period 1950–1965 to describe their development of aids to programmers. The evolution of the phrase is interesting in itself, in that each successive new terminology has defined a more complex entity, with the term "programming language processor" as it is used in this article actually encompassing all of its predecessors.

A programming language processor is considered to be a formal method for translating from any specified programming language to machine language or to some second language more closely resembling a machine language in its properties. Programming languages themselves came into being as a substitute for machine languages that would be more acceptable to users of computers in the sense that (1) they more closely approximated the natural language familiar to the user, (2) they permitted a problem to be stated precisely enough to be solved by a computer without requiring intimate detail of the machine language by the user, and (3) they enabled faster statement of a problem for computer solution than would use of machine language. It should be emphasized here that the limitations on the ability to design programming language processors impose the real limitations on the choice of programming languages. Thoughtful contemplation reveals that the reason natural English is not used as a programming language is that no language [3] processor has been designed that permits natural English to be translated into machine language or any second language which is both correct and nonambiguous. The fifteen years since 1950 have seen a series of approximations of programming languages to natural language or to subsets of natural languages peculiar to particular scientific disciplines. The approximations of programming to natural languages have become closer as the design of language processors has improved. It also appears apparent at this time that natural language will never be a programming language unless or until techniques for formalizing and mechanizing both syntactic and semantic analyses are developed. There are many, of whom Bar-Hillel is most prominent, who are convinced that such an eventuality will never occur. Regardless of this prediction, the present trend is that of compromise between the desired programming language and a feasible programming language with the design limitations of the language processor forming the basis for the compromise. Present limitations on design require programming languages to possess vocabularies allowing no synonyms, to possess vocabularies to each member of which may be ascribed only one "part of speech," to possess vocabularies of "fixed words" which may not be defined at the discretion of the user, and to have sentences of prescribed type and of predetermined format [41].

It is impossible to present a coherent discussion of programming language processors without a preliminary understanding of the features of language with which the processor must deal and without some introduction to notions of grammar, syntactic analysis, and semantic analysis. Sections 2 and 3 will deal with these topics. Section 4 contains a tabular presentation of the development history of programming languages and language processors, listing historical milestones. Section 5 discusses in detail types of programming language processors, along with typically ascribable features. Sections 6, 7, and 8 deal respectively with three major types of programming language processors—conventional processors, syntax-directed processors, and list processors. Section 9 treats the problem of evaluation of programming language processors, and Section 10 concludes with comments on the present status of programming language processors, on existing problem areas, and on apparent trends. Definitions are introduced as needed, and terminology is explained when first encountered.

2. Features of Programming Languages

2.1 Factors Related to the Effectiveness of Languages

Any language is an encoding of information for transmission between a sender and receiver. Either the sender or the receiver or both may be mechanical devices or human beings. For the transmitted information to be useful, the receiver must have a capability for decoding the language and for extracting meaning from the language for his own use [6]. The effectiveness of a language for communication of meaning or ideas is directly proportional to the degree of identicality between the meaning or idea originated by the sender and the meaning or idea as understood by the receiver. As such, the effectiveness of a language is dependent upon factors some of which are external to the language itself. Factors affecting the effectiveness of a language include the following.

(a) Internal properties of the language such as:
  (i) number and type of symbols permitted;
  (ii) vocabulary size and development potential;
  (iii) allowable ambiguity of an intentional nature as depicted by synonym density;

(iv) ambiguity of a nonintentional nature as exemplified by homography;
(v) structuring features including grammar, syntax, and number of word classes (sometimes subsumed under syntax);
(vi) relational features typified by semantics which is concerned with the relationship of the symbols of the language to the objects or "things" which the symbols are intended to represent;
(vii) pragmatic features which are concerned with the relationship of the symbols of the language to the actions which the symbols are intended to represent [28].

(b) The language encoding and decoding processes.

It is obvious that in the encoding of meaning or ideas into any particular language, much of value can be lost. In order to discuss this aspect coherently, it is necessary to introduce at this point some terminology and definitions, as follows:

Source language: the language being described. In the preceding discussion, the source language is the encoded language transmitted between sender and receiver. In general, throughout the chapter the "source language" will refer to the programming language under consideration.

Metalanguage: the describing language; that is, the language used to describe the source language. This language also, of course, has its conventions and restrictive features.

Linear language: a language which is comprised of a set of symbols arranged in a one-dimensional (linear) string in which the symbols are grouped into allowable combinations and sequences of combinations based on syntactic and semantic rules.

Target language: the language produced from the source language by the programming language processor or by the decoding process.

The sender or transmitter of information encodes meaning or ideas concerning a given environment into a source language which in this article will always be assumed to be a linear language. If this encoding is from an n-dimensional environment ($n \geq 2$), then the probability of loss of meaning is not negligible. For example, if one is translating a two-dimensional photograph into a linear language comprised of a set of 64 symbols (representing shades of gray, for example) governed by an almost trivial set of syntactic and semantic rules, an indeterminate amount of meaning is lost. If one is describing a particular event in real time in a linear source language, the presentation of all the three-dimensional detail and of all the background leading up to the event is normally impossible, so that much of the context of the event is lost in the encoding.

What is of more significance to a treatment of programming languages is the decoding process in which meaning is extracted from the source language for the use of the receiver. The decoding process may result in the production of a second language—the target language—for use by the receiver or for the purpose of triggering some action by the receiver. The decoding process, on the other hand, may simply be a mental extraction of meaning by the receiver from the source language into his own information set; e.g., into his own image of his world. Any decoding process which can be formalized can decode only a finite amount of source language in any single step. The smaller this amount is, the more restrictive the decoding process. If the decoding process can only treat a sentence at a time, for example, then it will be more difficult to extract meaning for use by the sender than if the decoding process can treat a paragraph at a time. Consider the discourse: "John is a very intelligent boy. He is always ahead of his friends." The meaning extracted from the second sentence differs depending upon whether it is decoded in context with the first sentence or as a separate entity. The effectiveness of the decoding process in extracting the meaning encoded into the source language by the sender is dependent upon the memory available during the decoding process, the capability of making more than one "pass" through the information transmitted on the basis of the information content itself rather than on predetermined rules, the "background" available to the receiver during the decoding process, the knowledge available of the "background" of the sender, and upon the depth of understanding of the source language. This is true whether the receiver, i.e., the decoder is a man or a machine. If the decoding is performed by a machine, then:

(i) Memory available during decoding is equivalent to the memory available to a computer in which to store the transmitted information in conjunction with the specification of a process to translate as an entity, i.e., in context, all the information held in memory.

(ii) The capability of making more than one "pass" is equivalent to the existence of a processing algorithm which back-tracks or is self-corrective during decoding, based on the information content being examined.

(iii) The "background" available during the decoding process is equivalent to the substantive data base available in the computer relevant to the information being transmitted which permits more meaning to be extracted from the source language.

(iv) The knowledge available of the "background" of the sender is equivalent to the substantive data base in the computer pertinent to the world of the sender which permits more meaning to be extracted from the source language.

(v) The depth of understanding of the source language equates to the extent to which the syntactic and semantic rules of the source language can be codified for use by the computer, the percentage of source language vocabulary available to the computer, and the parsing capability of the computer.

At the present time, most programming language processors decode or translate the equivalent of one sentence at a time from the source language where the sentence is considered as a self-contained entity with respect to meaning. Word meanings usually remain invariant during decoding for the equivalent of a paragraph. Many processors permit more than one pass over the source language being translated, but the occurrence and the number of passes is usually predetermined rather than being based on information content itself [*17*, *26*, *30*].

There are several theories which suggest that the encoding and decoding of language can be considered as sequential stratified processes with the major levels being *syntactic analysis* [*14*], *semantic analysis*, and *pragmatic analysis* [*46*]. This has been borne out in the translation between two natural languages, as well as in the design of the more sophisticated programming language processors. In both cases the semantic analysis level is virtually nonexistent or is highly artificial, being based upon specification of completely ambiguity-free vocabularies and syntactic structures. The pragmatic analysis in a programming language processor results in the specification of computer actions to carry out the actions demanded by the programming language being decoded. The syntactic analysis of a programming language is that portion of language encoding and decoding to which most effort has thus far been devoted. It is treated as a separate subject in Section 3.2.

2.2 Classifications of Programming Languages

In the Introduction a general definition of programming languages was given which emphasized their evolvement as a substitute for machine languages in order to obtain a closer approximation to the natural language familiar to the user of computers. Over the years several methods of classifying programming languages have been devised which amazingly enough have all been based upon the characteristics of the programming language processors needed to decode the source programming language into the target language more amenable to machine use. [*39*].

The first of these classification schemes divides programming languages into two types as defined below:

Procedure-oriented languages: programming languages which describe a process to be performed in terms of the data to be processed and the procedures to be employed in the processing. Some of the more obvious features of procedure-oriented languages are as follows:

(a) The user must be able to specify in detail all the mathematical, logical, statistical, etc., procedures to be used in the process he wishes performed. If a procedure has been already included in the vocabulary of the programming language, he need only use the exact vocabulary term assigned to that procedure in his statement of the problem. If he examines the programming language vocabulary and the desired procedure is not named and defined, then he must assign it a name, define it in all detail, and add it to the defined vocabulary before using it. For example, if one uses programming language A and finds in its vocabulary the term "sin X" along with a definition, then one need only ensure that the definition is adequate for one's purpose before using the term "sin X" in any problem statement. If, however, there is no such term in the vocabulary of programming language A, then one must add it and specify its definition both in the vocabulary and to the programming language processor in terms of series calculations, partial fraction calculations, or the like, before one can use it in any problem statement expressed in programming language A.

(b) The user must describe in detail the data to be processed. This he does by naming them mnemonically, if necessary, defining their dimensions, magnitudes, forms, format, bounds, etc. For example, if numbers are used, he must state whether they are real, complex, floating point, fixed point, and so forth. When matrices are involved, their dimensions and components must be listed. When data files are used, their contents, format, and size must be precisely delineated. All data must be named so that during the processing of some predetermined amount of the source programming language, a given proper name always refers to a unique set of data. As mentioned in Section 2.1, a proper name normally remains invariant, that is, tied to the same set of data for the equivalent of a paragraph. Thus if a 3×4 matrix is named "Mitsi," then for a paragraph's worth of source language, the programming language processor will always interpret the word "Mitsi" when it is encountered as a 3×4 matrix with stated characteristics.

Problem-oriented languages: programming languages which describe a problem to be solved in terms of problem statements or desired results. A problem-oriented language so defined is at a higher level of abstraction than is a procedure-oriented language. Its use implies that the programming language processor has the capability of decoding the source language into the equivalent of a procedure-oriented language during the process of producing a target language suitable for machine execution.

As a nonrigorous illustration for comparative purposes only, a problem-oriented language would permit a statement of the form:

Track the aircraft carrier Enterprise between Pearl Harbor and 30° N, 190° W printing hourly positions.

A procedure-oriented language expression of the same problem would demand statements of the form:

DATA
    SHIP = ENTERPRISE
    POSIT = (LAT, LONG)
    LAT = (0, 90° N (1°); 0, 90° S (1°))
    LONG = (0, 180° W (1°); 0, 180° E (1°))
    PORT = PEARL HARBOR
    PORT = FILE A (NAME (26), LAT, LONG)
    TRACK = $\begin{cases} \text{RHUMB LINE FOR (POSIT } x - \text{ POSIT } y \leq 1000 \\ \text{MILES)} \\ \text{GREAT CIRCLE FOR (POSIT } x - \text{ POSIT } y \geq 1000 \\ \text{MILES)} \end{cases}$

    GREAT CIRCLE = $D_1 = \frac{1}{2} \log \left\{ \frac{1 + \text{SIN LAT } x}{1 - \text{SIN LAT } x} \right.$
         $\left. - \frac{1}{2} \log \frac{1 + \text{SIN LONG } x}{1 - \text{SIN LONG } y} \right\} \cdots$

    .
    .
    .

PROCEDURES:
    CALCULATE GREAT CIRCLE DISTANCE D FROM PEARL HARBOR TO (30° N, 190° W)
    COMPUTE $\dfrac{D}{T} = W$
    FOR TIME $T_i = T_0, T_0 + 1, \ldots, T_0 + N, W, \text{w.1} \leq T_0 + N \leq W$
    PRINT D_i
    .
    .
    .

It can be readily seen that the existence of a problem-oriented language permitting statements even as simple as that illustrated above requires programming language processors of much greater complexity than does a procedure-oriented language aimed at the solution of the same problem. In the case of the illustration, the processor for the problem-oriented language would have to construct the equivalent of the statement of the same problem in the illustrative procedure-oriented language.

There are very few instances of problem-oriented languages in existence today, one major exception being process control languages such as APT developed for machine production applications. Another example is STRESS designed at MIT for mechanical engineering problems [5, 9].

The emphasis on and use of procedure-oriented languages has probably been a direct result of the von Neumann concept of digital computers adopted universally by the computer design industry. This concept is of course characterized by the sequential operation—the step-by-step sequential procedure of producing a problem solution, incorporated bodily by designers of procedure-oriented languages.

The most promising approaches to development of problem-oriented languages appear to be originating among those interested in designing question-answering languages [7]. There are obvious reasons for this. The purpose of most question-answering languages is to allow individuals to pose questions to a computer in a language as nearly like natural language as possible. Since questions can easily be transformed into declarative statements and vice versa in most natural languages through rearrangement of subject and verb, a question-answering language is closely akin to a problem-oriented language with respect to language features and with respect to demands on language processors or language decoders. A most heartening example of progress in this field is that work in DEACON by Thompson of GE Tempo [62, 64].

A second classification scheme for programming languages which again demonstrates the dependence of such languages on the capabilities of programming language processors is that which separates languages on the basis of the relationship between language structure and computer memory addressing [63]. This scheme divides programming languages into three types as indicated below:

Individual-memory-location-addressing languages: languages which permit only the naming or referencing of individual memory locations. The most typical examples of this type of language are machine languages and assemblers. Here the user must know the exact relationship between the data and procedures described and individual memory locations. In most cases, the vocabulary of the language and the language structure must be so simple that each word or statement references only one machine memory address. Such languages have little power and can never really approximate natural languages. The language processor is quite simple to design and has only trivial syntactic rules to handle with no semantic analyses even required.

Region-addressing languages: languages which permit the naming or referencing of regions of computer memory by a single vocabulary term or by a single phrase. Such languages begin to exemplify the power inherent in relating language structure to memory organization. The user of a region-addressing language need not know where in memory his data or procedures are in terms of fixed memory addresses. He can reference an entire region by the single letter A by saying in essence:

"ASSIGN THE AIRCRAFT CHARACTERISTICS FILE S' LOCATION A"

Then for the rest of his problem he may simply refer to file S', and the programming language processor will make the necessary correlation between file S' and memory region A. However, the user of the language must still know the size or magnitude of all data structures in order to know the total number of memory locations the structure will require and must ensure that there is indeed a region A of the desired size in the memory type specified. The region addressed by these languages is usually a single one composed of consecutive memory locations. Very rarely are provisions made in the programming language processor to permit the region addressed to be disjoint, that is, to be comprised of several nonadjacent subregions. Examples of region-addressing languages include a few assemblers and most procedure-oriented languages; e.g., FORTRAN, ALGOL, JOVIAL.

Scatter-addressing languages: languages which permit the naming or referencing of data structures, procedures, and problems without explicit reference to computer memory. Scatter addressing gives first evidence of the ability of a programming language to refer to complex interrelated information and to request processing of referenced information without a corollary requirement of the user that he be familiar with the magnitude of his data structures, with the availability of chunks of computer memory of the proper size, and with all the needed interrelationships between referenced information. The primary example of such languages is list processing languages. A secondary example is languages whose processors utilize associative memory techniques. It is apparent that any concerted development of problem-oriented languages will necessitate the use of scatter-addressing languages and of processors which can handle any referenceable information structures named by any allowable linguistic structure of a programming language.

Although this second classification scheme is not as commonly utilized as is the first one discussed, it is more useful in that it clearly ties the given type of programming language to levels of complexity of programming language processors. By so doing, it provides a clear indication of the features necessary in programming language processors to yield progress in the development of programming languages which more closely approximate natural languages. Immediate next steps to improve scatter-addressing languages and, concomitantly, problem-oriented languages are improvements in knotted list structuring, in threaded list processing, in back-referencing in list processing, and in associative techniques.

A third and final classication scheme presented in this article emphasizes applications [60] and as such does not reveal as clearly as do the first two classifications the dependence of programming language power upon the programming language processor capabilities. Programming languages ordered by application with an example of each follows:

(a) Algebraic and scientific languages (FORTRAN, ALGOL).
(b) Business languages (COBOL).
(c) Control languages such as process control and real-time system control (APT).
(d) Information retrieval languages (COMIT).
(e) List handling languages (IPL-V).
(f) Symbol manipulation languages (SNOBALL).
(g) Simulation languages (SIMSCRIPT).
(h) Natural language processing languages (COMIT).
(i) Question-answering languages (DEACON, BASEBALL).

There is no logical way to relate the first two schemes to this third classification scheme since the first two are based upon programming language structure and the last simply upon application area.

2.3 Dependence of Programming Languages upon Computer Design

There have been many demands and promises made for the design and development of computer-independent programming languages. One readily senses a feeling that the ideal programming language is an abstract language designed with no thought of any particular decoding or computing device in mind. This feeling appears, upon close examination, to be unfounded. All departures from natural languages to programming languages involve restrictions upon syntax, semantics, and vocabulary necessary to convert the natural language to a language suitable for processing by a machine visualized in considerable detail by the language designer. It may not be a particular model of a given manufacturer, but it will be one based upon the von Neumann concept, the parallel processing concept, the iterative logic concept, or the like. The restrictions imposed upon syntax, or semantics, or vocabulary will be tied closely in the designer's mind to his mental picture of memory allocation, of index registers, of sequential instruction counters, of arithmetic units separate from memory units, etc. Supporting evidence is found by noting that procedure-oriented programming languages based upon the von Neumann sequential computer concept comprise almost the total set of existing programming languages.

List processing languages based upon the more novel concept of scatter-memory addressing are more rare; programming languages [18] allowing full utilization of the parallel processing power of a modularly constructed multicomputer system are nonexistent. The reason is that these latter type languages are based upon programming language processors whose design principles differ from the von Neumann procedures, and very few individuals can as yet adequately visualize such novel new computer concepts. As such, it appears that Gorn had considerable support for his statement that "it is impossible to separate a language from its interpreting machine" made at the Working Conference on Mechanical Language Structure, Princeton, New Jersey, August 14–16, 1963.

3. Rules, Syntactical Techniques, and Grammatical Models for Decoding Programming Languages

3.1 General Comments

In Section 2.1, it was pointed out that the processing of programming languages, i.e., encoding and decoding processes, necessitated some syntactic, semantic, and pragmatic analyses. The explicit recognition of this fact has been slowly gaining a foothold among programming language designers. Prior to 1960, the use of such linguistic techniques was generally superficial and confined, as Perlis has said, primarily to a borrowing of terminology from linguistics. The design of programming languages and of the associated language processors was a nonseparable effort. The rules found necessary for incorporation into the language processor became by default the rules of grammar of the programming language. These rules in turn were a haphazard random collection dependent, in most cases, upon the engineering idiosyncrasies of the particular computer for which the language processor was being defined. One can summarize the period prior to 1960 by the statement that the structure of programming languages was based upon programming considerations rather than upon linguistic or computational linguistic considerations. Since 1960, a more formal liaison between linguistic and programming language design has not only been condoned but has been encouraged. One can note a trend of events which gives proof of a gradually evolving, more formal technique of programming language design and programming language processor design. It is still true that the design of language and language processor are often inseparable, although the design of ALGOL-58 and ALGOL-60 are notable exceptions. Before discussing in detail language processing rules, it might be helpful to review the trend toward more formality in language design by listing a few of the more important evidences of this trend:

(a) Language vocabulary terms were separated into word classes to permit different formal treatment during language processing.

(b) Relationships between members of given word classes were formalized by rules of mathematical logic, such as those of Polish notation and of operator precedence.

(c) Grammatical rules were developed for processing or decoding blocks of programming language. These rules soon resembled the parsing rules of linguistics.

(d) The relationships between different structural types allowed in the language were specified by models formal enough to allow analogies to be drawn between known linguistic syntax types and the structural models of those programming languages. The Backus normal form, a terminology in which the structure of ALGOL-58 was described, was the first such well-known model; and it has subsequently been shown equivalent to simple phrase structure grammars.

(e) Syntax has been formally imposed upon programming languages, permitting the development of syntax-directed compilers.

(f) Discussions and theories concerning ambiguities in programming languages have appeared.

(g) The role of semantics has been recognized, as has been the effect of inadequate semantic analysis techniques, upon the design of truly effective programming languages.

(h) A separation in the tasks of language design and of language processor design has occurred.

(i) The desirability, in fact the necessity, has been recognized of permitting semantic and syntactic ambiguity in the programming language which is resolved by the language processor through what can be termed a "contextual analysis"; that is, the ambiguity will be resolved through consideration of the context in which the ambiguous word or phrase is encountered. A language of any power must allow words to have more than one meaning or to belong to more than one word class if the vocabulary of the language is not to become ridiculously cumbersome [63].

(j) Relationships have been determined between the structuring of information in the data base of the computer or decoding device and the syntactic and semantic categories of the programming language.

3.2 Formal Description of a Programming Language

Any formal description of a programming language must address the subjects of vocabulary and syntax. Both vocabulary and syntax must be precisely defined as input data to a language processor.

3.2.1 Vocabulary

The vocabulary of a programming language will be considered as defined through the specification of:

(a) *An alphabetical or symbol listing.* This listing normally consists of letters, numerals, and signs or marks. Since a programming language always has associated with it a metalanguage, there will actually be two listings required—one for the source programming language itself and one for the metalanguage. Symbols for the source language may include $+, /, \$, =, [,], (,$ etc. Symbols for the metalanguage may include some not allowed for the source language such as $::=, \langle \ \rangle, |$ and $\rightarrow$. It should be noted that the vocabulary of the language processor is much more restrictive and is commonly referred to as the *hardware language* in that it is restricted by hardware aspects of the computer for which it is written. A part of the language decoding process is a decoding of the allowable set of programming language symbols into the normally much smaller allowable set of the hardware language. The specification of the syntax of the language is in the metalanguage; the statement of the problem to be solved is in the source programming language.

(b) *A lexicon or dictionary with construction rules.* The rules for word construction are specified usually in terms of bounds on number of symbols per word, constraints on types of symbols which may act as the first and last symbols of a word, and restrictions on symbol types which may comprise words. For example, a word formation rule might be:

> A WORD IS ANY STRING OF N SYMBOLS WHERE $2 \leq N \leq 25$ IN WHICH THE FIRST AND LAST SYMBOLS MUST BE LETTERS AND IN WHICH THE SYMBOLS $\$$ AND $+$ MAY NOT APPEAR.

The lexical or dictionary entries are usually subdivided into two types called "free identifier" and "reserved identifier." A free identifier is any allowable word denoting the various quantities, procedures, actions, or things which the language may represent. A free identifier may be assigned at the discretion of the user provided the construction rules are followed. Free identifiers name files; e.g., SHIP FILE; name procedures, e.g., CALCULATE; name mathematical entities, e.g., POISSON DISTRIBUTION; name actions, e.g., PRINT OUT; and name things, e.g., INCOME or TRAFFIC. Reserved identifiers are the lexical subset of words which are not assignable at the discretion of the user. They are normally assigned specific meanings during the specification of the syntax of the language and play a particular preset role in the syntactic analysis of the source programming language. Their definition and role are made known to the user in the language description. Typical examples of such words are: ASSIGN, IF NOT . . . THEN, ELSE, INTEGER, BOOLEAN, REAL, BIT, BYTE, etc. A very important class of reserved identifiers with a very particular function is known as the class of "delimiters." Delimiters are reserved identifiers which serve as the control elements of the syntax of the language. They serve as separators between words, sentences and other structural entities; and they serve as operators. Examples of delimiters are: [ ], ;, .,/, +, ×, −, ( ), and so forth. It has often been stated that the number of reserved identifiers and, particularly, of delimiters is a crude measure of the complexity of the programming language structure, which in turn often yields a measure of the power of the programming language.

Construction rules for lexical entries vary widely. They must prohibit the use of reserved identifiers by the user. They must exclude synonymy or provide a description of how synonymy will be treated by the programming language processor. For example, if "distance" is a lexical entry which has been defined as

$$\text{distance} = \text{speed} \times \text{time}$$

and the user wishes to define "distance" as

$$\text{distance} = \text{velocity} \times \text{time}$$

then either he must be told how to delete the first meaning and insert the second meaning or he must be told to name his "distance" something else such as "distanced" and to refer to the latter during his use of the source language. In addition, he must be informed as to how the language processor will handle two identical entries with different meanings. The processor may simply accept the first definition it finds during the dictionary search, or it may indicate an error and use neither definition in case of synonymy. The user must be told how to define a new lexical entry both in source language and in metalanguage in order to add it to the dictionary; he may be told, for example, not to use a word prior to the appearance of its definition in the source language statement of his problem. As can be anticipated, the addition of a lexical entry representing an action or a procedure normally requires the definition to be stated as a "program" in both the metalanguage and the source language. As a case in point, if the entry "curvature of a sphere" is made, a computer program resulting in the calculation of the "curvature of a sphere" must be written. If this is done, then later users may simply write in the source language the equivalent of

CALCULATE THE CURVATURE OF A SPHERE.

3.2.2 Syntax

The syntax of a programming language is the specification of the structure of the language along with a description of the structure. The structure of a natural language is comprised of words, clauses, sentences, paragraphs, and the like. The structure of programming languages as they have evolved over some fifteen years is quite analogous to that of natural languages. The syntactic description of a language does not, however, contain a set of rules for either generating or recognizing allowable structures. This is the function of a grammar which will be considered in a later paragraph. The diagraming or parsing of language structural units, such as sentences, is a syntactic technique for decomposing language structures into their smallest meaningful structural units, normally word classes. The first task in specifying the structure of a language, i.e., its syntax, is to assign all allowable sets of symbols, sometimes referred to as symbol strings, to syntactic classes. In particular, words are assigned to syntactic word classes, and sentences are transformed into strings of syntactic word classes. In both natural languages and programming languages a distinction is made between terminal-type classes and nonterminal-type classes where a terminal type is a single symbol from the source language alphabet or symbol set, and nonterminal-type classes are all other symbol classes. Functional word classes for programming languages have already been discussed in the paragraph on vocabulary and have been listed as reserved identifiers and free identifiers. Syntactic word classes for existing programming languages are not consistently analogous to those of natural languages.

In natural languages, syntactic word classes include:

noun
pronoun
verb
article
preposition
adverb, . . . , etc.

In programming languages, syntactic word classes appear to be either of the form:

    digit   — (1, 2, 3, ... , 9)
    letter   — (A, B, C, ... , Z)
    integer — a digit or group of several digits
    variable — a letter, possibly followed by one or more letters and/or digits
    etc.

or of the form:

    noun   — data name, procedure name, letter, register name, etc.
    verb   — designates any computer action
    qualifiers — serve the same role as adjectives in a natural language by making an ambiguous noun unique
    etc.

In natural languages the most important structural units are sentences which are either simple or compound; in the latter case, they are made up of two or more clauses. In programming languages the term "statement" has been universally used in direct analogy to sentence. A statement may be either simple or compound, where if compound it is composed of two or more "expressions." Expressions in programming languages play the same role as do clauses in natural languages. The role of the paragraph in a natural language is assumed by the "block" or the "procedure" in a programming language. A block or procedure consists of one or more statements preceded by an identifier, e.g., a name. The purpose of the block or procedure is to serve as an entity referenceable by other portions of the programming language, and hence it must have a title or name.

In natural languages, sentences are usually classified as: *declarative, imperative, interrogative,* and *exclamatory.*

Statements in programming languages are usually classified as: *declaration statements, assignment statements,* and *sequential or procedural statements.*

Here declaration and assignment statements correspond to declarative sentences, and sequential or procedural statements correspond to imperative sentences. Question-answering languages, of course, contain interrogative statements which are easily inverted into declaration statements as discussed in Section 2.2. Commonly found expressions in programming languages include arithmetic, logical, conditional, variable, and designational expressions. Table I presents the analogy between syntactic types of a natural language and typical syntactic types of a programming language.

Table I
Comparative Survey of Syntactic Types for Natural and Programming Languages

Natural language	Programming language

(1) Vocabulary
    Alphabetic symbols
    Marks and signs
 	
    Words
	(1) Vocabulary
	    Symbols
	        Alphabetic
	        Numeric
	        Marks and signs
	    Words
	        Free identifiers
	        Reserved identifiers

(2) Syntactic—word classes (examples)
    Noun
    Verb
    Adjective
    Adverb, etc.
	(2) Syntactic—word classes (examples)
	    Digit
	    Letter
	    Integer
	    Variable
	    Noun
	    Verb
	    Qualifier, etc.

(3) Syntactic subsentence classes
    Clauses (examples)
        Predicate
        Noun
        Dependent
        Independent, etc.
	(3) Syntactic substatement classes
	    Expressions (examples)
	        Arithmetic
	        Logical
	        Conditional
	        Variable, etc.

(4) Sentence types
    Declarative
    Imperative
    Interrogative
    Exclamatory
	(4) Statement types
	    Declaration
	    Assignment
	    Sequential
	    Procedural
	    Interrogative (for question-answering languages)

(5) Paragraph	(5) Block or procedure

One form for presentation of the syntax of a programming language which has become quite popular since its first appearance in 1962 [1] is known as the Backus normal form after one of its principal advocates, John Backus. The principal features of the Backus normal form are as follows:

(a) A definition has the form

(3.1) $\langle$name of syntactic type being defined$\rangle ::= $
$\langle$definition name 1$\rangle \mid \langle$definition name 2$\rangle$
$\ldots \mid \langle$definition name $n\rangle$.

(b) The symbol ::= is a separation symbol separating the right and left sides of a definition.

(c) The symbol | separates alternatives.

(d) The brackets ⟨ ⟩ are used to enclose nonterminal symbols.

(e) Terminal symbols stand by themselves without enclosing brackets.

(f) The syntactic type or the "thing" being defined is represented by a name as its nonterminal symbol in the definition statement.

As an example, consider the following specific definition:

(3.2)   ⟨procedural statement⟩ ::= GO TO ⟨variable⟩ | DO ⟨VARIABLE⟩.

Using the model of (3.1) and the explanation of the features of the Backus normal form, this example reveals that a symbol string in the source programming language is a procedural statement if it takes either one of two forms, namely:

(3.3)   GO TO ⟨variable⟩

where GO TO is a substring of terminal symbols and in particular, therefore, belongs to the lexical subset of reserved identifiers and where GO TO is followed by a free identifier naming a variable; or

(3.4)   DO ⟨variable⟩

where DO is again a reserved identifier. Thus, GO TO A23 and DO SQRT might be examples of procedural statements.

A second example illustrative of the Backus normal form syntax specification is:

(3.5)   ⟨assignment statement⟩ ::= ⟨expression⟩ → ⟨variable⟩ | ⟨assignment statement⟩ → ⟨variable⟩.

The definition of (3.5) shows the ability of the Backus normal form to incorporate recursive definitions. In (3.5) the symbol → would be a delimiter. As an indication of the simplicity of statement afforded by the Backus normal form, it has been shown [44] that all definitions so expressed can be transformed to one of the three following forms (except for the definition of ⟨empty⟩):

(3.6)
$$⟨A⟩ ::= ⟨B⟩ | ⟨C⟩$$
$$⟨A⟩ ::= ⟨B⟩ \ ⟨C⟩$$
$$⟨A⟩ ::= a$$

where A, B, and C are nonterminal symbol sets.

It is now possible to present the syntactic specification of a very simple but nontrivial programming language in Backus normal form

[22]. The recursive nature of the definitions and the typical interrelatedness of syntactic types should be noted:

(3.7)
⟨procedure⟩ ::= ⟨assignment statement⟩ | ⟨assignment statement⟩ ; ⟨procedure⟩
⟨assignment statement⟩ ::= ⟨variable⟩ = ⟨arithmetic expression⟩
⟨arithmetic expression⟩ ::= ⟨term⟩ | ⟨arithmetic expression⟩ + ⟨term⟩
⟨term⟩ ::= ⟨factor⟩ | ⟨term⟩ × ⟨factor⟩
⟨factor⟩ ::= ⟨variable⟩ | ⟨integer⟩ | (⟨arithmetic expression⟩)
⟨variable⟩ ::= ⟨letter⟩ | ⟨variable⟩ ⟨letter⟩ | ⟨variable⟩ ⟨digit⟩
⟨integer⟩ ::= ⟨digit⟩ | ⟨integer⟩ ⟨digit⟩
⟨letter⟩ ::= A | B | C | D | E | F | G | H | I | J | K | L | M | N | O | P | Q | R | S | T | U | V | W | X | Y | Z
⟨digit⟩ ::= 0 | 1 | 2 | 3 | 4 | 5 | 6 | 7 | 8 | 9.

It has only been recently that a concerted effort has been made to standardize the structural description of programming languages by informally agreed to standardization on metalanguage forms, vocabulary, terminology, and on the Backus normal form for syntactic specification. ALGOL, FORTRAN, NELIAC, JOVIAL, and COBOL have been so described [36, 42, 50, 61]. One might ask what one gains by the adoption of formal syntactic specifications for programming languages. Certainly, the earlier languages were described by manuals of rules and definitions bearing little resemblance to formal structural descriptions. In addition to the obvious observation that every manual was different, thus making the task of understanding and comparing programming languages quite cumbersome, it seems apparent that the ability to exploit a formal syntax makes the design of language processors simpler. The existence of formal syntax has, of course, made possible syntax-directed compilers. Further, such syntactic specification has bridged the gap between programming languages, language processor design, and the theories and techniques of mathematical linguistics and mathematical logic. It is certainly true now that as a result grammatical and syntactic theories pertinent to programming languages can be finally taught, and programming languages and their processors are being designed in a more rational way. What is of even greater import, however, is that more powerful programming languages in the sense of inclusion of more complex grammatical units can be designed and processed; and more efficient parsing or syntactic analysis techniques can be devised through allowable variations of a given syntax.

Because the recent literature on programming language processors exhibits extensive borrowing from that of linguistics and grammatical models and because the design of improved processors is so dependent upon understanding of grammatical models, syntactic types, parsing algorithms, and ambiguity considerations, it seems profitable to discuss here some of the prevalent concepts most relevant to those concerned with the design of programming language processors.

3.3 Grammatical Models and Ambiguity Considerations

As stated in Section 3.2, a grammar may be conceived as a model or a set of rules for either producing or recognizing the allowable sets of strings in a language. The more common and somewhat more restrictive use of the term "grammar" is due to Chomsky [13] who states that "a grammar can be regarded as a device that enumerates the sentences of a language. . . . We can investigate the structure of (a language) only through the study of the finite devices (grammars) which are capable of enumerating its sentences." As can be seen, this more classic definition of grammars restricts the strings analyzed to sentences. This, however, imposes no limitations on the applications of grammatical models to programming language design. It has been shown by a number of individuals that programming languages whose syntactic types are defined via the Backus normal form are equivalent to simple phrase structure grammars (in Bar-Hillel's notation), or type-2 grammars (in Chomsky's notation), or context-free grammars (in Gorn's terminology). A phrase structure grammar, of which the above-mentioned types are all subsets can be defined as follows [2, 47, 12]:

Phrase structure grammar: a grammar which consists of a finite set of rewriting rules of the form $P \rightarrow Q$ where P and Q are symbol strings. The grammar contains a special symbol S, standing for sentence, and a boundary symbol # indicating the beginning and end of sentences. Some of the symbols of the grammar stand for words. These constitute the terminal vocabulary of the grammar. (Note that the terminal symbols of the grammar differ from the terminal symbols of programming languages as defined in Section 3.2. This is because grammars do not normally deal with entities of smaller grammatical significance than words. Programming language processors, on the other hand, have to deal with individual symbols, e.g., $+$, $-$, $\rightarrow$, etc.) Given such a grammar, one generates a sentence by writing down the initial string $\# S \#$ and applying one of the rewriting rules to form a new string $\# P_1 \#$, i.e., the rule $S \rightarrow P_1$ has been applied. Then another rule is applied to form a new string $\# P_2 \#$, and so on, until a string $\# P_n \#$ is generated which consists completely of terminal symbols, e.g., words. Such a string cannot be further rewritten. The sequence of strings so constructed is often called a derivation of $\# P_n \#$. As an example, consider the following derivation sequence.

(3.8)
Step 1: $\# S \#$
Step 2: $\#$ noun phrase predicate phrase $\# \equiv \# P_1 \#$
Step 3: $\#$ article noun verb noun phrase $\# \equiv \# P_2 \#$
Step 4: $\#$ The dog bit article adjective noun $\# \equiv \# P_3 \#$
Step 5: $\#$ The dog bit the fat man $\# \equiv \# P_4 \#$.

Since P_4 consists completely of terminal symbols, it cannot be further rewritten. It appears evident that a grammar so defined by a set of rewriting rules can be implemented on a computing device which can, as a result, generate grammatically correct sentences. In actuality, different restrictions can be imposed on the set of rewriting rules to define a hierarchy of grammars. Chomsky has defined grammar types 0, 1, 2, and 3 where:

(a) Type 0 grammar is a Turing machine (remember that a grammar being a set of rules can be a device).

(b) Type 1 grammar has rules which are context-dependent.

(c) Type 2 grammars possess the requirement that the left-hand side of each rewriting rule must be a single nonterminal symbol and the right-hand side must be a string of at least one symbol. (Programming languages defined by Backus normal form are of this type.)

(d) Type 3 grammars are finite automata.

Chomsky's definition defines grammars as sentence generators. Grammars have been defined by others as sentence recognizers also. In any case, the process of sentence recognition is extremely important. The recognition process involves determination of the derivation sequence or derivation tree when given a terminal string, i.e., to determine $\# S \#$ when given $\# P_n \#$. The recognition process is exemplified in tree forms in Fig. 1 where it will be recognized as the parsing process known to most from elementary school days. The function of a programming language processor is to perform the recognition process as just exemplified. As will be seen in later sections, the processor examines the strings of language symbols, attempts to recognize them by syntactic type, adjoins them as in the tree derivation of Fig. 1, and continues the recognition of larger and larger syntactic types until, for example, it has recognized a statement. At this point it will not only have recognized a statement but will have a representation of the structure of the statement in terms of syntactic types and so will be able to determine what program or computer action is required [8].

It is quite apparent that since most (if not all) programming language

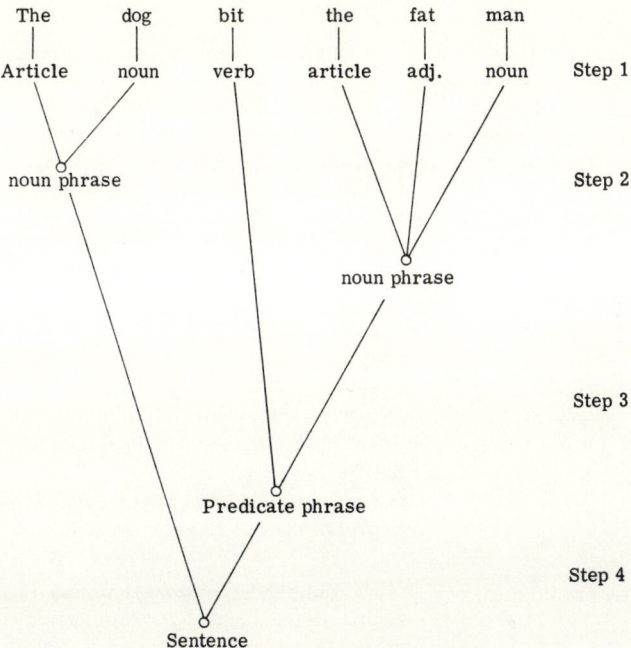

Fig. 1. Sentence recognition process.

processors perform a left-to-right scan of the language symbol string, it is important to know:

(a) how to recognize a syntactic type as soon as it is encountered as a symbol string;

(b) whether the determination of syntactic type may be changed based on later syntactic types encountered in the recognition process; and

(c) if (b) holds, then how much further in the recognition process must the analysis continue before all syntactic types thus far encountered can be uniquely identified, i.e., can be ensured to remain invariant regardless of the content of the remainder of the sentence.

The problem stated in (a) is resolvable through the use of parsing algorithms and of proper syntactic specification. The problem stated in (b) asks whether the language is free from syntactic ambiguity or whether it is context-dependent where the ambiguity must be resolved through contextual analysis. The discussion of (c) further refines the ambiguity question by inquiring as to whether syntactic ambiguity can be avoided within a bounded context. The questions of ambiguity and context dependence have been addressed with increasing frequency in

TABLE II
Survey Description of Selected Grammatical Models[a]

Grammar type	Grammar description
Dependency grammars[b]	Based on the principle that words in a language are mutually hierarchically dependent. Some approaches require any given word to be dependent upon only one other.
Finite state grammars	Based upon applications of information theory. Utilizes a probabilistic approach in that the expectation probability of occurrence of any given word is determined by the immediately preceding word. There is a given probability of occurrence for any word to be the initial word of a statement. Is more adequate for mechanical rather than for natural languages.
Formational grammars	Based upon a mathematical theory of the formation of symbol strings. Applications of the theory are few.
Glossomatic grammars	Based upon the principle that language structure can be determined by examination of a given corpus. Considers language as a system where the relationships between language units can be explicitly stated.
Immediate constituent grammars	Based on the principle that the analysis of language can be performed by successive analyses of language constituents starting with the largest and proceeding to the smallest. At each step the results of the preceding step are reanalyzed. They are somewhat akin to the phrase structure approach.
Phrase structure grammars	Based upon the theory that a grammar is a set of rewriting rules operating on the symbol strings of the language. Has been defined sufficiently to separate out four distinct types.
Stratificational grammars	Based upon the principle that language and, therefore, language analysis can be stratified into four levels: the sememic, the lexemic, the morphemic, and the phonemic. Each analysis level contains its own distinct set of rules.
Tagmemic grammars	Based upon the principle that sentence structure is comprised of functional slots into which proper syntactic types may be placed. The fillers are called "tagmemes." They are akin to immediate constituent grammars in many respects.

[a] See Postal [54].
[b] See Hayes [32].

the last several years, since most programming language designers would like to ensure that their grammar is unambiguous [10, 25].

Results that have been obtained thus far indicate that for arbitrary type 2 phrase structure grammars which are context-free there is no algorithm to determine whether or not they are ambiguous. However, for arbitrary type 2 phase structure grammars of bounded context, there are decision procedures to determine whether or not they are ambiguous. Fortunately, most existing programming languages possess bounded-context grammars. Returning to the problems posed by (b) and (c) above which center around resolution of ambiguity, one now states that for programming languages defined by bounded-context grammars, the structure of a substring of a language statement can be determined by considering only a bounded context of that substring. Further, it is possible for any specified bound on the number of characters considered to determine whether or not a given grammar is one of that bounded context. If it is, then one can ensure that it is not ambiguous. Finally, in this latter case of a nonambiguous bounded-context grammar, the programming language processor may perform a syntactic analysis where the number of operations needed can be shown to be proportional to the length of the statement analyzed [20, 21, 22].

It seems appropriate before leaving the subject of grammatical models to list some of the better-known grammars, if only to indicate the various modeling approaches open to designers of programming languages. A very cursory description is given and the listing is in alphabetical order for convenience in Table II [40].

The importance of the roles of rules of structure, syntactic specifications, and grammatical models in the construction of language processors should by now be somewhat apparent and will become more so in Sections 5-8.

4. Historical Development of Programming Language Processors

The formal, continuous history of programming language processors and of programming languages started around 1952 with the recognition and development of libraries of subroutines. The existence of subroutines organized in some semblance of a library so that they could be retrieved by an assigned tag—normally, a name—was essential for the development of macro-instructions. A macro-instruction, in this sense, is simply a set of machine instructions given a collective name. Macro-instructions over the years have become more complex and sophisticated, evolving into the "procedures" which can be named in procedure-oriented languages. The first programming language processors known as interpreters and compilers were also conceived during 1952 and 1953. Both of these allowed the use of very simple programming languages often referred to as machine-oriented symbolic languages. They were of the individual-memory-location-addressing type, but the addresses could be symbolic rather than the actual bit-address of the memory location. Operations to be performed were also given symbolic names but initially had a one-to-one correspondence with actual hardware operations. Macro-instructions were soon incorporated, however, into these simple programming languages permitting a functionally meaningful set of operations to be referred to by a single name. Interpreters scanned the simple symbolic programming language, translated it into machine language, and performed the indicated machine operations using subroutines during the actual language processing. Interpreters were deemed inefficient in that there was no final machine language translation of the programming language, and the interpretation process had to be repeated each time the same problem was solved. It is interesting to note in this regard, however, that list processors, now the most advanced language processors for nonnumerical applications, act essentially as interpreters. The first compilers were what are now termed "assembly routines" in that they processed these same simple symbolic languages, automatically assigned machine addresses to operand symbols, and "assembled" the resulting machine code into a machine language. Interpreters disappeared by 1956, and assemblers grew into compilers which could process procedure-oriented languages, first thought of as algebraic or algorithmic languages. During this period and even through 1958, languages were described in terms of rules which bore little resemblance to syntactic specifications or grammatical models. The first FORTRAN manuals, although complete, were far more complex than the language structure justified, simply because there was very little infiltration of linguistic knowledge into the programming field. Subsequent to 1958 and in particular since 1961, syntactic analyses and methods have more and more shared the spotlight in programming language development. The problem of removal of syntactic ambiguities and the extensions of phrase structure language theory to introduce more context dependence became highlighted. Different schemes of performing syntactic analyses were developed. After 1961 and particularly since 1962, programming language designers have become more and more involved with semantic and pragmatic considerations and most interestingly with the semantic specifications of languages and with types of pragmatic control. One of the most interesting and promising developments in the consideration of semantics is that of Thompson [64] in his DEACON question-answering system (DEACON stands for Direct English Access and Control). He introduces an equivalence between syntactic word classes of his programming language and the semantic categories of his computer data base. Then his language processor, which is a list processor, parses each sentence into syntactic classes which either name lists, sublists, or operations to be performed. His ideas, based on Tarski's logical truth theory appear to be the most advanced in handling semantic problems. In addition, Thompson makes clear the importance of permitting ambiguities in his programming languages which are later resolved by a semantic analysis which handles context-dependent grammars.

Although it is possible to list only a few of the major highlights in the development of programming languages and programming language processors, the presentation of these few in the years intervening between 1952 and 1965 is deemed useful in depicting the course of development and in anticipating future developments. Accordingly, the remainder of this section is devoted to this chronology of events.

1952–1953

1. Development of subroutine libraries.
2. Introduction of EDSAC and ILLIAC subroutine libraries by Wilkes, Wheeler, Booth, and Gill.
3. The Whirlwind computer at MIT was made available to users of an "open-shop" basis in the form of three pseudo-computers which existed as programmed interpreters. They included the Summer Session computer and the Comprehensive Algebraic computer (forerunner of ALGOL).
4. Development by Hopper of the A-2 compiler for the UNIVAC automatic coding system which produced a one-address machine code from a three-address pseudo-code.
5. Development of interpreter routines for the UNIVAC and the 1101, among others.

1954

1. Original concept of FORTRAN was developed by John Backus.
2. A "universal coding" experiment using the ENIAC, EDVAC, and ORDVAC at Aberdeen Proving Ground was made. The same simple general purpose, common pseudo-code was used as input to the latter two machines. For the first time the processes of "translation" and "assembly" were separated.
3. Research on programming languages for list processing and symbol manipulation was initiated at RAND and Carnegie Tech. It was part of a research effort on artificial intelligence and simulation of cognitive processes. These languages became the IPL (Information Processing Language) series.

1955–1956

1. Original FORTRAN language basically completed.
2. The first business-oriented programming systems were formulated. Those included the FLOW-MATIC by Grace Hopper of Remington Rand Univac and AIMACO, developed by Air Materiel Command. Both were simple procedure-oriented languages. They laid the groundwork for FACT—Minneapolis-Honeywell, COMTRAN (Commercial Translator)—IBM, NEBULA—Ferranti, Ltd., and COBOL—Department of Defense.
3. It became clear during this period that programming languages were information transformers or symbol manipulators and that the computers involved were of secondary importance.
4. The first process control system, APT, was coded for the Whirlwind computer at MIT [55].

1957

1. The initial FORTRAN system was issued. It was for the IBM 704 and was probably the most complex programming system ever produced. It comprised some 25,000 lines of code. It was released by IBM.
2. A FORTRAN primer was published.
3. The COMIT system, originally designed for mechanical translation and linguistic research, was initiated at MIT. It turned out to be a highly useful general-purpose symbol manipulation language. It is based on a notation due to Chomsky. It was first designed for use on the IBM 704.

1958

1. FORTRAN II, a new version with significant source language additions, was released. A SHARE users group for FORTRAN (704/9/90/94) was formed.
2. The preliminary report on ALGOL was published. The language described in this report was known as ALGOL-58. "Reference," "publication," and "hardware languages" concepts were introduced.
3. IPL-V, the first of the IPL series to be a "public" language was produced as a running system on the IBM 650. The first documentation was produced for IPL-V. Maintenance of each machine compiler rests with the originating group for that machine.
4. Work on the NELIAC language and the first NELIAC compiler was begun and completed. It was for the RRU M460 computer. NELIAC is a dialect of ALGOL-58.

PROGRAMMING LANGUAGE PROCESSORS

1959

1. The DOD hosted a meeting of 70 people to discuss possibilities of a common language for data processing. The CODASYL (Conference on Data Systems Languages) group was formed. The goal of a common language bridging all equipment was established.
2. Systems Development Corporation (SDC) began work on JOVIAL at Paramus, New Jersey. JOVIAL is a dialect of ALGOL-58.
3. The Conversation Machine, a program by Green, Berkeley, and Gottlieb allowed a computer to carry on a nontrivial conversation about the weather.

1960

1. A more definitive version of ALGOL known as ALGOL-60 was published.
2. The first implementation of a subset of ALGOL-60 occurred on a computer known as Electrologica XI in Amsterdam, Holland.
3. The specifications for COBOL were completed by an independent group and they were published by the Government Printing Office.
4. The first JOVIAL compilers were running on the IBM 709. SDC decided to adopt JOVIAL as a corporate-wide standard programming language.
5. The first available NELIAC documentation appeared.
6. Work on syntax-directed compilers by Irons progressed sufficiently to offer promise.
7. Development of question-answering systems became known. The Oracle, an experimental system to answer questions from simple English sentences was completed by Phillips at MIT.
8. Chomsky's work on models of grammar began to be advocated as useful for programming languages. Bar-Hillel, Rosen, and Gorn also contributed to syntactic analysis development.

1961

1. A revised version of COBOL specifications was completed and printed by the Government Printing Office. It was known as COBOL-61 [4, 16].
2. The first published documentation on COMIT was released by SHARE. It described the 7090 system. Maintenance of COMIT is by the Mechanical Translation Group at MIT, where a COMIT II system has since been completed.
3. The main documentation of IPL-V was considered complete, official, and almost fixed as a result of the publication by Prentice-Hall of an IPL-V manual.
4. The first documentation of JOVIAL appeared as publicly available.

5. The first DOD attempts to standardize on a single programming language were initiated [*31*].
6. The American Standards Association established a committee for the standardization of programming languages.

1962

1. An IFIPS working group to maintain ALGOL was formed.
2. A supplement of corrections to the ALGOL-60 report was issued, and IFIPS adopted the revised report as an official IFIPS publication.
3. The first COBOL-61 compilers were completed.
4. A JOVIAL maintenance group was formally established at SDC consisting of about 16 people.
5. The Backus normal form was "formalized" and its equivalence to type 2 phrase structure grammars shown.

1963

1. A revised report on ALGOL-60 was issued under IFIPS official sponsorship.
2. An IPL-V Secretary was established at RAND to act as a communication exchange agent. No language maintenance will be attempted.
3. A project to show a typical problem as implemented in various languages was started by Information International. Completion to be in 1964.
4. The Defense Communications Agency was asked to determine possibilities of standardizing on a command-control programming language.
5. Standardized presentation of programming language description was initiated by Association for Computing Machinery (ACM). ALGOL-60, NELIAC, JOVIAL, and APT were so described [*67*].
6. A listing of all known programming languages by application was compiled by ACM.

1964

1. The first limited test of DEACON, a question-answering system permitting ambiguities in language, was conducted.
2. Semantic and pragmatic considerations became widespread.
3. A survey of question-answering programming language systems was completed by Simmons, SDC.
4. Problem-oriented language development for other than control applications became popular. STRESS was designed at MIT.

5. Features of Programming Language Processors

5.1 Types of Language Processors

The preceding sections have revealed that any programming language processor must (it will be seen that list processors can also be made to comply with this description):

(a) linearly scan the given program written in the source programming language for symbol recognition,

(b) determine the syntactic structure by isolating all syntactic types based on the syntactic specification provided,

(c) discover all syntactic ambiguities and violations of vocabulary or grammatical rules and take remedial action,

(d) translate from the source programming language into the target programming language (e.g., machine language) where the syntactic and semantic specifications of the target language are provided,

(e) synthesize the resulting target language statement of the problem so as to take into account the machine operating environment, and

(f) either produce or provide for the production of machine code equivalent in result to the programming language input.

A language processor so designed will produce a target machine language which is syntactically perfect. Any errors in the target machine code must result from semantically incorrect statement in the original problem statement in the source programming language [56, 57].

The design and construction of programming language processors has been one of the main efforts of systems specialists since at least 1955 in the sense of expenditure of funds and of manpower resources. This construction effort has been matched by an equally gigantic demand for the processors. There is still enough aura of mystery about programming languages and processors that to most people associated in some way with data processing systems they represent a "folk-medicine-like" cure-all which will compensate for inexperienced programmers, non-understanding users, differences in computer equipment, lack of good data, lack of problem-definition, and so on. This sense of mystery has been both advantageous and disadvantageous to the improvement of languages and their processors. Money has, in general, been more available than has human talent so there have been no funding constraints to progress; overexpectations have, however, resulted in over-disillusionment in many cases. Due primarily to the continuing efforts of a staunch set of far-sighted and technically competent individuals, the development of languages and language processors has been one of the better features of software advancement.

Programming language processor development appears to have partitioned itself into three main approaches and one secondary approach. The three main approaches can be entitled: the conventional processor approach, the syntax-directed processor approach, and the list processor approach. The secondary approach, whose features overlap those of the conventional and syntax-directed types, can be entitled the intermediate language approach. There are a number who would add to this list that of the machine-independent processor approach. This title is so misleading, however, as to be dangerous in that the complete separation of processor from machine is impossible. It is only the manner in which the machine characteristics are introduced into the production of the target language by the processor that influences the amount of processor logic which is machine-dependent. It is for this reason that the machine-independent approach has been rejected. One universal property of programming language processors independent of type is that most of the difficulty in construction lies in the design logic. The operations performed during the language processing are normally quite simple ones; the majority are table look-ups, searches, comparisons, and symbol movements. The design logic in turn revolves around eight major considerations, namely, the manner of syntactic specification of the source language, the method of syntactic analysis, the means of error or ambiguity correction, the manner of specification of machine characteristics, the manner of specification of target language syntax and semantics, the means of translating between source and target language, the means for synthesis of target language, and means of optimizing the ultimate machine code production.

The conventional compiler approach is the oldest. It generally yields the fastest processor. There is also strong evidence that it produces the most efficient machine code, although this has not been factually proved either analytically or by equipment. In this approach, the design logic is such that a change in either the machine or the source language necessitates almost a complete redesign of processor logic with corresponding major changes in the processor program. This is because the translation process between source language, syntactic types, and target language, semantic and syntactic types, is accomplished via algorithms where the syntactic and semantic specifications, as well as the translation procedure, are frozen into the algorithms. These specifications and procedures are, in general, nonseparable so that a change in any one may have effects throughout any given algorithm and in more than one algorithm. The disadvantages of this approach have already been singled out as the large amount of change induced in processor logic and program due to any change in programming language or machine. The advantage of this approach is that the role of the programmer is greater than in the syntax-directed or intermediate language approach and is no less than in the list processor approach. This implies that the expert programmer can, by manipulating between the syntactic and semantic specification and hence taking more advantage of the peculiarities of an individual machine, produce a faster compiler and probably better machine code. An obvious corollary to this is that the construction of a conventional compiler is extremely demanding upon a programmer's skill.

The syntax-directed approach is more recent, only really being exploited since 1960. It is generally easier to write a syntax-directed processor program than a conventional processor program; but the processor will probably be slower and the resultant machine code less efficient. In this approach the syntactic specification of the source programming language is written in a form that can be converted into a set of tables for processor use. The design logic of the processor then defines a set of routines which will take source language program statements and perform table look-ups in the syntax specification table to determine the syntactic types involved so as to yield the structure of the statement or, in other words, to parse the statement. A second set of tables must also be provided which describes in terms of target language semantic and syntactic specifications the set of actions which may be indicated by any source language program. These actions are usually in the form of processing routines or machine code generators. The design logic must then outline analysis routines which will take the parsed source language statement and produce from it, based on searches in the tables describing the target language, the set of indicated processing routines or code generators. These latter are then synthesized and put into proper sequence to form the target language equivalent of the source language program. It should be noted that the routines of a syntax-directed compiler as described above can be made independent of the content of the specifications in the two sets of tables listed; namely, the source language syntax table and the target language syntax and semantics table. The routines need only be dependent on the format or form of the definitions [27] and can, therefore, be said to be independent of both the source programming language and of the machine. They are dependent only on the language which describes the contents of the tables; this language is occasionally referred to as the processor metalanguage. It can be seen that in this latter case a change in machine will change only the contents of the target language specification tables. Similarly, a change in source programming language will change only the contents of the tables containing the syntax of the source language. Two of the more useful characteristics of syntax-directed compilers are their ability to retrace steps in a syntactic analysis when an incorrect result has occurred and the recursive nature of their routines. Another useful feature which has not yet been fully exploited is that these processors are not restricted to the analysis of phrase structure languages of bounded context [23] but can perform a contextual analysis of any magnitude required, although at a definite cost in compiler speed.

List processors, as pointed out in Section 4, are interpretive. A list processing language itself is made up of lists. There is no rigid syntactic specification, and the structure of the language consists simply of lists. Rules governing the form of lists, the allowable contents of lists, and the linkages between lists and between the components of a given list replace the syntactic specifications of other types of programming languages. The vocabulary must be described, however, as discussed in Section 2, in terms of reserved and free identifiers, letters, symbols, digits, word types, and the like. A program in a list processing language is expressed as lists; data are lists of symbols. Verbs are program instructions in the list processing language. The list processor itself decodes the problem stated in the source language essentially by means of tables of processing routines or subroutines. Each verb in the program list is interpreted as a call to one of these subroutines to act upon the data list specified in the program list. The subroutine is executed by the machine as it is called up so that completion of the source language processing is synonymous with execution of the source language problem. As a result, no separate compilation process is needed. It is readily apparent that any change in source language vocabulary or in rules governing the structures of lists necessitates changes in the subroutines of the list processor and in the interpretation process itself. Comparison of list processors and the other three types of processors is a useless exercise since the purpose of list processing languages differs from that of the other programming languages. As expressed by some of the originators of list processing languages, these languages were intended to solve problems "sufficiently complex, ill-structured, and difficult" as to require human-like intelligence [51]. One of these difficulties involved the allocation of memory when the entities requiring memory only come into existence while the problem is being solved. In such a case, no predetermination of memory allocation can be made; and certainly no standard techniques would suffice. The solution was the organization of programs and data into lists which allowed scatter addressing of memory. Most of the use of list processing languages has been for non-numerical applications such as theorem-proving, chess-playing, mechanical translation, and symbolic calculation. More recently they have been found useful, if not essential, in the area of question-answering by computer. A list processor is much slower, as an interpreter, than are other types of language processors. A program written in a list processing language along with its associated data requires three or more times as much memory space as would the same program written in another type of language. The important point to note is that most problems resolvable by list processing could not even be written, much less solved, by use of the other types of languages.

The intermediate language approach emphasizes and makes rigid the role of the intermediate language in the translation from source programming language to target machine language. This intermediate language is specified in the same detail as is the source programming language. Its structure is closely akin to that of machine language, but it must at the same time be "machine-independent" because it plays the role of a universal intermediate language. The programming language processor in this approach is actually divided into two distinct language processors which can be labeled the source language processor (SLP) and the intermediate language processor (ILP). The SLP translates from a given source language to the intermediate language, and the ILP translates from the universal intermediate language to a given machine language. Both the SLP and the ILP usually approximate the syntax-directed approach so that only the source language specification tables change in the SLP with change in the source language; similarly, only the machine language specification tables change in the ILP with change in machine. The SLP and the ILP are normally written to operate on a particular specified computer which does not have to be any of the target machines. Thus, the resultant target machine language may be produced on a machine other than that on which it is intended to run. The source programming language, theoretically then, can be written with no thought of to which or how many computers it will eventually be translated. It is because of considerations such as these that the intermediate language approach is frequently termed the "machine-independent approach." Figure 2 illustrates graphically this approach. The total language processor (TLP), which is comprised of the SLP and the ILP (TLP = (SLP)U(ILP)) is cumbersome and slow compared to those of the other approaches. The machine code produced cannot be more efficient than those of the other approaches, and almost invariably will be less efficient. The influence of the expert programmer in the design of the TLP is quite restricted and is confined primarily to the design of the analysis routines linking source language description tables to intermediate language description tables and of analysis routines linking intermediate language description tables to machine language description tables. To the author's knowledge, no intermediate language processor types have been implemented, although at least one is currently in development.

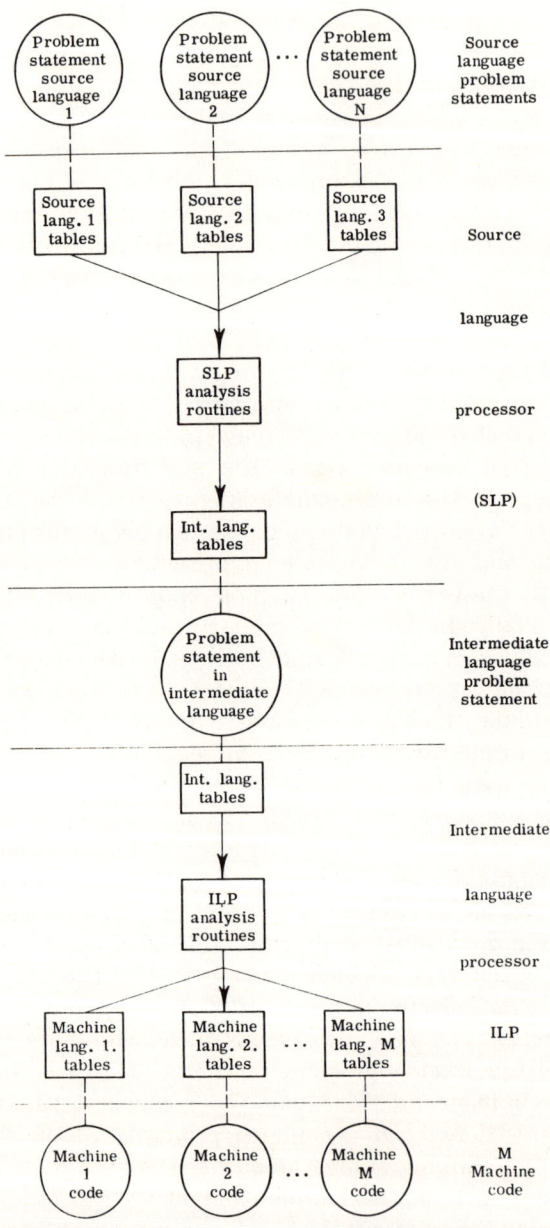

Fig. 2. Intermediate language processors approach.

5.2 Programming Language Processor Terminology

Before proceeding with more detailed discussions of specific processor types, certain commonly used phrases or terminology need to be defined and explained. This section will be devoted to such definitions.

(a) *A load-and-go compiler* is one in which source language statements are entered as input. The compiler then translates these into target machine language and immediately transfers control to this newly generated machine program. The first output of such a compiler consists of the actual answers to the problem, stated initially in the source programming language.

(b) *A self-compiler* is one which has the capability of compiling itself.

(c) *An n-pass compiler* is one which scans and analyzes syntactically the input source language problem string n times before producing the final output target language. The entire string of source language symbols need not be subjected to n analyses, nor do the same operations need to be performed in each of the n analyses in order for the term "n-pass compiler" to be applied. Using this definition, a load-and-go compiler is a zero-pass compiler. A rule of thumb in determining the number of passes needed is that if the target language programs produced in n passes are not noticeably better than those produced in $n - 1$ passes, there should only be $n - 1$ passes [*45*].

(d) *Polish notation* is a method of writing logical and arithmetic expressions without the need for parentheses. For example [*49*]:

Normal algebraic notation $(X - Y) \times (A - B)$
Polish notation $\quad\quad\quad\quad XY - AB - \times$

This notation was originated by the Polish logician J. Lukasiewicz. An expression written in Polish notation is called a "Polish string." In Polish notation the operators are written to the right of a pair of operands instead of between them. The rule for evaluating a Polish string is as follows:

(i) Scan the string from left to right.
(ii) Remember the operands and the order in which they occur.
(iii) When an operator is encountered, do the following:
 (1) take the two operands which are last in order,
 (2) operate upon them according to the type of operator encountered,
 (3) eliminate these two operands from further consideration,
 (4) remember the result of (2) and consider it as the last operand in order.

Consider the example:
$$a = bc \times ef \uparrow d \times +$$
where $\uparrow$ is the exponentiation operator. If one applies the rules for evaluating a Polish string one obtains:

Step 1: $a =$
Step 2: $bc \times$ becomes $b \times c$
Step 3: $a = b \times c$: intermediate result
Step 4: $ef \uparrow$ becomes e^f
Step 5: $e^f d \times$ becomes $e^f \times d$
Step 6: $(b \times c)(e^f \times d) +$ becomes $(b \times c) + e^f \times d$
Step 7: $a = b \times c + e^f \times d$: final result

(e) *A push-down list* is one in which the last item in is the first item out. It works, in principle, like the stack of plates in a cafeteria pile where the new plates put in last are the first ones taken out. It is the key to the success of most syntactic analysis techniques of language processing [52].

(f) *Crutch-coding* is the use of machine language in the statement of the problem in the source programming language. Its use immediately makes the programming language and the programming language processor machine-dependent.

(g) *Operator-precedence* analysis is a method of syntactic analysis which is a special case of bounded-context analysis. It may be used within the programming language processor whenever the programming language is a bounded-context type 2 phrase structure language. It is [15] dependent upon the establishment of a hierarchy of operator priorities which determines whether a given operator in the input string of a source language program should be applied before or after the next operator in the string when the sequence of required operations is established in the object language output. The operators referred to here are the mathematical and logical operators and the delimiters of the source programming language vocabulary. Illustrative of this concept, consider that when one manually evaluates an algebraic expression one observes (perhaps unconsciously) a hierarchical ordering of operators rather than just applying each operator in turn as it appears in the symbol order of the formula. For example, in computing
$$a \times b^3$$
one does not calculate $a \times b$ and then calculate $(a \times b)^3$. Instead, the exponentiation operator is given priority and one calculates b^3 and then $a \times b^3$. Consider the following example in which push-down lists are used and where operator precedences are given in Table III.:
$$\text{Equation I} ::= a \times b - 1/p \uparrow q$$

PROGRAMMING LANGUAGE PROCESSORS

Step 1: Take the first two operators ::= and ×. Using Table III, operator × has priority so it is applied prior to ::=. Therefore, put ::= and I in the push-down list.

Intermediate result	Push-down list
	::=
	I

Step 2: Take the second and third operators × and −. Using Table III × has priority so it may be applied. One obtains:

Intermediate result	Push-down list
$ab \times$	::=
	I

Step 3: Take the third and first operators − and ::=. The third has priority so the first will remain in the push-down list. Now take the third and fourth operators − and / where / denotes division. The fourth operator has priority by Table III so the third operator must be placed in the push-down list.

Intermediate result	Push-down list
$ab \times$	−
	::=
	I

TABLE III

OPERATOR-PRECEDENCE TABLE (ALGOL-LIKE SYMBOLS)
(INCREASING ORDER OF PRECEDENCE)

Operator	Priority	Operator	Priority
)	1	=	13
;	2	≤	14
,	3	<	15
::=	4	−	16
≡	5	+	17
⊃	6	%	18
OR	7	/	19
AND	8	×	20
NOT	9	↑	21
>	10	:	22
≥	11	(	23
≠	12		

Step 4: Take the fourth and fifth operators / and ↑ where ↑ denotes exponentiation. The fifth operator has priority so it may be applied and the fourth operator with its operand must be placed in the push-down list.

Intermediate result	Push-down list
$ab \times pq\uparrow$	1
	/
	−
	::=
	I

Step 5: Since the scan of the input string has been completed, the contents of the push-down list must now be scanned. Consider the first operator (last in) which is /. It has precedence over the next operator − so / is applied.

Intermediate result	Push-down list
$ab \times pq\uparrow 1/$	−
	::=
	I

Step 6: Consider the first and second operators, respectively, of the push-down list, namely, − and ::=. The first has priority so it is applied. One obtains:

Intermediate result	Push-down list
$ab \times pq\uparrow 1/-$	::=
	I

Step 7: Finally, one obtains:

Final result	Push-down list
$ab \times pq\uparrow 1/- \text{I} ::=$	empty

In practice the operator precedence analysis of the input source language string yields a Polish string representation of the operations to be performed. This provides an effective way of generating machine language output since the ordering of operations in a Polish string is that of most machine languages. The Polish string obtained in the above example:

$$ab \times pq \uparrow 1/- \text{I} ::=$$

is equivalent to a machine language output of the form:

clear add a
multiply b
store in w
clear add p
exponentiate q
divide 1
store in y
clear add w
subtract y
store in I

(h) *The consecutive operator bounded-context* analysis is a method of syntactic analysis which is like operator-precedence analysis—a special type of bounded-context analysis. It also may be used by a programming language processor whenever the programming language has a bounded-context type 2 phrase structure grammar. It is dependent upon the ability to determine a syntactic type of substring of the input source language through consideration of only two consecutive operators and the syntactic types between them. Instances where this is not true for any given programming language must be determined and identified so that special steps may be taken during the performance of this particular syntactic analysis. This analysis is commonly referred to as the Current Operator–Next Operator (CO–NO) analysis [35]. It requires the establishment of a CO–NO table analogous in function to the operator-precedence table. The CO–NO table may be set up as a two-dimensional array where the elements in the array usually reference processing routines or machine code generators to be inserted in the output target language to perform the actions indicated in the source language program. It is a more restricted method of defining the syntactic analysis required than is the operator-precedence technique. For illustration, consider the following example where Table IV is a sample CO–NO table only partially filled in; and Table V contains the list of machine code generators named by the elements of the CO–NO array [29].

PROGRAM STATEMENT
    PROCESS DECLARATIONS:
        SYMBOL STRING FIRST ADDRESS → I,
        SYMBOL → NOUN BUFFER ... ,

Step 1: Consider the first two operators : and → where : is the current operator and → is the next operator. From Table IV, we

Table IV
co—no Table

	Next operator															
		,	;	.	:	}	{	[	]	=	<	→	+	−	×	/
Current operator ↑ ↓	,	1		3	4	5				8	8	9	9	9	9	9
	;		1	3		5		7		8	8	9	9			
	.	1	1	3	4					8	8					
	:	1	1	3			6	7		8		9	9	9	9	9
	}	1		3						8		9				
	{															
	[															
	]	N^a	N				N			N						
	=						N									
	<						N									
	→	2	2					7								
	+									11						
	−									12						
	×									13						
	/									14						

N^a indicates that next operator is not reached directly

Table V
co—no Generator Listing

1. Generate return jump
2. Generate store instruction
3. Generate straight jump
4. Define entry point or label
5. End subroutine
6. Start subroutine
7. Set subscript
8. Set comparison
9. Generate clear and add
10. Transfer machine language
11. Generate addition
12. Generate subtraction
13. Generate multiplication
14. Generate division

find the corresponding array element to be 9 which calls up the GENERATE CLEAR AND ADD sequence so that one has the operation:

CLEAR AND ADD THE SYMBOL STRING FIRST ADDRESS

indicated.

Step 2: The CO now is → and the NO is , . The corresponding array element is 2 which calls up the GENERATE STORE INSTRUCTION. One then has the operation:

STORE SYMBOL STRING FIRST ADDRESS IN I

indicated.

One proceeds step by step in this way through the source language input string by referencing the CO–NO table and transferring control to the proper generator which inserts the necessary machine language instruction set into the object machine language program. The letter N of Table IV indicates the isolation of combinations of two consecutive operators such that the bounded context is insufficient to specify a particular action on the part of the syntactic analyzer. The bounded context must in such cases be enlarged to include the next two consecutive operators.

(i) *Recognition order* is the order in which the language processor scans the source program language input string to recognize syntactic types. Most processors, as well as all the techniques discussed in this article, are based on the premise that recognition order is the same as generation order. That is, if one scans a program statement from left to right, recognizes syntactic types as encountered, and generates the corresponding processing sequences in the output target language, then the order of these processing sequences will be essentially correct for problem solution. Variations and exceptions must, of course, be anticipated and planned for. Such a left-to-right scan recognition and corresponding generation of output target language would not handle a programming language whose syntax was modeled after the natural German language, for example.

6. The Conventional Programming Language Processor

It is difficult to fit the conventional processor into a single mold because, as was pointed out in Section 5.1, its design varies greatly with the individual programmer. However, there is a set of functions which it must accomplish; and these are generally performed in the same sequence. Accordingly, the conventional processor, for this discussion, will be assumed to be composed of five major components.

The first component is a load program which accepts the source programming language punched on cards or paper tape in hardware language. In many compilers, additional functions of a supplementary nature are performed by the load program. It may, for instance, be used to delete comments inserted into the problem statement by the programmer.

The second component may be considered as the first phase of the syntactic analysis. In this phase the string of source language symbols is separated into two parts: (a) the declaration statements which make use of the declarator delimiters of the reserved identifier lexical subset or which define identifiers used by the programmer at his own discretion, and (b) the procedural statements or imperative statements. In some cases, the set of declaration statements is called the "dimensioning set" or "noun list." Then the declaration statements or identifiers are examined for the purpose of:

(a) assigning them relative addresses for later storage in computer memories;

(b) tagging them with descriptors which, for example, determine the kind of arithmetic to be used;

(c) allocating computer memory to the various identifiers (nouns) and noun arrays;

(d) interpreting and storing numerical constants; and

(e) forming and storing the masks which may be required for arithmetic or logical masks.

The third major component which is the second phase of the syntactic analysis involves examining and interpreting the procedural statements of the source program. In this stage the analyzer separates out in sequential form the arithmetic or logical or manipulatory operations that must be performed in order to carry out the tasks specified in the procedural statements of the input source language. Unless great generalizations are used in memory allocation and mask formation and storage this phase of a compiler will become machine-dependent. Accordingly, these specific problems and the rather difficult problem of dynamic storage allocation are usually delayed and considered by the fourth component—the generator phase. There are a number of ways in which syntactic analysis of procedural statements may be carried out in order to recognize the syntactic types included. Two of these have been discussed in Section 5.2, namely the operator-precedence analysis and the two-consecutive-operator bounded-context analysis. The result of the first type of analysis is a Polish string equivalent of portions of the source language. In this procedure, applicable only to arithmetic or logical operations, a Polish string is produced through analysis of the input object language procedural statement string.

Since the command structure of most computers is probably best suited to the assembly of strings which are in the form of *operand-operator* pairs the Polish string created is replaced in turn by a string of operand-operator pairs; e.g., $bc \times ef \uparrow d \times + a ::=$ becomes "clear add b, multiply c, store w, clear add e, exponentiate f, multiply d, add w, store a." Such an operand-operator pair can be recognized as a permutation of the original source-language string with the insertion of certain lingual units of a bookkeeping type. This permutation and insertion process is handled automatically as the source language input string is scanned from left to right. It is controlled by the operator-precedence algorithm. The result of the second type of analysis is a listing of machine code generators in a proper sequence. Whatever method of syntactic analysis is employed, the output of the third component, i.e., the syntactic analysis, is a sequence of processing operations or code generators usually expressed in symbolic language structured like machine language.

The fourth component is the generator phase. The output of this phase is either an intermediate language or machine language. In either case the generator is machine-dependent. In this phase, individual addresses—either absolute or relative—are assigned; and arithmetic, Boolean, etc., processors are transformed into specific commands (machine language or assembly-like language) for a particular computer. The generator invariably makes use of tables containing most of the information required about the particular machine in question. There are two distinct modes in which output commands may be generated. In the one case the generator maintains tables containing the whole set of output commands which are equivalent to the various standard procedural statements in the input source language. In this mode one table look-up will retrieve the entire set of output commands which the generator merely completes by inserting the proper declarators and parameter values and then transfers as a block into the output target language. This mode makes use of a relatively large amount of computer memory. The other mode—the standard one in shorter generators—constructs output language commands individually as required so that less memory but a longer time of generation is used. Generalized algorithms exist for making efficient use of the special features (e.g., storage, index registers) of given computers. For example, for an n-register machine algorithms exist which scan formulas until they get to an expression which cannot be computed with less than n registers. Then the generator phase starts to produce target language output. These "n-register" algorithms minimize storage in that they permit the order of calculation to be reversed within the limit of n registers. Consider the expression:

$$A \times B + (C \times D + E \times F).$$

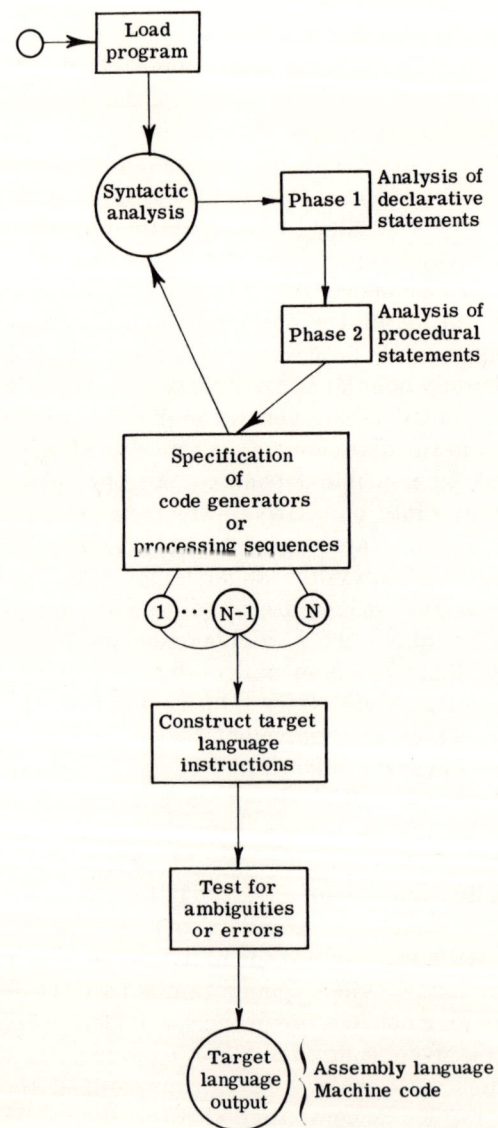

Fig. 3. Generalized conventional programming language processor structure.

Temporary storage can be saved if the order of calculation is as follows:

$$(C \times D + E \times F) + A \times B.$$

Similarly, a whole series of interesting techniques has been designed to optimize the use of index registers in loops. Most of these latter techniques, however, require several passes by the compiler through the input object language string [43].

The fifth component is concerned with the detection and correction of syntactic errors and ambiguities. It is often not a separate step in that its function may be accomplished as an integral part of the first four processor components. Detection of errors usually triggers jumps to fault routines or remedial routines. It appears desirable in many cases to permit the processor to continue even when faults are detected which cannot be corrected. This permits errors or ambiguities to be isolated with minimum use of computer time.

Figure 3 provides an illustration of the structure of an idealized conventional programming language processor. Most conventional compilers because of their structure are written either in assembly language or machine language itself. As noted earlier, conventional compilers do not permit scatter-memory addressing.

7. The Syntax-Directed Programming Language Processor

The syntax-directed compiler lends itself to a generalized description more readily than did the conventional compiler. The two primary reasons for this are that its structure is more rigidly prescribed and that very few syntax-directed compilers have been written about so there are few variations to consider. An excellent tutorial paper [11] has been written on syntax-directed processors, so this article will only treat them to the extent necessary for comparison with the other processor types discussed. The syntax-directed compiler can be subdivided into five major components just as was the conventional compiler [65].

The first component is the load program which performs the same functions as the load program of the conventional compiler. It accepts the problem written in source programming language and converted into hardware language for entry into the computer.

The second component is the syntactic analyzer. The analyzer parses the input string of the source language problem and produces a syntactical representation of the string structure generally in tree formation. The terminal nodes of the tree are vocabulary entries, and the nonterminal nodes are syntactic types. Figure 4 illustrates a typical example of a parsing of the ALGOL-like statement

$$P = q + (r \times s).$$

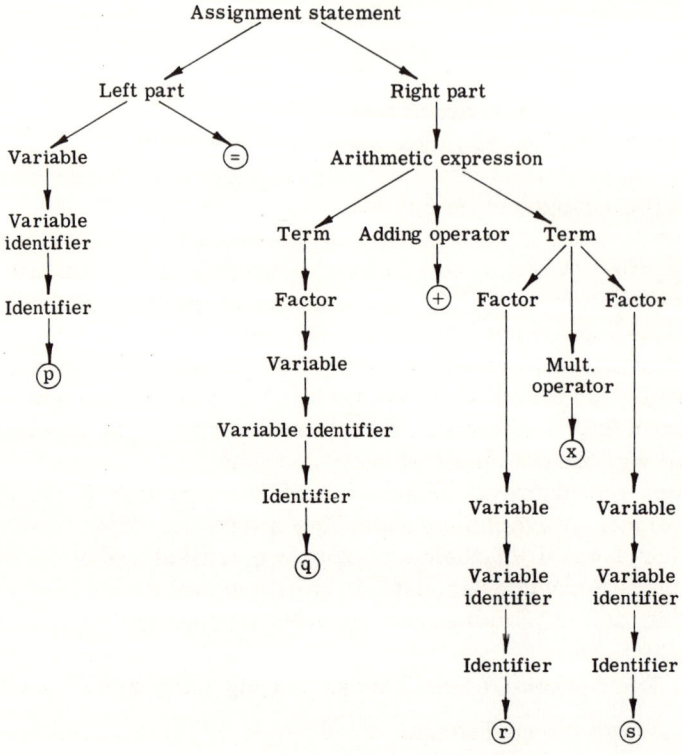

FIG. 4. Tree representation of parsing of $p = q + (r \times s)$.

In this case the syntactic specifications which fit the statement are:

⟨assignment statement⟩ ::= ⟨variable⟩ = ⟨arithmetic expression⟩
⟨arithmetic expression⟩ ::= ⟨term⟩ | ⟨arithmetic expression⟩ + ⟨term⟩
⟨term⟩ ::= ⟨factor⟩ | ⟨term⟩ × ⟨factor⟩
⟨factor⟩ ::= ⟨variable⟩ | ⟨integer⟩ | (⟨arithmetic expression⟩)

These are taken from the syntactic specification of Section 2 so that the reader has a statement in the programming language for which the syntax has already been defined. The syntactic analyzer must have available to it a set of tables which are an encodement of the syntax of the source language, normally given in Backus normal form. The syntactic analyzer always sets itself the goal of looking for a particular syntactic type. This goal is usually set for the largest syntactic type such as the Block or Procedure (equivalent of the paragraph in natural language). As the analyzer scans the symbols of the input string, subgoals are substituted for the initial main goal based on the syntactic types encountered. In looking for a Block, the analyzer will inevitably encounter elements of a statement and will, for instance, substitute "assignment statement" as a subgoal replacing its initial goal. This new goal leads in turn to new subgoals until one ends up with a tree representation of the assignment statement as illustrated in Fig. 4, having substituted as subgoals each syntactic type listed in Fig. 4 during the parsing process. The syntactic analyzer continues uninterruptedly in its recognition and parsing process until it has recognized a syntactic type of sufficient context that further scanning of the remainder of the source language symbol string will not affect its syntactic structure. This is normally a statement. At such a point the third component of the compiler is entered. It should be noted that there is a continual cycling between the analyzer component and succeeding components as each "complete-enough" syntactic type is first recognized by the analyzer and then processed by the remaining compiler components.

The third major component is the generator which takes as input the tree representation of the completed syntactic structure produced by the syntactic analyzer. The generator, in turn, uses a set of tables containing a generation strategy in order to determine what action to take at each particular node in the syntax tree. The generation strategy is simply a set of rules which (a) describes each possible type of node on a parsing tree, and (b) lists actions to be taken for each type of node encountered.

There are normally just two types of action: either to proceed to a neighboring node or to produce macro-instructions or target language code generators. The output, then, of the generator component is a set of code generators (or macro-instructions). The generator normally proceeds "up" the parsing tree from smallest syntactic type to largest syntactic type. When all possible macro-instructions have been produced from a given tree, the fourth component of the compiler takes over.

The fourth major processor component is known variously as the macro-accumulator, the in-sequence optimizer, or the generator translator. It shall be referred to here as the macro-accumulator as most expressive of its function. The macro-accumulator accepts as input the macro-instructions produced by the generator. It operates, as do the preceding two processor components, from a set of tables; these tables contain semantic descriptions of all the allowable macro-instructions. The semantic description actually defines the macro-instruction in terms of machine language or output target language and lists the rules for handling the macro-instruction. Examples of such rules include:

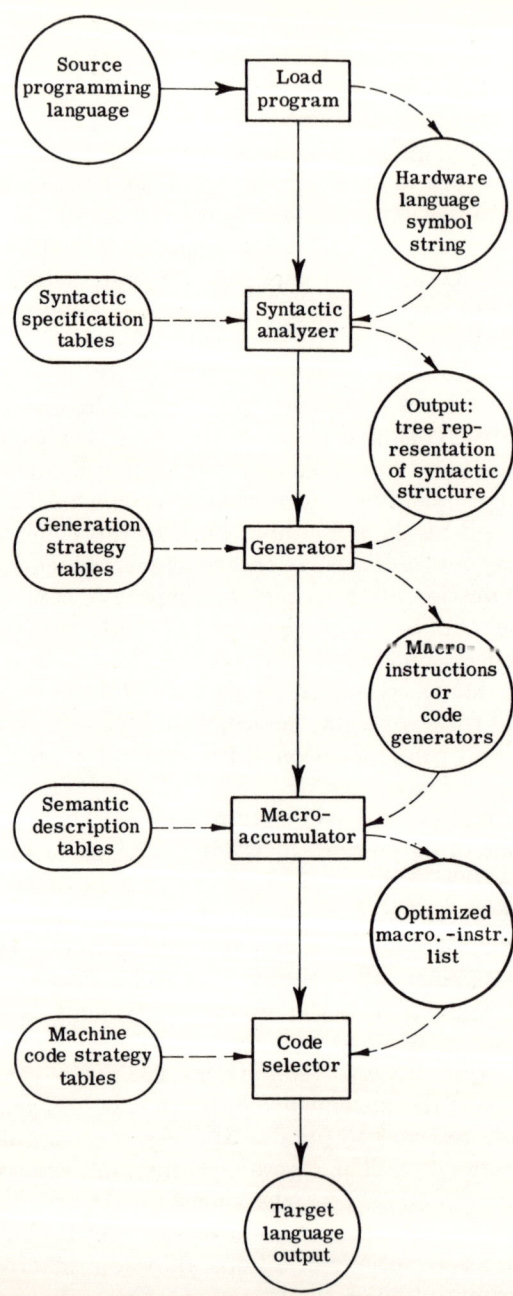

Fig. 5. Structural description of a generalized syntax-directed programming language processor.

(a) rules to determine whether or not the macro-instruction may be combined with other macro-instructions to yield a single combined macro-instruction;

(b) rules to recognize previous occurrences of the same macro-instructions and to determine whether the arguments in the two occurrences are identical; and

(c) rules to determine commutability properties of the arguments of any macro-instruction.

The macro-accumulator organizes the listing of macro-instructions for some large syntactic component such as a Block or Procedure, so as to reduce repetitions of the same process or computation, to optimize loops, to make best use of index registers and other special machine registers, and to minimize use of machine storage. Its output then is a listing of macro-instructions which makes best use of known machine features and which represents the equivalent of a large self-contained section of the source language program, usually a Block or Procedure.

The fifth major component of the syntax-directed compiler is most frequently known as the code selector. The input to the code selector is the optimized listing of macro-instructions produced by the macro-accumulator. The code selector makes use of a set of tables to produce target language output or machine code from the macro-instruction listing. The tables again contain rules which permit reordering of computation under given constraints, final register assignment, and maintenance of control over register usage. The code-selector component then produces the final target language or machine language output.

It should be noted that the syntactic analyzer may be dependent on the source programming language so that a language change would necessitate a change in it. The generator, the macro-accumulator, and the code selector are dependent in varying degrees upon the machine for which the computation is intended. The generator can be made independent of the machine through clever construction of the generation strategy. The syntax-directed approach, however, closely approximates the intermediate language approach described in Section 5.1. Figure 5 contains a structural description of a syntax-directed compiler, along with a listing of tables and outputs of the major components [37, 38].

8. List Processors

8.1 General Comments

As must be obvious from earlier treatments of list processors in this article, the conventions, terminology, and rules of language developed are only peripherally relevant to list processors. List processors are intended to process data via other than numerical, arithmetical, or standard logical techniques. The reason for development of list processing languages and of list processors was stated in Section 5.1. The essential ideas behind the concept which strongly affect the organization of list processors are:

(a) Data must be arranged in list structures that eliminate the need both for individual-memory-location addressing and for region addressing as a means of retrieval. These addressing schemes must be replaced by explicit links between data so that related data may be distributed randomly throughout the memory and so that data items may be added or deleted without disturbing the data list structure. The term "scatter addressing" has already been introduced to define this capability.

(b) All memory locations available for storage must be identified explicitly at all times.

(c) A set of processes for manipulating data arranged in flexible list structures must be designed and execution schemes must be devised. To allow real flexibility, the procedures to be accomplished must themselves have the same flexible list structure so as to permit self-manipulation [33].

The discussion of list processors cannot be separated from that of list processing languages since a list processing language is in essence the contents of the lists; its structure is the list structure; and its vocabulary is the vocabulary of the list processor. The list processor itself is an interpretive process which by means of several control lists simply interprets the procedures of the language lists by performing the required operations on the data lists. The output of the list processor is the solution of the source problem. To understand list processors is to understand the corresponding list processing languages. To do this the introduction of certain basic concepts is essential, and this is now attempted.

8.2 Fundamental Features of List Processors

The more essential features of list processors are as follows:

(a) List processors are interpreters which interpret procedures expressed as macro-instructions and perform them during the interpretive procedure as if they were machine instructions.

(b) All data and procedures (macro-instructions) are arranged in lists.

(c) All procedures involve manipulations of lists.

(d) All lists are push-down lists.

(e) A list is a set of words linked together by having the address of each word in the list recorded in the word immediately preceding it in the list structure. The name of a list is the address of the first word of the list. A list has the following form:

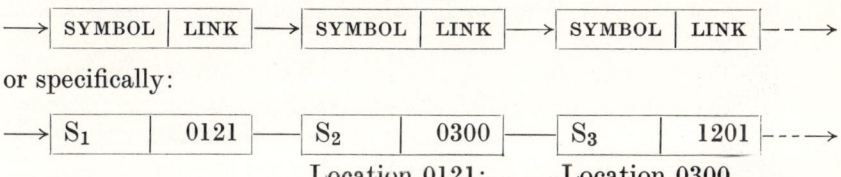

or specifically:

$\longrightarrow$ | S_1 | 0121 | — | S_2 | 0300 | — | S_3 | 1201 | $\dashrightarrow$

Location 0121:   Location 0300

(f) A list structure is a list with all its sublists and their sublists, etc. Any word on a list may refer to another list which is then a sublist of the given list. Figure 6 illustrates a list structure.

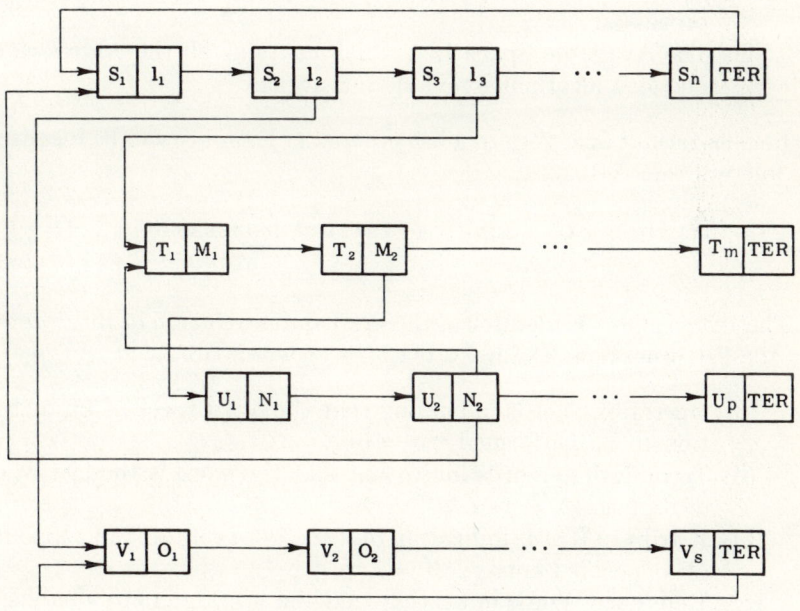

Fig. 6. A knotted list structure.

(g) A list structure is said to be a knotted list structure [34] if each list in the structure can be used as the sublist of any other list including itself.

(h) There are special lists which are essential as control lists to a list processor. Three such special lists appear frequently enough in list processors to be identified generically here as:

(i) The Communications List which serves a function analogous to that of the accumulator in a typical computer. It may be used as the operand for any list procedure. For example, if one wants to copy a word from list L_1 onto list L_2, then one first copies it from list L_1 onto the Communications List and from there to list L_2.

(ii) The Pointer List is a tracking list which points at any time to the word on a given list which is being processed. Its existence permits the procedures of a list processor to refer only to the top word in a list and then by advancing the Pointer List successively down the list being processed to perform the required manipulation on each word on the list in turn. The Pointer List permits processing to be interrupted at any time with later continuation at the interrupted point simply by referral to the Pointer List which has been tracking the on-going processes.

(iii) The Available Space List which contains all the addresses of memory locations available for storage.

(i) The format of a word in a list processing language can be idealized as follows:

ID	Q	LINK	OPERATION	OPERAND ADDRESS

The ID specifies the identity of the word and how it is to be interpreted by the list processor. Examples of types of words are:

(i) Operation Words indicating that the word specifies an operation to be performed; ID = OPP.
(ii) Termination Words indicating that the word is the last word of its list; ID = TER.
(iii) Attribute Words indicating that the word contains an attribute of a specified entity; ID = ATT.
(iv) Reference Words indicating that the word refers to a sublist; ID = REF.
(v) Data Words indicating that the word contains data such as decimal numbers and alphanumeric information; ID = DEC, BIN, ALP, etc.

The Q specifies a referencing technique known as indirection which indicates how to determine the address of the operand on which an operation is to be performed. The term "indirection" comes from the inherent ability to refer to a list indirectly. The indirection capability is one of the most powerful techniques of list processors. It can best be explained by example:

> If $Q = 0$ then the Operand Address field contains the address of the operand.
> If $Q = 1$ then the Operand Address field contains the address of the word in which to find the address of the operand.
> If $Q = 2$ then the Operand Address field contains the address of the word in which to find the address of the word which contains the address of the operand.

etc.

The Link field gives the address of the next word in the list.

The Operation field gives the symbolic name of the operation to be performed. The operation generally refers to a macro-instruction.

The Operand Address field references the address of the list on which the operation is to be performed, modified as indicated by the indirection specified in the Q fields. A list processing language word usually is comprised of two or three machine words.

In addition to the essential features of list processors listed above, there are certain others which deserve mention here. The erasure problem was a troublesome one in that the list structure imposed on the computer memory makes it difficult to determine what memory locations are available, particularly when the Available Space List is empty. One of the better methods for resolution of this problem is the "Garbage Collection" technique originated for IPL-V by J. McCarthy, now at Stanford University. Nothing is done until the Available Space List is empty. Then the program list structures required for the problem in hand are traced through by following the links specified. Each list word encountered in this tracing problem is tagged; both data and instruction words will, of course, be encountered. After the list structure has been completely traced through, then a linear scan of the entire memory is performed; and all words not tagged are placed on the Available Space List.

Some of the more common list processing macro-instructions are listed below in order to provide an indication of the types of manipulations which may be performed on data by list processors. These macro-instructions can be considered as comprising the reserved identifier lexical subset of the list processing language vocabulary. Examples are:

> preserve list L,
> restore list L,
> change the contents of a given field of the nonreference word of list L to zero,

move the first word of the Communications List to list L and place it just prior to the first nonreference word,

move the bottom word of the Communications List to the bottom of list L,

copy the first nonreference word from list L onto the Communications List,

exchange the positions of two consecutive words on list L,

find the attribute on the sublist S referred to by list L,

create a list S and put its name on list L,

erase list L,

erase list L and all its sublists,

branch if list L is empty,

branch unconditionally,

branch if the ID of the first word of the Communications List is not the same as the ID of the first nonreference word of list L,

execute list L,

execute the machine language routine at address R,

execute the first word of list L,

advance the Pointer List linearly along the list to which it points,

advance the Pointer List structurally along the list to which it points, etc.

8.3 List Processor Organization

Having gained some familiarity with list processor features in Sections 8.1 and 8.2, the list processor organization can now be described meaningfully. A list processor has three major components.

The first major component is the load program with functions completely analogous to load programs of conventional and syntax-directed processors.

The second major component is the translator which takes the hardware language statement of the source problem and translates it into symbolic machine language using simple semantic-syntactic translation tables.

The third major component is the interpreter which takes the symbolic machine language output of the translator as its input. It then proceeds down the Program list structure, interprets the macro-instruction it encounters, finds the data list on which it is to operate using indirections, fetches the machine language subroutines referenced by the macro-instruction, and executes the machine instructions requested. The output of the interpreter is the solution of the problem stated in the list processing language.

The use of a list processing language requires from three to eight times as much computer memory as would the solution of the same problem stated in other procedure-oriented languages. However, as emphasized in earlier sections, the problems for which list processing languages were designed cannot be reasonably solved using other existing types of procedure-oriented languages.

9. Evaluation of Programming Language Processors

A review of the evaluation efforts thus far attempted shows that until quite recently the evaluation of programming language processors had not proceeded in any methodical or organized fashion. In many cases, the evaluation considered both the language and the processor in a completely uncoordinated manner so that it was impossible to isolate the language from the processor. The first evaluations attempted in a scientific manner were initiated in the 1961–1962 era. One of these was an analytic evaluation, that is, a paper and pencil enumeration of the features of the processors and the languages in such a way as to permit comparison. The second was experimental in nature. It involved the programming of the same problem in the several languages being compared and running of the problem after compilation by the several processors under review. Neither attempt was really successful in that there were so many variables introduced that the results were inconclusive. Both were initiated by DOD governmental groups. It was obvious from these first attempts that any evaluation depended on the prior establishment of measures of effectiveness, of evaluation criteria, and of the development of measurable parameters, and on the separation of programming language processor from programming language [53]. Opler of the Computer Usage Corporation was probably the first to attempt to invoke such measures and criteria in evaluation; and the listing of measurable parameters of language and processors which he derived in conjunction with the author as early as 1962 is listed in Table VI for historical interest.

The analytic and experimental approaches to evaluation have already been mentioned. By now, there is sufficient experience in the use of several languages and of a multitude of processors to permit an empirical approach to evaluation. This involves merely the collection of data concerning operating, programming, and management experience in a manner which will permit statistical interpretation. Of the three approaches—analytic, experimental, and empirical—the analytic approach appears most amenable to prosecution at the present time. Shaw, SDC [59] has concentrated on the analytic approach and has worked out a questionnaire which attempts to make explicit and subject to quantitative measure all the more important features of procedure-

TABLE VI

MEASURABLE PARAMETERS FOR PROGRAMMING LANGUAGES AND
PROGRAMMING LANGUAGE PROCESSORS

A. The Programming Language
   1. Syntactic Properties
      (a) Formal construction aspects:
         (1) Clarity and simplicity of definition
         (2) Adequate syntactic specification
         (3) Avoidance of confusion between literals and comments, e.g., good vocabulary construction
         (4) Ability to add new definitions and new features to language
         (5) Ease of translation to other languages
         (6) Freedom from ambiguities
      (b) Readability—writability:
         (1) Optional (ignored) words
         (2) Optimization of character set
         (3) Avoidance of mixed dependency between symbols and written formats
      (c) Reliability:
         (1) Optimization of identifier lengths
         (2) Self-checking features
         (3) Avoidance of similar symbols (e.g., —, hyphen, or dash)
         (4) Minimization of special punching or typing requirements for production of the hardware language, e.g., multiple punches, half-spaces, etc.
      (d) Learnability:
         (1) Familiar character set
         (2) Familiar verb-operator set
         (3) Minimization of number of rules for statement construction
   2. Semantic Properties
      (a) Classification of language:
         (1) Problem-oriented (theorem proving)
         (2) Passive or goal-oriented (report generator)
         (3) Procedure-oriented (ALGOL, etc.)
      (b) Design (or selection) considerations:
         (1) Area of application (IR, scientific, etc.)
         (2) Level of user (novice, researcher, etc.)
         (3) Type of material (files, lists, trees, etc.)
         (4) Typical actions (compute, reorder, display, etc.)
      (c) Balance between size and scope of a language and that of its associated processor
B. General Features of the Programming Language Processor
   1. Logical capability
   2. Input/output capability
   3. Allocation capability
   4. Recursiveness

oriented languages and their associated processors. The questions are subdivided as follows:

(a) The Programming Language
  (i) Identity
  (ii) Applicability
  (iii) Origin
  (iv) Compatibility
  (v) Capability
    (1) Data type and structure
    (2) Operations
    (3) Decisions
    (4) Loops
    (5) Subroutines
    (6) Input and output
  (vi) Utility
    (1) Readability
    (2) Learnability
    (3) Usability
(b) The Programming Language Processor:
  (i) Identity
  (ii) Implementation
  (iii) Inputs
  (iv) Operation
  (v) Outputs
  (vi) Performance

where over one hundred questions are asked.

Neither the experimental nor empirical approaches have yet been exploited or developed in any useful or scientific manner. One must admit that as of today there is no meaningful or reproducible method for evaluating either programming languages or programming language processors. Anyone faced with selection of either must make his decision based primarily on qualitative descriptive data and on observations of competent, trusted individuals.

10. Concluding Remarks

It is difficult to predict the events to be anticipated in the future development of programming language processors and concomitantly, of programming languages. Certainly, the trend up to the present has been made evident in the preceding nine sections of the article. It does appear that question-answering languages will be concentrated upon heavily. With their reliance on mathematical linguistic techniques, the bridge between linguistics and programming language development will be strengthened. The question-answering languages, along with the evolvement of display languages, will advance the much-needed development of problem-oriented languages. These latter two types of languages, in addition to control languages, will comprise most of the problem-oriented languages for the next three to five years. Those additional problem-oriented languages which are designed will come primarily from universities for specialized applications such as mechanical engineering, architectural design, and musical composition.

Different grammatical models will be attempted for programming languages, and different techniques of syntactic analysis will be tried within language processors in order to allow programming languages to more nearly approximate natural language in vocabulary and in semantic considerations. Semantic models will receive as much attention as syntactic models have in the past. Means for allowing semantic ambiguities will be devised which are not based merely on the elimination of semantic synonyms.

There have been some [58], and there will continue to be, new computer designs attempted that will implement in hardware the more common macro instructions and procedural statements found in procedure-oriented languages. Certainly if basic procedure-oriented languages can be implemented in hardware, then problem-oriented languages can be more easily constructed than is now possible based on existing computer designs.

List processing techniques will evolve rapidly and will become operationally feasible as soon as memory costs decrease to one-fourth their existing level. When list processing techniques do become economically feasible, then most machineable data bases will be list-structured. Whole new concepts of data processing will result with a consequent rapid approach to more intelligent machine behavior.

The design of procedure-oriented languages must be expanded in concept to include multicomputer systems, parallel processing, and more effective time-sharing. The sequential processing concept must not continue to dominate procedure-oriented language processor design.

If distributed logic considerations, iterative computer concepts, and associative techniques of data processing can be advanced, then the need for procedure-oriented languages will be much reduced; and problem-oriented languages will be furthered.

Evaluation techniques must be developed before information processing can ever approach the status of a science. Formal educational institutions must emphasize evaluative methods, and management must be more insistent upon their use [19].

Standardization will come about in the areas of specific codes for specific subject areas, in terminology, and in methods of language and processor description. The cries for standardization of processing languages and of language processors themselves will disappear, due primarily to the tireless efforts of a few in the programming sciences who have continuously pointed out the dangers of such attempted standardization.

The programming aspects of data processing systems implementation and, in particular, the design of languages and processors to make possible the more effective use of Electronic Data Processing (EDP) equipment will continue to be the most costly. The resultant need for more types and better designs of programming languages and programming language processors will increase for at least the next five years.

References

1. Backus, J., The syntax and semantics of the proposed international algebraic language of the Zürich ACM-GAMM Conference. *Proc. 1st Intern. Conf. Information Processing, UNESCO, Paris,* 1959. pp. 125–132, R. Oldenbourg, Munich and Butterworth, London, 1960.
2. Bar-Hillel, Y., Perles, M., and Shamir, E., On formal properties of simple phrase structure grammars. Applied Logic Branch, Hebrew Univ. of Jerusalem, Tech. Rept. No. 4 (1960). *Z. Phonetik, Sprachwiss. Kommunikationsforsch.* **14**, 143–173 (1961).
3. Barnett, M. P., and Futrelle, R. P., Syntactic analysis by digital computer. *Commun. Assoc. Computing Machinery* **5**, 515–526 (1962).
4. Berman, R., Sharp, J., and Sturges, L., Syntactical charts of COBOL 61. *Commun. Assoc. Computing Machinery* **5**, 260 (1962).
5. Biggs, J. M., and Logcher, R. D., STRESS: A problem-oriented language for structural engineering. Project MAC, MIT Rept. No. MAC-TR-6 (1964).
6. Bobrow, D. G., Natural language input for a computer problem solving system. Project MAC, MIT Rept. No. MAC-TR-1 (1964).
7. Bobrow, D. G., Syntactic analysis of English by computer—a survey. *Proc. Fall JCC* **24**, 365–387 (1963).
8. Brooker, R. A., and Morris, D., A general translation program for phrase-structure languages. *J. Assoc. Computing Machinery* **9**, 1–10 (1962).
9. Brown, S. A., Drayton, C. E., and Mittman, B., A description of the APT language. *Commun. Assoc. Computing Machinery* **6**, 649–658 (1963).
10. Cantor, D. C., On the ambiguity problem of Backus systems, *J. Assoc. Computing Machinery* **9**, 477–479 (1962).
11. Cheatham, T. E., Jr., and Sattley, K., Syntax-directed compiling. *AFIPS Conf. Proc.* **25**, 31–57 (1964).
12. Chomsky, N., On the notion "Rule of Grammar." *Proc. Symp. Appl. Math. 1960,* **12**, (1961).
13. Chomsky, N., On certain formal properties of grammar. *Inform. Control* **2**, 137–167 (1959).
14. Chomsky, N., *Syntactic structures.* Mouton & Co., The Hague, Netherlands, 1957.

15. Chomsky, N., and Schutzenberger, M. P., The algebraic theory of context-free languages. In *Computer Programming and Formal Systems* (Hirschberg and Brafforts eds.), pp. 118–161. North-Holland, Amsterdam, Netherlands, 1963.
16. COBOL *1961—Revised Specifications for a Common Business-Oriented Language.* U.S. Govt. Printing Office, Washington, D. C., 1961.
17. Compiler organization, **4**, Issue 1, (1961): *Commun. Assoc. Computing Machinery.*
18. Craig, J. A., Pruett, J. and Thompson, F., DEACON breadboard grammar. GE TEMPO Rept. No. RM 64TMP-14. DIA Contract USAF 19(628)-3385 (1964).
19. Davis, R. M., Classification and evaluation of information system design techniques. *Information System Sciences, Proc. 2nd Congr.* pp. 77–84, Spartan Books, Washington, D.C., 1965.
20. Floyd, R. W., On the non-existence of a phrase structure grammar for ALGOL 60. *Commun. Assoc. Computing Machinery* **5**, 483–484 (1962).
21. Floyd, R. W., On ambiguity in phrase structure languages. *Commun. Assoc. Computing Machinery* **5**, 526 and 534 (1962).
22. Floyd, R. W., Bounded context syntactic analysis. *Commun. Assoc. Computing Machinery* **7**, 62–65 (1964).
23. Gilbert, P., On the syntax of algorithmic languages. Teledyne Systems Corp. Rept. under RADC contract AF 30(602)–2924 (1964).
24. Gorn, S., Specification languages for mechanical languages and their processors—A baker's dozen. *Commun. Assoc. Computing Machinery* **9**, 532–542 (1961).
25. Gorn, S., Detection of generative ambiguities in context-free mechanical languages. *J. Assoc. Computing Machinery* **10**, 196–208 (1963).
26. Gorn, S., Introductory speech: Common symbolic language for computers. *Proc. 1st Intern. Conf. Information Processing, UNESCO, Paris,* 1959. J. Oldenbourg, Munich and Butterworth, London, 1960.
27. Gorn, S., *The Treatment of Ambiguity and Paradox in Mechanical Languages.* Office of Computer Res. and Educ., Univ. of Pennsylvania, Philadelphia, 1961.
28. Gorn, S., Mechanical pragmatics: A time-motion study of a miniature mechanical linguistic system. *Commun. Assoc. Computing Machinery* **6**, 576 (1963).
29. Halstead, M. H., *Machine-Independent Computer Programming.* Spartan Books, Washington, D.C., 1962.
30. *Harvard Summer School, Lecture Notes for a Course in Language Data Processing (August 10–21, 1964).* Harvard Univ., Cambridge, Massachusetts, 1964.
31. Haverty, J. P., and Patrick R. L., Programming languages and standardization in command and control. RAND Corp. Memo No. RM-3447-PR, Santa Monica, California (1963).
32. Hayes, D. G., Grouping and dependency theory, RAND Corp Rept., Santa Monica, California (1960).
33. Holt, A. W., A mathematical and applied investigation of tree structures for computer syntactic analysis. Ph.D. Thesis, Univ. of Pennsylvania (1963).
34. Hsu, R. W., Characteristics of four list-processing languages. NBS Rept. No. 8163. Natl. Bur. Std., Washington, D.C. (1963).
35. Huskey, H. D., An introduction to procedure-oriented languages. *Advan. Computers* **5**, 349–377 (1964).
36. Huskey, H. D., Love, R., and Wirth, N., A syntactic description of B C NELIAC. *Commun. Assoc. Computing Machinery,* 367–374 (1963).

37. Irons, E. T., A syntax-directed compiler for Algol-60. *Commun. Assoc. Computing Machinery* **4**, 51 (1961).
38. Irons, E. T., The structure and use of the syntax-directed compiler. *Ann. Rev. Autom. Programming* **3**, 207–227 (1963).
39. Iverson, K. E., *A Programming Language*. Wiley, New York, 1962.
40. Joynes, M. L., and Lehmann, W. P., Linguistic theories underlying the work of various MIT groups. *Linguistics* **8**, October (1964).
41. Kay, M., Rules of interpretation: An approach to the problem of computation in the semantics of natural language. *Pro. Munich Congr. IFIP*, 79–83 (1962).
42. Kesner, O., Bibliography: Algol references. *Computer Rev.* **3**, 37–38 (1962).
43. Knuth, D. E., A history of writing compilers. *Computers Autom.* **11**, Issue 12 (1962).
44. Knuth, D. E., Backus Normal Form vs. Backus Naur Form (Letters to the Editor). *Commun. Assoc. Computing Machinery* **7**, 735–736 (1964).
45. Kuno, S., and Oettinger, A. G., Multiple-path syntactic analyzer. *Proc. Munich Congr.* IFIP, 1962. pp. 306–312.
46. Lamb, S. M., Outline of stratificational grammar. Univ of California, Berkeley, Rept. to the Natl. Sci. Foundation (1962).
47. Landweber, P. S., Three theorems on phase structure grammars of type 1. *Inform. Control* **6**, 131–136 (1963).
48. Lehmann, W. P., Computational linguistics: Procedures and problems. Linguistics Res. Center, Univ. of Texas Rept. No. LRC 65 WA-1 (1963).
49. Lukasiewicz, J., *Aristotle's Syllogistic from the Standpoint of Modern Formal Logic*. Oxford Univ. Press (Clarendon), London and New York, 1951.
50. McCracken, D. D., *A Guide to Algol Programming*. Wiley, New York, 1962.
51. Newell, A., Tonge, F., Feigenbaum, E., Shaw, J. C., and Simon, H., Information processing language V manual. RAND Corp. Rept. P-1897, Santa Monica, California (1960).
52. Oettinger, A. G., Automatic syntactic analysis and the pushdown store. *Proc. Symp. Appl. Math* **12**, (1961).
53. Opler, A., *et al*. Automatic translation of programs from one computer to another. *Proc. Munich Congr. IFIP* 1962.
54. Postal, P., Constituent structure: A study of contemporary models of syntactic description. *Intern. J Am. Linguistics, Part IV* **30**, No. 1 (1964).
55. Ross, D. T., The design and use of the Apt language for automatic programming of numerically controlled machine tools. *Proc. Computer Applications Symp.* 1959 pp. 80–99.
56. Ross, D. T., An algorithmic theory of language. Electronic Systems Lab., MIT Rept. No. ESL-TM-156 (1962).
57. Samelson, K., Programming languages and their processing. *Proc. Munich Congr. IFIP* 1962 pp. 487–492.
58. Schauer, R. F., and Mullery, A. P., The logic design of Adam, a problem-oriented symbol processor. IBM Rept. prepared for AFCRL Contract No. AF19(628)-1621 (1963).
59. Shaw, C. J., An outline questionnaire for describing and evaluating procedure-oriented programming languages and their compilers. Systems Dev. Corp., Santa Monica, Calif., SDC Working Paper No. FN-6821/000/00 (1962).
60. Intl. Standards Org., Tech Comm. 97, Subcomm. 5, Survey of programming languages and processors, *Commun. Assoc. Computing Machinery* **6**, 93–99 (1963).

61. Taylor, W., Turner, L., and Waychoff, R., A syntactical chart of ALGOL 60. *Commun. Assoc. Computing Machinery* **5**, 393 (1962).
62. Thompson, F. B., Craig, J., Gibbons, G., Gwynn, J., and Pruett, J. DEACON breadboard summary. GE TEMPO Rept. No. RM64TMP-9, ONR Contract Nonr-4101(00) (1964).
63. Thompson, F. B., The semantic interface in man-machine communication. GE TEMPO Rept. No. RM 63TMP-35, ONR Contract Nonr-4101(00) (1963).
64. Thompson, F. B., The application and implementation of DEACON type systems. GE TEMPO Rept. No. RM64TMP-11, ONR Contract Nonr-4101(00) (1964).
65. Warshall, S., A syntax-directed generator. *Proc. EJCC* **20**, 295–305 (1961).
66. Warshall, S., *A Syntax Directed Generator* (presented at Eastern Joint Computer Conf., December 1961). Computer Assoc., Inc., Woburn, Massachusetts, (copyright by AFIPS).
67. Yngve, V. H., A model and an hypothesis for language structure. MIT Res. Lab. for Electronics Tech Rept. No. 369 (1960).
68. Yngve, V. H., Sammet, J., Naur, P., Cunningham, J., Heising, W., Newell, A., Shaw, C. J., and Halstead, M., Towards better documentation of programming languages (ALGOL 60, COBOL, COMIT, FORTRAN, IPL-V, JOVIAL, NELIAC), *Commun. Assoc. Computing Machinery*, **6**, 76–92 (1963).

The Man-Machine Combination for Computer-Assisted Copy Editing

WAYNE A. DANIELSON

The University of North Carolina at Chapel Hill
Chapel Hill, North Carolina

1. Introduction 181
2. Computerized Line Justification 182
3. Computerized Hyphenation Programs 183
4. Advantages Claimed for Computerized Typesetting 187
5. Editing and Proofreading in Existing Systems 187
6. Editing in Experimental Systems 188
7. An Experimental Edition Planner 190
8. Conclusions 192
   References 192

1. Introduction

The printing and publishing industry was, in the early sixties, better prepared than some other industries for the introduction of the computer into the production process. This was because many plants had been using punched paper tape to operate line-casting machines for ten years or more. Employees were accustomed to preparing paper tape as input to machines. No great mental shift was involved, therefore, when punched paper tape was prepared for input to a computer and—moments later—another tape emerged ready for the machines in the back shop.

What happened *in* the computer, however, meant approximately 40% reduction in production time in the preparation of straight matter—because the computer, instead of a human operator, justified each line of type [1]. Beyond the immediate accomplishment, also, publishers (and printers) could see a time coming when the entire printing process might be automated [2].

As J. H. Perry, Jr., president of Perry Publications, Inc., West Palm Beach, Florida, put it:

"I can visualize a composing room of the future that will automatically compose a page in the newspaper starting from a typewritten page to a finished page without any human hands touching it until it is finished and ready for the press" [3].

In an even more utopian vision, L. B. Doyle foresaw ". . . multistory buildings in which computers and people are welded into a complex organism which feeds on verbal inputs from the outside world and emits an integrated output to which all elements of the system are able to contribute" [4].

Although some attention will be paid to hypothetical future systems, the main purpose of this article is to describe the *present* state of computer-based automation in the publishing industry. Particular emphasis will be placed on the relation of the editor to the computer in the production process.

2. Computerized Line Justification

Justification is the process of making a line tight in the column width being used. It is accomplished by placing extra spaces between words if the letters do not quite fill out the line or by slightly reducing the amount of space between words in order to get the last word into the line. Equal and even spacing is the goal, but it is not necessary to have exactly the same amount of spacing between the words if the words *appear* to be equally spaced. Insufficient spacing causes words to seem to "run together" and makes the line difficult to read. Too generous spacing causes "rivers" of white on the page which also reduce legibility [5].

Justification is ordinarily performed in machine systems by an operator who increases or decreases spaces between words (and sometimes inserts thin spaces within words) and who hyphenates words when necessary.

Obviously, programming a computer to adjust spacing is easier than programming one to hyphenate words. Indeed, one special purpose computer, the LINASEC, handles spacing only. If it finds that it must hyphenate a word in order to fill a line properly, it flashes a light to attract the attention of an operator who divides the word and then returns control to the machine [6].

At least one American newspaper has elected to forego hyphenation altogether and fill lines solely by spacing. Experimentation has shown that some space is wasted in this way and the appearance of some lines is bizarre, but readers are apparently quite unobservant (or tolerant) of such typographical irregularities.[1] Indeed, one major American

---

[1]See, however, the discussion of hyphenless justification in the article by W. R. Bozman in this volume.

newspaper, the *Denver Post*, has been published recently with an unjustified flush-left line and has had relatively few complaints.

Conservative spokesmen for the printing industry are understandably cool to such developments, arguing that "newer and poorer standards" of printing are being introduced by engineers and programmers. Speaking specifically of the elimination of hyphenation on an 11-pica column (the standard width of an American newspaper column today), Alexander Lawson says with some bitterness, "Such a solution would appear to run counter to all precepts of legibility." He concludes, "We need to attempt, at the very least, an improvement in quality in addition to an increase in production" [7].

Most computer programs for justification employ a subtractive process. The first information input specifies the type face to be used, the point size of the type (there are 72 points in one inch), and the width of the column. As characters are received, their widths are looked up in a table and then subtracted from the total width of the column. Each character, punctuation mark, and space is counted. When the number of units exceeds the capacity of a line, the last word is dropped and the computer attempts to fill the line either by expanding normal space bands between words or by placing additional spacing between words. It may also insert thin spaces between the letters of the longest word in an attempt to justify the line [1].

Although the spacing program will always fill a line eventually, the result will not necessarily be attractive. In other words, a hyphenation routine is needed to see whether the last word in the line can be split at a point which will help fill the line neatly.

3. Computerized Hyphenation Programs

Programming a computer to hyphenate words has proved to be a formidable task. The first programs went into commercial use in the United States in 1962. However, as recently as April 22, 1965, the first 50 transmissions on the Associated Press' afternoon Teletypesetter A wire (justified by an IBM program) contained these incorrect hyphenations:

Armeni-ans   Ir-ene
bludge-oned   li-teracy
Coqui-tlam (place name,   per-imeter
    British Columbia)   param-ount
cru-isers   rep-eated
devo-ted   spirit-ual
eleg-antly   sto-ry
implementi-ng   squa-dron

Why haven't errors been eliminated by now? One reason for the difficulty, of course, is that many hyphenation points in English have been determined more by literary tradition than by logic; there are many exceptions to the "rules" which do exist. It is very difficult to program for all the exceptions in a language which probably contains between 500,000 and 600,000 words. Then, too, the dictionaries used as "standards" often differ among themselves. Some take a "hard" line on division points while others are more tolerant. A program which gives acceptable results in the United States may give unacceptable results in England [8]. All in all, it is not only extremely difficult to write a hyphenation program, it is extremely difficult to test its validity. It has been estimated that skilled printers on American newspapers are correct in about 80% of their hyphenations. Developers of computer programs for hyphenation claim accuracies in the nineties. Both estimates are somewhat suspect for the reasons given earlier. It is this reviewer's opinion, however, that the errors made by a computer—even though they may occur less often—are likely to be more *noticeable* than the errors made by a human operator. Most printers for example would not split bludgeoned between the "e" and the "o" as the AP's computer did, nor would they take the "rep" break instead of the "re" break in repeated. In other words, most judges would probably still vote for hyphenation by human beings in a quality control test because of the "badness" of the computer errors when compared with the badness of errors made by the human operators.

How do computers split words? One of the American pioneers in computer applications to printing, the *Palm Beach Post-Times*, has adopted a dictionary approach to hyphenation [1]. That is, lists of some 25,000 words, with all possible hyphenations indicated, are kept on four duplicate reels of magnetic tape which can be read forward and backward at 10,000 characters per second. The dictionary is organized according to frequency of usage of initial letters. The most-accessed letter, "s," is in the middle of the tape and after executing a search for a word the tape returns to this position. Search times are fairly slow in computer terms, the average word being located in about one second. If a word is not found, it is stripped of certain endings—"s," "ed," "ing,"—and searched for again. If it is not found the second time, the word is split after the third, fifth, or seventh letter—supposedly good positions for hitting a true hyphenation point by chance.

The major difficulty with the dictionary approach—at least when the textual matter is news—is that the dictionary must be constantly updated to handle new names and new places in the news. If this updating is not built into the program as a matter of course, then the dictionary may rather quickly get out of date and give poor results. For example, in June 1964 when the author was in West Palm Beach, he found the newsroom chuckling over the latest "sin" of the computer's hyphenation routine. A previously infrequently encountered name had swiftly become important on the American scene and the computer—unable to find the name in its memory tapes—was hyphenating it "GOL-DWATER" with distressing frequency. Needless to say, the name with its proper hyphenation points was soon added to the dictionary.

An alternative to the dictionary approach to hyphenation is to use a "logical" approach. Certain prefixes and suffixes, for example, can be checked for and used with fair reliability as hyphenation points if they are present in the words to be split. A surprising percentage of hyphenations can be made in this way. Similarly, a large number of English words can be split between the double identical consonants which they contain—mat-ter, bal-let, mil-lion, etc.

If the words do not contain these "easy" hyphenation points, however, other approaches are needed. Published reports of logical programs sometimes become rather vague at this point because the real heart of each program (and the real commercial value) is here. One description of the IBM program in use on the Oklahoma City *Oklahoman and Times* is as follows: "The last word in the line is syllabified according to vowel and consonant patterns. Various techniques are employed in using letter sequences as a key to division, including table look-ups in which the cumulative effect of any three letters in the alphabet can be weighed and various paths taken" [1]. Another description says that the 1620 "scans a special hyphenation probability table to determine the best dividing point" [9]. A description of the NCR 315 system in operation as the Orlando *Sentinel-Star* says, in part, that hyphenation points are determined by asking the following questions:

"Is the word long enough to consider for hyphenation? Does the word contain an imbedded hyphen, capital, or punctuation? Is the word numeric? Does the word contain double identical consonants (pattern)? Does the word contain suffixes or prefixes? Does the word contain 'glottals'? What is the vowel-consonant pattern of the word?" [10].

The logical system devised by the National Computer Analysts, Inc. (the system used by Control Data computers) is perhaps representative. It is based upon: (1) the recognition and isolation of common word endings, (2) division of root words based on a specific set of rules and their exceptions, and (3) word division by recognition of group patterns of vowels and consonants [11].

Before any of the three methods is used, the program masks apostrophes and the letters S and T at the end of the word where S is a plural or possessive and T is a contraction. Consonants at the beginning of the word are also masked. If less than four letters remain after the masking, no attempt is made to hyphenate the word.

The search for splitting points begins at the right-hand end of the word. The last three letters are compared against a table of common three-letter endings. If no match is found, the last two letters are compared against common two-letter endings. Normal division points are assumed for each ending. For example, for the ending *ish*, the normal hyphenation point is XXX-ISH where XXX represents letters of the root word preceding the ending (for example, VAN-ISH). Certain specific letters preceding the common ending may require a different hyphenation point. An example would be VAN-QUISH (-XXISH). The program takes into account up to three letters preceding the common endings as exceptions to the normal division points, as follows:

    XXX-
    XX-X
    X-XX
    -XXX
    XX-
    X-X
    -XX
    X-
    -X

Each common ending is accompanied by a list of its exceptions and appropriate hyphenation points for each.

If no splitting point is found by the foregoing method the root word is searched to see whether certain rules of hyphenation are met. For example:

(1) Glottals (*L* or *R* preceded by *B*, *C*, *D*, *F*, *G*, *K*, *P*, or *T*) are carried as one consonant.

(2) Allophones—an *S* preceded and followed by a consonant has the hyphen preceding it. (The girl was CON-SCIOUS.)

(3) Double consonants—a root word is divided between like consonants.

(4) Letter *X*—root words containing *X* are hyphenated after the *X*. (TEX-AS, EX-TREME.)

(5) Special pairs—*CH*, *GH*, *PH*, *SH*, *TH*, and *WH* are considered as single consonants (GRA-PHIC, MO-THER).

If no hyphenation point is found after the examination of the root word, vowels and consonants are examined for the pattern CVC (consonant-vowel-consonant). If this pattern is found, the hyphen is placed before the initial consonant (-CVC). A series of consonants is treated as a single consonant. The ending letters of DIAPHRAGM (CCCVCC) for example, are condensed into the basic pattern cvc. If the cvc pattern cannot be found, the word is not hyphenated.

The logical programs offer the obvious advantage of being faster than the dictionary look-up systems. The NCR logical program claims output of 3 newspaper lines per second, the RCA logical program, 10 lines per second [*10, 12*]. They may be better, also, at handling new or "unexpected" words, proper nouns, etc. They have the disadvantage of making drastic mistakes over and over again unless an exception word list is built into the program.

Several of the recent hyphenation-justification programs offered to the printing industry might be classified as "mixed" types; that is, they use a logical program for speed, and a dictionary look-up program to take care of words which do not conform to the standard patterns. Their accuracy levels are determined jointly by the ingenuity and completeness of the logical system and by the size of the exception dictionary. C. J. Duncan, a British leader in computer applications to the printing industry, estimates that, ". . . by logical rule alone some 20 per cent of the vocabulary needs to be in an exception store if 100 per cent acceptable splits are desired" [*8*].

4. Advantages Claimed for Computerized Typesetting

Lest the over-all picture of computers in typesetting be regarded as somewhat dark, the following real advantages claimed by publishers should be cited:

(1) *Keyboarding of stories is faster and more accurate since operators are no longer concerned with justification and hyphenation.* C. B. Kelley of Palm Beach estimates, for example, that clerk typists can perforate tape at 500 to 780 lines per hour in the computerized setup in contrast with the old rate of 350 lines per hour of hyphenated and justified tape [*1*].

(2) *Loose and tight lines are eliminated by the computer programs.* This means that the typesetting machines into which the paper tapes are fed operate at higher speeds with fewer breakdowns and stops.

(3) *The computer output is more uniform in appearance.* This means that the final page of the book or newspaper is cleaner and more legible. Often, the computer packs more content into the available space than human operators can.

5. Editing and Proofreading in Existing Systems

Most editing in current operating systems in the printing industry is done *before* the copy is punched on tape. For a time, the *Los Angeles Times* experimented with having reporters produce a punched paper tape at the time they were writing their stories. Then editors had to prepare a correction tape which went with the reporter's tape to the computer. This experiment has now been largely abandoned and regular typists have been hired to punch tape on copy produced and edited in the normal way [13].

Since computers make few typographical errors, proofreading in the normal sense has declined in importance. The major new task is checking for lines with poor hyphenations. When a bad split is encountered, the line is reset, usually by an operator using a line-casting machine. In several shops proofreading has been virtually eliminated and the poor hyphenations (as well as mistakes produced by the tape-puncher) are simply allowed to go into print.

6. Editing in Experimental Systems

It is clear that some of the tasks which the editor now performs with a pencil, scissors, and paste pot on hard copy could also be performed electronically by an appropriately instructed computer. Although there is little reason to develop such systems now, they will become important as the publishing industry moves towards more complete automation. Experimentation is proceeding along two lines—toward the development of editing systems which depend primarily upon current general-purpose machines and rather elaborate *programs* and toward the development of editing systems which depend primarily upon new special-purpose subsidiary machines and associated programs.

John Diebold has suggested that the editor of the future will see copy displayed on TV screens that will be a part of every editorial desk. Deletions will be made with the use of a light pencil and additions will be made with an electric typewriter. Pages will be dummied on additional screens and committed to print automatically when the editor touches the final approval button. His is, essentially, a hardware approach to editing [14].

A data display subsystem which might have a place on such a future editor's desk was described in the October 1963, issue of the *IBM Journal of Research and Development* [15]. The DDS is capable of displaying on one tube a page of 4000 characters. The display permits real-time observation of data changes introduced by the operator through the extensive editing functions built into the system.

The basic unit of control is a single bit called the "X-bit" which is associated with each character of storage. It is used to denote the next character position that will be filled if a character is entered. Usually, therefore, only one character position in the entire memory will have a logical 1 in the X-bit position at any one time. On the screen the X-bit is displayed by a horizontal line if the character space is empty or by increased intensity if the space contains a character.

A character may be erased by positioning the X-bit properly and then depressing the blank character key. Characters may be inserted by moving the X-bit to the point at which the insertion is desired, depressing the INSERT key, and typing in the missing characters. All following characters automatically shift to the right. A DELETE AND CLOSE mode is also provided to delete regions of characters and close up the intervening space.

A somewhat similar approach to editing is being employed in the PENELOPE project (Pitt Natural Language Process) at the University of Pittsburgh [16]. There a specialized computer language designed to be closer to the natural language of the user is being developed in connection with a large-scale man-machine editing project.

An experimental approach to editing which relies mainly on programming a large general-purpose machine is the one developed at the University of North Carolina Computation Center for the UNIVAC 1105 [17]. The research has been supported in part by the Associated Press and uses as input already justified Teletypesetter tape.

Typically, all stories for an entire day are input at one time. As each character enters, it is converted to its corresponding computer printer code. Each line of the story is numbered. The dashes at the end of the story (- - -) initiate a story numbering routine. All transmissions are stored on a magnetic tape which is printed on an off-line high-speed printer.

Working with the print-out, the editor selects the stories he wishes to use, writes headlines for them, indicates lines he wishes to cut, prepares insertions, and writes directions for merging stories. His instructions are punched on cards as shown in Table I.

In operation, information from control cards is first stored in the computer's memory. Then the news tape is searched for the transmission number of the first story the editor wishes to use. That story is checked to see whether it is an original story or one to be merged. If it is an addition or correction transmission it is stored on a separate tape, tape B. If it is an original story it is stored on another magnetic tape, tape A. The process repeats itself until each story has either been stored or bypassed.

In the correction routine, each story is read into the computer and memory is checked to see whether any lines are to be deleted, correction lines added, or merges made. If corrections are necessary, the story is examined line by line and necessary deletions and additions are made. All finally correct stories are written on tape C. At this point stories may be sorted in various ways (according to news categories and

WAYNE A. DANIELSON

TABLE I

INSTRUCTION FORMAT FOR MACHINE EDITING

Column	Item
	Basic Control Card
1–6	Transmission number of story
7–8	News category of story (crime, war, etc.)
9–10	Rank of story in category (1 = most important)
21–40	First line of headline
41–60	Second line of headline
61–80	Lines to be *deleted* separated by commas; termination signal is a period (for example, 1, 2–6, 15–21, 72.)
	Line Correction Card
1–6	Contains 6 asterisks ******
11–16	Transmission number of story to receive corrections
17–20	Line number at which correction starts
21–56	Corrected line or lines of 36 characters each
	Story Merge Card
1–6	Transmission number of new material (the add)
11–16	Transmission number of old story to receive merge
17–20	Line number at which merge is to take place
61–80	Lines to be deleted in material to be added to original story (follow format of basic control card)

importance rankings, for example) and output on a magnetic tape capable of operating the high-speed printer. The final form is a page containing two 10-in. columns of type, all capital letters.

7. An Experimental Edition Planner

Looking toward the distant day when editors may be willing to allow the computer to enter further into the editing process than story correcting, the University of North Carolina editing program experimentally produces automated "editions" of news [17].

The first step of the edition routine is to input a data card containing the following information: (1) the size of the news hole to be filled (in Teletypesetter lines), (2) the per cent of news desired in each of two to eleven categories, and (3) the minimum allowable number of lines per story.

The computer first checks the number of lines it has available against the editor's requested edition size. If there is a shortage, it reports via the console typewriter. If the news hole exactly matches the number of lines available, editing is bypassed and the output routine is begun. If neither condition is met, as is usually the case, and the edition size requested is less than the number of lines available, the editing routine is entered.

First, the desired number of lines of each type of news is computed by multiplying the news category percentages supplied by the editor times the news hole figure. Next, a comparison is made between the available lines in each category and the desired lines in each category. If shortages occur, the computer adjusts the editor's desires to make them agree with the news it actually has on hand.

When a balance is struck at the news category level, the program moves on to story editing. The desired number of lines per story is calculated according to a formula which assigns more lines to those stories the editor has ranked as more important and fewer lines to those stories he has ranked as less *important*. The formula currently being used is:

$$b_i = B \cdot \frac{1}{\sqrt{a_i}} \bigg/ \left(\frac{1}{\sqrt{1}} + \frac{1}{\sqrt{2}} + \ldots + \frac{1}{\sqrt{N}} \right)$$

where

B = the total desired lines in the category as derived in the first part of the editing program;

N = the total number of stories in the category;

a_i = the *rank* given the ith story by the editor, $i = 1, 2, \ldots, N$ if desired (rank 1 = the most important story; rank N = the least important; the editor can repeat the numbers if he wishes to do so);

b_i = the desired number of lines in the ith story ($i = 1, 2, \ldots, N$).

If the initial calculation based on N stories in the category gives some stories fewer than the minimum allowable lines specified by the editor, the computer drops the lowest ranking story and recalculates using $N - 1$ stories. It repeats this process until the last story in the category meets the minimum length requirement.

After the desired lengths are calculated, the computer compares these with the actual story lengths. Discrepancies are treated in the way described previously for news categories. After necessary revisions have been made, the output routine sorts stories into categories, arranges them by rank within categories, and prints them on a two-column page. Each story carries a headline written by the editor. A category title appears at the beginning of each new category of news. As many editions as desired can be prepared using the same general supply of news.

The program cuts stories from the bottom in the editing process. This procedure, although it works well with regular news stories which are written to be cut in this manner, plays havoc with feature stories,

stories told in narrative fashion, etc. Obviously, a program which would cut paragraphs or lines in a preferential fashion (according to an editor's prior judgment) would be an improvement.

8. Conclusions

The progress toward automation in the printing and publishing industry has been called an evolution and not a revolution. Certainly, the computer applications mentioned in this paper are only part of the picture which has been marked in recent years by the introduction of new presses, new types of printing plates, new typesetting devices, and so on.[2]

The evolution may turn into a revolution, however, when one or two basic advances are made.

The first advance needed is a fully developed optical scanning device which can take copy directly from a variety of sources—reporter's typewriters, public relations releases, wire service transmissions, etc. Such a device would eliminate the double keyboarding which now handicaps all printing plants—even those using computers. It would also tremendously speed up the production process. The second advance would be a final output (printing) system capable of matching the computer's fantastic production capabilities. Experiments are under way involving photographic processes, laser milling of plastic plates, improved high-speed printers, and so on [14].

How will editors react to the revolution when it comes? If our student editors at the University of North Carolina are an accurate standard, then editors probably will appreciate any improvements in *production* which take place because they must struggle each day at present with an archaic, slow, incredibly complicated system. They will, however, resist any computer applications which go beyond production and begin to enter into the *judgmental* processes involved in editing. While such resistance will undoubtedly shape initial applications, the economic benefits to be derived from computer-editor teamwork will almost certainly determine the ultimate course of the industry.

References

1. Yasaki, E., The computer and newsprint. *Datamation* **9**, 27–31 (1963).
2. Parmullo, J. N., New computers are changing printing industry production techniques. *Inland Printer Am. Lithog.* **153**, 60–61 (1964).
3. Perry, J. H., Jr., *quoted in* Computers will be a major factor in tomorrow's typesetting. *Inland Printer Am. Lithog.* **151**, 66–67 (1963).

[2]For recent hardware developments see the article by W. R. Bozman in this volume.

4. Doyle, L. B., Expanding the editing function in language data processing. *Comm. ACM* **8**, 238–243 (1965).
5. Sutton, A. A., *Design and Makeup of the Newspaper*. Prentice-Hall, Englewood Cliffs, New Jersey, 1948.
6. Winkler, J. H., New developments in the printing industry today. *Inland Printer Am. Lithog.* **151**, 63–65 (1963).
7. Lawson, A., Computers lead to new standards of typesetting. *Inland Printer Am. Lithog.* **153**, 70–71 (1964).
8. *Proc. Intern. Computer Typesetting Conf.*, London, *1964*, Inst. of Printing, London, 1965.
9. First fully automatic computer-directed typesetting system. *Inland Printer Am. Lithog.* **152**, 63 (1964).
10. Orlando Sentinel-Star implements computerized typesetting. *NCR Total Systems News Rept.* September (1964).
11. *English Word Hyphenation Algorithm*. Nat. Computer Analysts Inc. (mimeographed).
12. *RCA 301 Computer for Newspapers*. RCA Cherry Hill, Camden, New Jersey (undated industry publication).
13. Typesetting in the computer age. *Print in Britain* Spec. Suppl. (1964).
14. Diebold, J., The editor and automation. Address presented before the *Am. Soc. of Newspaper Editors, Washington, D.C., 1963*. Diebold Group, New York, 1963.
15. Dammann, J. E., Skiko, E. J., and Weber, E. V., A data display subsystem. *IBM J. Res. & Develop.* **7**, 325–333 (1963).
16. Ohringer, L., Computer input from printing control tapes. Paper presented before the *16th Ann. Meeting Tech. Assoc. of the Graphic Arts, Pittsburgh, 1964*. Univ. of Pittsburgh Computation and Data Processing Center, Pittsburgh, Pennsylvania.
17. Danielson, W. A., and Briggs, B., A computer program for editing the news. *Comm. ACM* **6**, 487–490 (1963).

Computer-Aided Typesetting

WILLIAM R. BOZMAN

National Bureau of Standards
Washington, D.C.

1. Publication of Computer Output 195
2. Preparation of Computer Tapes for Typesetting 198
3. Examples of Computer-Prepared Typesetting 199
   3.1 Example I 199
   3.2 Example II 200
   3.3 Example III 201
   3.4 Example IV 202
   3.5 Example V 203
   3.6 Example VI 205
4. Hyphenless Justification 205
5. Conclusion 206
   References . . . ., . 206

1. Publication of Computer Output

The increasing speed of data handling and computing possible with modern electronic computers has been continually increasing the demand for speeding up the publication of the final processed data in the form of reports, numerical tables, and other documents. Data which can be calculated in only a few hours, or even a few minutes, may take weeks or sometimes months to be published and thereby be made generally useful.

One method of decreasing the time required has been to prepare offset printing plates from photographs of the final data as printed on a high-speed computer printer. These machines usually print with all capital letters, and even if they have both upper and lower case letters, they have only a small number of special symbols. This frequently results in the use of nonstandard notation which can be difficult to read, or in some cases misinterpreted.

The best results have usually been obtained from manually typeset material, but because of the increased time for the typesetting and extra proofreading which increases the costs, much of the material from data processing machines and computers has been published using the lower typographical quality, but faster methods.

This situation has been improved recently so that now it is possible to obtain high speed, yet to retain the typographical quality of manually typeset material. Several methods have been developed for preparing computer output for publication. The magnetic tape from the computer can be used to punch a paper tape which will operate a hot-metal typesetting machine which produces lines of type, such as the Linotype or Intertype machine. If more complex data are being typeset, requiring a large number of special symbols, the paper tape can be punched to operate a machine which casts individual pieces of type, like the Monotype. If necessary, certain characters can be inserted by hand into type which has been set by this method.

Another method for obtaining computer output in a form suitable for publication is to punch the paper tape for use on a phototypesetting machine. These machines produce high quality photographic images of the type in either galley or page form. Offset printing plates are made by using these as camera copy.

Recently an effort has been made to speed up the output of the phototypesetting machines. Notable in this improvement are the first Photon Zip 900, in successful operation since August 1964, and the first Mergenthaler Linotron, to be installed in the spring of 1966. These machines read the fully prepared data from magnetic tapes at rates up to 100 times faster than paper-tape operated typesetting machines. This tremendous increase puts the phototypesetters into the speed class of computer-printers, yet they give the high quality of conventionally typeset material.

Preparation of the magnetic tapes is relatively simple for tabular data. The page headings can be prepared on paper tape and read into the computer so that they can be written on the output tape without change, or they can be punched into cards or onto tape in a simple alphanumeric form, then converted by the computer into the proper codes for operation of the desired typesetting machine. The body of the data is prepared by using a table look-up method of conversion from computer language to phototypesetting language. A table of codes matches the input characters with the proper codes to be written on the output tape. A few additional instructions have to be given to the typesetting machine such as end-of-line codes, font changes, and page numbers. These are inserted in the proper locations by the computer's instructional codes.

The conversion routine for tabular data is fairly straightforward and

"There must be an easier way to do this."

FIG. 1. Reprinted by special permission of the *Saturday Evening Post*. Copyright 1963, The Curtis Publishing Co., New York.

is therefore quite rapid. As an example, the time taken to convert the 559 pages of NBS Monograph 53 [*3*] from BCD (Binary Coded Decimal) form to Linofilm form was only 13 min on an IBM 7090 computer.

More complicated material will take proportionately longer, depending upon the number of computer decisions required for each line. However, it is practicable to justify text,[1] generate page layouts, insert legends after leaving space for the illustrations, and even to compose pages complete with photographs.

This latter job should be possible with Mergenthaler's new Lexical-Graphical-Composer-Printer System now being built for the U.S. Air Force. The lexical part is to be phototypeset using the 1000-character/sec Linotron; the graphical portion, consisting of photographs, line drawings, etc., is to be printed out on the pages from information stored on videotape; the composer will be a special purpose wired-program computer which will be controlled by special input style codes in addition to the information to be typeset.

These and future machines will certainly change our present ideas about the publication of computer-processed data. In addition to the computed tables of numerical data, which naturally lend themselves to automatic typesetting or tape-controlled phototypesetting, most publications which need frequent revision will undoubtedly be more economically done by these methods in the future. Some examples are: telephone directories, catalogs, tables of technical and scientific data,

---

[1] See article by Danielson in this volume.

census data, and business data. Paperbacked editions of books can be reset in different page sizes and in different type faces than the original higher priced editions. Concordances, indexes, and other aids to reading can be prepared by computers for phototypesetting. Duplication of effort can be reduced in preparing the material for publication, thereby increasing output, yet maintaining high quality at reasonable prices. And finally, what promises to be a most welcome thing: computer-processed data will be printed with graphic arts quality of legibility and readability.

2. Preparation of Computer Tapes for Typesetting

The newer and faster typesetting machines are the phototypesetters which read directly from magnetic tapes at speeds of 300 to over 1000 characters/sec. The record holder for sheer speed, but somewhat limited versatility and image quality is, to the author's knowledge,[2] the Stromberg-Carlson microfilm printer. This machine will record digital computer output at the rate of 62,500 characters/sec in the form of 16 or 35 mm microfilm pages of 64 lines with up to 132 characters/line. However, most phototypesetters in use today are the medium speed machines which read paper tapes at 2 to 30 characters/sec. Many hot-metal typesetting machines also read paper tapes, and can operate up to about 5 characters/sec.

The basic principles of preparing a magnetic tape or a punched paper tape are the same, regardless of the machine for which the tape is to be used, but in practice the final tapes may be quite different since various machines use several different codes to represent the same typeset character, and use different control codes for the nontypesetting (control) operations of the machines.

The paper tapes are of several sizes: 5-, 6-, 7-, 8-, 15-, and 31-level tape codes are in use, and the same size tapes may even have the feed holes in different locations with respect to the code holes. Some paper tape readers require that the holes be punched completely out, whereas other machines can use the chadless tape.

Magnetic-tape-operated typesetting machines do not use a single standard either, but are designed to read the tapes from whatever computer system is being used. The majority of computers use $\frac{1}{2}$ in. tapes, and most of these are "IBM compatible," but even IBM has several "standards": 200, 556, and 800 bits/in. longitudinal density with 6 data bits and 1 check bit across the tape have been most widely

---

[2]With such rapid progress in this field, one can never be sure what the latest developments are.

used, but a newer magnetic tape system writes 8 data bits plus 1 check bit across the tape. This last tape can be used to record the data from an 8-level paper tape on a one-to-one basis. Probably most new systems, both computers and typesetting equipment, will use 8-level tapes with the ASCII (American Standard Code for Information Interchange) codes.

3. Examples of Computer-Prepared Typesetting

3.1 Example I

Monograph 53, *Experimental Transition Probabilities for Spectral Lines of Seventy Elements,* by Corliss and Bozman [*3*], Fig. 2, was the first computer typeset book produced by the National Bureau of Standards. It was published in July 1962 and contains 559 pages of data. Punched cards containing the data of the first three columns were read onto a magnetic tape, which was then used by the computer to calculate the values in the last three columns. These calculations took about 20 min on an IBM 7090. The output magnetic tape was in the proper form to operate the computer's high-speed (300 lines/min) printer. This BCD tape then had to be converted to the proper form to operate the magnetic-tape-controlled Linofilm phototypesetting machine which was located at the IBM Watson Research Laboratory. This conversion from BCD to binary Linofilm form took about 13 min on the 7090 computer. Details of this conversion method were described by the author in 1963 [*2*]. The book was phototypeset with 10 point Bodoni headings, 10 point Times Roman numerals, and a 10 point typewriter typeface for the element indications (second column). The book could

Wavelength A	Spectrum	Energy Levels K	gA 10^8/sec	gf	Log gf
3969.12	Co I	20501 − 45688	4.3	1.0	0.01
3972.53	Co I	28346 − 53512	16.	3.7	0.57
3973.15	Co I	15184 − 40346	0.85	0.20	−0.70
3974.73	Co I	4143 − 29295	0.038	0.0089	−2.05
3977.18	Co I	18775 − 43911	0.70	0.17	−0.78
3978.66	Co I	4143 − 29270	0.056	0.013	−1.88
3979.52	Co I	816 − 25938	0.018	0.0043	−2.36
3987.12	Co I	4143 − 29216	0.018	0.0044	−2.36
3990.30	Co I	15774 − 40828	0.73	0.18	−0.76
3991.54	Co I	29270 − 54316	15.	3.5	0.55
3991.69	Co I	4690 − 29735	0.032	0.0077	−2.12
3994.54	Co I	5076 − 30103	0.024	0.0057	−2.25
3995.31	Co I	7442 − 32465	6.0	1.4	0.16
3997.91	Co I	8461 − 33467	1.3	0.31	−0.51
4013.94	Co I	16196 − 41102	0.80	0.19	−0.72

FIG. 2. Portion of a page from NBS Monograph 53.

have been set in 8 point type and would have been adequately legible, but it was not realized until after publication that phototypesetting gave such excellent results. Some previous experience with photographs of computer print-outs led us to believe that the larger type should be used. A later publication [1] NBS Monograph 81, was set in 8 point Bodoni and is very legible.

3.2 Example II

The Fink Inorganic Index [9], Fig. 3, with 844 pages of data, was prepared from punched cards which had been sorted into proper order. The cards were written onto a magnetic tape in BCD form. The BCD tape was converted to Linofilm form and written in binary on an output tape.

2.56	2.48	2.42	2.05	1.73	3.45	3.07	2.95	RUBIDIUM FLUOBERYLLATE	10 - 146
2.56	2.48	1.93	1.67	5.47	3.28	3.18	2.76	PROUSTITE SILVER ARSENIC SULFIDE	9 - 110
2.57	2.48	2.38	2.16	2.07	4.14	3.20	2.99	LEAD BROMIDE PYRO PHOSPHATE	6 - 178
2.57	2.48	2.24	2.21	1.36	3.07	2.72	2.63	POTASSIUM SODIUM CARBONATE	1 - 038
2.57	2.48	1.95	1.80	1.71	1.65	1.46	3.87	BETA URANYL HYDROXIDE	9 - 239
2.57	2.48	2.06	5.17	4.29	3.83	3.08	2.98	POTASSIUM MANGANATE	12 - 264
2.57	2.48	1.88	1.76	1.70	1.60	1.44	2.84	RAMMELSBERGITE NICKEL ARSENIC 1 TO 2	7 - 319
2.57	2.48	4.26	4.00	3.67	3.19	2.92	2.61	SODIUM CHROMIUM SULFATE 12 HYDRATE	8 - 39
2.57	2.48	2.17	2.00	1.84	6.03	5.37	4.98	SHORTITE CALCIUM SODIUM CARBONATE	8 - 109
2.56	2.47	1.96	3.95	3.25	3.05	2.88	2.62	ZINC ORTHO ARSENITE FORM	1 - 943
2.56	2.47	1.78	1.72	1.68	1.54	3.15	3.09	LABUNTSOVITE	9 - 498
2.56	2.47	2.30	2.13	2.07	1.89	1.66	2.81	ZIRCONIUM SILICON	9 - 226
2.56	2.47	2.29	2.11	1.97	7.25	4.76	2.70	BASIC COPPER VANADATE HYDRATE	12 - 522
2.57	2.47	2.41	2.07	2.03	7.17	4.80	3.57	CALCIUM MANGANESE OXIDE 15 HYDRATE	4 - 149
2.57	2.47	2.21	1.65	1.49	1.43	0.80	2.85	COPPERCHROMITE	5 - 668
2.57	2.47	9.60	5.70	4.49	3.51	3.16	2.84	NONTRONITE HEATED 550 C	13 - 508
2.57	2.47	2.28	2.14	4.28	3.81	3.07	2.96	TARAPACAITE POTASSIUM CHROMATE	1 - 892
2.57	2.47	2.04	8.80	4.80	4.36	2.86	2.72	CALCIUM ALUMINATE 6 HYDRATE	12 - 8
2.57	2.47	2.44	1.78	1.53	5.15	3.11	2.90	CALCIUM GALLIUM SILICATE	14 - 383
2.57	2.47	2.02	1.93	1.56	4.02	3.26	2.84	SUANITE MAGNESIUM YRO BORATE	11 - 427
2.56	2.46	2.10	1.38	4.18	3.04	2.94	2.89	POTASSIUM FERRATE	3 - 650

FIG. 3. Portion of a page from Fink Inorganic Index.

At the time of this conversion, the computer code inserted spaces between the first eight columns. The cards had been punched without the spaces in order to save as many columns as possible for the names. Since different alphabetical letters can have different widths, it was necessary for the computer to add the width of each of the characters in a name and then to add sufficient blank space at the end of the name so that the tenth column would be properly aligned.

The computer also inserted the dashes in each line of the reference column, inserted blank lines between groups of 10 lines, generated a page number and centered it at the bottom of each page. If the last line of a group left room for 10 or more lines on the page, the code inserted the new group-range heading and continued to fill the page.

The computation, by an IBM 7094, took about 30 min to prepare the output magnetic tape for the 844 pages of the book. A 15-level paper tape was punched from the data on the magnetic tape; this punching took about 70 hr. The paper tape was then used to operate a standard phototypesetter. This took about 300 hr.

3.3 Example III

A new revision of *Crystal Data Determinative Tables* [4], Fig. 4, is being prepared at the National Bureau of Standards. This new revision is being punched onto paper tape using a phototypesetting keyboard. After the data for the complete book (about 1000 pages) have all been punched, the paper tapes will be written onto magnetic tape for input to a computer. The computer will cross-check some of the numerical data for consistency, compute additional numbers, and check various calculations. It will check the names of all the periodicals in the literature references to see whether the spelling is consistent with the given master

```
***A,ED,NM,IN,000485
```
Titanium oxide (5·9)
&&&.8386 .6560 7.120 8.490 5.569 P1 2 quant. 4.29 4.31
105°01′ 108°30′ 69°48′
 Pentatitanium nonaoxide, Ti_5O_9 (Andersson et al., Acta Chem. Scand. 11, 1641, 1957;
Andersson et al., ibid. 11, 1653, 1957; Westman & Magneli, ibid. 11, 1587, 1957: 5.569,
7.120, 8.865; 97.55°, 112.34°, 108.50°)$0\bar{1}0/101/\bar{1}00$. The cell dimensions reported earlier are
inaccurate (Naturwissenschaften, 43, 495, 1956). Structure by Andersson (Acta Chem. Scand. 14,
1161, 1960). Always twinned.
```
***A,ED,NM,IN,000489
```
Cadmium molybdo silicate (2·1·12·40) 22-hydrate
&&&.9082 .8754 13.85 15.25 13.35 P$\bar{1}$ 2 none 3.18 ...
106°42′ 107°06′ 81°52′
 Cadmium silicomolybdate 22-hydrate, $Cd_2Si(Mo_3O_{10})_4 \cdot 22H_2O$ (Ferrari et al., Gazz. Chim.
Ital. 81. 44, 1951: 13.35, 13.85, 15.25; 98°08′, 106°42′, 72°54′)$010/00\bar{1}/\bar{1}00$. Isotypic with
the tungstate.
```
***A.ED,NM,IN,000490
```
Cadmium tungsto silicate (2·1·12·40) 23-hydrate
&&&.9216 .8713 14.10 15.30 13.33 P$\bar{1}$ 2 none 4.47, 23° 4.51
108°10′ 108°14′ 80°47′
 Cadmium silicotungstate 23-hydrate, $Cd_2Si(W_3O_{10})_4 \cdot 23H_2O$ (Ferrari et al., Gazz. Chim.
Ital. 81, 33, 1951: 13.33, 14.10, 15.30; 99°13′, 108°10′, 71°46′)$010/00\bar{1}/\bar{1}00$. Designated
22-hydrate by Wyrouboff, 1896; 23-hydrate by Copaux, 1906; choice cannot be made on the
basis of the chemical analysis.
```
***A,ED,NM,IN,000491
```
Manganese tungsto silicate (2·1·12·40) 22-hydrate
&&&.9216. .8713 14.10 15.30 13.33 P$\bar{1}$ 2 none 4.33, 23° 4.34
108°10′ 108°14′ 80°47′
 Manganese silicotungstate 22-hydrate, $Mn_2Si(W_3O_{10})_4 \cdot 22H_2O$ (Ferrari et al., Gazz. Chim.
Ital. 81, 33, 1951: 13.33, 14.10, 15.30; 99°13′, 108°10, 71°46′)$010/00\bar{1}/\bar{1}00$. Isomorphous
with the Cd compound [the cell given here is that of the Cd compound].

Fig. 4. Sample of input to computer of revision of *Crystal Data Determinative Tables*.

list. Any discrepancies will be printed out and will then be hand-checked. The computer will also prepare two indexes by selecting out (1) all the names, chemical and mineral, and (2) all the chemical formulas. The computer tape will also be used for sorting various kinds of information by selected categories such as cell dimensions, space groups, and chemical composition.

The computer program can recognize various fields of the data by the type style (e.g., the names, in bold face), by commas, parentheses, brackets, and other typographical marks. In only two instances has it been necessary to supply a special "flag" to identify specific information for the computer. The triple asterisk, ***, identifies the line containing information for the use of the computer: *** A, ED, NM, IN, 000490. The A identifies the proper category for the particular crystal, in this case "anorthic." The ED instructs the computer to "EDit" the entry; NM indicates a "NON-Mineral," IN designates "INorganic," and "000490" is the accession number assigned to this particular crystal. The other flag, the triple ampersand, &&&, identifies the line of data which is to be tabulated by the computer. The individual values in this line are each separated in the input tape by a space. If a particular value is unknown, the column is punched with the code for a three-dot leader, ..., this being punched as a single character on the tape. If it is necessary to give two values in the same column, they are separated by a comma, but no space.

Since there are very few artificial flags, the "galley proofs" are nearly identical to the final printed pages. Thus proofreading, which is difficult enough with this kind of material, is not encumbered by the profusion of flags that would be necessary if this material were being punched by a method which had only a very limited character set.

3.4 Example IV

The sample of *Index Medicus* [5] shown in Fig. 5 gives some idea of part of the work of the very ambitious MEDLARS (Medical Literature Analysis and Retrieval System) project by the National Library of Medicine. MEDLARS is concerned with the collection, storage, and retrieval of bibliographic citations from over 2,500 of the world's biomedical journals.

The citations are prepared by a staff of literature analysts, stored on magnetic tapes, and sorted, processed, and made available for retrieval by a computer (Honeywell 800) for three main purposes: (1) the monthly publication of *Index Medicus*, (2) filling requests for information on individual questions (demand searches), and (3) preparation of recurring bibliographies in particular disciplines or areas of biomedical interest.

Each issue of *Index Medicus* contains about 600 pages in a three column format, listing current biomedical articles both by subject and by authors. Publication of *Index Medicus* is facilitated by the use of a high-speed (300 characters/sec) photocomposer system called GRACE (Graphic Arts Composing Equipment) built by the Photon Corporation. The information for each issue of *Index Medicus* is sorted and composed into page form by the computer. The output magnetic tape from the computer is then used to control GRACE, which produces page-size positive films ready to be sent to the printer for plate making.

TION

] Duchêne H, et al.
14:443-7, 1 Feb 64 (Fr)
ie problem in Austria] Beran F.
ev 4:82-95, 1963 (Ger)
situation in general: socio-legal
ons] Fechner E.
(Mex) 43:540-4, 10 Nov 63 (Sp)
mittee agenda of special interest to the
harmacy service] Ericsson R.
ırm T 68:145-52, 20 Feb 64 (Sw)
of drugs]
ırm T 68:165-6, 20 Feb 64 (Sw)

.TION, DENTAL (G2, I)

iiation control regulations of the state of
Holden FR, et al. **Oral Surg** 17:747, Jun 64

.TION, MEDICAL (G2, I)

aches to the narcotic problem. New
s at the national level. Javits JK.
Acad Med 40:292-8, Apr 64
ı the King-Anderson Bill (H.R. 3920). Doran
ıati **J Med** 45:189-91, May 64
k at the Illinois Medical Practice Act.
PG. **Illinois Med J** 125:345, Apr 64
he new drug regulations on teaching and
in medical schools. Kirby WM.
duc 39:355-9, Apr 64

INDEX MEDICUS

[Clinical case] Colle R.
 Belg T Geneesk 20:74-7, 15 Jan 64 (l
[Pregnancy, labor and the puerperium in my
patients] Osse K, et al.
 Zbl Gynaec 86:164-8, 1 Feb 64 ((
[Primary adenocarcinoma of the fallopian tu
Mazzella G. **Rass Int Clin Ter** 44:263-70, 15 Mar 64
[Benign nonepithelial tumors of the stomach] Ska
PB, et al. **Sovet Med** 27:78-82, Nov 63 (l
[Solitary pulmonary nodule] Díaz G, et al.
 Neumol Cir Torax 25:101-6, Mar-Apr 64
[A new case of gastric leiomyoma] Arnal P, e
 Rev Clin Esp 92:357-61, 15 Mar 64
[Benign gastric tumors] Moreno González-Bueno ı
al. **Rev Clin Esp** 92:333-7, 15 Mar 64

LEIOMYOSARCOMA (C2, C3)

Hemipelvectomy for the management of soft ti
tumors of the lower extremity. Phelan JT, e
 Amer J Surg 107:604-8, Apr 64
Primary leiomyosarcoma of the lung. Case re|
Rosen A, et al. **Dis Chest** 45:425-7, Apr 6
Myosarcoma of the bladder: report of two c.
Uehling D, et al. **J Urol** 91:354-6, Apr 64
Tumor seminar. Lattes R. **Texas J Med** 60:420-46, Ma
[Malignant tumors originating from the venous sys
Review and a case of leiomyosarcoma from the
saphenous vein] Christiansen J.
 Ugeskr Laeg 126:483-5, 2 Apr 64 (l

FIG. 5. Portion of a page of *Index Medicus*, by subject.

3.5 Example V

Example V, Fig. 6, is shown to indicate how a computer can combine implicit information with information explicitly punched in a card [6]. These names and addresses were punched into cards with no indication of upper or lower case letters. The computer capitalized only the first letter of each name and also each single letter (initials), inserted a period after each initial, set up the hanging indentations, substituted single and double asterisks for certain punches, and spaced vertically between entries.

Mihaly, Stephen Mark *
3781 East 77th St
Cleveland 5 Ohio
Pneumo Dynamics Corp &
 Cleveland Pneumatic
 Industries Inc

Mikesell, William A. Jr
Continental Oil Co
Drawer 1267
Ponca City Okla

Miketta, Casimir A.
210 West 7th St
Los Angeles 14 Calif

Mikulka, Charles *
730 Main St
Cambridge 39 Mass
Polaroid Corp

Miller, Arthur Banes
115 Grafton St
Chevy Chase 15 Md

Miller, Ausin R.
1815 Land Title Bldg
Philadelphia 10 Pa

Miller, Carl
36th Floor Woolworth Bldg
233 Broadway
New York 7 N. Y.

Miller, Clinton Frederick *
C. O. Hercules Powder Co
Delaware Trust Bldg
Wilmington Del

Miller, David Byron
1230 Ave Of The Americas
New York 20 N. Y.

Miller, Kenneth Lyall
Burroughs Corp
Patent Dept
Box 782
Paoli Pa

Miller, Kenneth W.
474 Overlook Rd
Mansfield Ohio
The Ohio Brass Co

Miller, Lawrence Gale
46 Lincoln Road
Wellesley Hills 81 Mass

Miller, Louis Allwine **
Patents Div
Office Of Naval Research
Washington 25 D. C.

FIG. 6. Sample of Patent Office Roster.

SIX-INCH TRANSIT CIRCLE OBSERVATIONS 1949–1956

SUN

Date U. T.		Julian Date 243	Obsr.	Cl.	Cir.	App. R. A. of Center			Corr. to A. E.	App. Decl. of Center			Corr. to A. E.
	m d					h m	s		s	°	′	″	″
1949	6 3.71	3071.21268	4	2	1	4 45	16.399		−0.058	+22	20		
	6 4.71	3072.21280	1	2	1	4 49	23.162		+0.106	+22	27		
	6 8.71	3076.21330	4	2	1	5 05	52.530		−0.002	+22	51		
	6 9.71	3077.21343	1	2	1	5 10	00.685		+0.089	+22	57	02.65	+0.38
	6 10.71	3078.21357	2	2	1	5 14	08.944		+0.041	+23	01	46.42	+0.18
1949	6 11.71	3079.21371	1	2	1	5 18	17.486		+0.060	+23	06	06.90	+0.90
	6 14.71	3082.21413	2	2	1	5 30	44.169		−0.007	+23	16	39.54	+0.53
	6 21.71	3089.21518	1	2	1	5 59	50.762		0.000	+23	26		
	6 23.71	3091.21548	1	1	1	6 08	10.053		+0.014	+23	26	05.27	−0.53
	6 24.71	3092.21563	4	1	1	6 12	19.562		−0.042	+23	25	05.23	+0.45
1949	6 26.71	3094.21593	1	1	1	6 20	38.478		+0.036	+23	21		
	7 3.71	3101.21690	1	1	1	6 49	38.215		−0.002	+22	57	28.13	+0.25
	7 5.71	3103.21714	8	1	1	6 57	52.779		+0.053	+22	46		
	7 20.71	3118.21838	4	1	1	7 58	48.473		+0.101	+20	38	39.25	+0.41
	7 24.71	3122.21849	9	1	1	8 14	44.232		+0.060	+19	50	43.10	−0.81
1949	7 28.71	3126.21849	8	1	1	8 30	30.661		+0.022	+18	57	30.25	−0.88
	7 30.71	3128.21845	9	2	1	8 38	20.248		+0.071	+18	28	59.95	−1.36
	8 1.71	3130.21838	4	2	1	8 46	07.232		+0.030	+17	59	19.19	+0.25
	8 3.71	3132.21828	4	2	1	8 53	51.748		−0.013	+17	28		
	8 7.71	3136.21800	4	2	1	9 09	13.462		+0.062	+16	23	19.44	−1.17

FIG. 7. Example showing use of overlay.

3.6 Example VI

Most of the heading of the example shown in Fig. 7 was prepared as a film positive overlay which was photographed superimposed on the paper page positives to make negatives to be used for the plate making. The parts of the heading which were not on the overlay, but photocomposed, were (1) the page number, which was generated by the computer, (2) the word "SUN" or other name which identifies the particular set of data, and (3) the line of letters and symbols which designate the units, just above the tabulated data. This line was fed into the computer and stored there in binary form, ready to be written on the output magnetic tape as needed.

4. Hyphenless Justification

Kunkel and Marcum [7, 8] have suggested a method "which may make the troublesome end-of-line hyphen a thing of the past in computerized

The American prairies are of two kinds. Those which lie east of the Mississippi are comparatively small, are exceedingly fertile, and are always surrounded by forests. They are susceptible of high cultivation, and are fast becoming settled. They abound in Ohio, Michigan, Illinois, and Indiana. They labor under the disadvantages of a scarcity of wood and water—evils of a serious character, until art has had time to supply the deficiencies of nature. As coal is said to abound in all that region, and wells are generally successful, the enterprise of the emigrants is gradually prevailing against these difficulties.

The second description of these natural meadows lies west of the Mississippi, at a distance of a few hundred miles from that river, and is called the Great Prairies. They resemble the steppes of Tartary more than any other known portion of the world; being, in fact, a vast country, incapable of sustaining a dense population, in the absence of the two great necessaries already named. Rivers abound, it is true; but this region is nearly destitute of brooks

The Great Prairies appear to be the final gathering-place of the red men. The remnants of the Mohicans and the Delawares, of the Creeks, Choctaws, and Cherokees, are destined to fulfil their time on these vast plains. The entire number of the Indians within the Union is differently computed, at between one and five hundred thousand souls. Most of them inhabit the country west of the Mississippi. At the period of the tale, they dwelt in open hostility; national feuds passing from generation to generation. The power of the republic has done much to restore peace to these wild scenes, and it is now possible to travel in security where civilized man did not dare to pass unprotected five-and-twenty years ago.

Recent events have brought the Grand Prairies into familiar notice, and we now read of journeys across them as, half a century since, we perused the narratives of the emigrants to Ohio and Louisiana. It is a singular commentary on the times that places for railroads across these vast plains are in active discussion, and

FIG. 8. Sample of work by Kunkel and Marcum.

photocomposition." The idea of eliminating end-of-line hyphens is not new, as they quickly point out, but has usually led to excessive interword spacing and/or letter spacing which may be so abrupt as to cause hesitation in reading. This may be justifiable in newspaper work, but it is certainly to be avoided in more permanent work such as book publishing.

In order to be able to justify a line which would have been too long, Kunkel and Marcum reduced the set size $\frac{1}{2}$ point smaller and then tried to justify the line. If the last word of the line was still too long, they moved the word to the next line, increased the set size $\frac{1}{2}$ point and then tried to justify the line. In the examples given in their paper, Fig. 8, they were able to justify all the lines without extra letter spacing or exceeding their chosen maximum for interword spacing. The basic type size used was 8 point. Those lines set in $7\frac{1}{2}$, or $8\frac{1}{2}$ point are indicated by a black dot. The use of this method gives a more subtle and pleasing effect than the usual method of letter spacing one or more words in a line.

5. Conclusion

The use of computers is one more step in the progress of printing which started over five hundred years ago with the use of hand cut movable type on a hand-operated press, and has progressed through many improvements in typesetting and press design to modern automated keyboards and high-speed multicolor presses. The judicious use of computers and automation may be a necessary step for many newspapers and printing and publishing companies to enable them to reduce the economic squeeze between rising costs and low enough prices to maintain profitable sales volumes.

It is now necessary for printers and publishers to learn about computers and their uses in order to be able to differentiate between what computers can *do*, and what computers can do *profitably*. Computers are not machines which will miraculously solve all the problems of a trouble-plagued company; they are tools which can be programmed to carry out designated tasks accurately and extremely efficiently.

References

1. Bhalla, C. P., Tables of electron radial functions. *Natl. Bur. Std. Monograph* **81** (1964).
2. Bozman, W. R., Phototypesetting of computer output, an example using tabular data. *Natl. Bur. Std. Tech. Note* **170** (1963).
3. Corliss, C. H., and Bozman, W. R., Experimental transition probabilities for spectral lines of seventy elements. *Natl. Bur. Std. Monograph* **53** (1962).
4. Donnay, J. D. H., and Donnay, G., (Eds.) *Crystal Data Determinative Tables.* Am. Crystallographic Assoc., 1963.

5. *Index Medicus*. Nat. Library of Med., U.S. Dept. Health, Educ. and Welfare (August 1964 and later).
6. *Roster of Attorneys and Agents Registered to Practice Before the U.S. Patent Office*. Patent Office, Washington, D.C., 1963.
7. Kunkel, G. Z., and Marcum, T. H., Hyphenless justification, *Datamation* **11**, No. 4, 42 (1965).
8. Kunkel, G. Z., and Marcum, T. H., Now: Hyphenless justification, *Printing Production* p. 44, Apr. (1965).
9. *Fink Inorganic Index to the Powder Diffraction File* (1964), ASTM Spec. Tech. Publ. 48-N3, Am. Soc. for Testing and Materials, Phila., Pa.

Programming Languages for Computational Linguistics*

ARNOLD C. SATTERTHWAIT

Washington State University
Pullman, Washington

1. Introduction 209
   1.1 Machine-Oriented and Problem-Oriented Programming Languages . 210
   1.2 Research Efforts in Computational Linguistics 210
2. Languages for Machine Translation 212
   2.1 General Characteristics 213
   2.2 COMIT 214
   2.3 SNOBOL 220
   2.4 The Linguistic Research System, University of Texas . . 221
   2.5 The Wayne State University Interpretive System . . . 225
   2.6 MIMIC 226
3. A Sentence-Parsing Program in COMIT 227
   3.1 The Program and Input Sentences 234
   3.2 The Output 236
   References 238

1. Introduction

Almost simultaneously with the advent of the digital computer, it was foreseen that this instrument might lend itself to the machine translation of natural languages. Exploratory research resulting from this initial forecast has gradually led most of those involved to believe that further research of considerable depth and variety will be necessary if the practical goal of machine translation is to be achieved. The initiation of broad research in what are essentially nonnumeric mathematical areas of some complexity has emphasized the need for programming systems with extensive capabilities for the manipulation of data in varied and intricate ways. This article discusses the major programming

*This is a revision of a paper presented at the Seminar on Mechanical Translation held in Tokyo, Japan, April 20–27, 1964.

systems currently in use in the United States for research in machine translation and computational linguistics. These systems belong in the same class as those discussed in the article by Bobrow and Raphael, "A comparison of list-processing computer languages"[1].

1.1 Machine-Oriented and Problem-Oriented Programming Languages

In general, programming languages are machine-oriented, problem-oriented, or combinations of the two. If the computer can be likened to a living organism, then the instructions given to it in a machine-oriented language correspond to the unconscious directions produced by the organism in order to establish pathways in the nervous system along which nerve impulses may travel. It is these impulses which stimulate the organism to activity. If the organism is a human being and the activity is "walking to market," a single instruction in a machine-oriented language will correspond to the unconscious order which selects a particular pathway in the nervous system. A large number of individual orders are required to produce one step.

In contrast to the machine-oriented programming languages the problem-oriented languages consist of rules which are frequently highly complex. In our example, a single problem-oriented rule will correspond to the more or less conscious impulse to walk.

1.2 Research Efforts in Computational Linguistics

In the early stages of research on machine translation, word-for-word translation devices which made use primarily of a dictionary look-up were proposed. In the course of the past fifteen years it has become apparent that far more sophisticated schemes than these will be required for the satisfactory translation of text from one language to another. Truly successful schemes may well have to include devices designed to supply a semantic analysis of the whole text and complete syntactic parsings of each sentence to be translated before the translation proper can be undertaken. The translation process itself will certainly involve reference to a bilingual dictionary with choices between alternate possibilities of target-language items. These choices will be determined by semantic criteria supplied by the source-language text and will in turn serve as one factor in the determination of the syntactic structure of the sentences in the target language. In one scheme for translation, the complete syntactic and morphological structure of the target-language sentence which translates the source-language sentence is constructed by the machine in the form of a specifier. The machine makes use of this specifier to produce the grammatical structure which terminates in the sentence which translates the source-language sentence.

A growing realization of the complexity of the problems presented by machine translation has compelled interested investigators to review past theories of language structure and semantics and sometimes to embark on the creation of new ones. These research workers are coming to agree that at the very least a thorough syntactic analysis of any sentence to be translated must be made by the machine. It has been felt that if the machine is to furnish such an analysis or parsing, it must be given access to a grammar explicitly detailing the syntax and morphology of the language of the sentences to be translated. On reaching this conclusion the researchers turned to the available grammars of these languages only to find them unsatisfactory. The best grammars in any language lack the detail required for machine translation, exhibit frequent lacunae in information offered, and fail to show the coherence required by our most sophisticated machines.

The inability of the available grammars to supply the required information has forced researchers in machine translation to undertake the preparation of grammars of their own designed to meet their needs. Research directed toward the composition of these grammars has forced some investigators to conclude that the general linguistic theory upon which the available grammars were based was frequently naive, confused, or even in some cases barely existent. To some it has seemed that the whole theory of communication among human beings by means of natural language needs reconsideration and further development before satisfactory translation by machine can be achieved.

Computers have offered the opportunity to test both old and new hypotheses concerning language theory, theories of linguistic structure, consistency and coherency of sets of rules in specific grammars, and so on. From the results of this testing new hypotheses may be formed, inadequate and naive ones refined and rendered more sophisticated, and false ones eliminated. On occasion these tests have taken the form of programs which produce grammatical though nonsensical sentences in a language through reference to a grammar which generates a large number, although not necessarily all, of the sentences of that language. Examination of sentences produced in this way indicates the degree of validity of the rules which make up the grammar. Besides being useful for testing purposes, programs which produce sentences may actually be used in the machine-translation process. In one translation scheme a sentence-production grammar is actually used to produce the target-language sentences which translate the source-language sentences provided it.

Sentence-parsing programs make use of similar grammars to provide syntactic analyses of any sentence provided them from a large set of sentences of the language specified by the grammar. In this case, the grammars are determined to be valid insofar as they parse any grammatical sentence and fail to parse any ungrammatical sentence submitted to the program. Sentence-parsing devices of this type are also used in actual, experimental machine-translation programs for the morphological and syntactic parsing of source-language sentences submitted for translation.

2. Languages for Machine Translation

The various research centers for machine translation in the United States are making use of machine-oriented languages some with special developments for machine translation, problem-oriented languages developed for purposes other than machine translation, such as ALGOL, AUTOCODER, and FORTRAN, and problem-oriented languages developed for research in machine translation, information retrieval, vocabulary analysis, machine production of grammatical sentences in natural languages, simulation of human problem solving, and so on. FORTRAN in particular has been used in linguistic research at the University of Pennsylvania and with increasing frequency at the Rand Corporation. The debate as to the respective advantages of machine-oriented languages and various problem-oriented languages may be expected to continue for some time. However, as more scientists drawn from areas outside of those utilizing traditional mathematics turn to the computer for research in linguistics and related fields, it is probable that the use of problem-oriented languages will increase.

Five problem-oriented programming systems developed specifically for symbol manipulation such as is required for machine translation will be discussed here; these are: COMIT developed at the Massachusetts Institute of Technology and used at over a dozen installations [4, 6], SNOBOL developed at the Bell Telephone Laboratories in New Jersey [5], the interpretive system developed at the Wayne State University [2], MIMIC developed by the Rand Corporation [8], and LRS, the Linguistics Research System, developed at the University of Texas [7]. All are implemented for use on one or more of the IBM 7000-series digital computers.

These various systems express two primary concerns. The Linguistics Research Center of the University of Texas is developing a broad system of research which should prove to be a powerful tool when completed. Its work includes the preparation of programming languages designed to serve the linguist as tools in the study of the structures of natural languages [10]. The entire system emphasizes the Center's feeling that the problems of machine translation will prove so intricate that a very broad, well-developed strategy will be required for their solution. Its strategy is based on the assumption that a moderately large team of researchers in diverse areas will be required. In order to facilitate its research, a carefully coordinated system of internally independent areas is being developed. One goal is the freeing of those working in one research area from the inconveniences of constant consultation concerning the minutiae of programming with those working in other, only distantly related areas of the machine-translation process.

The second, more restricted concern is represented by those who prepared COMIT, SNOBOL, the Wayne system, and MIMIC. The members of this group are interested in making computer research directly accessible to the nonprogrammer through the preparation of problem-oriented programming languages which are easy to learn, have broad applicability and, in the case of COMIT at least, furnish a check-out routine to assist in the detection of errors in the researcher's programs.

2.1 General Characteristics

In planning a programming language of the sort envisaged by the members of the last group, certain restrictions imposed by the machine-oriented language should be removed while care should be taken to avoid imposing any particular linguistic philosophy on the user. Among the inconveniences which any linguist would desire to avoid are those involving restriction on word length, the need to anticipate the length of the longest word, phrase, or sentence in the data, and the need for conscious shifting of data words back and forth to match them with computer words. The linguist wants to deal with the words of his data as units no matter what their length, but he also wants to be able to decompose these words easily and at will into their constituent characters for morphological examination and later to recompose the words of which they were originally formed. With this emphasis on language he wants to be able to form strings in the shape of natural language text. General and specific pattern matching is requisite. In order to avoid the necessity of examining all the data each time a pattern search is made, he should have available a number of temporary storage areas. Simple means of insertion, deletion, and replacement of data should be provided. Some dictionary device with automatic alphabetization and a fast binary search would seem convenient to any linguist. Simple arithmetical operations have proved useful enough to be included in at least two of the problem-oriented languages. A versatile and simple transfer control with conditional transfers of various sorts some of which may be data-dependent has also proved useful. As a research tool the programs should be capable of frequent change without continual drastic revision [*13*].

2.2 COMIT

In the following paragraphs the COMIT system, as the most widely used and thoroughly tested of these languages, will serve as an example. COMIT has been described as equivalent to a general Turing machine [*3*]. It is a general-purpose symbol manipulation programming language that favors a linear organization of data.

The data to be processed by the COMIT program are contained in three functionally different sections of the computer's core storage: the workspace, the shelves, and the dispatcher. The workspace is a string-form list structure. Data are contained in it in the form of constituents separated from each other by plus signs. The constituent is composed of a symbol of any number of characters which may have joined to it one or more logical subscripts and one numerical subscript. Each logical subscript may have one or more values, which are in effect sub-subscripts. The following is an example of a workspace expression:

VERB-PHRASE/ .2 + VERB/NUMBER SINGULAR, PERSON 3, TENSE PRESENT + GOES + ADVERB + SLOWLY

The symbols are VERB-PHRASE, VERB, GOES, ADVERB, and SLOWLY. VERB-PHRASE has a numerical subscript 2 identified by the prefixed period. VERB has three logical subscripts NUMBER, PERSON, and TENSE. In this case, each subscript has a single value, SINGULAR, 3, and PRESENT, although each could have several. The order of the constituents in the workspace is significant. A change in their order results in a different workspace expression. On the other hand, identical subscripts in various orders have the same meaning.

The workspace has subsidiary addressable lists, the shelves. These shelves, 127 in number, have several uses besides the storage of non-pertinent material away from current workspace operations. Data from the workspace may be placed on either end of any shelf, making of it either a push-down list or a queue line. Data are contained on the shelves in the same string-form list structure format as that in which they appear in the workspace. The shelves may also be used for further classificatory power and "since they are referred to by numbers, the shelves are addressable lists" which "can be used to set up matrices" [*3*, p. 115].

An example of the use of the shelves to set up a 4 by 13 matrix can be drawn from a routine designed to sort a deck of bridge cards into the four suits. In this case, the routine is furnished a shuffled deck in symbolic form; for example, HEART/ .2 + CLUB/ .3 + CLUB/ .6 + SPADE/ .6 + SPADE/ .14 + DIAMOND/ .12 + etc. The numerical subscripts represent the cards' ranks, e.g., 14 indicates the ace and 12 the queen. The routine is written to queue every SPADE on shelf 1, every HEART on shelf 2, etc. At the end of the routine a matrix is formed. The rows of the matrix contain the cards of the four suits and the columns show the cards in their order of occurrence in the deck. The three leftmost columns of such a matrix might appear as follows:

SPADE/ .6 + SPADE/ .14 + SPADE/ .2 + ...
HEART/ .2 + HEART/ .6 + HEART/ .3 + ...
DIAMOND/ .12 + DIAMOND/ .11 + DIAMOND/ .13 + ...
CLUB/ .3 + CLUB/ .6 + CLUB/ .8 + ...

Another routine creates a 13 by 4 matrix which queues all aces on shelf 14, all kings on shelf 13, etc., ending with all deuces on shelf 2. Each row of the matrix finally contains four cards of the same rank. The columns again show the cards in their order of appearance in the deck. The first four complete rows contained on shelves 2 through 5 appear as follows:

SPADE/ .2 + DIAMOND/ .2 + HEART/ .2 + CLUB/ .2
HEART/ .3 + CLUB/ .3 + DIAMOND/ .3 + SPADE/ .3
DIAMOND/ .4 + CLUB/ .4 + SPADE/ .4 + HEART/ .4
DIAMOND/ .5 + HEART/ .5 + SPADE/ .5 + CLUB/ .5
etc.

Besides the data, the core storage of the computer contains the COMIT program in compiled form and the COMIT interpreter, which executes the rules of the program. The COMIT program itself, composed of a series of rules, specifies the operations to be carried out on the data. The notation in which the full rules are formed is based on that used by linguists when they use rewrite rules of the sort, sentence → subject + predicate, where the arrow is read "is rewritten as." In COMIT the arrow is replaced by an equals sign.

The COMIT rule is composed of a rule name and one or more subrule names, a left half separated from a right half by the equals sign, a routing section and an optional go-to. If no go-to is provided, the next rule in the program comes into control after the rule has been executed. The routing section is devoted to the specification of operations not statable in terms of other parts of the rule. A simple rule follows:

rule name   *left half* = *right half*   *routing*   *go-to*
COMPLETE   A + C = 1 + B + 2   // *K1 2 3   NEXT

If the workspace expression before the execution of the rule were
A + D + A + C + F, it would be transformed to A + D + ABC + F
after successful execution of the above rule. The A + C of the left half
of the rule matches the A + C in the workspace expression and assigns
the temporary numbers one and two to A and C, respectively. The right
half of the rule then directs the insertion of the letter B between the A
and the C. The expression in the routing, separated from the right half
by the double solidus, orders the compression of the three constituents
already produced so that they form the one constituent ABC.

As most features of the COMIT rule are optional, it may be written in
many forms. Its authors feel that the COMIT system is probably easily
adaptable to research based on any linguistic hypotheses and general
theories of language. The author has found it most satisfactory not only
for syntactic analysis but also for the recognition and parsing of forms
exhibiting even the complexities of the staggered morphemes in Arabic.

The various operations to be performed on the data are frequently
determined by information furnished by the data *per se*. This information
is obtained by pattern searches made of the data proceeding from the
left to the right of the workspace. The pattern, a match for which is to be
sought in the data, is stated as the left half of the COMIT rule. This
pattern may consist of any specified or unspecified number of constituents from none to somewhere in the neighborhood of 10,000.
Certain or all constituents may be specified with several degrees of
definiteness. A workspace constituent matches a left half of a rule if it
has at least the mentioned subscripts and their values. For example, the
workspace constituent, MAN/ .3, NOUN COUNT, NUMBER SINGULAR,
GENDER MASCULINE will be matched by the left half of a rule which
directs a search for the symbol MAN or for any symbol with the subscript
NUMBER and value SINGULAR or for the symbol MAN with the subscript
NOUN or for any symbol with the subscript GENDER and the value
MASCULINE or for any symbol with a numerical subscript 3, or less than
5 or greater than 2, and so on. A search may also specify the constituents
identified by a left and right boundary, each of which may be described
with the various degrees of definiteness. Two noncontiguous constituents
with a specified or unspecified number of interposed constituents may
also be found through the statement of simple specifications in the
left half of the rule. The right half of the rule indicates operations which
are to be executed on the specified portions of the workspace expression
if the pattern search is successful. The workspace constituents may be
rearranged, deleted, inserted, and copied. Several symbols may be
compressed to make one symbol, or the characters of a single symbol
may be expanded, making a new symbol of each character. If, for
example, the workspace expression is −HE+ −CALLED+ −UP+ −

THE+ − GIRL, the following rule will rewrite it as − GIRL+ − HE+ − + C+A+L+L+E+D+ − GIRLS+ − UP.

DO $1 + $1 + $1 + $1 + $1 = 5 + 1 + 2 + 5 + S + 3 / / *E3, *K4 5, *Q1 2 END

In the left half, $1 finds a single constituent. The five $1 items find the five constituents in the workspace expression. In the right half, the fifth constituent located by the pattern search is written first. The first and second follow. The fifth is copied again and followed by an inserted s. Then the third constituent is placed at the end. In the routing, *E3 expands the third item written by the right half, in this case the constituent which was originally in the second position in the workspace expression and replaces − CALLED with − +C+A+L+L+E+D. *K4 5 compresses the second copy of the fifth constituent now in the fourth place and the constituent s which was added to the workspace expression to form the new constituent, − GIRLS. *Q1 2 queues − HE on shelf one.

Subscripts may be added to a constituent, deleted from it, and moved to another constituent. The values of subscripts may also be added, deleted, and inserted. Logical operations can be carried out on logical subscripts. Numerical operations on numerical subscripts include addition, subtraction, multiplication, and division. An example illustrating addition and various logical operations follow. Suppose the workspace contains:

P/ .3,A 3 5 6,C 2 3 + Q/ .6,A 4 5,B 2,C 2 4,E 1 3,F 1 3 4

Then suppose the rule is

CHANGE P + Q = 2/ .I. *1, − B,C*1,C 1 2 3,D 1 3,E 2,F*C SET

The result will be Q/ .9,A 4 5,C 2,D 1 3,E 2,F 2 5. First, the P is eliminated from the workspace as only the temporary workspace number 2 is recorded in the right half. The subscript .I.*1 increases the numerical subscript of the developing constituent by the numerical subscript found on the first constituent indicated by the left half. Subscript A is left unchanged; − B deletes subscript B with its values; C*1 forms the logical product of the values of subscript C attached to P and those of subscript C attached to Q. The product of the values of the two subscripts are those values common to both; C 1 2 3 forms the product of these values and those already on the Q in the workspace expression. As 2 is the only value held in common, the result of this operation is 2; D 1 3 adds this subscript to the symbol. The subscript E 2 in the rule replaces the subscript values of E, 1, and 3, in the original constituent since there are no common values; F*C complements the values of F in the original constituent. Assuming the total possible values of F are the integers 1 to 5, the complement of 1, 3, 4 is 2, 5.

The COMIT system includes a special rule called a *list rule*. The list rule consists of two or more list subrules and resembles a dictionary, the left halves of the subrules of which correspond to dictionary entries. The symbol of a given workspace constituent or the compressed symbol of a sequence of such constituents can be looked up in a list rule. The subrules of the list rule "are automatically ordered by the compiler so that the interpreter at run-time can use a fast binary search" of the list rule [13, p. 21]. The right side of the list rule is the same as the right side of other rules allowing the execution of any of the operations which may be carried out by the regular COMIT rule.

Multiple branching and determination of the flow of control are operations called for by the right half and the routing. Subscript names and their values are in the same class as rule names and subrule names which govern the flow of control in COMIT. Subscripts thus are available to the programmer for use in determination of the flow of control either immediately or by means of the dispatcher. The programmer can set the dispatcher at any point in the program by means of a routing direction. Then, when the rule specified by the routing direction is selected for execution, a specified subrule of that rule will be chosen. This same method can be used for selecting a subset of the subrules of a rule so that under control of the COMIT system one of the specified subset of subrules is randomly selected for execution. A subscript attached to a constituent in the workspace expression may be used to set the dispatcher for the execution of a subrule specified by the subscript. For example, if the workspace expression contains the constituent VERB/NUMBER PLURAL, the rule below will set a rule with the rule name NUMBER to the subrule name identical to the value of the subscript NUMBER.

```
    VERB    VERB   //*D1  VERB-STEM
```

If the program branch is not specified in some way, a subrule of a rule with multiple subrules is selected randomly under control of a built-in pseudo-random-number generator [13, p. 24].

Failure to find the pattern specified in the left half of a rule results in transfer to the next rule. This transfer is a conditional transfer on failure as exemplified by the following rules:

```
    READ    READ = WRITE
    NEXT           LOOK
```

In the first rule if the search does not find a match for the constituent READ, the rule fails in the left half and the next rule is executed. This rule merely directs the execution of the rule LOOK.

Conditional transfer on success may be to a specified rule as in the first rule above. If the constituent READ is found in the workspace expression, the go-to indicates that the rule named WRITE is the next to be executed. Conditional transfer on success may also be determined by the subscript on the leftmost specified constituent in the workspace expression. Suppose the workspace expression contains the following: READ + NOUN/GENDER FEMININE. Then suppose the following rule:

$$\text{READ} \quad \text{READ} + \$1 = 2 + 1 \,//\text{*}{\rm D}1 \quad \$$$

This rule reverses the order of READ and the constituent to its immediate right. Then, *D1 sets the dispatcher from the subscripts on the constituent indicated by the first item in the right half. In this case when rule GENDER is executed, its subrule FEMININE is selected. The $-go-to identifies the next rule for execution as the one named by the first subscript on the leftmost constituent identified in the right half of the rule. In this case the only subscript is GENDER so this rule will be executed next.

Input and output operations are quite adequate. Arbitrary strings of characters can be submitted to the computer equipped with the COMIT system without format restrictions. Also, instructions written in the symbolic notation used within the computer can be submitted as data. For example, the sentence "The boy hit the dog." can be punched on cards as THE BOY HIT THE DOG. and submitted to the computer. The computer will then record it in the workspace as T+H+E+−+B+O+Y+−+H+I+T+−+T+H+E+−+D+O+G+. Data may also be written in workspace notation as, for example, T+H+E+−+B+O+Y+−+H+I+T+−+T+H+E+−+D+O+G+.+, so that it will appear in the workspace in exactly this format. In like manner COMIT can write arbitrary records either unhampered by fixed formats or as an exact reproduction of the workspace format.

COMIT has been designed for ease of learning. A programmer can learn it in a weekend and a novice in a course of six lectures. Manuals are a necessary part of the system and are available. The system has been running for four years on the IBM 709-7090 digital computer and is in use at over a dozen installations. During this period it has been applied to the study of problems in many areas, among which may be mentioned two sentence-production programs for English and one each for German, French, and Arabic, a sentence-for-sentence mechanical translation program, information retrieval research, vocabulary analysis, simulation of human problem solving, simulation of games, logico-semantic investigations, theorem proving and mathematical logic, text processing-editing, automatic milling machine programming, electrical network analysis, maintenance of predominantly nonnumerical files, simulation of learning processes, alphabetizing lists of words [*13*, p. 19], problems with naturally two-dimensional data, problems involving the manipulation of plane figures [*14*], and the graph isomorphism problem [*11*].

2.3 SNOBOL

SNOBOL is another promising problem-oriented programming language recently developed by Bell Telephone Laboratories and implemented for the IBM 7090. This language has been designed for research in mechanical translation, program compilation, and combinatorial problems, being oriented toward the manipulation of strings of symbols. It has been tested over the past two years on a variety of symbol-manipulation problems including program compilation and generation of symbolic equations. In a recent article a program for the alphabetizing of a list of words was presented *in toto* and discussed [*5*].

The basic data structure in SNOBOL is a string of symbols. The symbols are formed with characters and space, which serves as a break character for distinguishing the concatenated elements. I SAW THE BOY is a typical string. Names are assigned to strings for the purpose of quick identification. Any sequence of characters including space may form a substring which is identified by specifying it and assigning it a name. A substring "R R" can be formed from the Arabic phrase BINTU R RAJULI 'the man's daughter' by naming the characters, including the intervening space, and assigning it a name, e.g., DEFINITE. This substring is composed of the word R 'the' followed by R, the first letter of the following word to which the definite article is assimilated.

Operations which can be performed with the SNOBOL system include string formation, pattern matching, and replacement. Substrings may be formed by specifying a sequence of contiguous characters or other substrings, by concatenation, and by reiteration. String formation by concatenation permits the formation of substrings composed of two or more strings of characters or substrings which were not contiguous in the original data submitted to the computer. This process also permits the formation of substrings whose elements appear in orders different from those which they had relative to each other in the original data. Reiteration permits the formation of substrings in which original data are repeated.

The pattern-matching process makes possible the identification of various patterns found in the data. By this process a specified string may be examined to determine whether or not it contains specified sequences of contiguous or noncontiguous characters or substrings or combinations of these. The SNOBOL system also provides a process called *back referencing* which examines a string to determine whether or not the repetition of a substring occurs in it.

The balanced string variables offer a device which has proved useful in analyzing algebraic structures. These variables can only match a nonvoid substring which is balanced with respect to parentheses. Fixed-length string variables match substrings which consist of specified numbers of characters. It is to be assumed, apparently, that in this case space is not considered a character.

The contents of any string or substring may be altered by total or partial insertions, deletions, or replacements. These operations are dependent upon the identification of a sequence defined by the pattern-matching process. Deletion or replacement can be made conditional upon the environment of the item to be deleted or replaced.

Simple arithmetical operations are possible with strings of integers. Binary operations of addition, subtraction, multiplication, division, and exponentiation may be performed on the right side of any rule.

The go-to specifies the rule to which control is to be transferred. Unconditional transfer, conditional transfer on success, conditional transfer on failure, or a combination of these are possible. If no go-to is given in the statement, control is unconditionally transferred to the next rule. A simple method for the alteration of the program flow depending upon the data is also provided.

The input-output process permits the reading of any arbitrary string of characters into the computer without format restrictions. The string is given a name at the time of reading. SNOBOL statements are formed so as to manipulate the data within the computer in the form in which they are submitted.

There is no indication in the description of the SNOBOL system of a method for alternative replacements of a substring. Such a process would appear to be useful, or even necessary, for the production of alternative strings in the synthesis of natural language sentences. For example, given a string ARTICLE NOUN VERB, the SNOBOL system can be used to form a new string, THE BOY RUNS. The author has been unable to find examples showing how several alernate strings could be formed from the single original one. For example, by making use of the COMIT system, one can form the following sorts of strings from an original, parallel to that above: THE GIRL TALKS, SOME PEOPLE RUN.

2.4 The Linguistic Research System, University of Texas

The developers of the Linguistic Research System have made two assumptions which have significantly influenced the system's form. They assumed in the first place that machine translation would be accomplished through application of a particular procedure and secondly that a considerable number of people would be involved in any effective machine-translation project.

The machine-translation procedure which has been incorporated into their system is divided into three parts. First the input-language text is subjected to a thorough machine analysis which will eventually include lexical, syntactic, semantic, and pragmatic levels. The second part transfers the structures of the input produced by the analysis into structures which specify the output text to be produced by the third part. The production section, finally, makes use of the structures provided by the transfer section to produce text in the output language equivalent to the original input. The system reflects in part the results of thought in the area of semiotic theory, particularly the work of Charles W. Morris.

The second assumption has resulted in an apparently successful attempt to isolate the various parts of the system so that changes in one part may be generally expected to require no changes in any other part. A like segmentation of any system similar to LRS would seem to be essential.

The various independent parts of LRS are brought into association by the central Control Program, which coordinates all other programs of the system, and by all data common to more than one program used in it. Such data must be defined so that they are utilizable by every program which may refer to them.

The Linguistic Research System is divided into nine distinct areas coordinated by the central Control Program. These nine areas fall into two sections, Linguistic Information Processing and Language Data Processing. Linguistic Information Processing is composed of Monolingual Recognition, Interlingual Recognition, Transfer, Interlingual Production, and Monolingual Production. Language Data Processing includes the areas of Request Maintenance, Corpus Maintenance, Grammar Maintenance, and Transfer Maintenance.

Work on the system has, to the present time, been concentrated on the Language Data Processing areas, most of the principal programs of which have been essentially completed. Development of the Linguistic Information Processing part of the system has been devoted primarily to Monolingual Recognition, a number of programs of which are currently operative.

The primary function of the Control Program is the coordination of all other programs in the system. This program, in addition, handles data tape distribution and takes measures to correct failures in input from data tapes and output to them.

All programs in Language Data Processing and Linguistic Information Processing may be technically considered subprograms of the Control Program. It is through the Control Program that the linguist or researcher communicates with the system by means of the Request Tape. This tape is prepared from a deck of cards furnished by the linguist. It indicates, among other things, the programs and the data tapes to be used. By reference to the Request Tape the Control Program is able to regulate the order in which the subprograms are operated, loading them into the computer from magnetic tape as needed. Just as the linguist communicates with the system by way of the Control Program the system, in turn, communicates with the researcher through the Display Tape on which the Control Program writes all information of interest to him.

Considerable savings in computer space and time are made by allotting to the Control Program the problem of handling the placement of the data tapes. The subprograms ask the computer to supply data by name rather than by location. The computer operator has the task of supplying the Control Program with information regarding the location of the data tapes named by the researcher. The Control Program thus is able to supply the location of the particular data requested by the subprograms. This allocation of responsibility relieves all other programs of the problem of taking corrective action on read-write failures, with the resultant saving of space which would have otherwise had to be duplicated in each subprogram. Other devices are provided which reprimand the operator if the wrong data tape is supplied and tell him how to correct the situation.

The Control Program also prints an operational history of each run on a log tape. From this tape the researcher may learn "the sequence of the System programs performed, changes in program status, error conditions and attempts at correction," etc. [7, p. 88].

An outline of the Linguistic Information Processing section actually consists of a statement of the machine-translation procedure advocated by the group developing this system. Input data processed here are received from Language Data Processing. The areas of this section are entered serially, Recognition being followed by Transfer which in turn is followed by Production. This serial feature does not prevent the researcher from stopping the process at any point. For example, he may specify that only the programs pertinent to Recognition be executed. At various points in the run displays can be requested and on the basis of these the linguist may decide whether or not to continue the computer process.

The recognition process is divided into two types, monolingual and interlingual. Monolingual recognition provides structures for the input at the lexical, syntactic, semantic, and pragmatic levels by reference to the grammar of the input language organized in the form of a recognition grammar. The analysis is sequential in that the lexical recognition section processes the raw data as input, providing lexical structure. The output of this section is input for the syntactic section which provides syntactic structure. The output of the syntactic section serves as input for the semantic section and so on.

The interlingual recognition procedure follows Monolingual Recognition. This process resolves the input into interlingual classes which are common to the input and output languages under consideration.

The Transfer area is planned so as to replace the structures of the input language with equivalent structures in the output language.

Production is, in general, the reverse of Recognition. It begins by selecting, through the use of transfer rules, the monolingual structures specified by the interlingual classes which form its input. Monolingual Production cascades down through the pragmatic, semantic, syntactic, and lexical levels selecting structures as it goes to produce finally the output specified by the structures previously selected at the various levels.

The four areas which fall into the section entitled Language Data Processing furnish the researcher with the facilities needed for the revision, display, and selection of data for use elsewhere in the system.

Request Maintenance allows the linguist to revise the Request Tape. This tape is produced from a deck of cards prepared by the linguist for the identification of the subprograms required, the calling of data tapes to be used in the run, and so on. After the Control Program has ordered the contents of the cards and verified them for format errors, the results are displayed so that the linguist can make corrections before the tape is introduced to the rest of the system.

Corpus Maintenance is the section designed to provide for the accumulation of text on tape for later introduction to the translation process. One master tape is provided for each language under study. This section is programmed so that material may be added, modified, and deleted as required. Corpus Maintenance includes a Corpus Selection function which selects excerpts from the master tape to serve as input data for Monolingual Recognition.

Grammar Maintenance contains three main subfunctions: Grammar Revision, Grammar Display, and Grammar Selection. Over fifty per cent of all the coding in LRS is to be found in this section. The predominance here is due to the fact that this function is essential to the meaningful use of any other portion of the system. Once these programs are operational, the linguist is able to "gather and revise his data for use in the Linguistic Information Processing section as those programs become available" [7, p. 96].

The Grammar Revision function contains the rules and procedures which allow the linguist to add rules to the grammar, delete them from it, or to change one or another of their features. This function also keeps track of the variables and constants in order to detect lacunae and incoherencies among the rules of the grammar. It is able to correct some errors by rejection of bad requests and to point out others by referring them to the researcher through the medium of the Display Tape.

The Grammar Selection function is designed to form two subgrammars, the Input Grammar used in Monolingual Recognition and the Output Grammar used in Monolingual Production. Considerable research remains to be done before this section of the system will perform both tasks.

Transfer Maintenance contains programs which process the interlingual data in much the same way as Grammar Maintenance processes the monolingual data. It is proposed that in order to transfer from the input language structures to the output language structures, "the structural information of the input language must be grouped into interlingual classes common to both languages" [7, p. 99]. This process is called Interlingual Recognition. To carry it out, the linguist prepares transfer rules which assign the monolingual structures to interlingual substitution classes. Transfer Maintenance then uses these rules to form automatically interlingual distribution classes which are defined as the units of replacement in the Transfer process.

2.5 The Wayne State University Interpretive System

Although this system has been composed for research in the syntactic analysis of Russian, it appears to be of a generality sufficient to make it useful in the analyses of texts in other languages. Its preparation has been inspired by the need for recursive subroutines and for more than the customary number of index registers.

To use the Wayne system the programmer prepares a syntactic analysis routine composed of sequences of instructions for direct SE9AP assembly or of pseudo-instructions. These routines apply to pre-edited input which consists of lists "of grammatical information code sets ... where each set corresponds to (or describes) a word or other symbol in a Russian sentence" [2]. This pre-edited input along with a set of computer words in binary notation called *masks* is processed by the system.

The Wayne system is composed of two computer programs. The first, the Input Translator, converts the pseudo-instructions of the syntactic analysis routine into a format suitable for SE9AP assembly. The other program, called the *Interpreter*, is an executive subroutine made up of a set of routines which recognizes and applies to the code set of the input the sequences of instructions composing the syntactic analysis routine.

The syntactic analysis routine prescribes tests to be performed on "elements (bit positions or clusters of bit positions) of the grammar sets" [2] as well as modifications of these elements. Examples of tests which may be used in the syntactic analyses include comparisons of elements of different sets or of elements of a set and specified masks.

The interpreter makes use of three main storage areas: one which preserves the code sets providing grammatical information about the sentence, a second which stores the masks, and a third which contains the index registers and other information.

The pseudo-instructions used in the syntactic analysis routine are divided into five classes: transfer, logical, testing, indexing, and miscellaneous instructions. The transfer instructions provide for unconditional transfer and two- and three-way conditional transfer within the interpretive routine as well as for transfer out of it.

The logical instructions include "and," "or," and "exclusive-or" operations which also specify tests utilizing various masks to determine whether or not the results of the logical operations meet required specifications. Two other more complex logical instructions are also provided.

The one specific testing instruction compares the contents of any two locations distinguishing one as greater than, equal to, or less than the other.

The indexing instructions are used to replace information in one location with information from another and to add to or subtract from the contents of one location the contents of another location.

The miscellaneous instructions specify right and left shifts of the contents of a location, the moving of a block of words, and the replacement of the contents of certain positions of a location by the contents of corresponding positions of a second location.

This system has been used for several years by the machine translation group at Wayne State University in the study of Russian syntax. It has proved to be a usable system for the syntactic analysis of Russian, but the pre-editing requirement would seem to present something of a handicap.

2.6 MIMIC

MIMIC is a member of the general class of languages to which the Wayne system and COMIT belong. It was prepared by the Rand Corporation "specifically to program the rules for insertion and inflection of English equivalents in the RAND Russian-English translation routine" [8, pp. 2 and 3]. Originally it was used for the production of English sentences but has since been retired in favor of FORTRAN and a new system in the process of development.

MIMIC represents a relatively early attempt to provide for the writing of computer programs composed of sets of rules which closely resemble English sentences. J-4 IF PART-OF-SPEECH = NOUN, GO-TO K-1 provides an example of such a rule.

The system is composed of a translator and an interpreter. The translator analyzes each rule and translates it into a pseudo-code which the interpreter uses to execute the programs specified by the linguist.

The three general types of rules allowed by the system are described as imperative, conditional, and definitional. The eight imperative rules consist of orders such as those expressed in go-to and exit statements. The conditional rules consist of tests which if met activate go-to instructions. These rules may contain imperatives to be executed before the rules indicated by the go-to's come into control. If the test fails, the next rule is executed.

The definition statement permits the programmer to define new terminology to be used in the writing of program rules. For example, D-6 DEFINE PART-OF-SPEECH AS POSITION-1 OF THE GRAMMAR-CODE is a definition statement which furnishes the programmer a term, PART-OF-SPEECH, with a greater mnemonic value than that possessed by the primitive term, POSITION-1.

Each word used in a program is found either in the translator's dictionary as a primitive term or entered into it by a definition statement. The words are classed as performing one of ten functions, examples of which are "imperative command," "item," "mask," and "relation." The inability of the definition statements to supply ambiguity in function and meaning to words in the program was felt to be overly restrictive. Kelly's illustration of the problem furnishes an interesting confirmation of the value of ambiguity in natural languages [8, pp. 4 and 5].

Although MIMIC is no longer used and is outclassed by the more elaborate and powerful COMIT and SNOBOL systems, it deserves recognition as one of the few systems the development of which was motivated specifically by the desire to carry on research in machine translation and the linguistic problems arising relative to this research.

3. A Sentence-Parsing Program in COMIT

In this section a program designed to parse sentences generated by a slightly revised version of a discontinuous-constituent phrase-structure grammar of a fragment of English written by Yngve [12, pp. 446 and 449] is presented as an illustration of the COMIT system. The grammar is composed of the following rules.

(1) *Sentences and clause*
- S   = NP1 + VP1
- S   = NP2 + VP2
- S   = S1
- S1 = NPP + VP
- CL = CT + S

(2) *Verb phrases*
- VP = VH + NPP
- VP = VT + NP
- VP1 = V1 + ADJ
- VP2 = V2 + ADV
- VP2 = V2

(3) *Nominals*
- NP = NPP
- NP = NPT
- NPP = T + N
- NPT = T + NT
- NP1 = PIT + ... + CL

(4) *Adverbials*
- ADV = ADV1 + ADV2
- ADV1 = COMP + ... + NP
- ADV1 = very
- COMP = COMP1 + ... + COMP1

(5) *Lexicon*
- ADJ   = true
- ADV2 = far
- COMP1 = as
- CT   = that
- N   = man, boy
- NP2   = he
- NT   = corner
- PIT   = it
- T   = the, a
- V1   = is
- V2   = went
- VH   = heard
- VT   = saw

Each rule consists of a left and a right half separated by the equals sign, to be read "is rewritten as." The symbol on the left side of this sign is the constitute or name of the construction produced by the rule. The symbol(s) on the right side composes the immediate constituent(s) of that construction. If there is more than one rule with the same left side, any such rule may be selected at random to expand the construction. The left branch is always expanded before the right branch, the expansion continuing to the left until the final constituent fails to match the left side of a rule in the grammar. At this point the next leftmost branch is expanded (Fig. 1).

The grammar is composed of three kinds of rules exemplified by the monadic rule S = S1, the dyadic rule S1 = NPP + VP and the discontinuous rule NP1 = PIT + ... + CL. The monadic rule, illustrated in Fig. 1, rewrites a constituent as another constituent. The dyadic rule expands a constitute into two consecutive constituents. The discontinuous rule braces the constituent to the immediate right of the constitute which matches its left side with the expansion of that constitute. If the discontinuous rule B = E + ... + F is applied to the sequence | B | CD, the result will be | E | CFD. Here the constitute B is rewritten as E bracing the C on the left and F bracing it on the right.

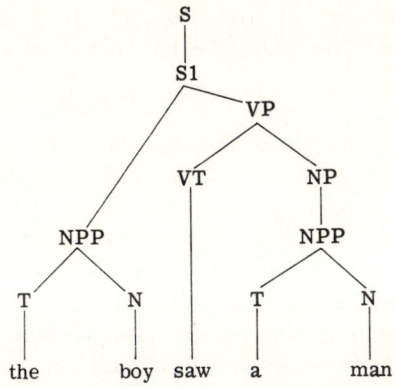

Fig. 1. Expansion of a simple sentence.

Figure 2 furnishes an example of an expansion of the discontinuous rule, NP1 = PIT + ... + CL. In addition to sentences like those in the figures, the grammar produces such sentences as: "He went as far as the corner"; "It is true that the man heard a boy"; and "It is true that it is true that he went very far."

Two interesting features of the grammar are found in its method of producing discontinuous constructions and its illustration of sentence embedding, a process which generates an infinite number of sentences. The grammar is described in considerable detail by Yngve [*12*].

The sentence-parsing program makes use of the immediate constituent method of syntactic analysis. According to this method the most deeply nested structures are first identified, the identification of the next most deeply nested structures following. In this way the tree-structure is built from the inside out. "Predictive analysis," the

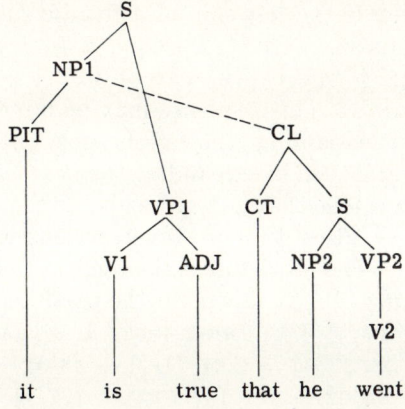

Fig. 2. Expansion illustrating a discontinuous rule.

"dependency connection" approaches, and "analysis by synthesis" are all distinct from the "immediate constituent" method of analysis [9, pp. 1–5].

The sentence-parsing program is divided into five sections: the four input rules (1–12), the three list look-up rules (21–23), the three BRACKET rules (24–26), the list rule (subrules L1–L16) and terminal list rule, the 53 sentence-parsing rules (31–217), and the output rule 218. In the course of the analysis the program requires the identification of various subtrees. The BRACKET subroutine illustrates the simple manner in which this identification is achieved by COMIT.

The sentences are read in, parsed, and written out one at a time. The list rule prefixes to each word in the sentence a constituent which indicates the grammatical class to which the word belongs. After all the words have been processed by the list rule, the sentence "The boy saw a man." reads T/.1 + THE/OT + N/.1 + BOY/OT + VT/.1 + SAW/OT + T/.1 + A/OT + N/.1 + MAN/OT. The numerical subscript indicates that the constituent bearing it matches the left side of a monadic rule. This subscript is used by the BRACKET subroutine explained below. The subscript OT identifies terminal constituents for the computer.

Rule 31 seeks something or nothing, an operation indicated by the dollar sign, followed by a T, followed by any single constituent ($1), followed by an N. If it finds such a sequence, it prefixes NPP/.2 to the construction and queues the evolving analysis through the N on shelf 1. The go-to indicates that the rule is executed repeatedly until it fails to find a match in the workspace. On failure, the next rule is entered and the workspace is restored by prefixing to it all on shelf 1 (through the routing instruction *A1 1). At this point the evolving analysis of the sentence is NPP/.2 + T/.1 + THE/OT + N/.1 + BOY/OT + VT/.1 + SAW/OT + NPP/.2 + T/.1 + A/OT + N/.1 + MAN/OT. The numerical subscript 2 indicates that NPP is the left side of a dyadic rule. The completely parsed sentence reads S/.1 + S*1/.2 + NPP/.2 + T/.1 + THE/OT + N/.1 + BOY/OT + VP/.2 + VT/.1 + SAW/OT + NP/.1 + NPP/.2 + T/.1 + A/OT + N/.1 + MAN/OT. This sequence may be interpreted two dimensionally (Fig. 1) by expanding the left branch until a terminal constituent is reached and then by expanding the next leftmost branch, etc.

The sentence "It is true that he went as far as the corner." illustrates the parsing of three discontinuous constructions and the use of the BRACKET subroutine. The procedure is the same as that for the preceding sentence through rule 112. At this point the parsing is PIT/.1 + IT/OT + V*1/.1 + IS/OT + ADJ/.1 + TRUE/OT + CT/.1 + THAT/OT + NP*2/.1 + HE/OT + V*2/.1 + WENT/OT + COMP*1/.1 + AS/OT + ADV*2/.1 + FAR/OT + COMP*1/.1 + AS/OT + NP/.1 + NPT/.2 + T/.1 + THE/OT + NT/.1 + CORNER/OT. (Fig. 3 below line A).

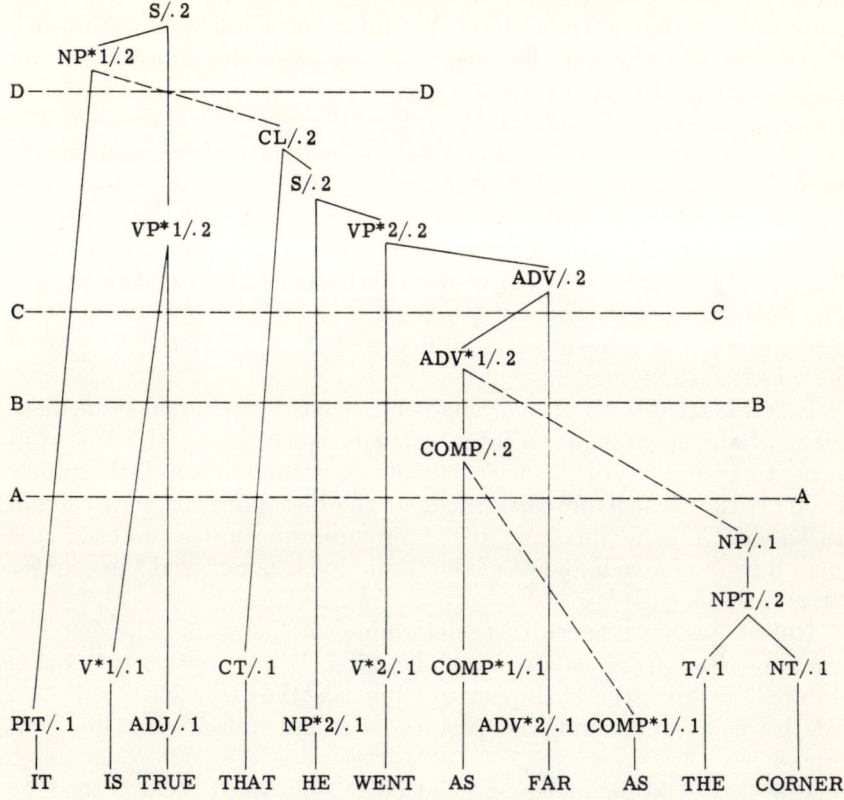

FIG. 3. Parsing of the sentence: "It is true that he went as far as the corner."

The grammar shows that COMP*1 is the left-hand constituent of a discontinuous construction. One of the axioms on which the grammar is constructed states that only one branch may occur between the left- and right-hand constituents of a discontinuous construction. Having found COMP*1, the computer is programmed to bracket the subtree to the immediate right of this constituent. After it has done so, it must discover whether or not the next constituent is the right-hand one of the discontinuous construction. If it is not, then the sentence is either beyond the competence of the program to parse or ungrammatical. The constituent *P/.2,123 is a counter placed to the immediate left of the analysis following AS/OT. Everything to the left of COMP*1 is queued on shelf 1 and the go-to calls for the execution of rule BRACKET. This rule first determines whether the numerical subscript on *P is one. It is not; therefore, the next rule is executed. This rule reverses the order of *P and the constituent to its immediate right, increases the numerical subscript of *P by the numerical subscript of the constituent with which it just reversed positions. The next rule decreases this sum by one and directs the repetition of the execution of rule BRACKET. The numerical subscript of *P is still not one; therefore, the next rule is entered. The constituent to the right of *P is now FAR/OT, with no numerical subscript; therefore, the subscript of *P remains two. The next rule reduces this to one and the rule BRACKET discovers this fact. The $-go-to now directs the execution of rule 123 named by the logical subscript found on *P, completing the execution of the subroutine BRACKET. The *P now lies to the immediate right of the subtree the left-hand constituent of which lies to the immediate right of COMP*1 + *P before the subroutine BRACKET was executed.

Rule 123 seeks to determine whether the constituent to the immediate right of the single subtree intervening between it and the left-hand constituent COMP*1 of the discontinuous construction is in fact another COMP*1, the right-hand constituent of the discontinuous construction to be identified. In this case it is; therefore, the constitute COMP/ .2 is placed to the immediate left of the whole construction and the counter *P is deleted.

Rule 121 is again executed to determine whether or not the sentence contains a second construction of this kind. It does not so rule 122 is entered, restoring the workspace and directing the execution of rule 131. At this point the parsing has progressed as illustrated below line B in Fig. 3.

Rule 131 seeks for the constituent COMP. This constituent is the left-hand constituent of the discontinuous construction the right-hand constituent of which is NP. The computer must be programmed by using the subroutine BRACKET to determine whether or not an NP occurs in the correct position to the right. In this case, both the discontinuous construction COMP and the construction it embraces must be bracketed. As these two constructions consist of two subtrees, *P is given the numerical subscript three (instead of two as in rule 121) and directed to execute rule 133 when the subroutine BRACKET is completed. These subscripts are placed on *P and everything to the left of COMP is queued on shelf 1. When subroutine BRACKET has been completed, rule 133 finds that NP does lie to the immediate right of COMP; and therefore, ADV*1/ .2, naming the discontinuous construction of which COMP is the left-hand constituent, is placed to its immediate left. At this point the parsing has progressed to the point shown below line C (Fig. 3). Rule 151 recognizes ADV*1 and ADV*2 as constituents of the construction ADV. From this point, the rules continue as before until 191 has been executed.

The situation immediately before the execution of rule 201 is indicated below line D (Fig. 3). The workspace contains PIT/ .1 + IT/OT + VP*1/ .2 + V*1/ .1 + IS/OT + ADJ/ .1 + TRUE/OT + CL/ .2 + CT/ .1 + THAT/OT + S/ .2 + NP*2/ .1 + HE/OT + VP*2/ .2 + V*2/ .1 + WENT/OT + ADV/ .2 + ADV*1/ .2 + COMP/ .2 + COMP*1/ .1 + AS/OT + ADV*2/ .1 + FAR/OT + COMP*1/ .1 + AS/OT + NP/ .1 + NPT/ .2 + T/.1 + THE/OT + NT/ .1 + CORNER/OT. Rule 201 is equivalent to rule 121. After the execution of subroutine BRACKET, rule 203 finds the right-hand constituent CL of the discontinuous construction to the right of the counter *P and marks the construction of which CL is the right-hand constituent as an NP*1. Rule 211 then recognizes NP*1 followed by VP*1 with two intervening constituents as a sentence. Rules 213–217 are used to identify embedded sentences of the type: "It is true that it is true that it is true that he went as far as the corner." The parsing of this sentence is left to the reader.

ARNOLD C. SATTERTHWAIT

3.1 The Program and Input Sentences

```
           COM C-0597 JUNE 14 1965 ENGAN SATTERTHWAIT    •                 0
  1  $//*RCR1                                           11                 1
                                                        FINAL              2
 11  $+.=A+1+2//*A1 1                                   21                11
  •   $//*Q1 1                                           1                12
 21  $+-=1//*L1                                         LIST              21
  •  $+.=1//*L1                                         LIST              22
  •  $//*A1 1                                           31                23
 BRACKET  *P/.1                            $            •                 24
  •        *P+$1=2+1/.I.*2                              •
  •        *P=1/.C1                      BRACKET                          26
 -LIST A       =T+1         •                           L   1
         AS    =COMP*1+1    •                           L   2
         BOY   =N+1         •                           L   3
         CORNER=NT+1        •                           L   4
         FAR   =ADV*2+1     •                           L   5
         HE    =NP*2+1 .                                L   6
         HEARD =VH+1        •                           L   7
         IS    =V*1+1       •                           L   8
         IT    =PIT+1       •                           L   9
         MAN   =N+1         •                           L  10
         SAW   =VT+1        •                           L  11
         THAT  =CT+1        •                           L  12
         THE   =T+1         •                           L  13
         TRUE  =ACJ+1       •                           L  14
         VERY  =ADV*1+1     •                           L  15
         WENT  =V*2+1       •                           L  16
  •      $1+$1=1/.1+2/OT//*C1 1 2                       21                L  END
 31  $+T+$1+N=1+NPP/.2+2+3+4          //*Q1 1 2 3 4 5   31                31
  •   $=A+1//*A1 1                                       •
 41  $+T+$1+NT=1+NPT/.2+2+3+4         //*Q1 1 2 3 4 5   41                41
  •   $=A+1//*A1 1                                       •
 51  $+NPT=1+NP/.1+2                  //*Q1 1 2 3       51                51
  •   $=A+1//*A1 1
 61  $+NPP+$4+VH=1+*Y+3+4             //*Q1 1 2 3 4     61                61
  •   $=A+1//*A1 1                                       •                62
 63  $+NPP+$4+VT=1+*Y+3+4             //*Q1 1 2 3 4     63                63
  •   $=A+1//*A1 1
 64A $+VH+$1+NPP=1+2+3+*Y             //*Q1 1 2 3 4     64A               64A
  •   $=A+1//*A1 1                     ,                 •                64B
 65  $+NPP=1+NP/.1+2                  //*Q1 1 2 3       65                65
  •   $=A+1//*A1 1
 67  $+*Y=1+NPP/.2//*Q1 1 2                             67                67
  •   $=A+1//*A1 1                                       •
 71  $+VH+$1+NPP=1+VP/.2+2+3+4        //*Q1 1 2 3 4 5   71                71
  •   $=A+1//*A1 1                                       •
 81  $+VT+$1+NP=1+VP/.2+2+3+4         //*Q1 1 2 3 4 5   81                81
  •   $=A+1//*A1 1                                       •
 91  $+NPP+$4+VP=1+S*1/.2+2+3+4       //*Q1 1 2 3 4 5   91                91
  •   $=A+1//*A1 1
111  $+S*1=1+S/.1+2                   //*Q1 1 2 3      111               111
  •   $=A+1//*A1 1                                       •
121  $+COMP*1+$1=1+2+3+*P/.2,123      //*Q1 1          BRACKET           121
  •   $=A+1//*A1 1                                     131               122
123  $+*P+CCMP*1=COMP/.2+1+3          //*Q1 1 2 3      121               123
131  $+CCMP=1+*P/.3,133+2             //*Q1 1          BRACKET           131
  •   $=A+1//*A1 1                                     141               132
```

```
133 $+*P+NP=ADV*1/.2+1+3              //*Q1 1 2 3          131         133
141 $+ADV*1+$1+ADV*2=1+ACV/.2+2+3+4    //*Q1 1 2 3 4 5     141         141
 *   $=A+1//*A1 1                                           *
151 $+ADV*1+$3+ADV*2=1+ADV/.2+2+3+4    //*Q1 1 2 3 4 5     151         151
 *   $=A+1//*A1 1                                           *
161 $+V*2+$1+ADV=1+VP*2/.2+2+3+4       //*Q1 1 2 3 4 5     161         161
 *   $=A+1//*A1 1                                           *
165 $+$1/OT+V*2=1+2+VP*2/.1+3//*Q1 1 2 3 4                 165         165
 *   $=A+1//*A1 1                                           *
171 $+NP*2+$1+VP*2=1+S/.2+2+3+4        //*Q1 1 2 3 4 5     171         171
 *   $=A+1//*A1 1                                           *
181 $+V*1+$1+ADJ=1+VP*1/.2+2+3+4       //*Q1 1 2 3 4 5     181         181
 *   $=A+1//*A1 1                                           *
191 $+CT+$1+S=1+CL/.2+2+3+4                                            191
201 $+PIT+$1=1+2+3+*P/.2,203           //*Q1 1             BRACKET     201
                                                           218         202
203 $+*P+CL=NP*1/.2+1+3                                    211         203
204 $+*P+$+PIT+$1=1+3+4+5+2/.2 //*Q1 1 2                   BRACKET     204
211 $+NP*1+$2+VP*1=A+1+S/.2+2+3+4      //*A1 1             213         211
213 $=*X+1                                                  *          213
214 *X+$+CT=2+3+1                                           *          214
 *   $+CL+CT+*X//*Q1 1 2 3                                 214         215
 *   $+CT+*X=1+2                                           191         216
 *   *X=0                                                  218         217
218 $=A+1+-*.*.//*A1 1,*hSM1 2,*WAM3                        1          218
FINAL              *                                                   FINAL
     END
A MAN SAW THE CORNER.
THE BOY HEARD A MAN.
A BOY SAW THE MAN.
HE WENT.
HE WENT VERY FAR.
HE WENT AS FAR AS THE CORNER.
HE WENT AS FAR AS A MAN.
IT IS TRUE THAT THE BOY HEARD A MAN.
IT IS TRUE THAT A MAN SAW THE CORNER.
IT IS TRUE THAT HE WENT.
IT IS TRUE THAT HE WENT VERY FAR.
IT IS TRUE THAT HE WENT AS FAR AS THE CORNER.
IT IS TRUE THAT IT IS TRUE THAT HE WENT AS FAR AS THE CORNER.
IT IS TRUE THAT IT IS TRUE THAT IT IS TRUE THAT THE MAN HEARD THE BOY.
```

3.2 The Output

```
S / .1 + S*1 / .2 + NPP / .2 + T / .1 + A / OT + N / .1 + MAN
/ OT + VP / .2 + VT / .1 + SAW / CT + NP / .1 + NPT / .2 + T
/ .1 + THE / OT + NT / .1 + CORNER/ OT +

S / .1 + S*1 / .2 + NPP / .2 + T / .1 + THE / OT + N / .1 +
BOY / OT + VP / .2 + VH / .1 + HEARD / OT + NPP / .2 + T / .1
+ A / CT + N / .1 + MAN / CT +

S / .1 + S*1 / .2 + NPP / .2 + T / .1 + A / OT + N / .1 + BOY
/ OT + VP / .2 + VT / .1 + SAW / CT + NP / .1 + NPP / .2 + T
/ .1 + THE / OT + N / .1 + MAN / OT +

S / .2 + NP*2 / .1 + HE / OT + VP*2 / .1 + V*2 / .1 + WENT /
OT +

S / .2 + NP*2 / .1 + HE / OT + VP*2 / .2 + V*2 / .1 + WENT /
OT + ADV / .2 + ADV*1 / .1 + VERY / OT + ADV*2 / .1 + FAR /
OT +

S / .2 + NP*2 / .1 + HE / OT + VP*2 / .2 + V*2 / .1 + WENT /
OT + ADV / .2 + ADV*1 / .2 + COMP / .2 + COMP*1/ .1 + AS / OT
+ ADV*2 / .1 + FAR / OT + COMP*1/ .1 + AS / OT + NP / .1 + NPT
/ .2 + T / .1 + THE / OT + NT / .1 + CORNER/ OT +

S / .2 + NP*2 / .1 + HE / OT + VP*2 / .2 + V*2 / .1 + WENT /
OT + ADV / .2 + ADV*1 / .2 + COMP / .2 + COMP*1/ .1 + AS / OT
+ ADV*2 / .1 + FAR / OT + COMP*1/ .1 + AS / OT + NP / .1 + NPP
/ .2 + T / .1 + A / OT + N / .1 + MAN / OT +

S / .2 + NP*1 / .2 + PIT / .1 + IT / CT + VP*1 / .2 + V*1 /
.1 + IS / CT + ADJ / .1 + TRUE / CT + CL / .2 + CT / .1 + THAT
/ OT + S / .1 + S*1 / .2 + NPP / .2 + T / .1 + THE / OT + N
/ .1 + BOY / OT + VP / .2 + VH / .1 + HEARD / OT + NPP / .2
+ T / .1 + A / OT + N / .1 + MAN / OT +

S / .2 + NP*1 / .2 + PIT / .1 + IT / OT + VP*1 / .2 + V*1 /
.1 + IS / CT + ADJ / .1 + TRUE / OT + CL / .2 + CT / .1 + THAT
/ OT + S / .1 + S*1 / .2 + NPP / .2 + T / .1 + A / OT + N /
.1 + MAN / CT + VP / .2 + VT / .1 + SAW / OT + NP / .1 + NPT
/ .2 + T / .1 + THE / CT + NT / .1 + CORNER/ CT +

S / .2 + NP*1 / .2 + PIT / .1 + IT / CT + VP*1 / .2 + V*1 /
.1 + IS / OT + ADJ / .1 + TRUE / CT + CL / .2 + CT / .1 + THAT
/ OT + S / .2 + NP*2 / .1 + HE / OT + VP*2 / .1 + V*2 / .1 +
WENT / CT +

S / .2 + NP*1 / .2 + PIT / .1 + IT / CT + VP*1 / .2 + V*1 /
.1 + IS / CT + ADJ / .1 + TRUE / OT + CL / .2 + CT / .1 + THAT
/ OT + S / .2 + NP*2 / .1 + HE / CT + VP*2 / .2 + V*2 / .1 +
WENT / CT + ADV / .2 + ADV*1 / .1 + VERY / CT + ADV*2 / .1 +
FAR / CT +
```

PROGRAMMING LANGUAGES FOR LINGUISTICS

```
S / .2 + NP*1 / .2 + PIT / .1 + IT / OT + VP*1 / .2 + V*1 /
.1 + IS / CT + ADJ / .1 + TRUE / OT + CL / .2 + CT / .1 + THAT
/ OT + S / .2 + NP*2 / .1 + HE / OT + VP*2 / .2 + V*2 / .1 +
WENT / OT + ADV / .2 + ADV*1 / .2 + COMP / .2 + COMP*1/ .1 +
AS / CT + ADV*2 / .1 + FAR / CT + COMP*1/ .1 + AS / OT + NP
/ .1 + NPT / .2 + T / .1 + THE / CT + NT / .1 + CORNER/ OT +

S / .2 + NP*1 / .2 + PIT / .1 + IT / OT + VP*1 / .2 + V*1 /
.1 + IS / CT + ADJ / .1 + TRUE / OT + CL / .2 + CT / .1 + THAT
/ OT + S / .2 + NP*1 / .2 + PIT / .1 + IT / OT + VP*1 / .2 +
V*1 / .1 + IS / CT + ADJ / .1 + TRUE / OT + CL / .2 + CT / .1
+ THAT / OT + S / .2 + NP*2 / .1 + HE / OT + VP*2 / .2 + V*2
/ .1 + WENT / OT + ADV / .2 + ADV*1 / .2 + COMP / .2 + COMP*1/
.1 + AS / CT + ADV*2 / .1 + FAR / OT + COMP*1/ .1 + AS / OT
+ NP / .1 + NPT / .2 + T / .1 + THE / OT + NT / .1 + CORNER/
OT +

S / .2 + NP*1 / .2 + PIT / .1 + IT / OT + VP*1 / .2 + V*1 /
.1 + IS / CT + ADJ / .1 + TRUE / CT + CL / .2 + CT / .1 + THAT
/ OT + S / .2 + NP*1 / .2 + PIT / .1 + IT / OT + VP*1 / .2 +
V*1 / .1 + IS / OT + ADJ / .1 + TRUE / OT + CL / .2 + CT / .1
+ THAT / OT + S / .2 + NP*1 / .2 + PIT / .1 + IT / OT + VP*1
/ .2 + V*1 / .1 + IS / OT + ADJ / .1 + TRUE / OT + CL / .2 +
CT / .1 + THAT / OT + S / .1 + S*1 / .2 + NPP / .2 + T / .1
+ THE / OT + N / .1 + MAN / OT + VP / .2 + VH / .1 + HEARD /
OT + NPP / .2 + T / .1 + THE / CT + N / .1 + BOY / OT +

22565 REGISTERS OF THE WORKSPACE WERE UNUSED.
```

Acknowledgment

The author is grateful to Ottis Rechard from whom he has profited greatly by discussion concerning the ideas presented in this article. The author is, of course, solely responsible for any errors or oversights to be found herein.

References

1. Bobrow, D. G., and Raphael, B., A comparison of list-processing computer languages. *Comm. ACM* **7**, 231–240 (1964).
2. Borris, M., *The Interpretive System*, 3rd Ann Rept. on Res. in Machine Translation. Wayne State Univ., Detroit, Michigan, 1961.
3. Bosche, C., COMIT: A language for symbol manipulation. In *Symbolic Languages In Data Processing*. Gordon & Breach, New York, 1962.
4. COMIT *Programmers, Reference Manual*. MIT Res. Lab. of Electronics and the Computation Center. Mass. Inst. Technol., Cambridge, Massachusetts (revised 1962).
5. Farber, D. J., Griswold, R. E., and Polonsky, I. P., SNOBOL, A string manipulation language. *J. ACM* **11**, 21–30 (1964).
6. *Introduction to* COMIT *Programming*. MIT Res. Lab. of Electronics and the Computation Center. Mass. Inst. Technol., Cambridge, Massachusetts (revised 1962).
7. Jonas, R. W., Computer programming. In *Symposium on the Current Status of Research*. Univ. of Texas Press, Austin, Texas, 1963.
8. Kelly, H. S., MIMIC: A translator for English coding. RAND Corp. Memo No. P-1926. Santa Monica, California, 1960.
9. Knowlton, K. C., *Sentence Parsing with a Self-Organizing Heuristic Program*. MIT Res. Lab. of Electronics. Mass. Inst. Technol., Cambridge, Massachusetts, 1963.
10. Pendergraft, E. D., Personal letter (1964).
11. Unger, S. H., GIT—a heuristic program for testing pairs of directed line graphs for isomorphism. *Comm. ACM* **7**, 26–34 (1964).
12. Yngve, V. H., A model and an hypothesis for language structure. *Proc. Am. Phil. Soc.* **104**, 444–466 (1960).
13. Yngve, V. H., COMIT as an information retrieval language. *Comm. ACM* **5**, 19–27 (1962).
14. Yngve, V. H., COMIT for n-dimensional problems (1962, unpublished).

Computer Driven Displays and Their Use in Man/Machine Interaction*

ANDRIES VAN DAM†

Moore School of Electrical Engineering
University of Pennsylvania, Philadelphia, Pennsylvania

1. Introduction and History 239
2. Display Technology 242
   2.1 Classification of Displays 242
   2.2 Human-Factors Dependent Parameters 243
   2.3 Task Dependent Parameters 254
   2.4 Display System Block Diagram 257
   2.5 Computer System (Block 2) 259
   2.6 Buffer (Block 3) 259
   2.7 Command Decoding (Block 4) 260
   2.8 Display Generation (Block 5) 261
   2.9 Display Presentation (Block 6) 267
   2.10 Multiple Remote Displays and Manual Inputs (Block 8) . 276
3. Man/Machine Interaction 278
   3.1 Introduction 278
   3.2 On-Line Programming 280
   3.3 Computer-Assisted Instruction 281
   3.4 Computer-Aided Design 282
   3.5 Conclusion 285
   References 287
   Bibliography 289

1. Introduction and History

Psychologists have estimated that as much as eighty per cent of our sensory data is received in the form of visual stimuli. It is therefore surprising to find that the field of computer driven visual displays has lagged behind the development of the computer complex as a whole,

---

*Adapted from "A Survey of Pictorial Data Processing Techniques and Equipments," August, 1965, prepared by the author for the Research Division of the Naval Bureau of Supplies and Accounts, and the Information Systems Branch of the Office of Naval Research, under Contract NOnr 551(40).

†*Present address:* Brown University, Providence, Rhode Island.

virtually since the birth of the computer in 1945. Recently, however, interest in extending the capabilities of the input/output (I/O) function of the computer system has been greatly stimulated. This has been done chiefly by the Armed Services through their need for real or nearly real time command and control display screens, and to a lesser extent by private research into graphic man/machine interaction such as that pioneered at MIT.

Electrically driven graphical output devices have, of course, been present for many years. Witness strip and circular chart recorders, and today's most prevalent display device, the cathode ray tube (CRT) console, a refinement of the oscilloscope which was known in the thirties and is still the tool most useful to electrical engineers. The development of radar and television was greatly responsible for increasing the power and corresponding potential of the CRT, and showed how information could be encoded electronically for display as part of a decision-making or information-gathering process. This indicated the possibility of a level of abstraction much above that of the waveform representation used by electrical engineers in their problem solving—mapping the behavior of circuits.

Despite such evidence, CRT technology was not used for the I/O function of the computer until the early 1950's. Until then, the principal I/O units were teletype printers and electric console typewriters, later augmented by off-line high-speed printers. Clever programs were written to format output so as to produce tables, charts, graphs, and even pictures of Alfred E. Neuman, which in effect amounted to a simulation of a latter-day plotter or cathode ray tube. These hard copy output devices, however, even in their vastly improved forms today, are only first generation devices limited by their mechanical nature to speeds of from tens of characters per second to twelve hundred lines per minute. They have minimal ability to handle graphical, non-alphanumeric information. Economy is their only advantage and explains the prevalence of teletypes in current multiconsole time sharing systems such as MAC at MIT.

In 1951 and 1952, the second generation "soft copy" CRT display made its appearance at a number of institutions simultaneously [1]. Operating at electronic speeds, it formed a much more viable interface between the user operating with extensive perceptive capabilities, but with a small instantaneous memory capacity, and the large information capacity milli- (or micro-) second computer. Cathode ray tubes (and other computer driven displays) allow real time display of much greater quantities of information than typewriters, and are much more flexible in the nature of the information which can be displayed or entered into the system, and the manner in which it can be arranged or manipulated.

Accordingly, in 1951, MIT utilized two 16-in. scopes as part of the output equipment of WHIRLWIND I. One maintained a visible screen, and the other fed a computer-controlled camera. An application was plotting the trajectory of a bouncing ball, while its equations of motion were solved by the computer. This produced output similar to that of a pen recorder driven by an analog computer. Another early application was the generation of antenna patterns to check design specifications.

During this same period, at the University of Illinois, ILLIAC was driving dual scopes (also one with a computer-controlled recording camera) with solutions of boundary value problems. The operator could monitor, on line, the progress of a calculation, detect obvious programming errors, and make better initial guesses during iterative computations or parameter-dependent procedures. This illustrated one of the earliest on-line man/machine interaction processes. The interaction concept became integral to what is the best known (and probably the largest) display center—that associated with the SAGE system (*circa* 1955). Tactical decisions related to the air threat at specified instants of time were made in a multiconsole, multiuser configuration with human feedback entering the system via light pens with pointing capability, toggles, and alphanumeric and function keyboards.

One of the earliest computer status displays was that associated with ORDVAC in operation in 1952 at the Aberdeen Proving Grounds. A CRT maintained a 1024-spot display, one spot per memory location. A memory access resulted in a spot's illumination, thus giving a representation of the internal action, and thereby making it easy to spot program break points or cycles. Later computers such as the LGP 30 and RPC 4000 continued this trend with small scope displays showing the actual bit contents of special registers. Scopes were abandoned in favor of status lights, however, until the CDC 6600 revived them by eliminating single bulbs entirely and installing two CRT's in its operating console.

In the mid-fifties, the use of displays became popular and a burst of activity resulted in a proliferation of equipment and techniques which has not yet abated. This was similar to the progress of computer technology itself, although on a smaller scale and from seven to ten years behind it. It is claimed that during the remainder of this decade the more noticeable advances in the state-of-the-art of computer systems will not be in the computer itself, but primarily in the area of peripheral I/O devices such as optical character readers, general-purpose display consoles, electronic printers, and microfilm recorders. Since the display is, in fact, the communication interface between the user and the computer system, today's emphasis on real time on-line computation, decision making, and design has made it important to use displays judiciously to "reduce the communications barrier," "increase the information throughput," and "match the impedance of man and machine."

The rapid expanse of equipment and techniques can then be interpreted as a response to this challenge. It is fashionable, for instance, to cite the so-called Rome Compendium [2], a *magnum opus* of somewhat less than a thousand pages of descriptions of automated display techniques and equipment. Another sign of the times and evidence of the popularity of man/machine communication through displays is present in the advertisements of some computer manufacturers, where mention is no longer made of the pedestrian console typewriter, but rather of the "man/machine communications device." A more serious indicator is the establishment, in 1963, of a very active professional society in the display field, the Society for Information Display (SID).

2. Display Technology

2.1 Classification of Displays

One of the primary purposes of the SID is the promulgation of research and formalization in the field of information display through the establishment of definitions and standards. This is appropriate since, beyond the cliché, "a picture is worth a thousand words," too little agreement exists within the field as to what constitutes meaningful descriptors or variables and how to measure their values. The interdisciplinary nature of the field has certainly been partially responsible for the lack of standards. Specialists have been culled from such diverse fields as psychology and the behavioral sciences, physiology, photometry, optics, electronics, and computer and information sciences, each field having its own vocabulary and standards. For the scope of this article some preliminary definitions are in order.

The field of *data display* is concerned with the assembling, transforming, and arranging of information for meaningful communication to human beings. *Visually displayed* information is detected by the eye basically by means of "angular and depth perception, luminance and chrominance discrimination, and coding in shape, size, orientation, blinking, and motion" [3].

The displayed information can be used for a variety of purposes, ranging from a static, one-way, man-to-man communication of a single fact or figure, to the dynamic man/machine dialog treated in Section 3.

It is obvious that the previous definitions subsume almost any type of visual data display, including blackboards and basketball scoreboards. For the purposes of this article, only computer (digitally) driven visual displays will be considered. Simple displays comprise several fields of their own, which are better treated elsewhere. For a listing of microfilm viewers, for instance, see the National Microfilm Association's 1959 and 1962 "Guide to Micro Reproduction Equipment." The television industry has produced handbooks on TV systems, both commercial and closed circuit.

Within the chosen category there still does not exist a formal, all-inclusive taxonomy in either structural or behavioral terms—displays can be classified in a number of different ways not mutually exclusive. The usual classification is that based on hardware mechanization, and displays are lumped into CRT, projection, and panel categories, which are further subdivided along the lines of the specific technologies used in implementation. Other ways of looking at displays are more user-oriented and less concerned with the technical performance. The function classification, for instance, regards a display as either a console for a single user or a large-screen, group display; or, as handling output only versus full-scale input/output for man/machine communication. The nature of the data partitions displays into those which present status information versus those which present real time, dynamic information, and those which display just alphanumerics or special symbols versus those which can display vectors and graphical information as well.

Only computer driven displays which are general purpose, i.e., displays which handle graphical as well as alphanumeric data, will be considered here. The emphasis will be almost exclusively on small-screen and CRT displays rather than on the large-screen command and control displays. Some of the newest panel techniques do appear to be equally applicable to both these areas, however. Not covered will be standard TV, three-dimensional displays, and special-purpose devices.

After a discussion of engineering parameters germane to all displays in this restricted category, a functional block diagram of a general-purpose display system will be shown, and typical implementations (mechanizations) of each block will be detailed. The classification will therefore be by mechanization of generic functions.

2.2 Human-Factors Dependent Parameters

2.2.1 Introduction

The types and values of engineering parameters desired in a display and indicative of its performance are determined primarily by human factors and the task to be performed. Most parameters, of course, are functions of both and are interdependent. As mentioned above, some of them do not lend themselves very well to objective measurement, and many of the units of those that do are ill-defined, contradictory, and lack compatible industry-wide standards. Luxenburg and Eberhardt illustrate the current situation:

"A wide variety of photometric units are in current use. Furthermore, many identical units have two or three common names, and it is not uncommon to see the units incorrectly used or defined in both technical papers and procurement specifications." [4]

"A confusing situation exists in the electronics industry with respect to specifications on the resolution of picture tubes, camera tubes, storage tubes, image tubes, and other related display devices. This confusion arises not only because of the variation of the ability of the individual observer to detect brightness changes in an image (a percentage modulation between 1 and 10 per cent being the usual minimum limit), but also because of the many alternative ways of expressing resolution." [5]

A vivid example is the following list—ten different units in which the resolution was specified in separate Request for Quote's (RFQ's) to one manufacturer: spot size, linewidth, number of TV lines, number of TV lines/inch, white lines/inch, optical line pairs, optical lines, lines/mm, per cent of character height, and shrinking raster lines/inch.

Even if one agrees on the appropriate variables, and the units in which they are measured, the method of measurement is often subjective and changeable. The measurement of those dependent on human factors is especially sensitive to the total environment and the observer. It is always necessary to treat each numerical specification with caution and to make detailed inquiry into the circumstances of its measurement.

Within the framework of these precautions, the following two sections will discuss the most applicable parameters and give some typical ranges of values under typical conditions: of the ambient environment of the typical well-lighted office, and of the average human observer (in the psycho-physiological sense). The purpose is not to prescribe design criteria, but rather to describe and catalog relevant parameters and their rule-of-thumb common ranges. Table I gives a summary.

TABLE I

ENGINEERING PARAMETERS OF DISPLAYS

Parameters determined largely by human factors	Parameters determined largely by task
(1) Brightness and contrast	(1) Display area size
(2) Halftone capability	(2) Message size
(3) Resolution	(3) Information type, format, and coding
(4) Color	
(5) Flickerless frame rate	(4) Symbol generation rate
(6) Readability	(5) Reponse time
(7) Visual fidelity	(6) Erasability, storage, and regeneration

2.2.2 Psycho-physical Photometry

Any human-factors discussion of displays relies on concepts of the *physics* of the information-carrying medium, light, the *physiology* of the visual receptor, the eye, and the *psychology* of the perception mechanism, the brain. Accordingly, variables are labeled as being physical, psycho-physical, or psychological depending on the stage of the information transfer from light source to mind in which they fall, and on the discipline of the scientist performing the measurements. The physicist regards light as a portion of the electromagnetic spectrum, and describes it in terms of such physical quantities as radiance, wavelength, and spectral distribution. The human perceptive mechanism is not an exact physical device, however, and while it does have "average" measurable physical characteristics, its psychological response to a given stimulus is heavily conditioned by the presence of other stimuli and by its history. Human beings perceive radiance as brightness, wavelength as hue, spectral distribution as saturation. Photometry and colorimetry are sciences which reside somewhere between the physical and psyhco-physical: average characteristics are measured under controlled conditions which eliminate conditioning effects and, whenever possible, the variables are measured objectively (physically) and independently of the observer. In the following few pages, several quantities which have come to be reasonably standard in the field will be defined, even though disagreement still exists as to the methods of their measurement.

Emissive bodies radiate power. That flux which is in the visible

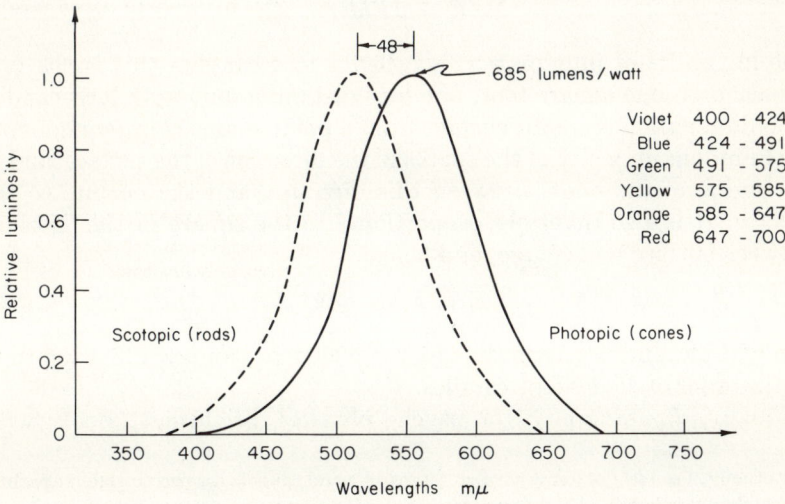

Fig 1. Relative luminosity curves of scotopic and photopic receptors.

spectrum (roughly 400–750 mμ) and produces the sensation of light is called *luminous* flux F, and is measured in *lumens* of luminous power. Luminous power does not correspond exactly to radiant (electromagnetic) power since it is a function of varying sensitivity of the eye to various wavelengths. "Relative luminosity" curves (Fig. 1) describe this spectral sensitivity for the two types of receptors in the human eye—the cones (color vision), and the more sensitive rods (black, white, shades of gray vision). At 555 mμ the *luminous efficiency*, the ratio of luminous power to radiant power, reaches a maximum of 685 lumens/watt. A typical incandescent bulb produces 100 lumens per *visible* radiant watt.

Actually, the luminosity curves and, in fact, other psycho-physical measurements do not measure luminous flux or power directly, but rather the psycho-physical objective correlative of psychological brightness, namely, *luminance*. Before defining luminance, it is useful to introduce the notions of luminous intensity and illumination. *Luminous intensity* I of a point source is defined as the differential flux *emitted*/solid angle in lumens/steradian:

$$I = dF/d\omega. \tag{2.1}$$

A source emitting 1 lumen/steradian is said to be a standard candle, radiating 1 candle[1] power. Since there are 4π steradians/sphere, a standard candle radiates 4π lumens. A 60-watt incandescent lamp radiates approximately 60 candle power.

Illumination E, of a surface, is measured by the differential flux of *incident* light/element of surface area:

$$E = dF/ds. \tag{2.2}$$

One lumen/ft^2 of illumination is called 1 foot-candle—this is the illumination on one square foot, one foot distant from a standard candle. The illumination of a unit surface from a point source is proportional to the luminous intensity of the source in the direction of the surface, and to the cosine of the angle between this direction and the normal to the surface. It is also inversely proportional to the square of the distance between surface and source, and hence

$$E = I \cos \theta / d^2. \tag{2.3}$$

Sunlight illumination is on the order of 9000 foot-candles; office lighting, on the order of 20–50 foot-candles.

Finally, *luminance* B, or psycho-physical brightness, deals with

---

[1] Actually, 1 *candela* power is correct, but candle and candela are used interchangeably. A blackbody radiator at the temperature of platinum solidification has a luminance (see below) of 60 candelas/cm^2 [4].

emission to the eye of extended surfaces which are self-luminous, or with *reflection* (re-emission) from surfaces illuminated by point sources. Luminance for extended surfaces is the luminous flux per unit solid angle per unit projected area of the surface, in candles/ft^2:

$$B = I/\cos \theta\, S, \qquad (2.4)$$

where

$$I = I(\theta). \qquad (2.5)$$

If it is the case that

$$I = I_0 \cos \theta, \qquad (2.6)$$

then

$$B = I_0/S. \qquad (2.7)$$

When (2.7) applies, B is independent of viewing angle, and the surface is said to be uniformly diffusing. An illuminated surface which reflects light perfectly and diffuses it uniformly has a luminance measured in foot-lamberts numerically equal to the number of foot-candles of illumination. Note that, contrary to illumination, luminance is not a function of distance. If a person moves closer to an illuminated surface, the amount of light entering the eye does increase with the inverse square, but so does the image on the retina. The flux per individual receptor is therefore unchanged and brightness remains constant. In actual practice, the foot-lambert is used for both self-luminous and reflecting surfaces, and is defined as

$$(1/\pi) \text{ candles/ft}^2.$$

Some typical values of brightness are shown in Table II [*4*]. The eye is an extremely sensitive and versatile brightness detector, capable of reacting over a wide range: from the order of 10^{-6} foot-lamberts (or even

TABLE II

Typical Brightness, Foot-Lamberts

Surface of the sun	4.8×10^8
Surface of a 60-watt frosted incandescent bulb ("hot spot")	36,000
Surface of a 60-watt "white" incandescent bulb	9000
Surface of a 15-watt fluorescent tube	3000
White paper in direct sunlight	9000
Clear sky	2000
Surface of moon, bright area	750
White paper on office desk	25
Pulsed EL mosaic panel	20
TV raster	20

a few quanta of light) to approximately 10^4 foot-lamberts, a range of ten billion to one. Brightness is normally measured by photocell or photomultiplier-tube spot meters, calibrated for luminous flux and having a spectral response similar to that of the eye [6]. Great care must be taken to evaluate the role of the environment in the use of these devices.

To summarize, *emission* from a point source is measured in lumens of luminous radiant flux or candles of luminous power. *Reception* or illumination from a point source is measured in foot-candles of incident light:

$$1 \text{ lumen/ft}^2 = 1 \text{ foot-candle.} \qquad (2.8)$$

Re-emission, or reflection of a surface illuminated by a point source (or a self-luminous surface), is measured in foot-lamberts. These units are in the English system; their cgs equivalents are lumen, centimeter-candle, and lambert. In the remainder of Section 2.2, parameters principally dependent on human factors will be discussed.

2.2.3 Brightness and Contrast

Objects are perceived insofar as their brightness exceeds the brightness of their background. The contrast between information brightness and background brightness of a display is usually a more meaningful parameter than information brightness itself, although the latter is often specified since it is relatively invariant to the equipment. Brightness is a function of, at least, ambient light, contrast, resolution, repetition rate, and nature of the display data. For instance, decreasing the area of the object necessitates an increase in brightness. For short flahes of light, more intense light is needed than for longer flashes. Isolated flashes below 0.1 sec duration are equally visible for equal energy (i.e., intensity × duration is constant). For flashes longer than 0.1 sec, intensity alone is a factor. Display brightness is usually on the order of 5–100 foot-lamberts, with 20–40 common for an average indoor display of nonrepetitive images.

Contrast is defined in terms of both brightness and color, but human beings are far more sensitive to brightness contrast which is therefore used for detail. Color contrast is often used for partitioning the displayed information into categories. Brightness *contrast* is defined as (information brightness − background brightness)/background brightness, where it is assumed that information is highlighted against a darker background. *Contrast ratio* is given as highlight brightness/background brightness. Contrast ratios of 5:1 to 30:1 are common, with 5:1 adequate for white symbols on black background, 25:1 for line drawings or text on white background. Too much contrast produces "dazzle."

The required brightness of a display can be roughly calculated by multiplying the ambient light level (as low a level as possible) by the desired contrast ratio, and dividing by the reflectivity of the surface attenuated by whatever filters and polarizers are used.

2.2.4 Halftone Capability (Gray Scale)

The continuum between lightest and darkest luminance is usually quantized in discrete levels called *halftones*—a term borrowed from the printing industry. The halftone printing process approximates areas of different shades of gray by a matrix of equispaced black dots which can differ in area but not shade of blackness. This creates a very fine binary image in which a given picture element is either black or white. In the display field, a halftone level or gray-scale step represents an increment in grayness of a given area over its surroundings. There is no formal unequivocal specification of how it is measured. The two most common ways are to define a halftone level (1) objectively, as an increase of 3 db (factor of 2 in luminance) over the previous level, or (2) more subjectively, as the Weber-Fechner fraction, which is measured as the ratio of a just noticeable change in luminance to the level at which this change is noted. This is measured for a small area test field, given background brightness and specified conditions of color.

For contrast ratios around 10:1 it has been found that on the order of 10 such shades of gray are discernible. Television displays have 5 to 10 levels of discernible gray scale, but few displays operate in other than a binary, highlight on background, mode.

2.2.5 Resolution

Resolution is a measure of spatial discrimination [as opposed to brightness (halftones), or color discrimination] and relates to the amount of detail that can be perceived by the observer. Two factors determine resolution: the resolution of the display itself, and the resolution of the human optical system, termed *visual acuity*. An ideal display should maximize information transfer by matching or exceeding human resolution; in actual practice, equipment limitations and the quantity of information to be displayed result in a lower resolution.

Visual acuity is defined as the reciprocal of the angle, in minutes, subtended by the smallest detail which can be resolved under standard conditions. It depends on the object, spectral distribution of the radiant energy, background luminance, contrast, duration of the visual stimulus, and the criterion used to determine whether the object is or is not seen. Visual acuity can be subdivided into the ability to *detect* single small objects, to *separate* (or resolve) two objects, and to *describe* the contour of a complicated pattern. *Detection* for high brightness objects, a star, for instance, takes place with angles measured in seconds of arc. A minimum white square on black background is detected at approximately 10 sec; a black square on white at approximately 30 sec (showing the effects of adaptation). *Separation* of black bars on white background is reported at $\frac{1}{2}$–1 min of arc. The interrelation between display variables, and the far stronger dependence of visual acuity on contrast than on brightness are shown in Fig. 2.

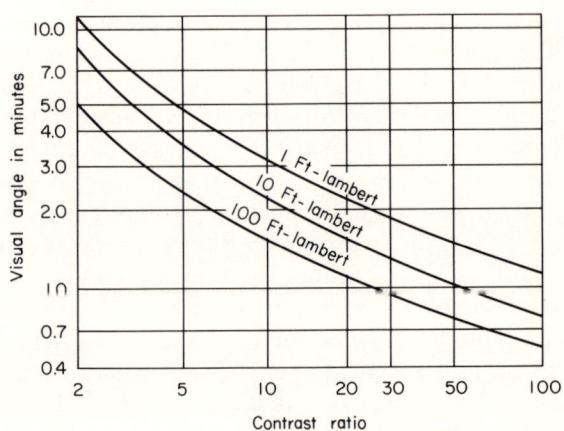

FIG. 2. Minimum visual angle for various contrast ratios [7].

A most interesting and valuable property of the eye-brain perception mechanism is that its great sensitivity does *not* cause it to be sensitive to errors or irregularities in patterns. Missing information is supplied and noise is suppressed, as anyone who reads handwriting can attest.

Display resolution is a function of the width of the "writing instrument" (cross section of the electron beam in the case of a cathode ray tube), the method of forming symbols, the granularity and diffusivity of the display medium (the phosphor, for instance), positioning accuracy and registration, etc. Resolution specified for a display is a function, then, of both eye and equipment and is measured in a variety of ways, as mentioned in Section 2.2.1.

Photographic resolution is specified in line pairs per unit length: "One hundred line pairs per millimeter," therefore, means that 100 black lines and 100 white lines of equal width, placed alternately, can be distinguished. Television resolution is expressed in lines per unit of length or image diameter, called *TV* or *total lines*. The number of lines is twice the number of line pairs, and one must know the size of the total image (often unstated and assumed to be 19 or 21 in.). Values of 50–200 lines/in. are common.[2]

Optical resolution is seldom used and is measured in minutes of arc, as mentioned above. Given the angle α (see Fig. 3) and the viewing distance, the object height or linewidth is $2 \times$ distance $\times \tan \alpha/2$, which can then be inverted to yield a rough measure of resolution in lines/unit length.

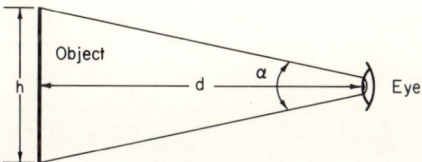

Fig. 3. Visual angle subtended by a small object.

Electronic resolution is measured by the spot size on the medium, assuming minimal diffusion. Typical spot sizes are measured in 10 or 20 mils. Again, simply invert to obtain approximate lines per inch. Shrinking raster lines per inch refers to a method of measurement whereby a 100-line raster, for instance, is shrunk to the minimal distinguishable size which is then measured. Percentage of character height resolution is useful since there are data on legibility of standard alphanumerics. For adequate brightness and high contrast 10 or 12 elements or lines (6 pairs) per dimension are satisfactory; on the order of 20 lines yield high quality. Given the viewing distance and a requirement of 12 to 20 min of arc character height for legibility, character size is determined.

Finally, a photo-optical concept finding some use in display work is that of the modulation transfer function (MTF). Unlike the shrinking raster method, bands of gray *continuously* varying in a sinusoidal intensity pattern from light to dark to light are imposed on the medium (photographic film or phosphor, for example). The output variation is then noted either by a microdensitometer or slit photocell. Thereafter the bands are compressed while the amplitude of the intensity is kept constant (see Fig. 4). The plot of the optical gain (output light level/input light level ratio) against the spatial frequency (lines per millimeter), is known as the MTF (see Fig. 5), and resolution limit can be defined similarly to cut-off frequency in the electrical analog.

---

[2]Strictly speaking, *at least* two television lines are required to display a line pair, since the desired vertical position of the line pair on the screen may not coincide with the TV raster. A correction, the Kell factor, gives the number of TV lines needed as approximately 2.8 TV lines/optical line pair.

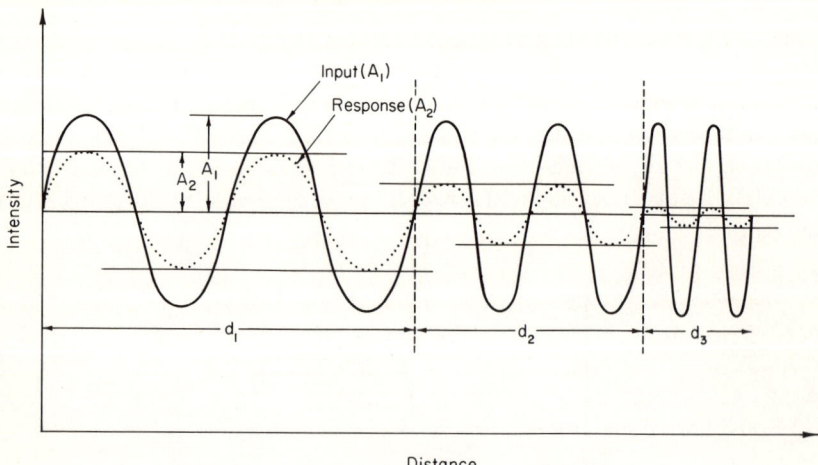

Fig. 4. Optical sine wave response.

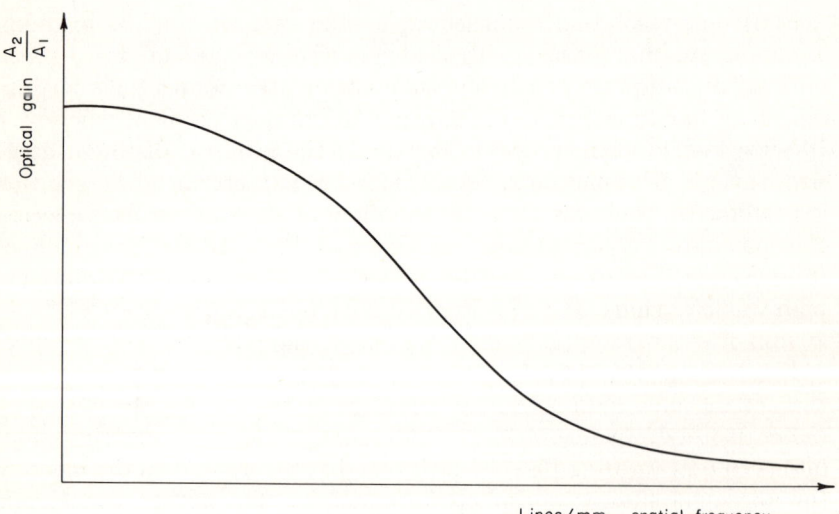

Fig. 5. Modulation transfer function.

2.2.6 Color

Color vision is determined by the three parameters mentioned in Section 2.2.2: luminance or brightness, dominant wavelength or hue, and purity or saturation. Purity describes the dilution of a spectrum color with white. There is, as yet, no single definitive theory of color vision, but the so-called trichromatic (Young-Helmholtz-Maxwell) system is used predominantly in colorimetry. This system allows the matching of any color by an appropriate mixture of three primaries, for instance, red, yellow, and blue. The eye is not a spectrum analyzer and may identify an indefinite number of spectra as the same psychological color. With a colorimeter, the observer compares the color to be determined with an adjusted mixture of reference colors: three primaries, for instance, or white light plus monochromatic light of controllable wavelength.

Studies have been made to determine the number of color tones that an observer can reliably recognize without reference to a standard. Reported values vary from around 7 to perhaps 11. In terms of ability to discriminate small variations in either hue or saturation, many colors can be distinguished when compared contiguously. Actually, the eye does not see colors in fine detail; as an example, it may be noted that the detail in color TV is transmitted in terms of shades of gray. Typically, a bandwidth of greater than 4 Mc is used for gray scale, and of only an additional 0.5 Mc for color. Accordingly, less than a half-dozen distinct colors are used on the average.

2.2.7 Flickerless Frame Rate (Volatile Display)

The flicker-fusion frequency is the minimum frequency of light flashes which appear to the viewer as continuous. It increases with increasing light intensity and decreasing proportion of the light-dark cycle occupied by the flash, reaching 50–60 cps at high intensities. The factors affecting it are the brightness of surrounding area, state of adaptation, and the area of the image on the retina. For useful brightness levels of 5–100 foot-lamberts, volatile screens are refreshed in the range of 30–60 cps to pass flicker–fusion.

2.2.8 Readability

Readability is a measure of the speed and accuracy with which an observer can detect and correctly interpret information presented on the display. Readability is affected by brightness, contrast, resolution, flicker, screen and character size, height/linewidth ratios, and types and fonts of symbols projected. Symbols should be chosen which are familiar to the user, implying that the use of English alphabet and Arabic numerals probably is more desirable than that of abstract symbols. Characters having sharply pointed corners are read more easily than those with rounded corners, as this predistortion of characters tends to compensate for the limited resolving power of the eye. Alphanumeric characters having a width/height ratio of about 3:2 to 3:4 are generally regarded as optimum in typical circumstances, and those having height/linewidth ratios of 30:1 or 40:1 are more legible, especially at high contrast levels, than those of 10:1 to 15:1 since the letters do not fuse or blur at a distance. It is usually quite expensive, however, to achieve this high a ratio; smaller spot size for CRT's is required, for instance.

2.2.9 Visual Fidelity

The following quotation is from Loewe *et al.* [8]:

The display must allow the user to properly interpret quantitative data (e.g., the distance between items or their relative position). A military ground unit, for example, should not be represented on the wrong side of a river. The necessity for proper interpretation leads to specific requirements for linearity, accuracy, and registration. Distortion in a display (e.g., pin cushion distortion in a CRT) must be kept to a level which will not bother the user, nor cause concern as to the adequacy of the display. Character spacing and alignment must be reasonably uniform on tabular displays; lines which the user expects to be straight should appear so.

Obviously, the system must be accurate in the sense that the data displayed truly represent the data which were received from the processor. Dropped bits, drift in analog units, etc., may cause as much trouble in a display system as in a computer.

Registration refers to the ability to place information with accuracy and repeatability anywhere on the screen. Static distortion or dynamic distortion (wobble) may result from inadequate registration.

2.3 Task Dependent Parameters

2.3.1 Display Area Size

Display area size is determined by the size and geometric disposition of the audience, the quantity and organization of information to be displayed, the human factors limiting the minimum character size and the maximum simultaneous viewing angle of an observer, and equipment factors. An ideal display has a step function directivity, that is, constant light output within the useful radiation angle and zero output outside of it. A display area having less than 2:1 variation of brightness over an angle of $\pm 45°$ gives good results in typical applications. The screen must be large enough to display the volume of data and degree of detail required by the task. It must also be large enough that its details are easily seen by the most distant observer—an observer can scan $\pm 30°$ horizontally without undue fatigue and about three-fourths of this range vertically. The cost of a display, of course, is a function of screen size and is considered in the determination of size in most cases. In general, screens are either group (large screen) or individual (small screen, less than 500 in.^{2}).

2.3.2 Message Size

The information capacity required in a display is largely a function of the task which the display is expected to perform. Human factors do impose limits since the amount of data placed on the display should not exceed that which can be comprehended and utilized by the observer. Assuming one minute of arc as the eye's resolving power and a maximum observer scan angle of $\pm 45°$, up to 60 lines/degree $\times$ 90° = 5400 total lines can be resolved by a single observer. Unless the display is to be viewed in sections by several observers, there is little advantage in providing for an information capacity requiring greater resolution. In terms of the number of alphanumerics permissible in a display, the upper limit is therefore about 40,000 (i.e., 5400 lines $\times$ 1 character/10 lines = 500 character rows; 500 rows $\times$ 80 characters/row = 40,000 characters, counting spaces as characters). Past experience has indicated that a capacity of 10,000 characters is suitable for most tasks. Large screens are naturally required for such tasks. Cathode ray tube consoles may handle up to 1000-character messages without difficulty.

2.3.3 Information Type, Format, and Coding

Information may be presented on a display as alphanumeric or symbolic characters, vectors, points, continuous curves, grid lines, map outlines, area shading, or coloration, and may be randomly located or arranged in orderly fashion (as in a table). It may be produced in discrete quantities of one character, vector, etc., at a time, or by an over-all scanning of the display area, as in TV or scanning radars. Semifixed images may be superimposed by overlays or by optical combinations of images from slides or film strips. A display should be capable of accepting discrete information, as this method is best suited to operation with a data processor.

Information format refers to positioning of information within the display. A fixed or typewriter format is one in which the locations of various elements of the display are predetermined and cannot vary. Free or random access format is one in which the positions of elements are not fixed and may be a function of time, or of the information itself. Vector and line drawing information is written in the latter mode. Increased preorganization lowers the requisite bandwidth and therefore cost and flexibility as well.

Information coding takes place when the graphic capabilities of the two-dimensional screen are utilized to convey information symbolically. The mass of raw data that a computer has manipulated can be then expressed tersely to achieve maximum information transfer. The following variables can assume different values in the encoding process: size, shape, position, orientation, brightness, color, number, line structure (width, length, dotted or dashed), movement, blinking, etc.

The number of different values for each variable differs depending on the human recognition process and ease and cost of implementation. Shape recognition admits the largest number of alternatives—200 to 1000 with some practice. (The Chinese language has approximately 40,000 separate ideographs, many of which are partially similar.) Color coding should use 3–10 levels and is quite meaningful. All the other variables are less desirable and are used on approximately 2–5 levels.

2.3.4 Symbol Generation Rate

Symbol generation rate measures the number of standard symbols (characters, vector strokes, etc.) that can be written per unit time. The generation rate is a function of the average time required to form a symbol at a specified location, at the minimal required brightness level, plus the average time required to move to the specified location from a previous one. For character generators operating in typewriter format, writing speeds range from 20,000 to 200,000 characters per second, with 50,000 average. The larger the message size (i.e., the more information per frame), the faster the generation rate must be to shape all symbols within the on portion of one refresh cycle.

2.3.5 Response Time

The speed of response required in a display is a function of the task and of human response times. Response time must be defined separately for each of three modes of operation: tracking, updating, and replying. Tracking response is a measure of the ability of the display to show virtually instantaneously and continuously the changing positions of moving targets or cursors. Tracking response is measured by the frequency of motion and by the delay in displaying a new position. In an operational mode involving surveillance or the presentation of data indicating the progress of a computation, the significant measure of speed is the update time, or the delay in presenting fresh data after it becomes available to the system. The update response time is measured simply in seconds of delay. In an operational mode involving "query and answer" routines, the significant measure of the response of the display system (including an associated data processor and memory) is the reply time, which is the time from the generation of a request for new data by the operator to the appearance of the data on the display. Ideally, it should be about a second, since research has shown that users start forgetting what they asked for or become bored or frustrated with longer delays. In either the update or reply modes, the response time of a display is usually a function of the organization of the data.

2.3.6 Erasability, Storage, and Regeneration

Erasability refers to the ability to obliterate old data to prevent its interference with new data. Erasure may be accomplished by complete and instantaneous deletion of the old image, by causing the old image to fade with time, or by instantaneous deletion of a selected portion of the old image. The nature of the task determines which of the three methods is preferable. If the erasure time is short enough to be compatible with the response time criteria, it can be considered to be instantaneous. In the case of fading images, the optimum rate of decay is a function of the task.

An image must be maintained until it is either updated (i.e., replaced or selectively erased) or is no longer of interest. Volatile displays require constant regeneration of input information above the flicker-fusion rate. Nonvolatile (storage) displays, by their nature, preserve the information.

2.4 Display System Block Diagram

Having discussed at some length the parameters appropriate to displays, it is now time to turn to a discussion of the structure of the general-purpose display itself. Since the display system is computer-based, one must examine not merely the display function itself but also the prerequisite functions of processing, storing, and generating of the digital information which drives the display. Whereas there are considerable differences in the techniques of presentation of information on the display surface, the functional block diagram of Fig. 6, as a whole, applies to most types of display systems with minor changes.[3] There is no method of mapping functions onto subsystems uniquely and without overlap. It must be realized, then, that the block diagram is more a behavioral rather than a structural description. There is also considerable choice in the specification of the functions to be included. Specifically, display is often treated as one of the functions in a general-purpose, on-line information storage and retrieval or decision-making system. Here we consider bulk digital and pictorial data storage as auxiliary to the display system since, in reality, it is difficult to delineate which functions are subservient to which.

The computer system (block 2) delivers processed and digitally encoded information to the rest of the system directly or via inter-

---

[3]The discussion in the following sections, though based primarily on CRT technology, is quite representative of other technologies as well—only in the nature of the display surface itself is there sufficient difference to itemize the differing technologies (Section 2.9).

mediate storage on magnetic tape. This information results from internal computations or from externally supplied information (block 1—from secondary storage, or for example, via dataphone from another computer in a multicomputer complex). Information also comes from the user's own action and reaction (block 8) in the form of keyboard entries, cursor, light pen, or "crystal ball" manipulations. This manual input is first decoded in block 9 for input to the computer, or is applied directly to the display as is the case with background generators (for example, slides for projection displays).

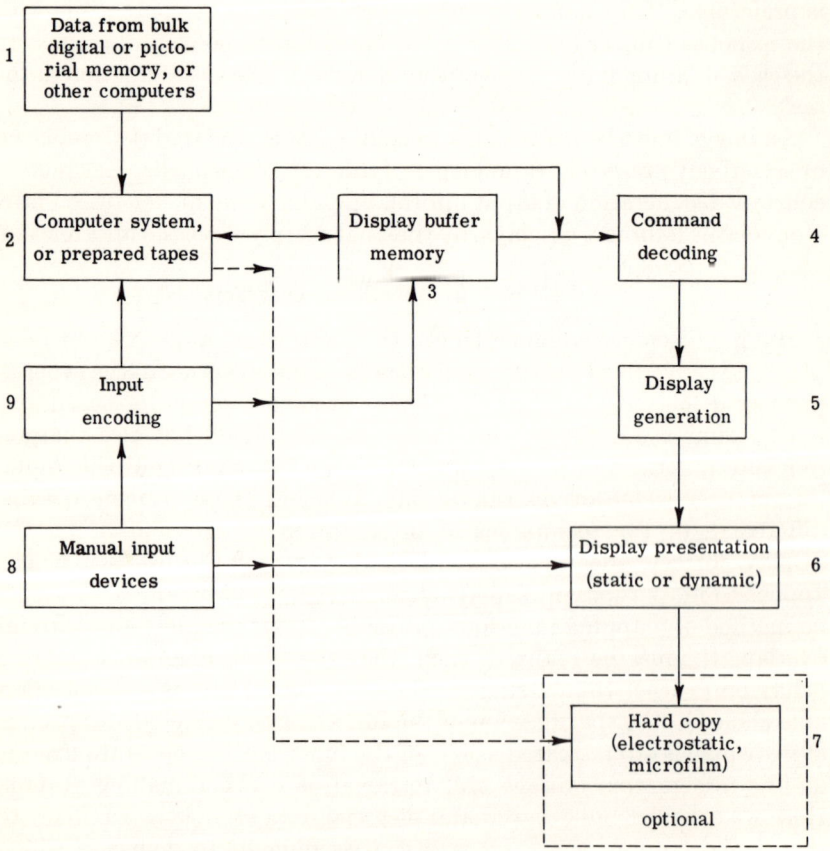

Fig. 6. Block diagram of a generalized display system.

The buffered or unbuffered digital information is then decoded (block 4) and converted to analog signals which are applied to the symbol generation circuits (block 5). These "paint" the display surface with the soft copy data presentation (block 6), from which hard copy may be produced (block 7).

2.5 Computer System (Block 2)

The computer system, while peripheral in a sense, to the actual display function, is nonetheless a most important subsystem for the execution of any task beyond brute force point plotting. The computer system (and its auxiliary digital and pictorial storage) contains the data base from which the display information is derived, and manipulates this information, often under direct control of the user in a man/machine interchange system, to produce the display records which will be exhibited. The power of the display and its corresponding utility vary directly with the power and complexity of the system's file structure and of the appropriate retrieval and manipulation algorithms. There is naturally a trade-off between increased utility and the cost of time and money to program and maintain the system. Also to be considered, however, is that the development of elaborate display and picture processing languages allows the computer and display to be used in entirely new ways which can produce savings in time and money well beyond original expenditures.

2.6 Buffer (Block 3)

If the display surface retains the impressed information (i.e., if it has storage capability), then the computer's digital information is applied directly and only once per message to the command decoding circuits. If the display is volatile, however, the information must be refreshed periodically above flicker-fusion rates. In this case a portion of the internal computer memory, or a separate buffer, is used to maintain the display. If, for instance, the display operates in a random format mode (arbitrary positioning of successive symbols) and must be refreshed fifty times each second, a 1000-symbol message would require the transmission of 50,000 instruction words per second to an unbuffered display, probably tying up one data channel almost completely.

A separate buffer can reduce this load by several orders of magnitude if the pictures do not change too rapidly. The justification for the use of such a buffer depends on trade-offs between buffer cost and computer time and flexibility, the nature of the displayed information (size, update frequency, etc.), and the number of displays time-shared by the computer.

A local buffer can also be used profitably to accumulate information to be transmitted from manual inputs to the computer. Typically, an entire message is typed, formated, accumulated, and then edited, prior to transmission *en masse* to the computer. In this fashion, the computer is interrupted only once per message. Display buffers today are often core, rather than synchronous drums, disks, or delay lines, since usually several modes of display format are used, each with its characteristic operating time, and the synchronous devices do not operate fast enough for the random scan mode. Where single, nonrandom formats are used, the synchronous nature of drum or disk can be used to good advantage for timing purposes. Core buffers operate typically at the 2- to 5-μsec level. Their input and output signals are sometimes interlaced to minimize discontinuities in the pictures.

As an alternative a small computer used as a local processor may provide buffering of the display, as well as input and output editing, format conversion, light pen tracking, and scheduling and controlling priority for multiple users of a central processor. This is especially useful where the data source is a telephone bandwidth channel or is otherwise restricted in transmission capacity.

The digital information, buffered or unbuffered, is next applied to the command decoding blocks.

2.7 Command Decoding (Block 4)

The simplest type of display, which operates in the *point plotting mode*, plots single points under direct program control typically on a 1024 by 1024 grid [9]. Command decoding in this case takes the form of simply converting two 10-bit numbers to the appropriate position on the grid at which the point is to be written. The simplicity and corresponding low cost of this system are its only virtues; the computer is directly tied up with the display, each symbol must be laboriously constructed with subroutines, and even at high point plotting speeds, the amount of information that can be written without overloading the computer and without causing flicker or blinking is minimal. For example, at 50 μsec/point and a 50 cps refresh rate, only 400 points can be written. Vectors must be composed of many points so that this number can represent only very limited line drawings.

A more useful mode of operation is to program the formation of symbols directly without resorting to plotting their individual components. In this case the output of the computer takes the form of a special-purpose display machine language which describes the symbol, its location on the surface, and relevant control information. The command decoding circuitry, then, functions very much like the equivalent circuitry inside the computer—the instruction is dissected, the operation and operand are established, the appropriate registers in the display generation section are filled with the corresponding bit patterns, and selective gating of the actual symbol generation circuits takes place.

The most general display machine language instruction can specify successive symbols in random positions on the display surface. A display using this format is said to operate in the *random scan mode*. A typical instruction can be written as $\boxed{S \mid X \mid Y \mid C}$ where the S field represents the symbol (alphanumeric character, or vector of specified length and orientation), and where X and Y are 10-bit Cartesian coordinates; C labels a control field which can be used for a variety of purposes such as to specify symbol size or font, linewidth, brightness, color, or time-dependent variations of these parameters.[4]

Vectors of arbitrary length can be handled in a specialized fashion by specifying their end points (or one end point, a magnitude, and an angle), and asking the symbol generator to draw a straight line between them. For piecewise linear approximation of free forms another format is useful. A starting point is defined, and then the successive (Δx, Δy) strokes are added contiguously by digitally accumulating resultant end points. In this mode of operation, vectors are produced very quickly by restricting their length to a small fraction of display surface proportions (as fast as 3 μsec/stroke with an electrostatically deflected CRT).

If the information to be displayed is highly structured, as is the case with alphanumeric messages or tables, a format is often used which represents a compromise between point plotting and random scan in terms of economy and flexibility. In the *typewriter mode* the buffer contains either a map of the entire display area which must be filled for each grid point, or, as is far more common, a typewriter-like message. This message is a string of code which includes the first symbol in random scan format, followed by a set of zero or more symbols to be contiguously and evenly spaced, and control information such as "space," "carriage return," "line feed," "tab n spaces," or "change brightness to level n." This pattern may be repeated a number of times to produce the entire display. In addition to the instructions for producing actual symbols, special control codes are used. They usually sandwich the coded message and are of the form "start of message," "end of message," "transmit," "verify," "erase character," "erase line," "clear screen," etc.

2.8 Display Generation (Block 5)

2.8.1 Introduction

Command decoding circuits deliver digital symbol identification, symbol position, and control information to the display generation circuits which convert them to (analog) driving voltages which, in turn, "write" the information on the surface.

---

[4] For example, a technique to call attention to a specified symbol is to blink it, or to modulate its size with a slowly varying sine wave.

There are two ways to fill a screen such as a CRT: the "XYZ" and "TV" scans. In the XYZ scan, a separate position generator and symbol generator are used (often dependent on the same basic circuits), one to provide "gross" positioning (X,Y), whether in typewriter or random scan format, the other to form the symbol once it has been positioned, by controlling the intensity (Z) of the writing beam while it makes local X,Y excursions. In a TV scan, the beam is swept across the entire screen in a fixed, interlaced television raster, and only the intensity Z is continuously modulated. This latter type of display has been interfaced less commonly with digital computers, and will be discussed last, in Section 2.8.5.

For the more common XYZ displays, most of the position and symbol generation techniques evolved with CRT technology and are routine—character and vector generators are commercially available to be added as packages to separately purchased CRT's. Some of the techniques are equally applicable to other technologies; for example, the programmed dot generators are used in the solid state panel (matrix) displays. The remainder of Section 2.8 is written in the context of CRT displays, but it is to be remembered that most of these techniques carry over to other display media.

2.8.2 Position Generation

The position generator is often merged with the symbol generator, especially if they use the same type of XY deflection techniques. In CRT's (see Section 2.9.2), the electron beam can be deflected either magnetically or electrostatically to an accuracy of $\pm 0.1\%$ or better. Magnetic deflection is more common since it is appreciably less costly to design and manufacture and tends to have higher resolution. Electrostatic deflection, however, is approximately an order of magnitude faster so that it is used for the high-speed (high bandwidth) requirements of random scan. Much larger deflection voltages (greater than 1 kv) must be generated, however, requiring the use of expensive vacuum tube circuitry. If a large number of symbols need to be displayed in typewriter format, high bandwidth is required to draw individual symbols, but relatively low bandwidth is required for gross positioning. A combination, dual deflection, can be used in this case: magnetic for gross positioning, electrostatic for symbol generation.

2.8.3 Symbol Generation

There are primarily three parameters in a CRT which can be controlled in order to form symbols. These are the electron beam cross section, the X and Y deflections, and the intensity. In the context of XYZ CRT displays, Fig. 7 gives a classification [10] of symbol generation techniques according to the way in which these parameters are controlled.

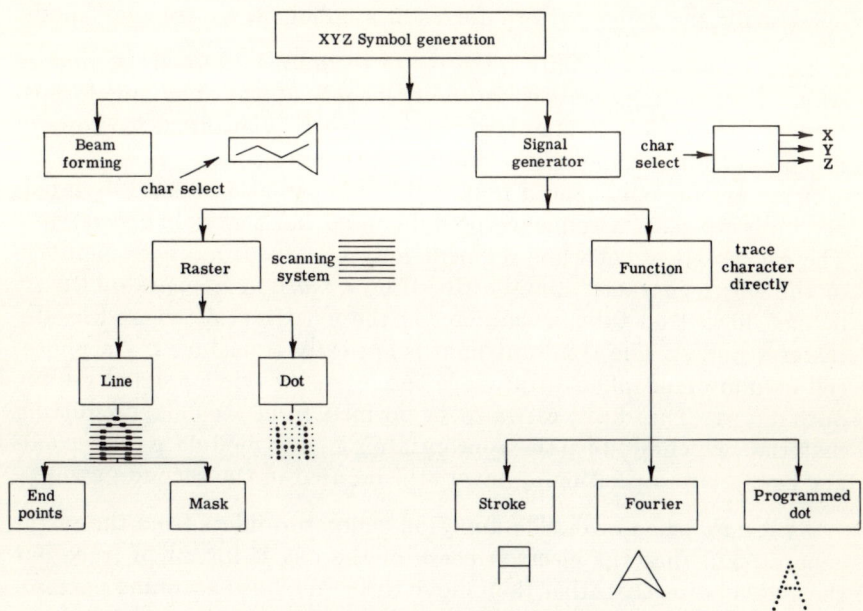

Fig. 7. XYZ symbol generation techniques.

2.8.3.1 Beam Shaping. The first of two basic techniques is to modify the cross section of the CRT electron beam. A special CRT is used which has a stencil mask through which the electron beam is directed or "extruded." The cross section of the emerging beam has the shape of the particular stencil. The beam is then deflected to the appropriate position on the screen while retaining the shape of the desired character. The Charactron is a typical tube utilizing this technique.

2.8.3.2 Signal Generation. The other basic technique is to simultaneously affect the two other parameters, by generating X and Y deflection voltages which force the beam to trace some particular pattern on the screen, while also generating Z intensification voltages which turn the beam on and off (unblank it) at the correct times. The result is the desired figure or symbol.

Within this category, there are primarily two methods which are used in generating symbols. One is a *raster technique:* the beam is forced to follow a fixed scanning pattern locally, analogous to a TV raster scan. While the scan is not a function of the symbol, the symbol itself is formed by intensity modulation.

The second technique is called *function generation*. The beam is forced to follow some particular function or group of functions, not necessarily the same pattern for each symbol, in a "tracing" mode.

2.8.3.3 Raster Scan. Within the raster technique, there are again two ways of generating symbols. In the first method, the symbol is formed from groups of *dots*. A standard raster is used, typically seven rows of five dots. Many airline status boards use this principle.

A raster of evenly spaced horizontal *lines* can also be used. Symbols are built up with a sequence of unblanked horizontal line segments. The *end points* of each line segment may be stored in a core memory, or the entire character may be stored on a *mask* in a separate CRT. As in the Charactron tube, a character in the mask is selected, and locally raster scanned. The resultant light is optically transduced, via photocell or photomultiplier, to produce the intensity (video) signal for the output CRT. The mask can also be formed from secondary emitting materials which produce the appropriate signal to modulate the secondary beam. Gross positioning must still be used in the second CRT.

2.8.3.4 Function Scan. The function generator differs from the raster generator in that the electron beam of the CRT is forced to trace out the symbol directly rather than move through a fixed scanning pattern. In this method, the deflection voltages are generated by stored magnetic, resistive, or diode logic. There are three main techniques.

The first is to form characters from groups of connected *strokes*. In a representative system, a vocabulary of strokes at some eighty angular orientations and five or more magnitudes is used. Individual strokes are written in fractions of microseconds, and a symbol constructed of a maximum of 24 strokes can be written on the average in less than 3 μsec. There are two ways of generating strokes such that the brightness is constant for all strokes regardless of length—constant time plus intensity compensation, and constant velocity. These methods are discussed more fully in Section 2.8.4, entitled "Vector and Line Generation."

A second technique is to use *Fourier methods* in a manner quite similar to that for producing the familiar Lissajous patterns, where two frequencies out of phase by 90° are applied to the X and Y deflection plates of the CRT to form a circle (provided the input signals are identical and the gain of the two channels is identical). The symbol repertoire is built from a variety of sines and cosines of fundamentals and of some harmonics, including appropriate phasing and clipping of waveforms.

A third technique uses *programmed dots*. An array of, say, 15×16 dots may be used, of which some fixed number, less than 20, are used for forming each symbol. Instead of scanning through the entire matrix of 240 dots, as in the raster dot method, the CRT beam is directed in sequence to only those dots which are needed to form the desired symbol. In some programmed dot systems, the beam is unblanked only as it reaches the programmed dot. In others, the beam is left on during its excursions from one dot to another so that the symbol has the appearance of being drawn with a continuous line.

2.8.3.5 Comparative Performance of CRT-*Based Symbol Generators.* It is customary to evaluate the different symbol generation techniques according to speed, symbol quality (esthetic and legible), ease of changing repertoire, and cost. This evaluation is relatively easy when the generators are self-contained units, but they are often part of an integrated system. An important *caveat* applies especially to speed—some figures are quoted for writing repeatedly at the same coarse screen position, while others include average deflection time as well.

Character generation speeds in typewriter format vary from several thousand per second to several hundred thousand per second. In general, the speed varies fairly linearly with cost of the deflection circuitry—increased speed requires greater (and costlier) bandwidth. Speed is not an immediate function of the method of symbol generation.

Quality is also directly related to cost. The off-the-shelf Charactron probably offers the best quality, but is relatively expensive and suffers from the severe limitation that a change in symbol repertoire requires a new tube. Equivalent quality can be obtained by increasing the customary resolution of dot or stroke symbol generators. Increased resolution calls for finer spot diameters and great position and linear accuracy. Since a larger number of components per symbol are used, the speed (and bandwidth) of the deflection circuitry must be correspondingly increased to keep character generation rate constant.

The dot and stroke generators tend to be most modular in the sense of symbol repertoire change. The cost of generators varies, in general, from several thousand dollars to well over ten thousand dollars.

2.8.4 Vector and Line Generation

Techniques for generating arbitrary line drawings are not as plentiful as those for symbol generation. There are essentially three methods: (1) the "pencil writing" curve-tracing mode which requires continuous simultaneous X and Y deflections, (2) dot pattern approximation, and (3) straight line or vector approximation, in which lines are drawn either between specified points, or starting at a given point, in a particular orientation, with a particular magnitude. Of these, the last is most commonly used, since it is the easiest to mechanize, and is quite similar to stroke symbol generation.

In a synchronous mode, the beam moves in constant time, i.e., the time to traverse a vector of arbitrary length is kept constant. If there is a large variation in length, the shorter vectors will be drawn at lower beam velocity, and therefore with proportionately higher intensity. The lines will appear to vary in brightness, and a compensatory modulation proportional to line length is therefore applied to the Z axis. Brightness compensation has the disadvantage of affecting spot size, hence resolution, and of requiring a wide-band linear brightness amplifier. Long lines can also be written by concatenating shorter ones but this requires a larger number of instructions. A more elegant approach is to move the beam asynchronously with constant velocity, independent of size or orientation of the vector. With this approach, additional logic is required to determine not only length and direction, but also length of time for deflection. Stroke symbol generators work with either method and usually accumulate successive end points of short strokes as the symbol is traced out.

2.8.5 TV Scan Displays

Previous sections described XYZ displays requiring XY position generators and XYZ symbol and vector generators. A TV scan display, while not as easily interfaced with a computer, has distinct advantages accruing from the fact that only Z is modulated. A large quantity of information can be written with relatively low bandwidth for producing the TV raster deflections, and with high bandwidth for the brightness (video) channel. This latter bandwidth is neither difficult nor costly to achieve, as demonstrated by the low cost of commercial or even closed circuit TV monitors. The data conversion from digital computer output to analog TV video, however, is often a complex and costly task. Television scan is very attractive in the type of application where computer-generated information must be distributed to a large number of low cost terminals located at a distance (NASA ground control, for instance). The data conversion need only take place once, and the resultant video can then be transmitted and mixed with standard video using routine methods.

The spot on a TV screen moves very quickly horizontally, slowly vertically, and covers approximately 10,000 in. for a single 525-line raster on a 21-in. screen. A deflection speed of several hundred thousand inches per second is therefore required to eliminate flicker. This speed is fast compared to that produced in XYZ deflected CRT's. To increase the symbol quality, a larger raster is needed, thus increasing the necessary deflection speed. The deflection amplifiers are optimized for their specialized tasks, and can therefore still be of relatively low bandwidth. Even at higher than commercial resolution, most XYZ displays tend to have higher quality than TV displays since symbols can be constructed from continuous lines rather than spaced horizontal line segments or dots.

The purpose of data conversion circuitry is to change computer instructions to Z information, thus combining the function of command decoding and display generation. Random scan information must be reduced to typewriter format due to the time-dependent sequential nature of the display generation process. A nonlogic circuit approach that is frequently taken is to use a scan converter tube (see the following section) driven by a standard symbol generator. With this method, the display surface is "read out" by a second beam scanning in the raster mode. The first stage CRT can also be read out electro-optically with a high resolution vidicon.

2.9 Display Presentation (Block 6)

2.9.1 Introduction

We will now consider the actual method of displaying the previously generated information, i.e., of creating the visual stimuli at the display/user interface. The effort to improve old and to develop new display media is probably the most active one in the entire display field, and is therefore often the most interesting. In the introduction to this article, it was mentioned that the block diagram would be discussed in terms of mechanization of generic functions. The mechanization of the display presentation function is usually classified according to Table III. As mentioned previously, the CRT display is still the workhorse of the

TABLE III
CLASSIFICATION OF DISPLAY PRESENTATION TECHNIQUES

Cathode ray tube[a]	Projection[b]	Panel[c]
(1) Conventional	(1) Mechanical inscription	(1) Electroluminescence
(2) Memory	(2) Slide projection	(2) Laser luminescence
	(3) Film projection	(3) Reflective or transmissive matrices
	(4) Light valve	

[a] Small screen, individual console (normally).
[b] Almost exclusively large screen, multiple users.
[c] Either small or large screen.

computer driven display field, and, therefore, it will be discussed more thoroughly than the other techniques.

2.9.2 Cathode Ray Tube Displays

2.9.2.1 Principles of Operation. Cathode ray tubes operate at extremely fast rates (write times measured in fractions of microseconds) because the entire mechanism operates nonmechanically. The only moving component is the electron beam which has virtually no inertia. Figure 8 shows a standard electrostatically deflected CRT. As in any tube, the heated cathode emits electrons which are drawn to the more positively charged anodes under control of the grid (Z modulation). Other electrodes help to focus the stream of electrons into a "beam" and accelerate the individual electrons to increase the beam's energy and hence the intensity. Deflection of the beam (XY modulation) is accomplished by creating time varying electromagnetic fields which affect its trajectory. In electrostatic deflection a high voltage differential is placed on the internal plate pairs, whereas in electromagnetic deflection a current-induced magnetic field is created by yokes (coils) placed externally on the neck of the tube. As mentioned previously, electromagnetic deflection is cheaper, slower, and tends to produce somewhat better resolution. Often combinations of both techniques are used.

The deflected beam impinges on a screen of emissive materials such as phosphors. Electrons in these materials absorb energy from the bombarding beam and are excited to energy levels higher than those they occupied in the so-called ground state. As they fall back to this unexcited state, they emit radiation with a frequency f characteristic of the difference in energy between ground and excited states (a fixed quantity for any given material):

$$\Delta E = hf, \qquad (2.9)$$

where h is Planck's constant and f for CRT phosphors is in the visible region.

The brightness of the resultant spot of light is a function of the energy or intensity of the beam, the duration of the bombardment, the density and shape of the beam's cross section, and the efficiency and persistence of the screen. Phosphor efficiency is much the same quantity as luminous efficiency and describes the amount of luminous radiation produced per unit of electron radiation. Persistence describes the decay rate of the trace on the screen as a function of the speed with which the excited electrons revert back to equilibrium level—the higher the persistence, the lower the brightness, since the amount of releasable energy is constant.

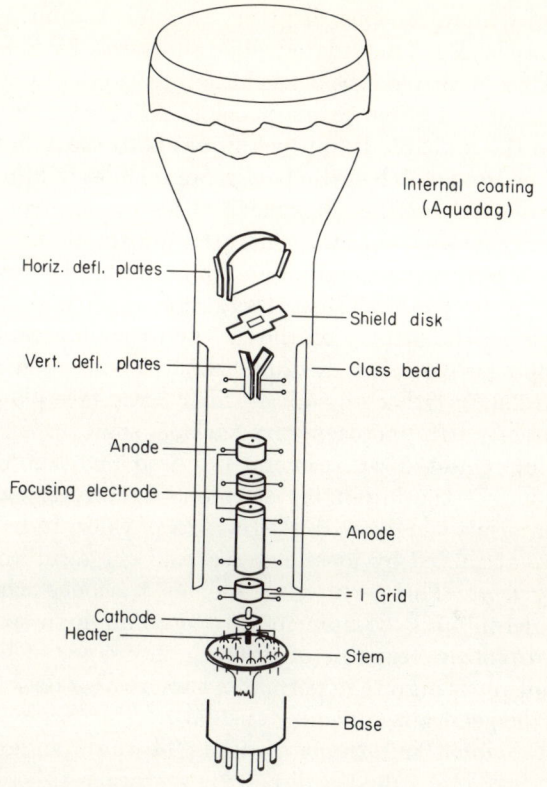

FIG. 8. Electrostatically deflected cathode ray tube [11].

Resolution of a CRT is often defined in terms of beam or spot size—a smaller beam cross section will produce a larger number of resolvable elements, provided that "cross-talk" (leakage) between neighboring phosphors is minimal. Brightness and resolution are inversely related in that greater brightness requires greater beam intensity, while this intensity widens the beam and hence the spot.

2.9.2.2 Options and Variations. While the operating principles are virtually the same for all types of CRT's, there is great variety in implementation and special effects. Tubes come in all sizes and shapes; from 1 to 19 or 21 in. in diameter for both types of deflection, round or square, long-necked or flat. Aiken "thin" tubes, for instance, produce a beam directed in the plane of the screen to one corner to be deflected by an array of horizontal and vertical deflection plates. Beam shaping or stencil tubes have been discussed above. Some tubes have multiple electron beams, up to a dozen or so, each separately modulated to produce many simultaneous displays. In such a multi-gun assembly, one beam may be XYZ modulated while another is TV video modulated. Other CRT's use multiple beams and different types of phosphors which emit light in one of three primary colors to effect a color display. A variation on the multiple beam techniques is to use a "window" in the back of a tube from which static background slides or film strips may be optically projected on the phosphor, while the electron beam superimposes the dynamic computer generated information.

Some CRT's have exceedingly high luminance and are used for large-screen theater projection. Most large-screen projection, however, is done by forming the display on the CRT and then optically transducing it to microfilm or a similar medium which can be used for projection (see Section 2.9.3). Other CRT's have fiber optic face plates to conduct the light directly to a photosensitive surface; some have special screens which are impregnated with several hundred fine wire styli per inch. The styli conduct the impinging electrons directly to electrostatically sensitive materials which are dusted with a powder. Individual "toner" particles are attracted by local charges, and the resultant pattern can be fixed by heat. These CRT's, as well as the ones which feed high precision microfilming equipment, are used in high-speed electronic printers and plotters, capable of printing thousands of lines (or ten or more drawings) per minute in permanent archival or dissemination form (block 7 of the generalized display system).

One of the most important variants of the standard CRT is the "memory" CRT, also called a direct view storage tube (DVST). These tubes extend the persistence or temporary storage property of the phosphor by incorporating a separate storage surface. The principal advantage is the elimination of the refresh cycle since persistence is on the order of several minutes. A bonus is provided by the much higher brightness capability (several thousand as opposed to roughly a hundred foot-lamberts), though at considerably lower resolution than present in an ordinary CRT. Also, halftones are more easily available—five 3-db levels are common.

Typically, the storage grid is a fine mesh of several hundred thousand holes per square inch, a fraction of an inch from the phosphor screen. The side of the mesh opposite the phosphor screen is coated with a dielectric material having a high ratio of "secondary emission" electron radiation—secondary electrons are knocked loose and are discharged at a rate greater than that at which the primary electrons arrive at the dielectric surface in the writing beam. The initially negatively charged surface thus comes to carry a net positive charge. A collector mesh placed between gun and storage mesh captures the secondary electrons to prevent their returning to the storage mesh. A second electron gun, called a "view" or "flood" gun, in turn produces a large flood of low velocity electrons which are attracted by the positive collector mesh and become distributed uniformly over the entire storage screen. Where there appears a positive charge on the storage screen due to the writing gun, the flood electrons pass through and are accelerated toward the phosphor; where there is no positive charge, the potential of the dielectric is lower than that of the flood cathode, and hence the electrons are repelled and collected at the collector mesh. The flood gun, therefore, produces the actual phosphor-activating electrons while the write gun causes the storage mesh to modulate the flood beam to produce the pattern. Since the flood gun provides the constant mass of activating electrons, much greater brightness can be obtained than with the conventional low volume, high velocity electron beam which must move across the phosphor screen at high speed, dwelling on each phosphor neighborhood substantially less than a millisecond each second. The halftone levels are obtained by varying the intensity of the write beam current.

The entire display is erased by causing the storage mesh to return to a potential negative with respect to the flood cathode. Selective erasure can be accomplished in some types of DVST's. Degradation of the image is the limiting factor in the storage time. Flood electrons ionize residual gases in the tube, and the ions migrate to the predominantly negative dielectric where they then, in turn, attract flood electrons, and lower the contrast. Eventually, the entire screen reaches maximum brightness, and contrast disappears. Color and stencil symbol generation techniques can also be used with this type of tube.

Scan conversion tubes (SCT) are a variation on the DVST and are used to convert one type of scan (conventionally, polar radar) to another (conventionally, TV). These tubes are also used to convert from an XYZ computer driven scan to a TV scan (see Section 2.8.5).

A typical SCT is a double-ended tube with a write gun at one end, and a read gun at the other. The write gun patterns the charge on a storage mesh in the input scan mode, while the read beam scans in a different mode and is modulated by the deposited charge pattern. A collector electrode on the write side receives the resultant signal which can be fed to the actual display tube. The read beam is additionally modulated so as to provide separation from the write signal.

An interesting application of CRT technology is the approximate 3-D display produced by sandwiching a number of thin CRT's. This is still very much an experimental project. There are a number of other techniques such as dark trace writing, and bombardment-induced conductivity storage which are too specialized to be discussed here.

2.9.3 Projection Displays

These displays are used typically for large-screen command and control (of the SAGE variety) and far less frequently for individual user/system interaction.

2.9.3.1 Mechanical Inscribing. A servo-controlled inscribing system permits the large-screen display of real-time dynamic information at a relatively slow rate. A glass slide coated with an opaque material is inserted into a projection system, while another glass plate with a stylus mounted in its center is positioned parallel to the first slide so that tipping the glass plate causes the stylus to penetrate the opaque material. Under the control of external signals, the stylus is moved in the X and Y directions and a pattern is inscribed in the opaque material on the face of the slide and focused on a projection screen in real time.

Color filters can be added, and a composite multi-input or multicolor display can be generated by superimposing the dynamic images from several projection systems or static backgrounds. No external memory is required for this type of display, since the inscription remains on the glass slide.

2.9.3.2 Slide Projection. Conventional slide projectors can be computer-controlled only in the sense that the computer can activate a servo-system which selects one slide from a standard library and position it. These projectors are naturally very limited.

2.9.3.3 Film Projection. Film projection systems generate the display on a CRT, photograph it, or otherwise transduce it onto hard copy film, rapid-process the film, and project it, all in real or nearly real time. Again, multiple images are available. A new, "lenticular" film has been developed which can contain three separate color images on the same black and white film frame. This film consists of a film base with a standard black and white emulsion on one side and lenticular elements (i.e., minute, parallel cylindrical lenses) embossed on the other. The optical image of the subject is separated by color filters into a large number of minute parallel strips, corresponding to the actual number of lenticules in the picture area, and each of these strips is subdivided into red, green, and blue components. Projection inverts this operation. A 30 by 40 mm lenticular format will provide resolution better than 3000 lines in the 30-mm direction, and up to 2000 in the other.

Photochromic film also appears promising for future display systems. Photochromic materials are grainless organic dyes which become opaque when exposed to ultraviolet light, and return to the transparent state when exposed to heat or infrared light. The chemical process is reversible, techniques to reduce capacitive coupling or cross-talk (nonlinear loading resistors, for example) single elements can be uniquely pulsed. An advantage of this technique is that it is all-digital and no D/A signal conversion need take place, as in a CRT. Much effort is going into the design of the appropriate switching logic. Electroluminescence techniques and variants thereof (such as those which provide storage or halftone capability), seem promising because of their inherent advantages—parallax-free viewing over a wide angle, low power consumption and heat generation, reliability and long life. Electroluminescence has not become competitive with other display techniques as yet, however, because of relatively low brightness (in the tens of foot-lamberts) and resolution (around 10 lines/in.), and development and manufacturing complexity and cost.

2.9.4.2 Laser Luminescence. The highly directional, extremely fine laser beam could be used to activate light-induced luminescence materials or to expose silver halide or photochromic film, and holds great promise as an electron beam replacement. Various electronic methods for controlling laser output in both deflection and modulation are now available and provide the potential to control light at multi-megacycles per second rates, with high radiant energy concentrated in micron-sized spots, yielding a high speed/brightness/resolution display. The experimental technology will remain costly for a few years to come.

2.9.4.3 Reflective or Transmissive Panels. These panels contain elements which reflect (or alternatively, transmit) light in a threshold fashion depending on the applied voltage. An external illuminating source is therefore required, and individual elements may control the pattern in which the light is reflected, say, to a screen. A promising example of a reflective matrix which is coincidence current controlled, is based on magnetic properties of certain thin film materials that affect their reflection of light. The technique uses a vapor-deposited thin magnetic film that is a colloidal suspension of magnetic particles. Magnetic film elements are switched with an XY matrix array of access wires, and the film element causes the magnetic particles to reflect incident light or not, depending on the state of the film element. Simplicity and low cost of batch fabrication and operation, high speed, brightness, and resolution are possible with this technique, as are inherent memory and lack of cross-talk.

In general, panel techniques are not now competitive in performance and cost, but may become so within this decade, especially when batch fabrication becomes economical. Until then, the CRT console will remain the principal computer driven display. A further reason for the deserved popularity of the CRT is the ease and flexibility with which the options of hard copy output (block 7), time sharing of multiple monitors, and manual inputs (block 8) are added.

2.10 Multiple Remote Displays and Manual Inputs (Block 8)

2.10.1 Multiplexed Consoles

It is desirable to be able to drive a number of remotely located displays in a time sharing mode with other output devices such as teletypes. Multiplexed consoles are usually fed from a single distributor or control unit which may contain a buffer and command decoding/display generation circuits in addition to the appropriate timing and gating circuits. This control unit can be located remotely from the computer, and can accumulate its digital information over cable or voice circuits, or perhaps from an intermediate scheduling computer or the manual inputs of the consoles themselves. The buffer, in the simplest case, holds only one display field which is distributed in turn identically to each console. A more useful method is to partition the buffer into sections, one per display, so that each display may show different information. Another technique is to associate a local buffer and decoding/generation circuits with each console, increasing flexibility and cost per unit accordingly, but reducing the cost and complexity of the control unit. A useful compromise is to use a common buffer and decoder, and to transmit still digital information to local generation circuits. The resultant analog signals from the generation section can then be applied directly or via short lengths of coaxial cable to the actual display.

2.10.2 Manual Inputs

The ability to use a display console not merely as an output device but as an extremely versatile real-time, on-line input medium as well, is provided by a variety of devices under human control: keyboards, light pens, cursors, and tablets.

2.10.2.1 Keyboards. The principal means for human input to the display system console is usually a pair of keyboards. The typewriter-alphanumeric keyboard allows formation of requests or procedures in the computer language, and the input of substantive information. A control keyboard with toggle switches and push buttons allows extensive manipulation and user control of the display information. The functions of all controls on this keyboard usually are labeled, and if the function of a control changes, its label can be changed also. Lights or message indicators can also be a part of such a control (function) keyboard.

If a console is to be used for different functions, provisions can be made to relabel a group of keys for each function. Labels are placed on of hard copy output (block 7), time sharing of multiple monitors, and manual inputs (block 8) are added.

2.10 Multiple Remote Displays and Manual Inputs (Block 8)

2.10.1 Multiplexed Consoles

It is desirable to be able to drive a number of remotely located displays in a time sharing mode with other output devices such as teletypes. Multiplexed consoles are usually fed from a single distributor or control unit which may contain a buffer and command decoding/display generation circuits in addition to the appropriate timing and gating circuits. This control unit can be located remotely from the computer, and can accumulate its digital information over cable or voice circuits, or perhaps from an intermediate scheduling computer or the manual inputs of the consoles themselves. The buffer, in the simplest case, holds only one display field which is distributed in turn identically to each console. A more useful method is to partition the buffer into sections, one per display, so that each display may show different information. Another technique is to associate a local buffer and decoding/generation circuits with each console, increasing flexibility and cost per unit accordingly, but reducing the cost and complexity of the control unit. A useful compromise is to use a common buffer and decoder, and to transmit still digital information to local generation circuits. The resultant analog signals from the generation section can then be applied directly or via short lengths of coaxial cable to the actual display.

2.10.2 Manual Inputs

The ability to use a display console not merely as an output device but as an extremely versatile real-time, on-line input medium as well, is provided by a variety of devices under human control: keyboards, light pens, cursors, and tablets.

2.10.2.1 Keyboards. The principal means for human input to the display system console is usually a pair of keyboards. The typewriter-alphanumeric keyboard allows formation of requests or procedures in the computer language, and the input of substantive information. A control keyboard with toggle switches and push buttons allows extensive manipulation and user control of the display information. The functions of all controls on this keyboard usually are labeled, and if the function of a control changes, its label can be changed also. Lights or message indicators can also be a part of such a control (function) keyboard.

If a console is to be used for different functions, provisions can be made to relabel a group of keys for each function. Labels are placed on techniques to reduce capacitive coupling or cross-talk (nonlinear loading resistors, for example) single elements can be uniquely pulsed. An advantage of this technique is that it is all-digital and no D/A signal conversion need take place, as in a CRT. Much effort is going into the design of the appropriate switching logic. Electroluminescence techniques and variants thereof (such as those which provide storage or halftone capability), seem promising because of their inherent advantages—parallax-free viewing over a wide angle, low power consumption and heat generation, reliability and long life. Electroluminescence has not become competitive with other display techniques as yet, however, because of relatively low brightness (in the tens of foot-lamberts) and resolution (around 10 lines/in.), and development and manufacturing complexity and cost.

2.9.4.2 Laser Luminescence. The highly directional, extremely fine laser beam could be used to activate light-induced luminescence materials or to expose silver halide or photochromic film, and holds great promise as an electron beam replacement. Various electronic methods for controlling laser output in both deflection and modulation are now available and provide the potential to control light at multi-megacycles per second rates, with high radiant energy concentrated in micron-sized spots, yielding a high speed/brightness/resolution display. The experimental technology will remain costly for a few years to come.

2.9.4.3 Reflective or Transmissive Panels. These panels contain elements which reflect (or alternatively, transmit) light in a threshold fashion depending on the applied voltage. An external illuminating source is therefore required, and individual elements may control the pattern in which the light is reflected, say, to a screen. A promising example of a reflective matrix which is coincidence current controlled, is based on magnetic properties of certain thin film materials that affect their reflection of light. The technique uses a vapor-deposited thin magnetic film that is a colloidal suspension of magnetic particles. Magnetic film elements are switched with an XY matrix array of access wires, and the film element causes the magnetic particles to reflect incident light or not, depending on the state of the film element. Simplicity and low cost of batch fabrication and operation, high speed, brightness, and resolution are possible with this technique, as are inherent memory and lack of cross-talk.

In general, panel techniques are not now competitive in performance and cost, but may become so within this decade, especially when batch fabrication becomes economical. Until then, the CRT console will remain the principal computer driven display. A further reason for the deserved popularity of the CRT is the ease and flexibility with which the options and an image can be exposed with ultraviolet light and erased with infrared light, all with extremely high resolution. The image will decay at room temperature at a rate depending upon the particular chemical compound. To achieve persistence longer than a few minutes, cooling is required since the photochromic decay is inhibited by cold temperatures. Several hundred reversal cycles are possible without fatigue.

A special CRT with a phosphor radiating strongly in the ultraviolet region pipes the image through fiber optics to the film. A special mirror which transmits ultraviolet but reflects luminous light is sandwiched between the film and the fiber optics. To project the image, light is passed through the film and is reflected by the mirror onto a screen. Where the film is opaque, the light does not reach the mirror, and therefore does not impinge on the screen, leaving a dark trace reproducing the image. Several hundred symbols can be recorded and updated per second, and faster photochromic materials will make this electro-optical, nonmechanical, projection technique quite competitive with contemporary CRT systems.

In general, film devices provide high resolution and brightness, easy color, and image superposition, at high cost and low speed.

2.9.3.4 Light Valves. Light valves are a variation on film projection and are based upon the technique of light refraction by a grating, rather than by transmission through transparent regions. In one approach, deformations or ripples are formed in a Schlieren medium consisting of an oil film, after the medium is bombarded by an electron beam formed by a conventional electron gun. These deformations produce varying refractions which allow light to pass through a grating or set of bars to the screen. In the absence of these deformations, all light would have been stopped by the grating. A variation of this technique involves the use of reversible thermoplastic tape as the Schlieren medium. The thermoplastic layer receives an electrostatic charge which causes corresponding deformations in the material when it is heated. The deformations remain when the tape is cooled after which the grating technique may be used. Heating is also used to erase the lines for reuse of the tape.

A display in the first category, such as the "Eidophor," has nearly real time response (30 frames/sec) and reasonable resolution, but a short life (20 hr/cathode, 3 cathodes). The second category is still experimental and promises real-time high resolution projection, but also at high cost.

2.9.4 Panel Displays

The panel display is a flat device (flat in the sense that the depth is considerably less than any area dimension), and is primarily solid or liquid state, though electromechanically controlled basketball scoreboards could be considered as panel displays. The size may vary from square inches to many square feet depending on the application. An "ultimate" panel display may be described as an individual *or* group display assembled from batch-fabricated standard-sized modules, with high resolution resulting from the use of a very large number of elements individually controlled in real time, and with built-in storage, immediate read-out, and selective erasure. Four different types of techniques are listed below.

2.9.4.1 Electroluminescence. Electroluminescence (EL) is an electrochemical process which converts electricity directly into luminous light without an intermediate conversion to heat (incandescent light) or ultraviolet light (fluorescent light). The plug-in night light is an example of a commercial lighting application of EL. In general, the light is emitted by a thin layer of crystalline phosphors, usually zinc sulfide, placed between two closely spaced capacitor electrodes, and "excited" by a time varying field. Such a capacitor sandwich can be made from a transparent supporting material (glass or plastic), a transparent electrode (often stannic oxide, or a metal film deposited on glass which combines support and conductivity), a dielectric material, the phosphor (usually containing catalytic impurities such as copper, gold, or silver), the other electrode, and a protective coating or second support.

The luminance output of the phosphor is a nonlinear function of the amplitude and frequency of the applied electric field. Both the brightness and color of the light are more sensitive to frequency variations than to amplitude. Brightness varies approximately linearly with frequency, while it exhibits a form of threshold response to amplitude. Color, while most often in the blue-green region, also can vary extensively with frequency, although it is insensitive to amplitude. For typical plate separations of the electrodes measured in mils, applied voltages are of the order of a hundred volts, though the panels can be made to operate in the 5–10-volt range; frequencies are generally in the audio range. Life of the element is roughly inversely proportional to frequency.

Since individual elements must be used to compose symbols on the surface, the primary problem with EL is the distribution of the generated signal for presentation. In other words, how can a large number of randomly spaced small elements be individually addressed in rapid sequence? This problem is generic to all panel displays and the usual, expensive solution is to operate display elements on a threshold basis, using very fast XY coincidence logic for selection much the same way that single bits are accessed in core storage. The signal on an individual column or row is somewhat below the threshold, and with special a plastic overlay, one for each of the keys which protrude through it. The overlay may also contain coding along its top edge in the form of small buttons which actuate switches built into the keyboard, or conducting strips which can make electrical contact. When the overlay is in place and a button is pressed on the keyboard, binary identification of the overlay as well as of the key pressed is sent to the computer. Thus, different programs may be called into the computer by simply changing a plastic overlay on the keyboard, making the display system behave in a special-purpose manner for the duration.

2.10.2.2 Cursor and Light Pen. The cursor and light pen form a most powerful way of communicating with the display console/computer system since, unlike keyboards, the information they provide is in graphic form. The terms *cursor* and *light pen* mean different things to different people, but at least their mechanization is unambiguous. Light pens work with light; cursors are moved about with electromechanical controls. A cursor, here, means a cross or a caret on the screen which indicates and possibly digitizes a position (i.e., stores its x,y location in memory); or, it may be a circle, perhaps with variable radius, which indicates and digitizes an area on the screen. The cursor may be moved on the screen by means of four types of controls: (1) velocity control, typically a "joystick" which moves the cursor in the X or the Y direction, or both, with a velocity proportional to the position of the joystick; (2) a stepping control which paces the cursor horizontally or vertically at a constant rate as direction labeled keys are depressed; (3) a position control which moves the cursor in the X, Y, or both directions, for a distance proportional to the distance the control is moved (a "crystal ball" control, consisting of a sphere suspended so as to be free to rotate in any direction about its axis, is typical, as is a shaft encoder); and (4) a direct manual control such as a light pen (or gun), which optically draws the cursor along to the new position. In effect the cursor indicates at any given time the XY coordinates of current interest to the computer; lines may be drawn between two cursor positions upon depression of appropriate function keys, or a curve may be encoded simply as a succession of closely spaced points.

The light pen can be used not merely to *draw* by controlling a cursor, but also to *point* at areas or objects of interest to the user so that further computer generated information about them may be displayed. The light pen is a cylindrical device, roughly pen sized, which houses a light sensitive element having a very narrow field of view. The pen is held close to the screen, is aimed at a bright spot (presumably a symbol or a piece of a complex drawing), and an electrical pulse is developed at the instant that the spot is activated by the beam. This pulse can be used to cause an interrupt in the display cycle, or to load a special register with the address of the current display instruction or the exact X, Y address of the spot on the screen, etc. The program can then cause the designated symbol to blink or intensify (especially useful in case of ambiguity), or it can output additional alphanumeric or graphical information pertaining to the symbol, or take some other action on the symbol itself, such as transforming its position or orientation, or deleting it. The console may incorporate special hardware to perform light pen "tracking" (i.e., servoing its position) or to perform coordinate transformations of designated objects, since these tasks are very time consuming to the computer and are not difficult to implement in hardware.

2.10.2.3 Tablet. The Rand tablet [12], currently being manufactured under the name GRAFACON, can be used as an alternative to light pen input of graphic materials. It consists of two layers of Mylar with coordinate lines etched on each. One layer has 1024 lines in the X axis, the other 1024 in the Y axis. The tablet measures 10.24 by 10.24 in. giving a high resolution of approximately 100 lines/in. To write on the tablet the user moves a special stylus on its surface. The stylus picks up the signals which occur at an intersection of two grid lines and sends them through an interpreter to the computer which stores the coordinates of the point. As the user writes, a record of the stylus movement may be shown on a CRT display screen in front of him. This same screen can also display computer-generated information. The primary advantages of the Rand tablet are its fairly low production cost, high resolution, and the convenience of a horizontal as opposed to a vertical writing surface.

With the addition of the manual input capability, and a large amount of supporting software, the display becomes a most effective and congenial device for man/machine interaction.

3. Man/Machine Interaction

3.1 Introduction

In the old days of computing, one became a machine language expert and sat down at the computer console to control the input and computation processes with control keys. Testing and debugging took place on line and several alterations of the program could be entered sequentially in the allotted time span. When the number of users and the cost of computing time became too large to allow individual "diddling," this open shop, hands-on approach was replaced by the more efficient closed shop, batch-processing operation. A sense of intimacy with the machine and the progress of the problem solution was lost in the change-over, however, and turn-around time came to be measured in days, or at best hours. Programming was delegated to programmers more familiar with the intricacies of the machine and its operating system than with the problem to be solved.

As a solution, FORTRAN and other procedure or problem-oriented languages were developed to allow the user to solve the problem naturally and efficiently without having to become a machine programmer. This approach still does not allow for the type of iterative, "by feel" programming that seems to be so often necessary for the solution of problems not easily algorithmized. The current popularity of "public utility" time sharing, and the resurgence of the small personal computer with algebraic compiler, are therefore both easily explained. The user can still program in a language convenient to him *and* he gains immediate access to and response from the computer. The multiconsole, multilanguage situation is typified by Project MAC [*13*]: close to a hundred teletypes and teletypewriters, and several display consoles are remotely tied to a large computer system with bulk storage. These multiplexed terminals will come close, in the future, to meeting Mooers' specification of a "reactive typewriter," a device "almost as cheap to have and as easy to use as the phone" [*14*]. In terms of operating time and efficiency, time sharing is still noncompetitive with batch processing; but what price tag should be put on user convenience, interest, and ability to solve problems faster than could be done ordinarily (or problems which would not have been solved with batch processing)? There is one severe limitation of this type of console—it provides only alphanumeric communication, restricting the types of problems that can be solved to ones easily articulated and digitized. The general-purpose display console discussed in the previous sections, although more expensive to construct and operate, can provide man/machine interaction in the two-dimensional language of graphics and text which is natural to most problem solutions and solvers.

What are the requirements on a system so as to make meaningful discourse technically and economically feasible in real time?

(1) The display subsystem(s) must operate in a time and memory sharing environment, simultaneously with other processors and input/output units. Multiprogramming/processing rather than mere time sharing may eventually make operating cost viable.

(2) There must be efficient, dynamic, and flexible storage and retrieval system programs available to access the collection of bulk storage, which contains the data base of the display information.

(3) Transmission of information must become more economical at higher speeds.

(4) A flexible and powerful pictorial data structure must be used to

model both the syntax and the semantics of the information displayed on the screen. This data structure must be able to represent graphical as well as textual information in exactly the same way, and must be invariant to the nature of the input process: light pen actions, alphanumeric instructions, and function key depressions specifying an identical process in each case must result in identical representations in memory. At times a user may wish to be verbose and state a very general problem in a problem-oriented display language; many other times he may wish to be terse and economical, and merely "grunt" by pointing with the light pen or by pushing function keys. Either way, similar requests must produce similar results, and therefore require similar internal organization.

(5) The display language must allow intermixed execution of picture processing procedures, and other types of computations; the same system monitor must handle the intertwined statements.

(6) The data structure and the commands operating on it must be iteratively and recursively usable in a boot-strapped open-ended fashion. Entities defined on one level must be applicable without limit as building blocks on successively higher levels, while still represented as single instances in the data structure. Procedures must be able to call on other procedures, and on themselves. Threaded list structure techniques and associative memory organizations are conventionally used to provide this capability.[5]

Condition (1) is the most difficult to fulfill since consoles are still very expensive, and multiprogramming/processing still experimental. The other conditions are being met, at least for the most part, in a number of highly imaginative and productive research projects, such as those pioneered at MIT. In the following sections a few examples of such promising man/machine interaction experiments will be given.

3.2 On-Line Programming

An extension of conversational programming which takes place via teletype is the use of the console to display a "menu" of available commands and operands. The user points with the light pen to successive items on the screen which are then concatenated into syntactically meaningful commands ready for compilation or interpretive execution. The WHIRLWIND computer [17], still in use after fifteen years of operation, can display its order codes, eight octal digits, and six control instructions for light pen pointing. The previously drawn ten lines of coding are displayed, as are the contents of the A and B registers. The

---

[5]The Massachusetts Institute of Technology has developed the "plex" structure [15]; the University of Pennsylvania, the "MultiList" memory organization [16].

program is stepped through under a form of automonitor or trace routine, and results are displayed on the screen.

A more problem-oriented approach is to display subroutine calls which can be assembled on the screen as a sequence of procedures to be executed at the user's request [18]. The display tells the user how many operands are needed, what transformations are allowable, and in general permits him to make only syntactically correct statements. Extensive checks and balances, and diagnostics are employed, and the output on the scope can be quite explicit in its explanations. This English language system is very easy to use and provides a good example of Licklider's "terse in—verbose out" rule of thumb [19].

At the University of California at Santa Barbara, Culler, one of the originators of the on-line computing movement [20], is constructing small storage tube consoles with alphanumeric and function keyboards for use in classroom situations [21]. Function keys are used to program the solution of complex mathematical problems, and certain "level" keys introduce modalities which determine whether the rest of the function keys are to make the system behave as a calculus, a numerical analysis, or a complex variables tool.

Thus, the pointing ability of a pen, or the unique identification provided by a button, allows for very fast input of highly encoded and compressed information so that a running "conversation" can be handily sustained.

3.3 Computer-Assisted Instruction

The consoles at MAC, for instance, are used for homework assignments as well as for research computation, and an interest in the educational and instructional aspects of the remote console is rapidly developing. Displays can be used not merely as more versatile teaching machines but as two-way teaching devices. The far larger data base and manipulation capabilities of the computer system make it possible to extend the notion of programmed-instruction *branching* into general-purpose *decision making*. Feedback from the user to the system can be used not only for recording his performance, but also for heuristic modification and revisions of the curricular materials or the program itself. Furthermore, could not, for instance, the Socratic System interaction [22] be made more valuable by the ability to interact graphically as well as in natural language? X-rays could be "discussed" in much the same fashion used by doctors and interns: talking while using pencils to point at cogent areas. Omar Khayyam Moore's Talking Typewriter [23] could be used not just as a reading or spelling machine, but as an arithmetic or space relations machine.

Experimental data on the cost/effectiveness of displays in this new application is now being gathered in a variety of locations. Stanford is starting a "computer-based laboratory for learning and teaching" [24] with six student stations, each equipped with a CRT/keyboard/light pen/ microfilm viewer console. Prior experience was obtained with twelve multiplexed scopes in the Computation Center [25]. The Carnegie Institute of Technology is also acquiring general-purpose scopes for "programming and debugging, engineering and scientific calculations, and classroom instruction" [26].

3.4 Computer-Aided Design

The use of computers to carry out some phases of a design process dates from the fifties. At that time the APT language for numerical control of machine tools was developed at MIT, and there were early efforts by the large aircraft/aerospace companies and computer manufacturers toward automating portions of the circuit design, layout, and back plane wiring problems. Today computer-aided design (also called *design automation*) provides one of the most fruitful applications of man/machine interaction via displays, as shown by the large amount of research being conducted in the area. This is the case, due to the nature of the typical design task. The design of a circuit or a truss bridge, or of a free form for a fuselage or car door, is not a cut and dried procedure except in the most trivial instances. Instead, the designer must go through an iterative procedure, stages of which may require a large number of rather routine calculations. He starts out with a vague notion of the problem and potential solutions. A first stage articulation of both produces a crude approximation of the answer. This preliminary design is analyzed, the structure or parameters are changed, and a more refined design may be tested. The process cycles until a satisfactory design results. The computer driven display is very useful in its ability to show the designer, in the graphic two-dimensional language fiducial to him, what the intermediate design "looks like." The analysis of the design can be carried out partially by the computer, under direct supervision of the designer. For instance, it can perform parametric and iterative computations, drawing results immediately, and allowing the designer to change values and to recompute in real time. A great variety of techniques, heuristic, as well as algorithmic, can be tried out in this immediate feedback mode. The computational and data processing capability of the computer can be effectively coupled in this interchange with the user's ability to make educated guesses and to generalize.

Two parallel projects at MIT helped to establish generic techniques for computer-aided design. In the SKETCHPAD [27] program at Lincoln

Laboratory, a TX-2 with large core, and many toggles and buttons, was used to investigate the problems of circuit design, stress calculations on truss bridges, the drawing of views from perspective, the rotation of constrained linkages, and the conversion of flow charts to coding. The computer-aided design group at MIT's Electronic Systems Laboratory has generalized experience with APT and is very active in the area of developing theories underlying display and computational languages and data structures, and in the design process itself. They are also developing special- and general-purpose display hardware and software [28]. Figure 9 shows part of their current equipment, time shared in the MAC system. The "crystal ball" can be used with the built-in hardware rotation matrices to tumble the 3-D-in-perspective object in all directions. Note the use of the teletype for hard copy output. Preliminary ship design [29] was selected as a test of the ability to work with general space curves and surfaces, and their stress distributions. Similar work on automobile surfaces has been done at General Motors.

FIG. 9. MIT's Electronic Systems Laboratory display console.

In such programs and in other computer-aided design programs of the future, the scope may be used under cursor/light pen/keyboard control to provide some of the functions in the following sample sequence:

(1) The screen is cleared.
(2) Points, and the lines and arcs defined between them, are drawn either by light pen or keys.
(3) Geometric constraints (equal angles or lengths, parallelism, perpendicularity) are imposed.
(4) Smoothing and linearizing take place.
(5) Previously defined "macros" or drawn subpictures may be retrieved from memory and connected into the assembly.

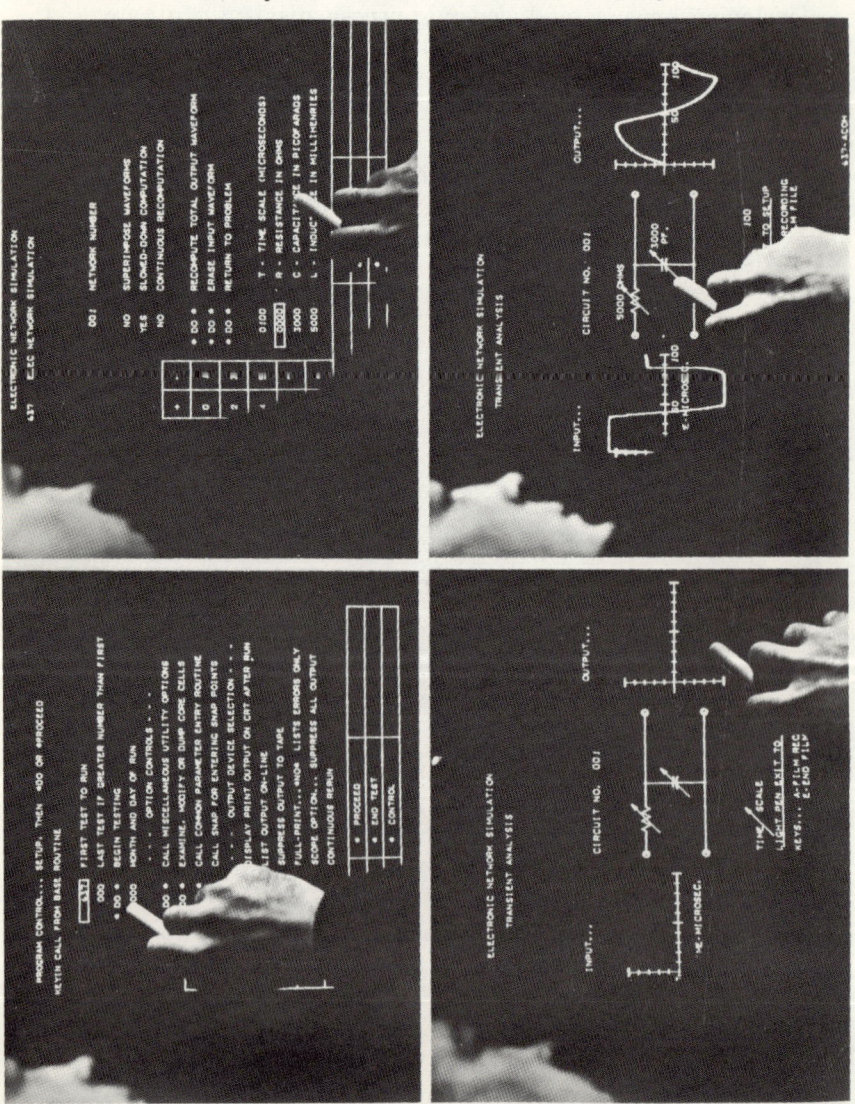

FIG. 10. Transient analysis of a linear circuit.

(6) Selective erasure is used to alter the configuration.

(7) Entire subpictures or portions of the screen may be translated, rotated about any arbitrary axis, or nonuniformly scaled about an arbitrary axis.

(8) The contents of the entire screen may be tumbled through a perspective three-space.

(9) The display may "zoom" in or out on an arbitrary region or component.

(10) On the basis of function keys, overlays, or selections from a scope menu, standard computations may be performed on the picture in the screen [30]. Figure 10 shows a transient analysis made of a linear circuit. The values of the parameters can be varied by pointing the light pen at various parts of the arrows. Pointing at the head will cause the parameter to increase at a preset rate until the pen is removed, at the tail it decreases at the same rate, and in between, proportionally to the distance from the center.

(11) A detailed drawing suitable for output to a drafting machine, or instructions to a numerically controlled tool or wire wrap machine, or a complete parts order list, etc., may be produced.

(12) A finished screen drawing may be appropriately labeled and stored away for future use.

An exceedingly powerful capability is that of making a change in a single component, which is then reflected in all higher level components utilizing the first. This uniform substitution option makes updating and graphic file maintenance very easy.

The design process will come to have the aspect of a one-man show: the original designer participates in the complete design process, doing most of his laboratory work through display monitored simulation. He will also carry out the drafting and documentation chores. This total involvement will be an extremely valuable asset of the method.

3.5 Conclusion

Below are listed a small number of problems to which displays in a man/machine interaction mode may be applied.

(1) Nonlinear problems solved by iteration and varying parameters (lens design [31], nuclear phenomena, heat transfer [32], etc.)
(2) Problems for which it is easier to draw than to write (information retrieval based on drawn chemical structures) [33].
(3) Optical alignment or digitizing of bubble chamber tracks and general curve fitting [34], and pattern recognition in general [35].
(4) Architectural layouts [36].
(5) Layout drawings for chemical plants.
(6) Logical design.

Fig. 11. The ALPINE pictorial data processing system.

(7) Editing and composition [37].
(8) Producing animated cartoons [38].

The only reason that techniques discussed in this article are not more widely used is cost. To paraphrase: "What this country needs is a good five hundred dollar display console," driven over voice circuits, with built-in storage, and all the requisite manual inputs. In addition there is a need to expand existing machine-dependent display languages to machine-independent "display compilers." Users still need to know too much about the pathologies of the system, and cannot program for the display in a strictly problem-oriented language. Special-purpose languages such as AUTODRAFT [39] for specifying drawings for precision drafting, the Norden/IBM [40] circuit analysis and layout encoding language, and COGS [41] for formating of various types of output, are only a step in the right direction. Finally, further advances in the state-of-the-art in pattern recognition will be looked to for circumventing the present need of specifying in detail through keyboards what is on the screen.

Activity in the field is profuse: SID, SHARE design automation conferences, IFIP sessions on man/machine interaction and displays, and two-week courses in pictorial data processing. Furthermore, commercial versions of entire graphic data processing packages are now being marketed, and displays in themselves are becoming even more popular—over fifty manufacturers are producing them. As an example of a commercial package, Fig. 11 shows a version of the ALPINE system: film scanner (for input from hard copy microfilm), recorder (for microfilm archival and dissemination copies produced on line in less than a minute from the CRT), ground glass microfilm viewing screen, and flexible display console with light pen, alphanumeric keyboard, and labeled overlay with function keys. The DECADE system [42] is a commercial computer-aided design system which omits some of the recursive forms of generality to attain current economic feasibility. It would seem difficult to overestimate the potential of graphic man/machine interaction.

REFERENCES

1. Davis, R. M., A history of automated displays. *Datamation* 11, No. 1, 24–28 (1965).
2. RADC, *Compendium of Visual Displays*. Rome Air Development Center, Rome, New York, 1964.
3. Display Glossary. *Inform. Display* 2, No. 2, 24–25 (1965).
4. Luxenberg, H. R., Photometric units. *Inform. Display* 2, No. 3, 39–41 (1965).
5. Eberhardt, E. H., Resolution specifications. *ITT Ind. Lab. News*, April (1962).
6. Akin, R. H., Photo sensor problems in display luminance measurement. *Inform. Display* 2, No. 1, 26–30 (1965).

7. Smith, Y., Air Force research underlying the specifications and test of display requirements. *Proc. 2nd Natl. Symp. Soc. Inform. Display, Washington, D.C., 1963*, 45–62 (1964).
8. Loewe, R. T., Sisson, P. L., and Horowitz, P., Computer generated displays. *Proc. IRE* **49**, 185–195 (1961).
9. See, for instance, Dennis, J. B., A multi user computation facility for education and research. *Commun. Assoc. Computing Machinery* **7**, 521–529 (1964).
10. After Machover, C., Converting data in human-interpretable form. *Data Systems Design* **1**, No. 9, 17–24 (1964).
11. Darne, F. R., Cathode-ray tubes. In *Electronic Information Display Systems* (J. H. Howard, ed.), pp. 87–109. Spartan Books, Washington, D.C., 1963.
12. Davis, M. R., and Ellis, T. O., The Rand tablet. A man-machine graphical communication device. RAND Memo No. RM-4122-ARPA. Rand Corp., Santa Monica, California, 1964.
13. Samuel, A. L., Time-sharing on a multiconsole computer. MIT Project MAC Rept. MAC-TR-17. Mass. Inst. Technol., Cambridge, Massachusetts, 1965.
14. Mooers, C. N., The reactive typewriter program. *Commun. Assoc. Computing Machinery* **6**, 48 (1963).
15. Ross, D. T., and Rodriguez, J. E., Theoretical foundations for the computer-aided design system. *Proc. AFIPS Conf.* **23**, 305–322 (Spring 1963).
16. Prywes, N. S., and Gray, H. J., The organization of a multilist-type associative memory. *Proc. Session on Gigacycle Computing Systems AIEE Pub.* No. S-136, 87–101 (1962).
17. Shortell, A. V., On-line programming. *Datamation* **11**, No. 1, 29–30 (1965).
18. Goodenough, J. B., A lightpen-controlled program for online data analysis. *Commun. Assoc. Computing Machinery* **8**, 130–134 (1965).
19. Licklider, J. C. R., Problems and principles of console design. *Proc. IFIP Congr., New York, N.Y.*, 1965 (in press).
20. Culler, G. J., and Fried, B. D., The TRW two-station, on-line scientific computer: general description, *Computer Augmentation of Human Reasoning* (M. Sass and Wm. Wilkinson, eds.) pp. 65–87. Spartan Books, New York, 1965.
21. Culler, G. J., On the logical structure of the communication in a highly interactive on-line system. *Proc. IFIP Congr., New York, N.Y.*, 1965 (in press).
22. Feurzeig, W., The PDP-1 computer as a teaching aid in problem-solving. *Proc. DECUS Symp.* 203–213 (1963).
23. Pines, M., What the talking typewriter says. *The N.Y. Times Mag.* May 9, 1965.
24. Stanford's computer-based classroom on the air. *Datamation* **11**, No. 5, 65 (1965).
25. McCarthy, J., Stanford timesharing system. *Proc. DECUS Symp.* 13–18 (1963).
26. Carnegie Tech. to get computer-driven display. *Datamation* **11**, No. 6, 76 (1965).
27. Sutherland, I. E., Sketchpad: A man-machine graphical communication system. MIT Lincoln Lab. Tech. Rept. No. 296, Lexington, Massachusetts, 1963; see also, Sketchpad: A man-machine graphical communication system. *Proc. AFIPS Conf.* **23**, 329–346 (Spring 1963).
28. Ross, D. T., Coons, S. A., and Ward, J. E., Investigations in computer-aided design for numerically controlled production. MIT Interim Eng. Progr. Rept. No. ESL-IR-221. Mass. Inst. Technol., Cambridge, Massachusetts, 1964.

29. Hamilton, M. L., and Weiss, A. D., An approach to computer-aided preliminary ship design. MIT Tech. Memo. No. ESL-TM-228. Mass. Inst. Technol., Cambridge, Massachusetts, 1965.
30. Branin, F. H., Jr., D-C and transient analysis of networks using a digital computer. *Proc. SHARE Design Automation Workshop, Atlantic City, N.J., 1964* (1964).
31. Shannon, R. R., and Radkowski, E. J., Graphics in optical design. *Proc. IFIP Congr., New York, N.Y., 1965* (in press).
32. Holstein, D., Computer-aided design. *Product Eng.* 66–76 (November 1964).
33. Lefkovitz, D., The input and output display and manipulation of chemical structural formulas by cathode ray tube with light pen. Proposal to Natl. Sci. Found., by the Inst. for Coop. Res., Univ. of Pennsylvania, July, 1965.
34. Conn, R. W., and von Holdt, R. E., An online display for the study of approximating functions. *J. Assoc. Computing Machinery* **12**, No. 12, 326–349 (1965).
35. Teitelman, W., New methods for real-time recognition of hand-drawn characters. Bolt, Beranek, and Newman Rep. No. 1015, June 1963.
36. Souder, J. J., *et al.*, Planning for Hospitals. Am. Hospital Assoc. Chicago, Illinois, 1962. Mr. Souder's firm (Bolt, Beranek, and Newman) uses these procedures commercially today.
37. Samson, P., Type justifying program. MIT Dept. Elec. Eng. Memo. No. PDP-9-1. Mass. Inst. Technol., Cambridge, Massachusetts, 1963.
38. Knowlton, K. C., A computer technique for producing animated movies. *Proc. AFIPS Conf.* **25**, 67–87 (1964); see also *Proc. Spring JCC* (1964).
39. Harris, H. R., and Smith, O. D., Autodraft—A language and processor for design and drafting. *Proc. SHARE Design Automation Workshop, Atlantic City, N.J., 1965* (in press).
40. Development of techniques for automatic manufacture of integral circuits. Interim Eng. Progr. Repts. IR-8-167 (I), (II), (III), (IV), May 1964—April 1965.
41. Dinwiddie, J. H., and Mullens, R. C., Color output generation system. *Inform. Display* **1**, No. 2, 32–36 (1965).
42. Stein, C. W., DECADE, Digital Equipment Corporation's automatic design system. *Proc. DECUS Symp.*, 1965.

Bibliography

1. Davis, R. M., The information display field as it exists today. *Inform. Display* **1**, No. 1, 28–30 (1964).
2. Howard, J. H. (ed.), *Electronic Information Display Systems*. Spartan Books, Washington, D.C., 1963.
3. *Pocket Data for Human Factor Engineering*, Cornell Aeronaut. Lab., Ithaca, New York, 1960.
4. Luxenberg, H. R., and Bonness, Q. L., Quantitative measures of display characteristics. *Inform. Display* **2**, No. 4, 8–14 (1965).
5. Walter, C. M., Color—A new dimension in man-machine graphics. *Proc. IFIP Congr., New York, 1965* (in press).
6. Thoman, R. E., A computer-generated television display system. *Proc. 3rd Natl. Symp. Soc. Inform. Display, San Diego, Cal., 1963* (1964).
7. Edwards, A. W., High-speed electronic printer. *Electronics World* **72**, No. 12, 26–48 (1964).

8. Pegram, J. B., Direct-view storage tubes. *Electronics World*, **73**, No. 2, 25–28 (1965).
9. *Proc. 4th Natl. Symp. Soc. Inform. Display, Washington, D.C., 1964* (1965): Morrison, D. J., Utilization of lenticular film for full color display systems. 181–210; Fuller, H. W., and Spain, R. J. A thin magnetic film technique for wall panel display. 171–180; James, P., and Dittenberger, D., Display requirements of the intergrated management information system of 1968–1970. 73–97; Stetten, K. J., Real time CRT photochromic projection display. 59–72; Acton, B. E., Displays for control center management. 211–266.
10. Strock, L. W., Electroluminescence. *IEEE Spectrum* **1**, No. 11, 68–83 (1964).
11. Coons, S. A., An outline of the requirements for a computer-aided design system. *Reprint Proc. AFIPS Conf.* **23**, 299–304 (1963 Spring Joint Computer Conf.).
12. Stotz, R., Man-machine console facilities for computer-aided design. *Reprint Proc. AFIPS Conf.* **23**, 323–328 (1963 Spring Joint Computer Conf.).
13. Johnson, T. E., Sketchpad III: A computer program for drawing in three dimensions. *Reprint Proc. AFIPS Conf.* **23**, 347–353 (1963 Spring Joint Computer Conf.).
14. Rowe, A. J., The ADMA automated system of design and drafting. Hughes Aircraft Co., No. PB-87R Culver City, Cal., May 1964.
15. Lang, C. A., and Polansky, R. B., Graphical language—A step towards computer-aided design (MIT. Conf. Paper No. CP-64-575). *Proc. IEEE Machine Tools Ind. Conf.*, Hartford, Connecticut (1964).
16. Jacks, E. L., A laboratory for the study of graphical man-machine communication. *Proc. Fall JCC* pp. 343–348, San Francisco (1964). See also the four companion articles pp. 349–410.
17. Digital Equipment Corp. (Staff), Displays for individual use—CRT consoles. *Data Systems Design* **1**, No. 9, 29–30 (1964).
18. Smith, C. F., Graphic data processing. *Proc. SHARE Design Automation Workshop, Atlantic City, N.J., 1964* (1964).

Author Index

Numbers in parentheses are reference numbers and indicate that an author's work is referred to although his name is not cited in the text. Numbers in italic show the page on which the complete reference is listed.

A

Acki, M., 71 (1), *113*
Acton, B. E., *290*
Akin, R. H., 248 (6), *287*

B

Backus, J., 134, *177*
Bar-Hillel, Y., 137 (2), *177*
Barnett, M. P., 46, *113*, 118 (3), *177*
Barnum, A. A., 11 (4), 59, *113*
Berman, R., 145 (4), *177*
Bhalla, C. P., 200 (1), *206*
Bibb, T., 79 (21), *114*
Biggs, J. M., 125 (5), *177*
Bobrow, D. G., 119 (6), 125 (7), *177*, 210, *238*
Bonness, Q. L., *289*
Borck, W. C., 11 (60), *115*
Borris, M., 212 (2), 225 (2), 226 (2), *238*
Bosche, C., 214 (3), *238*
Bourne, C. P., *113*
Bozman, W. R., 197 (3), 199, *206*
Branin, F. H., Jr., 285 (30), *289*
Brick, D. B., 66 (6), *113*
Briggs, B., 189 (17), 190 (17), *193*
Brooker, R. A., 138 (8), *177*
Brown, S. A., 125 (9), *177*
Burks, A. W., 33 (7, 8), *113*
Bussell, B., 79 (1, 21), *113*, *114*

C

Cantor, D. C., 141 (10), *177*
Carroll, A. B., 25 (9), *113*
Cheatham, T. E., Jr., 163 (11), *177*
Choisser, J. P., Lt., 63 (56), *115*
Chomsky, N., 122 (14), 137 (12), 154 (15), *177, 178*
Chow, C. K., 64, *113*

Cohen, L. J., *115*
Comfort, W. T., 25 (9), 27, 96, *113*
Conn, R. W., 285 (34), *289*
Conway, M. R., 76 (12), *113*
Coons, S. A., 283 (28), *288*, *290*
Corliss, C. H., 197 (3), 199, *206*
Craig, J. A., 125 (62), 128 (18), *178, 180*
Crane, B. A., 46 (13), *113*
Critchlow, A. J., 68 (14), *113*
Culler, C. J., 281 (20, 21), *288*
Cunningham, J., 146 (68), *180*
Curtin, W. A., 68, *113*
Cutrona, L. J., 59 (16, 17), *113, 114*

D

Dammann, J. E., 188 (15), *193*
Danielson, W. A., 189 (17), 190 (17), *193*
Darne, F. R., 269 (11), *288*
Davies, P. M., 39 (24), 42 (18), *114*
Davis, M. R., 278 (12), *288*
Davis, R. M., 176 (19), *178*, 240 (1), *287, 289*
Dennis, J. B., 260 (9), *288*
Diebold, J., 188 (14), 192 (14), *193*
Dinwiddie, J. H., 287 (41), *289*
Di Henberger, D., *290*
Donnay, G., 201 (4), *206*
Donnay, J. D. H., 201 (4), *206*
Dorn, W. S., 109, *114*
Doyle, L. B., 182, *193*
Drayton, C. E., 125 (9), *177*

E

Eberhardt, E. H., 244 (5), *287*
Edwards, A. W., *289*
Ellis, T. V., 278 (12), *288*
Estrin, G., 42 (22), 79, *113, 114*
Ewing, R., 39 (24), *114*

AUTHOR INDEX

F

Falkoff, A. D., 104 (25), *114*
Farber, D. J., 212 (5), 220 (5), *238*
Feigenbaum, E., 150 (51), *179*
Feurzeig, W., 281 (22), *288*
Floyd, R. W., 136 (22), 141 (20, 21, 22), *178*
Ford, D. F., *113*
Fried, B. D., 281 (20), *288*
Fruin, R. E., 41 (50), *115*
Fuller, H. W., *290*
Fuller, R. H., 42 (22, 26), 109, *114*
Futrelle, R. P., 118 (3), *177*

G

Garner, H. L., 90, 92, 95, 96 (27), *114*
Gibbons, G., 125 (62), *180*
Gilbert, P., 150 (23), *178*
Gonzales, R., 29, *114*
Goodenough, J. B., 281 (181), *288*
Gorn, S., 118 (24), 120 (28), 122 (26), 141 (25), 149 (27), *178*
Gray, H. J., 40 (51), *115*, 280 (16), *288*
Gray, S. B., 66 (6), *113*
Griswold, R. E., 212 (5), 220 (5), *238*
Gwynn, J., 125 (62), *180*

H

Halstead, M. H., 146 (68), 157 (29), *178*, *180*
Hamilton, M. L., 283 (29), *289*
Harris, H. R., 287 (39), *289*
Haverty, J. P., 146 (31), *178*
Hawkins, J. K., 60 (29), *114*
Hayes, D. G., 140, *178*
Hechtel, J. R., 54 (30), *114*
Heising, W., 146 (68), *180*
Hennie, F. C., 38 (31), *114*
Holland, J. H., 23 (32, 33), *114*
Holstein, D., 285 (32), *289*
Holt, A. W., 168 (33), *178*
Horowitz, P., 254 (8), *288*
Howard, J. H., *289*
Hsu, R. W., 169 (34), *178*
Huskey, H. D., 136 (36), 157 (35), *178*

I

Irons, E. T., 167 (37, 38), *179*
Iverson, K. E., 122 (39), *179*

J

Jacks, E. L., *290*
James, P., *290*
Johnson, T. E., *290*
Jonas, R. W., 212 (7), 223 (7), 224 (7), 225 (7), *238*
Joseph, E. C., 42 (35), *114*
Joynes, M. L., 141 (40), *179*

K

Kaplan, A., 42 (35), *114*
Karplus, W. J., 57 (38), *114*
Kay, M., 119 (41), *179*
Kelly, H. S., 212 (8), 227 (8), *238*
Kesner, O., 136 (42), *179*
Kiseda, J. R., 42 (36), *114*
Knapp, M. A., 11 (4), 59, *113*
Knowlton, K. C., 230 (9), *238*, 287 (38), *289*
Knuth, D. E., 135 (44), 163 (43), *179*
Kosarev, Yu. G., *116*
Kron, G., 55 (37), *114*
Kunkel, G. Z., 205, *207*
Kuno, S., 153 (45), *179*

L

Lamb, S. M., 122 (46), *179*
Landauer, W. I., 40, *114*, *115*
Landweber, P. S., 137 (47), *179*
Lang, C. A., *290*
Lawson, A., 183 (7), *193*
Lee, C. Y., 44, *114*, *115*
Lee, E. S., 42 (42), *115*
Lefkovitz, D., *115*, 285 (33), *289*
Lehmann, W. P., 118 (48), 141 (40), *179*
Leith, E. N., 59 (17), *114*
Leondes, C. T., 51, 79, *113*, *115*
Lewis, D. R., 68 (44), *115*
Liebmann, G., 55 (45), *115*
Liklider, J. C. R., 281 (19), *288*
Lindquist, A. B., 71 (46), *115*
Logcher, R. D., 125 (5), *177*
Love, R., 136 (36), *178*
Lowe, R. T., 254 (8), *288*
Lukasiewicz, J., 153 (49), *179*
Luxenberg, H. R., 244 (4), 246 (4), 247 (4), 287, *289*

AUTHOR INDEX

M

McCarthy, J., 282 (25), *288*
McCormick, B. H., 35 (47), *115*
McCracken, D. D., 136 (50), *179*
Machover, C., 263 (10), *288*
McReynolds, R. C., 11 (60), *115*
Marcum, T. H., 205, *207*
Mellen, G. E., 68 (44), *115*
Minnick, R. C., 42 (48), *115*
Mittman, B., 125 (9), *177*
Mooers, C. N., 279 (14), *288*
Morris, D., 138 (8), *177*
Morrison, D. J., *290*
Mullens, R. C., 287 (41), *289*
Mullery, A. P., 176 (58), *179*

N

Narasimhan, R., 89 (49), 109, *115*
Naur, P., 146 (68), *180*
Newell, A., 146 (68), 150 (51), *179, 180*
Newhouse, V. L., 41 (50), *115*

O

Oettinger, A. G., 153 (45), 154 (52), *179*
Ohringer, L., 189 (16), *193*
Opler, A., 173 (53), *179*

P

Palais, S. M., 31 (65), *116*
Palermo, C. J., 59 (17), *114*
Parmullo, J. N., 181 (2), *192*
Patrick, R, L., 146 (31), *178*
Pegram, J. B., *290*
Pendergraft, E. D., 212 (10), *238*
Perles, M., 137 (2), *177*
Perry, J. H., Jr., 182, *192*
Peterson, H. E., 42 (36), *114*
Pick, G. P., 66 (6), *113*
Pines, M., 281 (23), *288*
Polansky, R. B., *290*
Polonsky, I. P., 212 (5), 220 (5), *238*
Porcello, L. J., 59 (17), *114*
Postal, P., 140, *179*
Pruett, J., 125 (62), 128 (18), *178, 180*
Prywes, N. S., 40 (51), *115*, 280 (16), *288*

R

Radkowski, E. J., 285 (31), *289*
Raphael, B., 210, *238*
Rice, T., *115*
Rodriguez, J. E., 280 (15), *288*
Rosin, R. F., 41 (54), 112 (55), *115*
Ross, D. T., 144 (55), 147 (56), *179*, 280 (15), 283 (28), *288*
Rowe, A. J., *290*
Rubinoff, M., 51, *115*

S

Samelson, K., 146 (57), *179*
Sammet, J., 146 (68), *180*
Sammon, J. W., Lt., 63 (56), *115*
Samson, P., 287 (37), *289*
Samuel, A. L., 279 (13), *288*
Sattley, K., 163 (11), *177*
Schauer, R. F., 176 (58), *179*
Schutzenberger, M. P., 154 (15), *178*
Schwartz, J., 73, *115*
Sebestyen, G. S., 61 (59), *115*
Seeber, R. R., 71 (46), *115*
Seeger, J. A., 54 (30), *114*
Seelbach, W. C., 42 (36), *114*
Shamir, E., 137 (2), *177*
Shannon, R. R., 285 (31), *289*
Shapiro, R. M., 99, *116*
Sharp, J., 145 (4), *177*
Shaw, C. J., 146 (68), 173 (59), *179, 180*
Shaw, J. C., 150 (51), *179*
Shortell, A. V., 280 (17), *288*
Sisson, P. L., 254 (8), *288*
Simon, H., 150 (51), *179*
Skiko, E. J., 188 (15), *193*
Slotnick, D. L., 11 (60), *115*
Smith, C. F., *290*
Smith, O. D., 287 (39), *289*
Smith, Y., 250 (7), *288*
Souder, J. J., 285 (36), *289*
Spain, R. J., *290*
Spangenberg, K., 55 (63), *115*
Squire, J. S., 31, 110 (64), *116*
Stein, C. W., 287 (42), *289*
Stetten, K. J., *290*
Stotz, R., *290*
Strock, L. W., *290*
Sturges, L., 145 (4), *177*
Sutherland, I. E., 282 (27), *288*
Sutton, A. A., 182 (5), *193*

AUTHOR INDEX

T

Tankca, R. I., 49, *116*
Taylor, W., 136 (61), *180*
Teig, M., 42 (36), *114*
Teitelman, W., 285 (35), *289*
Thoman, R. E., *289*
Thompson, F. B., 125 (62, 63, 64), 128 (18), 129, (63), 142, *178*, *180*
Todd, J., *116*
Tonge, F., 150 (51), *179*
Turn, R., 70 (69), 79 (21), *114*, *116*
Turner, L., 136 (61), *180*

U

Unger, S. H., 34, *116*, 220 (11), *238*

V

von Holdt, R. E., 285 (34), *289*

W

Walter, C. M., *289*
Ward, J. E., 283 (28), *288*
Warshall, S., 99, *116*, 163 (65, 66), *180*
Waychoff, R., 136 (61), *180*
Weber, E. V., 188 (15), *193*
Weiss, A. D., 283 (29), *289*
Winkler, J. H., 182 (6), *193*
Wirth, N., 136 (36), *178*

Y

Yasaki, E., 181 (1), 183 (1), 184 (1), 185 (1), 187 (1), *192*
Yevreinov, E. Z., *116*
Yngve, V. H., 118 (67), 146 (68), *180*, 214 (13), 218 (13), 220 (13, 14), 227 (12), 229, *238*

Subject Index

A

A-2 compiler, 143
Adaption, 60
Adaptive networks, 107
AIMACO, 144
Algebraic equations, 112
Algebraic structure, analysis of, 221
ALGOL, 84, 85, 90, 126, 127, 129, 136, 143–146, 212
Algorithm, 7
Algorithmic decomposition, 96–99
Allophone, 186
Alphabet, of a programming language, 130
Alphanumeric keyboard, 276
ALPINE, 286, 287
ALPS, 71–73
Ambiguity of programming languages, 139–141
Amplitude modulation, 60
Analog-digital techniques, 57
Analog mechanization, 48
Analog optical processor, 59
Analysis-by-synthesis method of translation, 230
Analytic evaluation of programming language processors, 173
Antenna pattern, 241
APT, 125, 127, 144, 146, 282
Arabic 216, 219
Array,
  rectangular, 14
  module, 23
  iterative, 38
  solenoid, 66, 67
  data, 85
Array processor, 50–53
ASCII, 199
Assembly routines, 118, 142
Assignment statements, 133
Associative
  computer, 39, 42–44
  Logic Parallel System (ALPS), 71–73

memory, 39, 40–42, 71, 77, 126
search, 104
technique of data processing, 176
Attribute words, 170
AUTOCODER, 212
Autocorrelation, 60
AUTODRAFT, 287
Automata, 138
Automobile surface, 283
Available space list, 170

B

Back referencing, 221, 227
Backus normal form, 90, 129, 134, 135, 137, 146
Barrier, 92
BASEBALL, 127
Batch fabrication, 3
Block, 133
Boolean function, 58, 90
Boundary value problem, 57
Bounded context, 139, 141
Brightness, 248, 268, 273, 275
Broadcast register, 16, 100, 104
Bubbling, 35
Buffer, 259, 260

C

CAL-TECH, 57
Cartons, 287
Cathode ray tube console, 240, 255; see also CRT
Cellular logic, 33
Channel, 82
Character generator, 262
Characteristic value problem, 57
Charactron, 265
CHILD, 63
Chinese, 256
Clock rate, 14, 25
COBOL, 127, 136, 144–146

SUBJECT INDEX

CODASYL, 145
Code generators *see* Macro-instructions
Code selector, 167
Coding, information, 255
COGS, 287
Coherent optical techniques, 59
Coincidence logic, 274
Color, 252, 253
Colorimetry, 245
COMIT, 127, 144, 145, 212, 214–220, 227–238
   rules, 215, 216, 218
Communication, theory of, 211
Communications list, 170
Compilation aids, 96
Compilers, 118, 141
Comprehensive algebraic computer, 143
Compressible fluid flow, 57
Computational linguistics, 210
   programming languages for, 209, 238
   research in, 210–212
Computer-aided design, 282
Computer-assisted instruction, 281, 282
Computer characteristics, specification of, 148
Computer-independent programming languages, 127, 128
Computer typesetting, 187–207
Computing power, 2
COMTRAN, 144
Concurrent ALGOL, 90
Conditional probability, 61
Configuration statement, 86
Consecutive operator bounded-context analysis, 157
Consonant patterns, 185
Construction rules, *see* Lexicon
Context-dependent and context-free grammars, 137, 138, 141
Contextual analysis, 129, 139
Contrast, 248, 249
   ratio, 248
Control, distributed, 21
Conventional programming language processors, 148, 159–163
"Conversation machine", 145
Conway's system, 76–79
Correlation, 60, 104
Cost, 2, 5, 6, 22, 26, 53, 78, 265, 282
Cost effectiveness, 3
Cross-correlation, 60

CRT console, 240, 255, 270, 282
CRT display, 243, 267, 268
Crutch-coding, 154
Cryogenic processor, 40, 71
Cryotron, 40
Crystal ball, 258, 277, 283
Current operator—next operator analysis, 157
Cursor, 258, 277
Curve generator, 265

D

D-825, 58
Data
   array, 85
   conversion, 266
   description, 85
   display, 188, 242
   retrieval, 39
   words, 170
DEACON, 127, 142, 146
DECADE, 287
Decision-making, 257
Declaration statements, 133
Decoding of languages, 130
Delimiters, 131
Dependency connection, 230
Dependency grammars, 140
Design automation, 282
Design limitations of language processors, 118, 119
Diagramming *see* Parsing
Dictionary, 218; *see also* Lexicon
Dictionary hyphenation, 184
Differential equation processors, 49–58, 102, 106
Diffusing surface, 247
Digital-analog techniques, 57
Digital optical processor, 58
Discontinuous-constituent grammars, 227–233
Dispatcher (in COMIT), 218
Display, 267–276
   CRT, 243, 267
   data, 188, 242
   graphical, 243
   panel, 243
   projection, 243
   real-time, 240
   vector, 243
   visual, 239

SUBJECT INDEX

Display
　area, 254
　capacity, 255
　language, 260, 280, 283, 287
　parameters, 244
　presentation, 267
　resolution, 250
Distributed control, 21, 22–34, 91–96
Distributed logic, 176
Dot generator, 265
Double consonant, 186
Drum array processor, 51–53
Dual scope, 241
Dynamic storage allocation, 160

E

Editing, 187–190, 287
Edition planner, 190
EDSAC, 143
EDVAC, 143
Elasticity, 57
Electrologica XI Computer, 145
Electroluminescence, 274
Electromagnetic deflection, 268
Electronic resolution, 251
Electrostatic deflection, 268
Elliptic equation, 113
Emission, 248
English sentence production, 219
ENIAC, 143
Erasure, 257
Evaluation of programming language processors, 173–175
Expressions, 133

F

FACT, 144
Film projection, 272
Finite automata, 138
Finite-state grammars, 140
Flicker, 253, 257, 259
Floating point arithmetic, 20
FLOW-MATIC, 144
Fonts, 253
Foot-Lambert, 247
Fork instruction, 76
Fork-join pair, 76
Formational grammars, 140
FORTRAN, 96, 99, 112, 126, 127, 136, 142–144, 212, 227

Fourier transform, 60
French sentence production, 219
Function keyboard, 276, 280
Function scan, 264
Functional unit modular machine, 81–84

G

Gamma-60, 68
"Garbage collection", 171
Gaussian elimination, 68
Generalized Horner's Rule, 109
Generation order, 159
Generation strategy, 165
Generation vector, 261
Generator phase of processor, 161
Generator translator, 165
Geometry control, 86
German sentence production, 219
Glossometric grammars, 140
Glottal, 185, 186
GRACE, 203
GRAFACON, 278
Grammars,
　finite-state, 140
　formational, 140
　for natural languages, 211, 212
　for programming languages, 137–141
　glossomatic, 140
　phrase-structure, 137–141, 146, 227 ff.
　sentence-producing, 212
Graphic language, 282
Graphical display, 243
Gray scale, 249

H

Halftone, 249, 270
Hard copy, 240, 258, 270, 272, 283
Hardware language, 130
Hardware-oriented terms, 84
Hardware utilization ratio, 70
High-speed printer, 240
Holland machine, 23–29, 96
Hooks, 82
Horner's Rule, 109
Human factors, 243
Hybrid techniques, 57
Hyphenation,
　dictionary, 184
　logical, 185

SUBJECT INDEX

Hyphenation
  program, 183–187
  routine, 183
  rules, 186
Hyphenless justification, 205, 206

I

Ideal Multifunction Machine (IT), 70
Identifiers, free and reserved, 130
ILLIAC, 34, 35, 89, 143, 241
Illumination, 246
Immediate-constituent grammars, 140, 229, 230
Impedance network, 55–57
Incident flux, 246
Index Medicus, 202, 203
Indirection (indirect addressing), 170
Individual-memory-location addressing languages, 115
Information
  coding, 255
  format, 255
  retrieval, 39, 219, 257
  type, 255
Initial value problems, 57
Input/output, 19, 78
In-sequence optimizer, 165
Integrated circuit, 4, 6
Intercommunicating cells, 44–46
Interlingual production, recognition, transfer, 222–225
Intermediate language approach (to processors), 151
Interpreters, 118, 141, 172
Interpretive System *see* Wayne State University
IPL, 127, 144–146
IT, 70
Iteration, 282
Iterative array, 38
Iterative computer concepts, 176

J

Join instruction, 76
JOVIAL, 126, 136, 145, 146
Joystick, 277
Justification of margin, 182, 183, 197
  hyphenless, 205

K

Keyboard, 258, 276, 282
  alphanumeric, 276
  phototypesetting, 201
Knotted list structure, 127, 169

L

Label, 86
Lambert, 247
Language,
  display, 260, 280, 283, 287
  graphic, 282
  theory of, 211
Language data processing, 222–225
Languages *see* Natural l., Programming l.
Laplace's equation, 84, 112
Laplace transform, 60
LARC, 68
Large-screen projection, 270
Largest syntactic type, 164
Laser luminescence, 275
L-buffer, 16, 101, 104
Lenticular film, 272
Letter sequence, 185
Letter X, 186
Lexicon, construction rules for entries to, 129, 130
Libraries of subroutines, 141, 143
Light pen, 241, 258, 260, 277, 280, 282
LINASEC, 182
Line generator, 265
Line justification, 182, 183, 197, 205
Linguistic
  hypotheses, 216
  information processing, 222–225
  Research System (LRS), University of Texas, 212, 221–225
  structure, theories of, 211
  techniques in programming language processing, 128
Linguistics *see* Computational linguistics
Link field, 171
Linofilm, 197, 199, 200
Linotron, 196
List
  processing, 210
  processors, 39, 126, 127, 150, 167–173
  rule (in COMIT), 218
  structures, 214
    knotted, 169
    threaded, 127

SUBJECT INDEX

Load-and-go compilers, 153
Load program, 159, 160, 163, 172
Lockheed Machine, 49
Logical hyphenation, 185
Logical program, 187
Look-ahead capability, 29, 31
LRS *see* Linguistic Research System
Lumen, 246
Luminance, 246
Luminous intensity, 246, 268

M

MAC, 240
Machine editing, 190
Machine-independent processors, 148
Machine language *see* Hardware language, Display language
Machine translation of natural languages, 150, 209–211, 219
   programming languages for, 212–227
Macro-accumulator, 165, 167
Macro-instructions, 141, 165
Man-machine interaction, 240, 278–287
Manipulation
   of lists, 168
   of plane figures, 220
Manual input, 258, 259, 276–278, 287
Matrix multiplications, 68, 100
Maximum likelihood processors, 60–64
Maxwell's field equations, 57
Measurable parameters (for programming languages and processors), 173, 174
Mechanical translation *see* Machine translation
MEDLARS, 202
Memory, associative, 39
Memory, sharing, 279
Memory speed, 7
Mergenthaler Corp., 196, 197
Message size, 255
Metalanguages, 120, 130
Microfilm, 270, 282
   printer, 198
MIMIC, 212, 226, 227
Mixed expressions, 87
Mode control, 14, 18, 19, 87
Modular computing system, 22
Modular retrieval device, 44
Modulation transfer function, 251
Module, 23, 49
   adaptive, 107

   arithmetic, 83
   control, 82
   functional unit, 81
   input-output, 83
   memory, 83
   predecessor, 24
   successor, 24
Module array, 23
Monolingual production, recognition, 222–225
Monte Carlo methods, 112
Multiaperture ferrite core, 40
Multidimensional machine, 31–33
Multimodule unit, 49
Multiple-function machines, 68–84
Multiple instruction stream, 21, 68–84
Multiprocessing, 279, 280
Multiprogramming, 279, 280

N

NEBULA, 144
Neighbors, 20
NELIAC, 136, 144
Network control unit, 15
Network sequencer, 15
NIKE X LARC, 68
Nondestructive read, 40
Nonrandom format, 260
Nonterminal word classes, 132
n-pass compiler, 153
n-register machine algorithm, 161
Numerical tool control, 219, 285

O

On-line, 276
On-line programming, 280–281
Open-shop computing, 143
Operand-operator pairs, 161
Operation words, 170
Operator precedence, 129, 154
Optical
   character reader, 241
   density, 60
   processors, 58–60
   resolution, 244
   scanning, 192
   thickness, 60
Optimization of computer codes, 148
Ordinary differential equations, 106
ORDVAC, 143
Oscilloscope, 240

SUBJECT INDEX

P

Panel display, 243, 273, 274
Parallel
  machine organization, 7–10
  network computers, 10–22
  Network Digital Computer (PNDC), 22
  network language, 85–89
  network processing, 100–109
  networks, 14, 16, 17
  Network Signal Processor, Westinghouse, 65
  network translator, 99
  processing algorithms, techniques, 100–113
  search, 104
Parsing, 129, 132, 139, 212
Partial differential equations, 102
Path
  building, 25, 29, 31, 33, 96
  structure, 94
  tracing, 95
Pattern,
  antenna, 241
  consonant, 185
  vowel, 185
Pattern
  articulation unit, 35, 36, 89
  language, 89
  matching, 213, 220, 221
  processing language, 89, 90
  processor, 34
  recognition, 89, 285; *see also* Shape recognition
PENELOPE Project, 189
Perception mechanism, 250
Persistence, 268
Perspective drawing, 283
Phase modulation, 60
Phosphor efficiency, 268
Photochromic film, 272
Photographic resolution, 250
Photometric units, 243
Photometry, 245
Photon, 196
Phototypesetters, 198, 199, 201
Phase structure grammars, 137–141, 146, 227 ff.
PILOT, 68
Pitt Natural Language Process, 189
Plotter, 170
Point plotting mode, 260

Pointer list, 170
Polish notation, Polish strings, 129, 153
Position generator, 262
Pragmatic analysis of programming languages, 122
Precedence *see* Operator
Precedence scan, 98
Predecessor module, 24
Predictive analysis, 229
Pre-editing (for machine translation), 225, 226
Prefix, 185
Printer, 270
Problem-oriented programming languages, 84, 123, 124
Procedural statements, 133
Procedure, 133
Procedure-oriented programming languages, 123, 124
Process control languages, 125
Processing element, 14, 17, 18
Process-oriented languages, 84
Processors for programming languages,
  design limitations, 118, 119
  evaluation, 173–175
  history, 141–147
  syntax-directed, 163–167
  terminology, 153–159
  types, 147–153
  see also Programming, List processors
Program,
  hyphenation, 183–187
  edition, 190
  logical, 187
Program memory, 15, 19
Programming element, 21
Programming languages, 84–91, 117–141
  alphabet, 130
  ambiguity, 129, 139–141
  classification, 122–127
  complexity, 131
  decoding, 130
  dependence on computer design, 127, 128
  description, formal, 130–137
  effectiveness, 119–122
  for computational linguistics, 209–238
  for list processing, 210
  for pattern processing, 89, 90
  for machine translation, 212–227

SUBJECT INDEX

grammatical models, 132, 137–141; see also Grammar
hardware, 130
machine-oriented, 210
problem-oriented, 123, 124, 210
procedure-oriented, 123, 124
process control, 125
question-answering, 125, 133
syntax, 132–136
vocabulary, 130
see also Processors
Projection display, 243, 270, 272, 273
Proofreading, 187, 188
Propagation delay, 2, 7
Psycho-physical photometry, 245–248
Push-down lists, 154, 168, 214

Q

Question-answering languages, 125, 133

R

Radiance, 245
Random format, 259
Random scan mode, 261
Random walk solution, 52, 53
Rand Tablet, 278
Raster, 262
Readability, 253
Real-time
command and control, 240
display, 240
editing, 188
Reception, 248
Recognition, 60, 64
of patterns, 89, 285
of sentences, 138, 139
Recognition order, 159
Rectangular array, 14
Redundancy, 96
Re-emission, 248
Reference words, 170
Reflexive panel, 275
Regeneration, 257
Region-addressing languages, 126
Registration, 254
Repetitive structure, 4
Reply time, 256
Resistance network, 54
Resolution,
CRT, 269, 270

display, 250
electronic, 251
optical, 244, 249–252
photographic, 250, 273
symbol, 265
Response time, 256
Retrieval, 39, 257
Rivers of white, 182
Routine, hyphenation, 183
Roots of algebraic and transcendental equations, 112
RW-400, 68
Russian, 225, 226

S

SAGE, 272
Scalar-potential equation, 57
Scan conversion table, 271
Scatter-addressing languages, 126
Schrödinger's Wave Equation, 57
Schwartz's Machine, 73–76
Self-compilers, 153
Semantic analysis
of natural languages, 210, 219
of programming languages, 122
Semantic models, 176
Semiotic theory, 222
Sentence
generators, 139
production, 219
recognizers, 139
Sequential statements, 133
Sequential stratified processes, 122
SE9AP assembly, 225
Shape recognition, 256; see also Pattern recognition
Shelf, 214 ff.
Ship design, 283
Signal processors, 65–67
SIMSCRIPT, 127
SKETCHPAD, 282
SMI, 46–48
SNOBOL, 127, 212, 220, 221, 227
Soft copy, 240, 258
Solenoid array, 66, 67
SOLOMON, 3, 11–20, 35, 66, 86, 87
Space surface, 283
Spacing, 182
Spatial frequency, 251
Special pair, 186
Spectral distribution, 245

SUBJECT INDEX

Standardization of programming languages, 136, 176
Statements, types of, 133
Status tests, 87
Storage tube, 270, 281
Story editing, 191
Stratificational grammars, 140
STRESS, 125, 146
Strings, 137, 138
Stroke generator, 264, 265
Stromberg-Carlson, 198
Subjective measurement, 244
Sublists, 169
Subroutines, libraries of, 141, 143
Successor module, 24
Suffix, 185
Superconductivity, 40
"Summer Session" Computer, 143
Symbol
  generation rate, 256
  generator, 262
  resolution, 265
Symbols of a programming language, see Alphabet
Synonymy, 131
Syntactic
  ambiguity, 139
  analysis
    of natural languages, 211, 216
    of programming languages, 160, 163
    of Russian, 225, 226
  types of programming languages, 134
  word classes, 132
Syntax-directed programming language processors, 90, 149, 163–167
Syntax of programming languages, 122, 132–136
Synthesis of target language, 148

T

Tagmemic grammars, 140
Target language, 161
  specification, synthesis of, 148
Teletype, 240, 279
Terminal word classes, 132
Terminal symbols, 135
Termination words, 170
Texas, University of, see Linguistic Research System
Theorem proving, 150
Threaded lists, 127

Time sharing, 240, 259, 279
Total lines, 250
Tracking response, 256, 278
Transcendental equations, 112
Translation see Machine translation
Translator (component of list processor), 172
Translator for parallel networks, 99
Transmission panel, 275
Tree decomposition, 98
Turing machines, 138, 214
TV lines, 250
TV scan, 262, 266, 271
Types of grammars (Chomsky), 137, 138, 141
Typesetting, 187, 287
Typewriter mode, 261

U

UCLA Machine, 79–81
Unger Machine, 34, 35, 37, 38
Uniformly diffusing surface, 247
UNIVAC, 143
Update response, 256
Utilization ratio, 70

V

Variable structure computer, 79
Vector
  display, 243
  generator, 262, 265
  potential equation, 57
Visible spectrum, 245, 246
Visual
  acuity, 249
  display, 239
  fidelity, 254
Vocabulary
  of programming languages, 130
  of natural languages, analysis of, 219
von Neumann concept of digital computer, 125
Vowel patterns, 185

W

Wavelength, 245
Wayne State University Interpretive System, 225, 226

SUBJECT INDEX

Weber-Fechner, 249
WHIRLWIND, 143, 241, 280
Wire wrap machine, 285
Word classses, syntactic, 132
Word length, 213

Words, types of, 170

X

XY Coincidence logic, 274, 275
XYZ scan, 262, 266, 271

QA
76
A3
v.7

JAN 14 1969